PADRE

from the

MONASTERY

to the

FOREST

*A memoir of my life journey in a war torn Eritrea
and my immigrant life in USA*

HIABU H. HASSEBU

iUniverse, Inc.
New York   Bloomington

PADRE *from the* MONASTERY *to the* FOREST

A memoir of my life journey in a war torn Eritrea and my immigrant life in USA

iUniverse books may be ordered through booksellers or by contacting:
iUniverse
1663 Liberty Drive
Bloomington, IN 47403
www.iuniverse.com
1-800-Authors (1-800-288-4677)

ISBN: 978-1-4502-3682-9 (pbk)
ISBN: 978-1-4502-3683-6 (ebk)

Printed in the United States of America
iUniverse rev. date: 07/23/2010

Dedication,
To....

Saron my daughter, the desert flower.

Made in the desert, with perfume power.

Daddy smelled your fragrance, in substance.

My life allowance, my only rememberance.

As far as my mind, reaches your beauty.

From the diaspora, the land of prosperity.

You are there, my life consolation.

Here I dedicate the book, as a love promotion.

To you only my life champion.

Prologue

The day I concluded my first book, "Fagret: The Female survivor" I said, "Bravo" to myself. It was my first time to congratulate myself to myself. I started to include my thanks, to all who helped me realize the book. To do my homework, to write a decent book, on a forgotten experience of war and a people, motivated me greatly. The first thing I decided, when I was getting ready to write my second book, was to begin with hope and proceed with courage to reach my goal.

The idea of writing a book was for a long time in my mind. But I needed better time, place and opportunity. To say the truth, in the monastery where I was living, I wouldn't express my self in writing, as I am doing now. My conscience was not free. If I did so I would lose my reputation. As the Abysinian saying goes, " Be free, then act, for your acts are now changed". I followed the exact letters of the Abysinian sayings.

Let me get this straight, I have dragged for a number of years, chopping life, thinking that this way it would function. During all those years, my spirit was fluctuating up and down a dozen times. I firmly believed, while I was in the monastery, I wouldn't express my self in writing, about a subject that never mattered the religious concept.

Let me tell you some thing. The local's experience of the war was always in my mind. I was born in war, grew in war, until I embraced the liberty in 1991. Thanks to the heroes of the land, at last the people were able to be free, once and for all.

I am writing this book being in my room 3mX3.5m square. My bed was messy. Everywhere you find papers. The room was not inviting, but it was my favorite room.

Appropriately enough, it was three years since I started it. I have lost so many times and then I just stopped writing. On and off, the good thing everything was on file. I needed only to open the files. I stored all the contents with out any order in my files. It was very recently that I started to order it into my computer and began to compile it as a book. Thanks to the technology and to the computer I used to write with, I was able to accomplish some thing. Above all I thank Brother Dominic Ehrmanthraut who donated me such a fabulous instrument.

My tendency was a comedian rather than a novelist. My profession was more a preacher than a writer. I had a good technique of speech but never realized that my writing ability would give such an effect. To prove my self I have started it, but some times in the middle, I felt a sense of non-sense.

I was totally encouraged for a simple reason of my friends advises. I really appreciate their advise and very skill full manner of helping me to continue with my project. Since my mind approved the ideas they were giving me, I based my self on the amount of a success, I would acquire in the future.

For years I was trained to imitate the Saints, the Angels and Jesus, in the congregation I used to live as a monk. On the other hand, the society where I grew up, in it self limited my thought only to copy the others. I always hated to copy and imitate. I am original, I said. God created me to be original. I believed hardly in that. The philosophy of creativity opened my mind to go to the imaginary field to enrich my mind. I liked to go beyond the actual discoveries, of day to day life experience, and used the common sense of my creativity. I knew that this attitude would disturb many of my friends. People are scared of being original. They only like to imitate.

I remember when I was doing grade eight, my English teacher gave us an essay to write about a title: "Whom would you like to be if you were born again". Most of the essays were various and identical. Some of the students liked to be famous Presidents, like John Kennedy and some others picked different celebrities and did their essays. My essay was very strange, particular and out of the environment. I wrote, if I was going to be born again, I would like to be born like Hiabu. The teacher rewarded my essay for its content originality but my classmates neglected me.

One thing I was very conscious about was not to write a fiction. What I wanted was to convey, one story with two different experiences, one identical crises with two different environment, one dream with two separate aspirations, one Institute with two different identities.

My exposure in the field of authors, might fail to excite an audience that expected much from me. On this field I started to look very preoccupied. At times, I seemed to have lost interest in what I was doing but my will never deterred.

When I started writing, the first thing that came to my mind was not what would be the content to transmit but rather how to transmit the message. I knew I had plenty of content to write, so I was not bothered about what to write. From my profession as a beginner, I had never had difficult in transmitting the content matter. It was in the technique of methodology on how to deliver the message that I found it difficult. In the end I learned that one has to know how to transmit the message. The content is one, it is about the local's experience..

Writing about two stories at the same time, for me meant dealing with two stories, two files, two works, two preoccupations with one mind, one person. Of course, for me it was not easy. It was very time consuming. I looked very disorganized. I learned a lot.

My focus was one, telling the experience of the war and the locals struggle for their independence, and my main interest was not the individual stories, but the local's experience of the struggle as a whole.

The first story was about a female survivor of Ona- Keren Eritrea, a novel story I composed based on true a story. The book is already in the market, since June of 2007. The second book titled, "Padre, from the monastery to the forest" was my memoir as an author, born and grew in war.

I did not follow the chronology, and it was neither as it comes to my mind. My expectations around the writer's set were running high and optimistic. I said it was really something to start up, since I had trained my brain to analyze, plan and learn, to distinguish the real from the imaginary. I didn't try to accomplish something out of nothing. On this part I was very sure. The philosophy and the ways of my dealing to the matter, may seem one sided and some times very exaggerated. And I will accept all comments. I know I would be under the attention of my readers. I never thought besides the local's experience.

For what ever it might be, I was spinning around the same experience of the local's war experience. I had only written down, the things that my mind had dictated me. The words were definitely mine, but the experience was of the locals. It is all about the locals dedication and sacrifice. Their work didn't lie in ruins. The locals reasoned the right way and they interpreted the situation through their life.

When yesterday was still in my remembrance, to recount the past experience of the local's, would be one of my priority job, I said. It took me so many years to realize it. One thing I learned within the process was to begin and proceed with hope.

I programmed my mind to that fruitful experience, since I wanted to learn some thing of their experience. The lesson was gratis, for this reason I began it immediately. My advice to you is to read the two stories one after the other. It would be a difficult assignment. Never get confused.

I have a certain perspective that had guided my thought into a sharper focus of the war experience. The long experience of war, had taught the locals how to engage in armed struggle, and fulfill the wish of the people. Speaking about the armed struggle and the local's, who realized it within the context of historical framework, encouraged my mind to do something about it.

I adopted the local's view of a struggle in which so many excellent ideas came into my mind. I sorted out, that this story will not be dealing with the individual life experience.

Full of my best intentions, I began it, my will supported me to bring it to completion. I adjusted my mind so well, in fact I began with good frame of mind. To write about the locals was something to be proud of and I have more reason to feel satisfied in writing about the locals. Although a more detailed discussion of Sewra's (Arabic word for revolution) distinctive armed struggle was needed to be recounted, on my part I was very limited.

To do so, I needed to reconstruct those days and years of struggle. Admitted my self as part of the story. Welcomed my mind and tried to listen back, the out standing experience of struggle. I didn't need help remembering. I had a local talent. I could engage my mind and imagine the right way. From the beginning I figured out that it would be a lengthy business, but for whatever reason, the local's struggle, was getting more to my urgent attention.

✱✱✱✱✱✱✱✱

PART I

My Life Journey

When my mother's womb relaxed for seven years, after which her pregnancy surprised all the neighbors, I was conceived. I was born seven years after the last son. I'm the last child of seven. I checked my mother's womb before her womb said enough. I became a clear fact to be born in this world without my consent. My parents have never expected the pregnancy to happen. When it happened they accepted it spontaneously with happy attitude. My mother said "Yes", to bear me in her womb and my father became pregnant in his mind. After nine month I became natural. Three years before the armed struggle started, I was born. The year was 1957.

I was lucky enough to be baptized in the Parish of Saint Michael. Those who were born in 1956 one year before me were baptized in their houses, since it was closed for any pastoral services, for more than one year.

During the first 12 years of mommy's motherhood, a perfect rhythm of two years span was followed. Every two years my mother conceived and gave birth to all six of her children. It was too late, for a mother who was giving birth at that pace of two years, to expect me in the world. My birth renewed my mother's life. It gave her a new life

1

and a new discipline. I was keenly aware, that I was being accepted with different attitude and renewed spirit. I enjoyed the particular care I got from my mother. I pay respect to my parents.

The relationship my mother had with me, was totally different from the other of my brothers and sisters. I don't say this lightly. I saw it during my childhood. I was enjoying the many benefits of the last son as hirer. She never called me by my name Hiabu. The Bilen culture wouldn't allow her, since I was named by the name of my grand father. She instead was calling me, Paulos or Paulino.

The last shot at the last minutes counts very much. It really made a difference. The family number was supposed to be an even number but I made it odd. Seven is a blessed number as we learn it from our tradition and the Bible. Whenever our elders exchange their cultural blessings they say: "Ade wey Abo shewate ygberKa yegberKi" (Let you be the Father or Mother of seven).

I was born when tradition was respected to its maximum level and the attitude of surprise was practiced day by day. No monogram, no for telling of the sex of the baby to be born. Mrs. Hawa was the traditionally professed nurse around Keren. She volunteered to be on this profession for more than thirty years. She was present at my birth time to help my mommy deliver.

I was born where social facts count more than economical facts. "Multiply and fill the World", is the biblical saying, accompanied by a traditional saying, "Quelas kem Mibayu yAbi ", (The baby will grow as he or she grows without our consent), so never to be worried, "God will provide", was the main belief, and that made sense.

The women congratulated mommy with the usual cultural benediction by saying, "Anqua Mariam Mharetki,", (It is good that you are under Mary's mercy). They shared their happiness by shouting seven times "Ellelta", (a monotonous shout of joy, emitted by vibrating their tongues under their teeth), to show that the newborn baby was a male. No one thought my mother at that age to be pregnant and give birth to me. Mrs. Barhet mommy's best friend indicated that my name be Hiabu which means a gift, just to take the name of my Grandfather. Mrs. Gabru voiced differently, my name to be Icquar, which means (Reserved for later).

As the Italians say "Chi vine tardi o gode o perde", (The one who comes late either wins or loses), on my part I was a winner. At the time I was born, all my brothers and sisters were already grown up. My next older brother Amman, was seven years older than me, so everybody was taking care of me. I became the center of attention of all.

My eldest sister Haimin was grown up ready to be married. My next eldest sister Mihru, she left for Addis Ababa- Ethiopia to live with our cousin. My eldest brother Norai joined the seminary to be a priest. When my brother Norai heard the pregnancy of my mommy he was very concerned and said, "why does mommy commit a sin again". Seven years passed, so he never thought, that my mom would be pregnant again. He never thought I would be born in the world. He thought that my mother's womb had given up.

Ande my brother, who was handsome and very liked by outsiders, he was never able to make a connection in our family circle. His friends they called him by his nickname Napoleon. You always see him fighting. He never allowed himself to be provoked. If he wanted to raise his voice he didn't need help. He ignited very quickly. He couldn't control his emotions. There were times that he paid for the uncontrolled outbursts. One time during a fight between the Keren Lalai youth and Gezabanda, he became a victim. He was beaten to death.

He quit his school, while he was in the elementary and entered in the world of earnings. At that age to have money on your own, was quite distracting life and the consequences were not good.

I have special remembrance of my deceased mom who disciplined me to be my self. By this time she would be 94 years if she was still alive.

She used to read a lot. She had her own small library. She collected all the newspapers, and she read them again and again. When I was a kid, she was reading for me the short stories of the bible in Tigrinya, written by Abba Adhanom Siilu.

I was lucky enough, when I was in my high school to have Abba Adhanom as my moral teacher. Very scholarly and intelligent as he was, one day he told me that, during his entire career, as a writer he was not able to write a book for children. He frankly told me that he tried it many times. He said, whenever I started to write a book for children, the content always ended up to be for the elders. The opposite thing happened to me, when I started to direct my self into the world of writers. I started to write the content regarding the adults but the message ended up being for children. I was trained like that. By chance to be the opposite of Abba Adhanom.

Reading was a lesson I learned from my mommy. It was the first down payment, I received as a gift from her. Whenever she was not doing housework you see her reading something. She knew the basic math of calculations, additions and subtractions. On the other hand daddy was not able to read and write. I remember one day how mommy had helped daddy. He had a court hearing, which he had forgotten the day of the appointment. When she was doing laundry she found a paper of the appointment in his pocket. She kept it in a safe place and when it was due time she surprised daddy the day before.

****

Kindergarten

The entire period, from my birth until I reached age 6, I was enjoying my mothers loving pre school care. She invested all her energy, to bring me up in the world and never hesitated to restore the mission she initiated responsibly. She took her time to instruct and lead me in the right path. When I thought of leaving my mother going to school, I felt emotionally like guilty.

There was plenty to do at home. In the area, there was no established pre school care. No hired baby sitter to take care of me. If there was one, everything was gratis. A conducive environment of the neighborhood was one of the guaranty in growing children. Everything was covered by mommy. A simple life in a simple society. No recited rules and regulations. If I walked to another family house on my own, there was no preoccupation of being kidnapped. It is true I was always free to walk any where, any place and any time on my own.

My house was located two blocks from the Parish of St. Michael. No street name but we shared the same wall with the seminary of St. Michael. One could easily hear all the movement of the seminarians.

I remember there were two sounds of bells ringing at intervals. The first bell was very loud and I could hear it only three times a day, early in the morning, at noon and late evening. The second one, I could hear it at an hourly intervals ringing in a low sound. At home we did not have a watch. We did not need one. My mother was following the hours of the seminary discipline time. She knew when to start cooking, when to go for shopping, thanks to the seminary bells. She was tuned so eloquently that everything was done on time.

It was around September of 1965. The gracious rain had stopped raining. All seasons were disciplined to respect each other. The mountains and the valley's were amazingly covered by green grass and wild flowers of different colors. It was the beginning of harvest. The engaging time of the rain season, with all its challenges was forgotten.

One could see farmers running to their fields, charged with the positive power.

September first according to the Geez calendar is the beginning of the year. It is the largest annual commemoration, which every Habesha celebrated. The day is celebrated under the patron St. John the Baptist. It is the most important festival for the followers of the Geez calendar. All 12 months of the year share equal days of 30. To complete the year, there are five or six days which are called by the name as "Pagumen", (The last days of the cleansing days). On those days, people go to the river bank for a bath (a sign for a spiritual renewal).

A thanksgiving day, celebrated by all the faithful Christians, It was my favorite day. The festival is called Hoye- Hoye, and it began on the eve of "Kidus Yohannes", (St. John the Baptist) and it lasted for two weeks until the day of "MesKal", (the commemoration of the founding of the holy cross).

When the sun goes down, most of the families and their children come out and gather together in one place. One of the male elders initiates the celebration by singing a hymn of forgiveness from the Lord. A litany of prayers accompanied by singing follows, after which the elder male would start the fire. All with a happy and renewed faces they exchange their blessings, by repeating "Amet n'amata yedgmena" (May this coming year be repeated the same like this year).

That year my brother Tecle who was living in the seminary, came to pass the summer vacation with us. He was wearing a white rob (garment) which the seminarian wore. The way I saw him, it made me laugh. Everything about him, I found it laughable. He was different from every body. Curiously, I grabbed his rob and said, you became like mommy with her high heels.

At the age of six, I was circumcised, by a traditional circumciser Aboy Musie Kifl. It was like a celebration, a painful in its procedure. All my family gathered together to accompany and help me it done.

On my part, I was repeatedly told to repeat the word "Wuhir" (a word of encouragement). That time me and my elder brother Ande were to be circumcised. I followed the exact advice of my parents and when it was done, though painful, I repeated the word Wuhir. When it was the turn of my brother Ande, he said "Wedi Shermuta" (son of a b....), to Aboy Mussie the performer of the circumcision.

The first time, I put my feet at saint Joseph school Keren, was around the first week of September of 1965. After the festivity of the new year older student and new students were flocking towards the school. The main street of Keren Lalai was crowded. On the street you see many students, wearing their colorful blue and grey school uniform. Me and Yohannes Zerom (who was called by his nickname John Kennedy), were accompanied by our mothers. Together with my favorite childhood friend, hand in hand we were welcomed to kindergarten. Our home room teacher was Mr. Dirar. Mr. Dirar who came from the suburb village of Jufa was from Bilen tribe.

Me and John were living in the same area only two blocks apart. Our childhood friendship was so intimate. John's behavior was extroversive, to the opposite, I was introversive. After 6 months going to school together, once and for all I was to lose John. After two days of staying in Keren hospital, he died of meningitis. The day before his death, we were playing together. In my mind, I never entertained death, until I learned about John's death. Though, I became so sorrowful, it was from that day, that I started to accept it as one of human destiny.

The end of the school year was nearing. Since John's death, I was to be alone. His sudden death affected my life. The next three months before the school was to be closed, I was to be on my own, walk alone. It was a misfortune. A bad luck. It was one of the childhood terrible remembrance I had ever had in my life.

June was the last month of the school year. I was to hear about my school results. Despite everything, I was the first in the class. Padre Chahma a Spanish missionary (a monk serving as the principal of St.

Joseph school), was to distribute the report cards. As he was covering the distribution of the report cards, I raised my voice and demanded to be given the report card of my friend John, just to give to his mother. "He already took his report card to heaven" he said, to calm my mind. I started to cry and I said, "John why don't you take me to heaven" to be together.

When I was a child, the only hair style I used to cut my hair was the style of "Ghiset" (a rectangular shape, uncut hair on the upper part of the head), mostly seen around Keren area. My mother was my hair stylist. She shaved around all my head using a blade, only leaving a portion of my hair on the upper part. "Kellela" (an arrow shape, style that looks like the Punks style), was the other style which was used by the highlanders. We could easily differentiate, who was who by the hair style.

The girls also had different hair styles, each reflecting to a tribal back ground. Girls from low land, specially the Bilen and Tigre tribes, they used the style of "Shelli" (a thinly braded in front and left unbraided at the back part). Most of the time, the style was decorated by real gold. On wedding days or other special events, the Bilen women, accompanied by "Shellil dance", by moving their head left and right with the drum beat, they heat up the dancing group

As I grew up my hair stylist was Iyasu Beraki. He had a home based business as a barber. Age wise he was three years older than me. He was into the business for family reasons. His father was in Jail for more than 15 years. He was the only bread winner of his family. He was doing the job of barber, on part time basis, since he was going to school. Every week end we gathered in his small house, some to cut our hairs, some to chat. Iyasu around 1975, he joined the ELF (Eritrean Liberation Front) at his early age. He died three years later in Denkel area, while he was accomplishing the duty of a freedom fighter.

"Aboy" (father) Ricab was the professional soul mate finder around Keren Lalai. He had no particular office. No place of advertisement. Un paid job. His expected tip was "Melelik Sua" (a local jar full of a local beer). To fulfill his duties as soul mate finder he used to meet people in Inda Sua (local bars). Inda Tzigeweini was his favorite place. The deal was done in the absence of the becoming soul mates, by the elder male parents. My two older sisters Haimanot and Mihret were the victim of the local deal of soul mate finder Aboy Ricab.

My mother used to buy her ornaments and beauty supply from the down town of Keren. But some times she was buying it from a Tequrir, (a home delivery business). The home delivery beauty supply items were such as, Zeiti (hair ointment), Kuhli (eye coloring substance), Hinna (hands and feet coloring leaves). The ornaments were "Inqui Bahri" (the beads) collected from the sea shore, used for different decorations of "Mahzel", (the baby carrier) and for bed rooms.

Hilet Tequarir was called the zone near the mountain of Etabir. It was inhabited by the Tequarir, immigrants from Nigeria the Hausa tribe. Tall and dark skin Tequarir, almost more than two centauries ago they came to the land of Eritrea. All the Tequarir were Muslim by faith. The main reason for immigrating to Eritrea was the Hajj (Muslim holy pilgrim) to Mecca. At that time there were no air planes. The male individuals all their way from Nigeria they crossed on foot to reach the coastal land of Eritrea. To reach their destination to cross the red sea, they used small wind boats. When the holy pilgrim was terminated they came back to the main land of Africa. Again to make all that journey back home on foot was not feasible. So they chose to remain on the coastal lands of Eritrea.

Binamir they were called the tribe that lived along the Barka region. A nomadic population of Binamir, they raised cows for their living. Every rain season, they used to come to Keren town suburbs and sell their milk to the people. A natural fresh milk, sold in "Kuro" (a circular container), by the Beniamir, was circulating in exchange of cash. I used to enjoy the fresh milk, without any preservatives. "Birah" (a processed sour milk), was my favorite drink. The Bilen girls, from the surrounding villages, they used to come to Keren Lalai, to sell the sour milk of Birah. The sour milk "Birah", I liked it more than any food, when it accompanied "Geat" (porridge) for a sauce.

Inda Fratelli

A very handsome monk returned from Rome Italy, after finishing his initial religious formation program. He was assigned to teach in St. Joseph School Keren. His Name is Afewerki.

No other distinguishing title was given to individual besides being a monk (Brothers). They could be with their PhD, or other professional degrees. What ever it be, the name "Brothers" was the designating common name, in which some times in Italian language, our fathers were calling them "Fratelli". As their name indicated the De La Sale Christian Brothers were always to be called by the name brothers.

The good soul, brother Afewerki, when he came back from Rome, he became my homeroom teacher. That year, I was doing grade one. Very dedicated and spiritual as he was, he had good class management. He spoke Italian very fluently. He was very much liked by all his students. He was like a teacher, father, mentor and a counselor.

I had good chance, at my early age to capture some Italian words and phrases. Brother Afewerki (which we mostly called him by the name Affie), used to be very creative, and that helped him to discover the difference. I could have gone, on and on, to describe the different good qualities of the gentle Brother. I just kept it on hold for the time being, for my pages were contained.

This was the entire setting of St. Joseph school. The whole area of the compound was about 15,000 square meters. A rectangular big building with two floors and a basement occupied almost 1/4 of the totality of the compound. In front of the building at the entrance there was volley ball, basketball, and tennis field. A medium soccer field stretches in front of the building, the length being equal to the main building.

There were twelve spacious classrooms inside the building. My classroom was located at the corner of the corridor. What made it different from other classroom, was the paint and the inside decoration it had. There was a big watch, right in front, above the blackboard. Symmetrically, two identical bird cages, were set on opposite sides. The canary birds, accompanied the class by their beautiful songs. We were the only lucky class, to hear the voice of birds. Some times when the class was silent the birds revived our spirit.

Out side of the classroom, under the open sun light, there were three big cages, full of different kind of birds.

Brother Afewerki's all in all, in his educational philosophy, was a holistic one. The class room was like a home, recreational unit and educational facility. It was a natural classroom. The whole setting of our classroom lectured peace and joy. It was a privilege to be in that class. I considered it as God's gift. After school most of our classmate remained in the class for hours to enjoy the birds.

During the rain season we organized a "Haden" (hunting's) of the wild animals. Our hunting tools were sticks, knives, and dogs. Every hunter was equipped with this hunting tools. Every one had to wear shorts. No trained dogs for the hunt, besides the natural ability of running. The hunting was like a game. There was a group leader. Communication was by whistling. The group had to follow certain hunting rules. The group leader had to assign the different positions.

This was how we enjoyed the hunting game. The place was in the vast plain area of Golgol Megarih. It was like a soccer game, our ball being "Mantle" (a wild rabbit). Each hunter had to be alert and ready to run with his dog besides him. The wild rabbit was smoked out, from the bushes and as it attempted to flee, the dogs run one after the other as a relay. Since the wild rabbits run faster than dogs, the dogs run one after the other until the wild rabbit gives up running. Before the animal falls under the dogs teeth, each hunter had to run faster to get hold of the rabbit either alive or dead. We were having fun under the sun, all the day playing the hunting games.

Every Saturdays of the Summer, when the school was closed, we played soccer games until noon. When the sun picked with its heat until it got weak, we played games, like Palina (little glass balls) , Korer (a round spinning thing), Gebeta, (14 holes dug superficially on sand), under a tree shade. In the evening before it got dark, teamed up into two equal groups, we played a game of defense and offence by fighting with "Ingule", (a wild inedible fruit). For face and head protection every one used a shield made of tin. The "Ingule" was considered as a bullet and to each fighter an equal share of ingule was given. A rank was given by how many one hits his target. If one was captured by either group, he was to get a punishment. The rubbing with "Ame" (wild leaves that caused an acute pain on the skin), was the punishment applied to the captured member of the enemy.

Almost, every Summer, my childhood friend Miku Neguse, used to come from Addis Ababa, just to pass his vacation in Keren. Upon his first arrival to Keren, I introduced him to the Keren Lalai group, and once he got used with the group, I was taking him every where I was going. One time, one of the Keren Lalai group member rubbed Miku's body with "Ame". Miku was crying and crying because of the pain he got from the rubbing. I immediately came to his rescue. I rubbed him with unti-Ame (a special red sand used as a medicine).

Every Sunday afternoon, from three to six, the soccer tournaments were going on, at the soccer field of Joko. There were four very known soccer teams. They were the team of La sale from Keren Lalai, Al-hilal from Shuk, Anseba form Hilet Sudan and Stella from Ghezawereket. The teams were formed based on the zone where the players lived. La sale team being the team of Keren Lalai, it was my favorite team. All the people of Keren Lalai they were cheering for the team of La sale.

During the foot ball match, the people from Keren Lalai controlled everything, if their team was losing, they disrupt the game. They enter into the field with their sticks. No one can resist. The police themselves were scared.

From all the players of La sale team, the most fun I had with, were Tewelde Yohannes (the team leader) and Yohaness Karkas Joker (the goal keeper) . Both of them were selected, to join the famous team of Hamasien, in the capital city of Asmara. In short time, Joker became a very known goal keeper nationally and internationally. He was the number one goal keeper of Ethiopia. He played with the national team of Ethiopia, in different countries, before he joined the Eritrean liberation front.

In the outskirt of Keren town, twenty minutes walk from "Shuk" (the down town), there is the shrine of Mariam Deari. Inside a holed baobab tree, there is the statues of the miraculous black Mary. This was how the first miracle happened. Two Italian soldiers, to avoid of being targeted by the British jet fighter, they hide themselves under the baobab tree. While they were under the tree, they were reciting their rosary. The British jet fighter, though it dropped the bomb, exactly at where they were hiding, the bomb shell hit the baobab tree, without being exploded. That was the time, the survivors realized, that a miracle had occurred.

It was during the second world war, when the British soldiers were advancing towards Keren town, that this happened. The two Italian soldier survivors, when they returned back home, they made a pledge to put a black statues of our Lady inside the holed baobab tree. From that day on the shrine of Mariam Deari had welcomed millions of people. The devotion to the Black Lady of Deari, at the beginning it became very popular among the local people, but in time the devotion was diffused to many countries.

If I could design the entire strategic position of the shrine. From the main entrance gate to the baobab tree the distance is about 400 meters. As you enter from the main southern gate, two streets divide at an angle, at which when they reach to the big tree of baobab, they form a complete figure of an isosceles triangle. Along the sides of the two street, there are "Mim" (azadiracta indica) trees, planted parallel to each other. The view from the air, is like a triangular cathedral. A cathedral made of natural plants. There is a seasonal river that passes near by the shrine. At the back of the baobab tree there is a big plantation field run by the Cistercians monastery.

The annual commemoration of the shrine is May 21. From different part of the world, people came to the shrine, only for one reason, to be endowed the gracious grace of the mother of God. After the holy mass the colorful procession was held. The "Debteras" (professional Geez rite singers) raised their voice in singing accompanied by the big drum. The scouts and spiritual associations with their distinctive uniforms lead by the cross, lead the procession. Older women with their rosary in their hand and the sole women's gift of "Elelta" (a monotonous joyous voice), they awakened the spirit of the pilgrims. When the processions was ended, a preaching by a known preachers followed. After the preaching the people flocked towards the baobab tree, some to offer their gift and some to pray in solitude.

All the social activity and festivity continued on the river bank. Another world another space to discover. It all seemed pointless, to change the spiritual atmosphere, suddenly, into a mundane activity. The people looked like they had been born without any notion of having faith, I said, a self-disapproval of the situation. All in all I was convinced positively if all things were done with discipline.

The river bank, it looked like an open exhibition of different cultures, entertaining their minds. In a matter of minutes, it turned to a big market, of some selling goods and some buying, some getting high in dancing and some in drinking alcohol. The fresh cold water of the natural spring, served as a natural freezer. The beautiful and sexy Bilen girls, accompanied by the handsome boys, they echoed their songs in "Golia" (dance party). With their colorful dresses and the competition less dance, they stayed all the day and night dancing. Bilen were born with the drum. The dance was not artistic in its kind, but it was in their blood. From the beginning of the dance party, until they get tired, they danced "Golia" (usually dancing in a circle with the female drummers being in the middle).

Three months before the annual feast of Mariam Deari, in groups of five or six, we raised money by selling home made "Fofol" (a candy made of sugar and flour), and "Mikli" (a sandwich). The money we collected, we put it in one common box and every time the elected treasurer gave an account of the money. Our grouping was male with male and female with female. On the eve of the feast we made everything ready, the food, the drinks and other entertaining materials.

Before the summer of 1969 was to end, a group of Italian film makers, came to Keren to realize their film. The heavy clouds of the rain season cleared, leaving the ground dry and making way for the film makers to shoot their pictures easily.

One day, as we were playing soccer, in front of the church of Kudus Michael, from far we saw about four big trucks coming towards us. At first, we were scared, because we thought the trucks might be those of the Ethiopian military, which everybody was allergic. As they came, they parked along the side of the soccer field.

Suddenly, we interrupted playing and as we saw the crowed were white people we assured our safety. From one of the truck, two white gentlemen with an interpreter came out, to meet all the soccer players. The interpreter (a handsome Eritrean which was not from Keren area) had started to communicate with us about the film project they had.

After introducing himself and the purpose of their coming to Keren Lalai, he immediately went to the deal of taking our pictures. You will be compensated, for whatever you do for us, he added to persued every body. On consensus we accepted the deal.

Three older youth of Keren Lalai, took the responsibility of making the deal and all the follow-ups. The picture the film makers expected from us, was very simple and needed no rehearsal. In the middle of the soccer field, they put some benches where we were to sit all in a "C" shape position. A young beautiful lady from Asmara, was to accompany the show as a teacher. Being in the middle she was showing us the pictures of different animals by asking us, "What is this".

We were under four big cameras, being taken pictures from different angles. The director of the film was moving here and there, to see the perfect performance of the action. Some times he was too loud speaking in his native Italian language. We were able to differentiate Italians from British, by the language they spoke. When they spoke Italian language, we said "Tiliano Meakor Hibey", (Italians monkey's ass) and when they spoke in English language, we said "Ingliz Korkar" (Britain stingy).

As an actor I was so exited. I tried to match my self to the known actors of the world. That time, the movies that were circulating around Keren, most of them were Indian films. I enjoyed the Indian films, and when ever I got chance, I used to go to the movie house, in down town of Keren.

The movie, I was part of as an actor, was about a certain Italian General who had died around kKeren, during the second World. It was the General's daughter, the author of a book, who attempted her father's story to be on the screen. I was particularly impressed about the young Italian lady who was on her late thirties, as an author of a book. Her look was beautiful and sexy. Seated under a tree she observed all the actions to be taken as pictures.

After our performance of the movie was accomplished, according to the will of the film makers, the compensation of the money was given to the older boys (the dealers). Since the majority of the participants were under 10 years age we knew nothing about what was going on. With the money we were compensated, we planned to buy a sport equipments. We bought two soccer balls, shoes, and sport shirts.

The Associations

The day I started to associate myself for the first time, was with the association of Legion of Mary. That year I was doing grade three, and I was 9 years old. When I grew up in Keren Lalai, there were different social aggregations organized spontaneously. Some of our groupings, were definitely wrong, as I see them now. Fighting with different entity of different counties was wrong. Disrespecting and abusing the mentally ill individuals, for the sake of entertainment was also wrong. I couldn't clear myself from that of wrong doing, but I feel regretted.

Two religious lay associations were founded in St. Joseph school Keren. The first association named by "Jesus the crucified", the origin being from Italy, was founded by the deceased Brother Daniel Misghina. The association was mostly dominated by female members. My mother was one of the members. The second association was "The Legion of Mary", the source of the foundation being Dublin Ireland, it was started by Brother Ghebretensaie and brother Yemanu. Two spirituality, two devotions, two services in one community. Not rivals in essence. No competition, since the members in age wise they were different they wouldn't match. Age wise, the members of the Legion of Mary were very young, compared to the association of "Jesus The Crucified". The youth generation of Keren Lalai was spiritually infiltrated by these associations. There was a spiritual campaign going on, for recruiting other individuals, to join the association.

This was how the weekly meeting held. The meeting was done inside one of the classrooms with the statues of Mary placed in a visible place. All the members sat in circle. The president, the vice president, the secretary and the treasurer sat together completing the circle. The president after greeting all the attendants, he started the meeting with prayer. After singing the opening song all are sited. With a convincing tone, the president greeted all the new comers. The new comers were invited to briefly introduce themselves. The vice president explained, the aims and the goals of the associations with brief history.

After taking the names of the attendees, he proceeded recording the participant presence, for the update of the next meeting. The president invited, to all members to kneel down and started the recitation of the holy rosary. After the rosary, every member sat down and an assigned member for the day began a spiritual preaching. After the preaching the secretary read the recorded meeting items, of the past week. It was the secretary's job to assign the weekly voluntary jobs or actions of mercy. The weekly voluntary duties were like helping senior citizens, helping the poor families, teaching, cleaning the parish church, visiting the sick in hospitals. The members were to express or give testimony, to the action of mercy they have accomplished. Before the meeting was to close, the treasure acknowledged the participant about the financial situations. After some announcement given by the president the meeting was closed by short prayer.

I was lucky enough, at my early age, to grasp a civilized way of associating myself to the others. At that age to speak, about the terms, president, vice president, secretary and treasurer for me was an extraordinary thing. At the beginning of every year elections were taking place. By a secret ballot democratically we were electing our leaders. I remember I was elected twice as a president and one time as a secretary.

After each spiritual weekly meetings we had a social times where we used to play indoor games, like playing cards and dominos. During weekends soccer tournament were organized. Twice a year we had a social outing or a picnic.

The discipline to freely aggregate and express one self I learned it from the association. Misbehaviors were discussed and self correction was available. There was a secret campaign going on to eliminate bad behavior of the community, such as not drinking alcohol, not using tobacco and street fighting. The school of St. Joseph was greatly helped by the lay association. Our teachers figured out spontaneously who was who by the way we disciplined ourselves.

I was a member of the association, for six year, until I decide in 1975, to join the De La sale Christian Brothers.

The "Zema" (Geez rite singing) group, was another association, I was affiliated with. It was not a well organized association. The group was smaller in number. The aim of the Zema group was to help during the holy mass in singing. To master the unique Geez Zema was not simple. Everything we had to learn by heart. To master the whole Zema, it was very demanding and some times it took years. Good voice with good will, was the criteria of endurance, to finish the program. There were no grades to follow but a classification of "Anagustis" the beginners, "Nifki Diakon" intermediate and "Deacon" professionals. Only one master, one teacher. The classes were taken in an open air. Aboy Mario, we used to call him (the instructor of the Geez liturgy songs), a blind man from his birth.

Everyday, precisely at 4:30 in the morning, Aboy Mario, rushed towards the parish church of St. Michael, to ring the big bell. It was one of his everyday duty. With no traffic to fight, he was always there before everyone. Though physically blind, his inner senses of recognizing people, was very much developed. He managed to recognize each of his students, either by our voices or by touching our heads. One day to test his inner insight of recognition, I approached him silently without emitting any voice. Once my head was under his hand, he immediately recognized me by saying my nick name "Hibabu" (in Tigre language meaning hyena). He was the one who gave me this nick name. From that day on, I believed in his inner capacity of recognizing people.

Aboy Mario was never dependent on others, for his day to day life. To go from one place to another, he didn't need any help from other people to be guided. The power of intuition was highly developed in his mind. Every afternoon from six to seven, for one hour he was teaching the male children, to be able master the Geez song by heart. The class was an out door class under a shade of a tree with no light. The discipline was performed under a blind man. Being seated on a stool, all the attendee had to voice their presence. Once he knew who was sitting where, without a monitor, he accomplished his job. Everybody had to sit, within the reach of his "Mekomia" (a long stick), on the sand. Even if we tried silently, to move from one position to another, he could easily follow all our movements. No one escaped from his inner surveillance. I remember one day, while we were in the session, Abreda and Kelati switched their position. As he noticed the illegal movement, he stretched his long stick to strike the head of one of the perpetrators.

He was expert in cooking the spaghetti. My mental assessment of his cooking performances was excellent. He was to the point, specially when he prepared the spaghetti sauce. He knew exactly, the whole procedure of cooking, without reading any recipe.

One day, to satisfy my curiosity, I asked him a tough questions. How do you explain happiness and unhappiness, I asked. He answered, despite of my being blind, I can be happy or unhappy, in relation to what my other senses dictate my mind. I have all the preferences, the attractions and the satisfactions of life, with the exception of my sight which is only darkness, he added. I never heard Aboy Mario feeling bad, about his being blind. Though being blind from birth, was a painful experience, his mind had concluded that life was like that, after all, he had the guts to go through with it.

The color and the beauty of the world with all it's textures were obscured. For him everything was dark. He was able to distinguish the day from the night by the sense of heat only. The degree of the heat as it increased from the time of the sun's rise to about 3:00 o'clock, it gave him a chance to calculate the hours of the day. Though, he had an old alarm clock, time wise he was only assisted by his creative mind.

His sense of direction was formidable. He set his walking steps, block by block, to reckon the distance from his house to the church. He managed to go back and forth by counting the blocks of "Inda" (house of) Ukbamariam, Inda Nisur, Inda Abbe, Inda Reda, Inda Gafo.

"Micael Hiabu", called by his nick name "Wuriu", was my deceased uncle who died when I was about ten years old. He was very well known in Keren Lalai for his bravery. He had a combative attitude, and he had associated himself with the drinkers of Keren Lalai. In the evening after he got drunk with so many "Wanchas" (a cone like container) of Sua (local beer), he controlled the whole community of Keren Lalai. He abandoned himself to the world of drinkers at his early age. No one had to be on his way. My grandfather was not happy with my uncle for his drinking habits. In order to get him disciplined, my grand father preferred to mention the name of my uncle Wuriu, for the forced military service ordered by the Italians, a possible attempt, designed by my grandfather, to change his character, through military discipline. My uncle refused to join the Italian military and physically to avoid it, he escaped towards Sudan. My grandfather was obliged, unwillingly, to give his beloved son my father Hassebu. Before he left for the military training, my grand father blessed my father for a safe come back.

My daddy, at the age of 21 he became one of the "Ascari" (as the Italians were calling to the local's military recruits). He fought in three big battles, the battle of Kesela, Berentu and Keren against the British. He was a radio operator in the brigade 110. He knew some Italian language. He saw many of his friends dying in the battle. Thanks to God he survived the war. If he didn't I wouldn't be in the world.

When the Italians were defeated at the battle of Keren (the last front), he took the opportunity to escape the situation by going to hide himself in a village called Ashera, where my aunt Lettemicael lived. He made a deal, in selling his rifle of "Carben" (Italian made rifle), to a Welkait fellow, for 300 hundred shillings. After staying for a couple of weeks with my aunt, he decided to go to Keren to join his family. My mother was pregnant to her first child Haimin. During the war, all our family moved to a way distant village of my grand mother's, in Tzeazega. The day of the reunion was so great and so blessing. "Resi Ahwatka Yegberka" (be on the top of your brothers and sisters) was the blessing of my grand father to my father. When he saw the new blessing of a new baby born girl, my father got exited and became very happy. With the money he earned, by selling his rifle, he started to reinstate his family life. He opened a small convenient shop and maintained it until I was born in1957.

Wuriu my uncle had a famous female rival. Her name was Lijajet. Besides Lijajet no one could confront him. He often got drunk in the afternoons and then he raved against Lijajet. When he was immersed into the ocean of alcohol, cursing after cursing flowed from his mouth, before he slowed down as the Tigrinya saying goes, "Ziaklen TiHinen BeAle Mariam yibla" (after grinding enough they make an excuse of saying it is a holiday). In her turn Lijajet, by getting up early in the morning, while my uncle was still in the status of hangover, she rained him with all colors of curses. Mornings were for Lijajet as evenings were definitely favorable time for my uncle. At Lijajet's funeral one of my uncle's friend Aboy Meskel Hammad raised his voice in the middle of the people by saying "Woe to you, the dead in the cemetery of Megarih, as for us we got a great relief" .

"The Geometra" (an Italian word to mean an architect), was the name given to the drinkers who used to zigzag the main road of Keren Lalai. After drinking alcohol heavily, to balance their walk was impossible. The good thing, there were not these much cars to be blocked by the drinkers. Aboy Paulos Ghebray was one of the many of Keren Lalai's Geometras. One day he bought a goat and tied it to a tree near the bar of Tzigheweini. After drinking so many Wancha Sua he got over drunk. He untied the goat and let it free, by saying, "go to Keren Lalay and be ready to be cooked as Himito" (the internal intestine cooked and sauced with local spices). The next day there was no goat in the house and no "Himito".

Coprifuoco

King Haile Silasie had ordered, a decree of emergency, for Keren and it's surroundings. The town fall under a military siege. It was guarded under a heavy curfew. From six o'clock in the afternoon till six O'clock in the morning any movement was forbidden. The locally recruited commandos were ready to apply the order. The commandos most of them who came from a rural and the surrounding villages, were trained by Israel. Militarily they were far more able than the regular Ethiopian soldiers. Because they knew the place very well, they were able to resist the freedom fighters for a while, until they were infiltrated by the ELF and EPLF, between 1973-1976.

1969 before it was to end around the fall, my cousin Tekie was killed by the soldiers. He was among the 47 villagers, who were massacred in the environ of Shinara. Tekie very gentle and happy in all his manners, was performing a farmers job in his own village. At his young age he was married, and before his death his wife was six month pregnant. Three month later, the child was born and they named him Fikri which means love.

I was used, to see camels carrying woods and other stuff, but when I saw the cadaver of Tekie, being carried by a camel I was shocked. I looked very scared. My first reaction was revenge. A revenge to the merciless commandos the perpetrators. They became savages knowingly, to harm their own people.

A forced relocation of the villagers was implied, to all the surrounding villages of Keren. My aunt Leteghiorghis with all her remaining children and grand children came to Keren. The little compound of our house was not able to accommodate to all. My father built a "das" (a temporary rectangular shape shelter), made of straws and "Tencobet" (a rag made of palm tree leaves).

My mother gentle in her nature, she provided a small kitchen, to be used by all the family of my aunt. She was not from a Bilen tribe, she was a Tigrinya speaking, from Hamasien. Her lack of understanding the Bilen language, made her live in the loneliness of the wide Belen's. Language wise she was easily communicating with the children by signs.

I had three aunts on my fathers part. All three were married to farmers from the environ of Keren. Every week end we had a visit from the family of my aunts from Shinara, Ashera and Halibmentel. When they come to visit our family they came with their farming products, such as "Tzeba" (milk), "Tesmi" (butter), "Birah" (sour milk), "Ful" (peanuts), "Gaba". Our culture was so well versed by this "InKa Haba" (give and take), generous action. My mother in return she gave them, "Shikor" (sugar), "Bunn" (coffee) and "Berbere" (a spiced hot paper flower).

Our house was always open to all. One day my aunt Medhin from Halibmentel she came to our house. After a brief discussion with my mother, my aunt had agreed, that Meiso her daughter would live with us in order to follow her studies. Meiso my cousin, came to keren Lalai when I was almost eleven. I was so exited to see her being part of our family. Me and Meiso were around the same age. She started school in Halibmentel when she was a little older.

The beauty of the Bilen unfolded my eyes, the first day I saw her. She easily slipped into the routine of our daily family life. Due to the age gap I did not enjoy my older sisters as I enjoyed Mieso. My youngest sister Lette was 11 years older than me. Besides Aman my older brother all my brothers and sisters were living away from Keren lalai. Tecle, Lette and Ande they moved to the capital city for a better life. Haimin and Mihru both of them married, they were living in the surrounding village of Begu. My mother became very happy about my new situation. I finally found some one to talk to, to play with.

All my attention fall on Mieso's new life in town. She was satisfied with my reception. She was very much pleased, with all the attention I was giving her. For me, Mieso, to be part of our family, was a great favor. Upon the whole, I was much pleased for her gentleness. On her part, she turned her attention almost entirely on me. To see her settled in our house with that serenity added my affection to her.

To distract the Keren Lalai youth eyes, from labeling Mieso as "Haggie" (villager), "Felestin" (people without land), I gave her used cloths of my sister Lette. Every cloth fit to her. She looked different as the Habesha say "Zenita" (became beautiful).

As we walked together, I was always presenting Mieso, to every member of Keren Lalai's youth, as being one of my niece. We walked alone to the neighborhood of Keren Lalai and to down town "Shuk". She taught me about the village life, how they lived, and on my part, practically, I shared with her the towns life. I always enjoyed my stay with Mieso. Her honest mind taught me a lot. I was proud of her. I knew how Mieso was struggling, to learn Keren Lalai's ways. She missed a lot from her village life.

The day she was to leave me once and for all I started to cry. The connection we made in a year time, it was such a comfort of mind. I fought to my best to make her remain with me. I promised her a lot. I did not want to lose her. The gleam of hope I shared with her was about her education and the success she would gain if she remained in Keren. We built a good connection of being brother and sister. I was taking care of her more than any one. The day my aunt came to pick Mieso from our house, I started to yell at my aunt. Mieso cried with me as she saw me crying. She knew the decision was against her will. I wish she transgressed the Biblical commandment to honor your father and mother.

In vain did I try to convince my aunt, or persuade her. My deeply felt influence couldn't work. She became a victim of her parents decision. Her father was asked by a family, to engage Mieso to be wedded to a farmer in the village.

****

Kerenini

Keren town is 91km distant from the capital city of Asmara. It is located in the middle of Eritrea and it is 1600 meters above see level. Four big mountains surround the town; on the east Mt. Etabir, on the west Mt. Senkil, on the north Mt. Lalumba and on the south Mt. Ziban . It looks like it is built inside a big volcanic crater. It is a very charming town and most of the doctors prescribe their patients to live there. It is a place where Muslims and Christians live together harmoniously.

There are two claims about how the town took its name, the Tigrigna version and the Bilen version. The Tigrigna version says the word Keren came from the word "Keren" meaning "mountain". The Bilen version says the word came from "Krin" a Bilen word for " stone". The town was subdivided into seven administrative zones, Keren Lalai, Ghezabanda, Ghezawereket, Hilet Tequarir, Hilet Sudan, Daari and Shuk.

At Keren, fruits-town, life was very different from the capital Asmara. People made their living working as farmers, raising animals, or employed by the Italian landlords on the fields. The town was built at the time of Turkish dominion, more than two centuries ago.

The military base known by Forto was built by Turkish, during the Ottoman Empire, more than three centauries ago. It is located at the center of the town and looks like a center point of a circle. Surrounded by four big mountain, it issued the panoramic view of the whole town and the surrounding mountains.

The main street of Keren Lalai extends from Forto (dead end to the north), to the Church of Kudus Michael (dead end to the south), in a straight line. One sitting in front of the Church would have a direct straight view of the fort and vice versa.

For centauries the "Momona" trees planted along side the soccer field of Joko, were the natural law edifice, that served the locals as a court house. Planted on the river bank, they were green for the entire year. "Shimagle" (Elders), from different places of Keren surroundings, were coming to the place, for different kind of meetings. Land dispute, family issue and tribal problems were discussed under the trees. Decisions were given on consensus. What the majority accepted was applied. Case was closed democratically. Verdict was carried out without prison facility. Punishment was handled accordingly. Social alienation was the main substance of a punishment. Appointment were respected. No rush judgment. Settlement was a process. Some times it took for years. A full session of the Elders was required to open and close a case. When ever it was necessary hearing was conducted in absence.

Singing birds accompanied the whole session of a verdict. It was a place were wisdom was explored and the culture of dialogue nurtured. All sat harmoniously in a circle on stones, though uncomfortable to sit. No chair available. There was a moderator Shimagle, with no case recorder. The exchange was heart to heart. No interruption. Social seclusion was the main discipline.

One day while we were playing soccer, the kicked ball hit the ground, where the elders were gathering. The player who went to recover the ball, on his way curiously asked to one of the elders, by saying "why they were patiently staying for long hours sitting on circle, unmovable on a stone". The wise elder answered, my son as you kick the ball the whole day, we too kick a case till we arrive on a deal.

The day I learned, that the Momona trees were cut down once and for ever, under the order of the Government, I was totally shocked. What made me mad was not only the destruction of the trees, but the loss of the whole tradition. The Government cut the trees without the consent of the people. The voiceless natural trees, once and for all they were destroyed. I wished the procedure of a referendum was conducted, I would have cast a "No", vote. The natural court building, as they collapsed under the government axes, I felt very sad.

About four blocks from the parish of St. Michael, there was an orphanage for female orphans. The orphanage was run by the Santa Anna nuns. From all corners of Eritrea, female orphans were accepted to the program without considering their religious and ethnic background.

The community as such was so united, since the majority of the neighborhood inhabitant were of one ethnic and religion group. The Catholic missionaries had made their base in that neighborhood more than two centauries ago. I felt safe, in my own hometown. I had friends, which I belonged to, with different mentality. I was born form a practicing Catholic parents. I used to go to Church everyday. Our family was disciplined in that way.

No sense of fundamentalism everything was normal. I have Muslim friends. Most of them go to the Catholic schools; even the Muslims who were sons of Sheik or Sidi were joining the Catholic school. I understood exactly how the community was organized. Everyone was either a Christian or a Muslim, Bilen, Tigre, or Tigrigna. My only remembrance was the harmonious co-existence between the people.

Coming from down town on the main street, St. Joseph school and Santa Anna school, lied parallel. At the dead end of the street on the left there is the orphanage of St. Agnes. Facing straight to the main street there was the church of St. Michael, with the Seminary behind it.

On the street you don't see many cars running, beside the truck of Mr. Ghinbot, Mr. Dirar and Mr. Tewelde Seber. There was only one taxi in the whole town owned by an Italian half cast, and one horse cart owned by Abrahim Arej. Heavy load transportation was accomplished, either by donkey's or camels.

At the corner of Gira fiori, a convenient tea shop owned by Ajak, used to serve breakfast meals. Mr. Ajak was very well known for this special menu of Shihanful, (Boiled beans served with aromatic sauce and yogurt). There were two famous local bars, (Inda Suwa), run by Mrs. Tzigheweini and Mrs. Abeba, in Shuk down town. After four o'clock in the afternoon you see people running towards the local bars. All the customers were male and no female was allowed to be there.

My father was one of the favorite customer of Mrs. Tzigheweini. Specially, the last day of the month of his pay day, he was coming home very drunk. Early in the morning, on the street of Keren Lalai, we were enjoying counting the caravan and when the sun goes down, we were counting the drinkers.

Sheik Zaid was his name, the famous psychiatric local doctor, near down town of Keren. People with mental disorders they were going to Sheik Zaid, an illiterate individual with a special power. He used to exercise his healing profession without any license. He had the power of manipulating minds and was able to foretell, the future fates of his clients. Though, I couldn't tell the procedure of his healing method, the business was working in his favor. Even, people from the capital city, they were going to Keren to pay a visit for their psychiatric problems. As the Abyssinian saying goes "Ab Adi Uwurat beal Hade aini ymerih" (in the land of the blinds the one with one eye leads). Sheik Zaid was the only available doctor without prescriptions.

Adey Werku, was the traditional acting healer for different internal diseases. Her expertise in healing people was by home made herbal prescriptions. Over eating and stomach problems were cured by "Metekosta" (a sharp heated iron rubbed against the lower foot). Another traditional medical intervention, she used to cure infectious disease, was by mixing herbal and roots boiled or un boiled ready to drink. Backache, rheumatism and acute pains, were cured by " Mahgoma" (a blood letting from the veins by means of a cone shaped instrument and sucking the blood).

Two modern pharmacies located at the downtown were giving services, one owned by Mr. Mohamed Hiabu and the other by Mr. Fesehaie. The majority of the population they used the traditional medicine. Said Kasim was the traditional pharmacist. In his shop he had, "Lihtit" (Genus Malva), "Kerbe" (Commiphora Erythrea), "Karfa" (Cynamon tea spices), "Chena adam" (Ruta chalepesis), Ointment oils, "Himor" (Tamarind), "Gingibil (Ginger), Sono (Sena Alexandria)

Sibirsikirti (a white mineral). My father was proficient in healing the "Timto" (the finger toe infection). He had a hidden pharmacy locked in a box very securely.

"Kudar" (an open vegetables market) was my favorite place. If I ever went with mommy, the spare change of money I was getting from her, I was buying it fresh "Zeitun" (guava). There was one junkyard where the owners had used their creative mind to produce house utensils, like "Menkeshkesh (coffee roaster), "Menkerker" (fire mixer), "Sherekrek" (a coffee can mixer), "Jebena" (a coffee maker).

I liked a lot of things about Keren Lalai. I don't want to put Keren Lalai out of my heart. I am not exaggerating. After all it was this neighborhood that initially fashioned my mind.

What made the neighborhood more livable was the absence of the bars, restaurants and nightclubs. There were only three grocery stores owned by Mr. Kelifa, Mr. Michael Adem and Mr. Dirar Ashera. No other competitors.

The shop owners were running their small business, on the premises of "Maalesh", an Arabic word, which has no literal translation in English. The word maalesh is a customer satisfying word. Maalesh and a good sense of humor, would create a confident relationship between the customer and the shopkeeper. After Maalesh there was no satisfying word. The customer would come again without being invited to shop again. No need of publicity or advertisement. No price label. But it was drilled into the mind of the customer orally. Different place and different world to discover. Confidence was created face to face. What counted most, was the direct acquaintance between the creditor and the debtor. The physical contact played a great role. No, telephone deal. No contract and no paper work to sign. There was no hidden creditor. Every relationship was based on trust. One debtor and no flow of bills. No fear of identity theft. One trust built day by day. If one looses trust he or she would never be back again. The deal was " I will give you the honey, be ready with the money". Pay as you go without interest. A collection was made face to face. The trust was measured on monthly bases.

The market of Maalesh was all about exploring, the culture and the custom of Keren people. The local people from all the surrounding villages, they came to exchange not only their goods, but their daily life experiences. In its structure, the market being in an open field, one can hear only the natural noises of people talking or the noise of animals. The traders wearing their colorful cloths, to their utmost selling ability, tried to communicate with their customers.

Let me step up here, and tell my experience in USA with my immigrant mind. It all started when I was living in Gaithersburg Maryland. One day in the middle of 2001, I received a letter from an unknown creditor. It was my first credit card. It was a surprise for me. Before that time I only heard about it from friends jokingly. Let me phrase the joke. An old lady from Eritrea came to visit her children in USA. After living for a while she helped her self going out with her children every where. She never had an experience of the use of the credit card, besides the every day cash transaction she was used to. She saw many times her son milking cash from an ATM machine. She never stopped from asking out of curiosity. Specially she was very curious to ask about the smart box, (the ATM machine). In her mind she started to compare two experiences. Her mind was floating, one time in the ocean of USA and another time back home. Her limited mind set wouldn't let her navigate. She said, it would be great if my son gives me the money milking card (the credit card). When it was time to go back home at the air port she insisted and demanded to have one of the credit card instead of being given the cash.

Unless accompanied by elders, no one was allowed to go to "Shuk" (down town) of Keren. If one was under age he/she had to manage wisely otherwise he/she was to be considered as "Uwala" (vagabond). For the fear of not being labeled as "Uwala" I preferred to be accompanied always by my mother or my eldest brothers.

Along the sides of the street there were the ever green trees of Mim, planted almost three meters apart. The trees were the main ornament of the street. People walked under the tree shade just to avoid the sun's heat. Keren was very well known by it's hot weather. I was very dis-appointed, once again, when I learned about the destruction of the trees. All the trees where cut by the government to make asphalt road. I wondered if the government was thinking the right way. As the Tigrinya saying goes, "KneTzeBik KinBil KeyNeKfi" (to make it better we made it worse), for me their action totally seemed anti-green. What blinded the authority not to see the beauty of the street with its natural trees, I said, filled with true sentiment by reacting differently, disposed to rage.

Saint Agnes orphanage, being only two blocks from my house, I was able to hear all the movement of the orphans, playing, singing and praying. The orphans were only orphans, and their status as orphans was well respected. No religious indoctrination, to convince them to join the nuns and no special act of recruitment was applied.

My mother was doing business with the Saint Agnes orphanage. At home she was raising chickens and selling the eggs to the community. I never asked my father for my educational needs. My mother was the one providing and always ready to pay for my books, pen and pencils. When ever they needed eggs I was the one who went to deliver to the nuns. When I was little child I was doing it without precondition, because it was my business. But as I grew up, I stopped going to the orphanage to sell eggs. The main reason was the presence of Tirhas in the orphanage. Since she was my childhood girl friend, I didn't like to expose my self in that way.

In 1970 while I was doing grade six, I happened to be in the same classroom with Tirhas Adem. Tirhas originally from Tesenei town, she was living in the orphanage at St. Agnes. Her step father was a well to do Italian land lord, in the town of Tesenai. As long as my remembrance goes, I was well acquainted with Tirhas. Her quite and reserved character, wouldn't allow her to be social with others. Besides smiling she never multiplied words, to communicate with others. If my child hood attraction was explainable, I would happily do so. The Keren Lalai conservative attitude, I grew up with, added to the nuns way of life, didn't allow us to freely express our inner most attraction.

Out of 38 student in grade seven, there were only five female students in St. Joseph school. A male dominated school, at that time to break the usual policy and open up for female students was so unusual. Three of the female students, Letekidan, Letekristos and Marta, were from Santa Anna formation house program. Muza Amid was lucky to join the school through the affiliation of the nuns. Though she was not in the formation program, somehow she was living with the nuns. A very charming, down to earth lady she was always shy. She did not look, that she was born in Keren Lalai. The interesting thing, she was not baptized by Keren Lalai's holy water.

My first English classes, I had them, with my home room teacher brother Pedro Arrambide. Brother Arrambide, was a sort of a teacher, who kept his students with good discipline and respect. His class management was beyond expected. I am the fruit of brother Arrambide. For me it was such a big deal to be one of his students. I feel proud of him. He was always in good mood, to make his students happy.

"Tzibuk Nzigeberelka wey gberelu wey Ngerelu" (Either do a good deed or tell to the others about the good deeds you received), as the Abysinian saying goes, for me the good deed of Bother Pedro, was still in my mind. In 1972, when I was doing grade eight, brother Pedro from his own good will, he organized a school trip to Masawa (the sea port of Eritrea). He made everything ready by him self. All the trip cost was covered by him. None of the students paid a dime. It was the first good luck, I had ever to tell. For me to go to Masawa was a dream.

Early in the morning, one day of March of 1972, a local bus parked at the soccer field of St. Joseph school. All my classmates, with a happy face talking and chatting in groups were showing up at the gate of the school. Masawa, for every body, was a mysterious sea port town, to be discovered and be enjoyed. Besides the five female students all the other of my classmates were ready for the trip. Me and Yobiel Kidane had shown up together. We were close friends and always we had to do things together.

Though I was very exited, for some reason some thing in my mind was disturbing me. It was the absence of Tirhas. She was one of the female classmate, I had ever being in love. I asked about the situation to Tirhas the day before our trip. I wish I would have come, but the superior nun decided not, she said.

The night before the departure day to Masawa, Yobiel's mother gave birth to a baby boy. That morning when I met him he was so exited. He couldn't wait to tell me about the surprise. By taking out from his pocket "Kitcha" (a local dried bread), surprise! Surprise! he shouted. The only thing, I certainly knew about Yobiel's family was that his mother was pregnant. Could you figure out what the surprise was, he asked. No, I said. Try to guess, he said. After guessing for several minutes, I lost my patience. Please tell me the surprise, I said, since I surrendered not to proceed guessing. In our house we got a new baby, he said. You mean your mother gave birth, I responded. You got it, he said. Congratulation, I said shaking his hand. In one mind at the same time, two excitement were rambling. I could see on his face.

While both of us were running towards the school, suddenly we heard the honk of the bus. On the way Yobiel stumbled and fall on the ground. He hit his head with a stone. As he fell, I saw blood coming out from his head. We did not have the first aid. A quick solution was to bandage his head with a white cloth. I took out one extra white shirt from my bag and bandaged him. Time for departure was approaching. Besides me and Yobiel all of our classmate were inside the bus waiting for us. Yobiel joined the Eritrean liberation front around 1977 and he was sacrificed after a couple of years.

Brother Pedro, at the beginning he got angry, but when he saw the situation he cooled down. After a brief prayers we proceeded to Asmara the Capital city. The time was around eight in the morning.

The bus driver had made his music selections before hand. Most of the songs he selected were Tigrinya and Tigre songs. None stop with the music he had entertained all of us. Two hours after our departure we arrived Asmara. We took our breakfast in a small tea shop in the down town of Asmara. As it was organized by brother Pedro, the next move was to go to Melotti Beer Factory. We were lucky enough, for the first time in our life, to see a big industrial establishment. The managers and the workers had welcomed us, after which they gave us a tour with explanations. For all of us it was a big deal. We never saw such an enormous factory in Keren area.

That year, for the first time, the facility of Asmara Expo was opened by King Haile Selasie. It was opened for the duration of six month. People from different locations of Ethiopia were coming for the show. I was very interested in the cultural dances that were performed in the stages, by different ethnic groups and regions. What most attracted me, was the show of the different cultures, showing their farm product, the village life, and the history of different ethnics. After staying for four hours in Expo, we proceeded to our destination Masawa. From the inside of the bus, some were enjoying the panoramic view of the landscape, some were discussing about the exiting scene of the Expo and some were listening the music. The level of excitement was so high, some time our voice was so loud, we couldn't hear each other. Almost we forgot the entertaining music, composed by the DJ the driver. The twisting road of Libi Tigray (Asmara-Keren) was far more better than the road from (Asmara-Masawa). Before we reached Masawa, while we were in the bus brother Pedro started to explain about Masawa, it's history, the population, the sea out let. In the middle of his discussion, to pick the class, in a question form "Do you know what the color of the red sea looks like?" he asked. All of us in one voice said, blue, blue, since the color of all oceans was blue. Just to make things different and curious, you see from its name (Red sea), it's color is red , he said. Every body believed brother Pedro, despite his occasional teasing campaign. Again to be more believable, insistently, "All of you are wrong, the color of red sea is red", he said.

It was Friday around seven in the evening, it was before the sun had to lose it's power. The opened case of the color of the sea, it was still in the mind of every student. Everyone's expectation was to see a red color. As we reached the city of Masawa, most of the students stopped chatting and concentrated on viewing the panoramic view of the old city. The city of Masawa, is built of two islands, Tualet and Resi Midri connected by a straight asphalted road to the main land Edaga.

In the city we saw a mixture of an old and modern buildings. Finally we reached our destination. The house that looked like a big sailing ship in the middle of an ocean, was the De la Salle Christian Brother recreation house. We stayed for three days in that magnificent house. The three sides of the compound was surrounded by water. Inside the compound there was a volleyball field, out door shower place and a parking place.

The next day we were to go to Gurgusum (a swimming area located distant from the main city). To connect our soul with the nature, the ocean, the sea plants and fishes every one was getting ready. Equipped with swimming tools we departed towards Gurgusum refreshed by the usual MTA (Asmara Theatre Association) songs of the time. At that time in Gurgusum, there was only one moderate hotel with it's restaurant. The whole day we passed our day, some times swimming, some times laying on the sand and some times playing either soccer or volleyball.

About three to four miles distant from the shore, I saw a big ship floating on the sea port of Masawa. Later in the evening the whole class was surprised, when we went to down town. We got a permission to go and see the inside of one of the big ships that were anchored near the loading dock. The captain of the ship was from Keren area and his name was Abraham. He let us inside his ship and gave us a detailed explanation, of how the life on the sea was different from land. I personally enjoyed the tour.

Coup d'etat

After collecting enough wood from the mountain Senkil, I was very tired and thirsty. I was all alone. In my mind I decided to rest for a while. It was around mid day and the sun was over my head. I was on the mountain top, sitting alone on a huge rock, under an acacia tree.

From a distant, I could see villagers walking along the twisted road of Tinkulhas. One after the other, many caravan of camels, carrying wood, grain and other food stuff were passing. I started to play a guess play in counting the numbers of the camels in each caravan. I was counting in the absence of my friend, Abraha Woldesus, who still was collecting wood. It was a bit relaxing. I wish I had a camel, I said, entering into a deep thought, the long way I had to walk, carrying the heavy load of wood on my head. If you don't have a donkey you become a donkey, I was saying in my mind.

I could hear people talking. All the villagers were heading towards Keren town, speaking their mother language of Bilen. While I was entertaining the view, suddenly, Abraha my best friend approached me. Time to go, he said, in a low voice, with a loaded wood on his head. I didn't expect from him to be greeted and neither to be shaken my hands.

The sun was equally shining to both of us. We walked about half a kilometer down the steep slope. With the heavy load of wood on my head, I was staggering. Both of us we were not talking to each other. Every one was engaged. My face was paled out from the sun's heat. I was breathing rapidly. I wished my breathing was under my control.

When we reached at the bottom of the mountain, before joining Tinkulhas road, we headed to a natural fountain across the street to quench our thirsty. The stream flowing over a big rock made a natural light waterfall. I rushed towards the fountain. After drinking enough water, to refresh my body, I went to the water fall to take a shower.

After entertaining near the fountain, we started to have a conversation. As usual our conversation was centered on the school and family affairs. In the middle of the conversation, I lost my mind. I was totally disarrayed from the conversation. I kept silent. My friend Abraha, was not happy about my being silent. Though he tried his best to revive the conversation, I was not in a position to give him an ear.

What is wrong with you, what is going on, Abraha said, whispering near my ear. I never wanted to share with any one of what had happened to my family. The sense of guilty covered my conscience. I deed as I was told. I did not want to dishonor mommy. Secrecy about the situation, was promoted as a warning by mommy.

Unconsciously, I began to recite the family affair which I kept it secret from Abraham. I was always cautious not to tell family affairs to others. Though, I was entitled not to tell, this time I did. I told him about the disappearance of my sister Lette.

My eldest sister Lette, lived with my brothers in Asmara, before she disappeared, in 1974. Very religious and responsible Lettina, she was the one who took care of me, when I was a baby. I could remember all her good attention she had on me.

To help our family, she interrupted her school at grade eight. She was helping in Italian school as a kindergarten teacher. She really encouraged me in my studies and fulfilled all my needs. When the Italian school was closed, Lettina left for Asmara to seek for a job. She started to work in a shop and started over time job, helping Arab girls, learn the art of sewing. While she was working in the shop, a certain guy had introduced himself to Lettina, which later he fell in love with her. Lettina had hidden all this relation she had from my brother Norai. When she got pregnant, since she couldn't hide it she fled with out any trace to the village of her husband. We did not hear about her whereabouts for two years. My mom got sick because of her disappearance. I tried to console mom, some times by going to Asmara and bringing some news, which in effect they were not true. After two years Lettina was found in far village married to a Muslim guy. No one had expected from her to act in this way. My mom did not accept her choice. But daddy as usual who takes things as they come, he became more tolerant.

It was 1974. The first year of the birth of "Abiot" (the revolution) and the last year of king Haile Selasie dominion of his kingdom. The king was deposed by "DERG" (a military junta). The organizers of the revolution, were the university students mainly from the two capital cities of Asmara and Addis Ababa. The students movement, was suppressed by the military, at it's early stage. The turmoil changed the peaceful environment of the country from bad to worse. Peaceful rallies and demonstrations of innocent students were paid by mass killings. Almost about 10,000 innocent souls were perished for nothing.

The military Junta, the day it took power by force, it made a false pronouncement to the people of Ethiopia, under the banner "Forward Ethiopia without bloodshed". When, opposite or contrary things happened, the Tigrean people from Eritrea they say "Babur Ighebeiki" (Train it is not your way). The military junta on it's way it lost it's direction.

The Eritrean armed resistance, was greatly helped by the coup d'etat. Many students escaped to save their life and those who were Eritrean by birth, they joined the Eritrean Liberation fronts. All high schools and the universities were closed for two years. A "Limat Zemecha", (a green campaign) program was designed by the Derg, everything to be accomplished by force.

Asmarini

I could have been any where, any place, but I was in Asmara, the capital city. It is a good opportunity, I have chosen to be there not other else. I don't know, why I thought, it would be a good idea to spend my summer vacation in Asmara. I guess, one thing I know was, to brake the monotony. I planned for a visit, just to spend some quality time around the city. Every summer, I pass my summer vacation, with my brothers and sisters. I decided to go to Asmara after the school closure. I was sure about my bus ticket. I had only to notify before time. My daddy doesn't like surprises. I planned ahead of time. At the end I succeeded.

The night before my departure to the capital, I slept for the whole night. I didn't want to get up late and miss the first bus of 5:00 am, so I went to bed early.

The next morning, I went to the bus station. The bus was almost full, ready to depart. Ashera was the name of the driver. Very famous Ashera, one time he was the candidate, to be elected for the house of representative in Addis Ababa. Unfortunately, he was not able to win. He was the friend of my father and we were neighbors.

The ticket man refused to let me in the bus. I shouted and called the name of Ashera. The engine was running. When Ashera saw me from the mirror, he ordered the ticket man to let me in. The ticket man objected, for a simple reason that there was not a space for me to sit. Ashera took a pillow from his under seat, and let me seat on the motor of the bus. The problem was solved.

Next, he put gear on the first, then second and then third. He played the tape recorder. Every body inside the bus started to be entertaining by the songs. One after the other by changing the cassettes he relaxed passengers minds. Since, I was seated in front besides the driver, I was talking the whole time with Ashera.

When we reached Libi Tigrai, a very twisted road, everybody kept silence and controlled his body. Many of the passengers were getting through their windows and vomiting.

After twenty minutes of driving, we stopped by AddiTekelezan for our breakfast. Ashera invited me for breakfast. Most of the stomachs were empty, so the refill was a necessity. After 30 minutes of break we proceeded our journey to the Capital.

Addi Tekelezan, is 40 km far from Asmara, and it took us forty minutes to be in Asmara. At the bus station of Edagahamus, I heard behind me some one, saying 'welcome contrabandist'. I looked around and it was my brother's friend Afom. He saw me struggling to take out my things from the inside of the bus. He tried to help me and invited me to eat with him some 'Schehanful' (the Kerenini favorite food made of beans, yogurt and hot stuff).

I tried to walk like the Asmarini, so that no one would suspect, where I came from. If I didn't do that, I would have seen the consequences of being robed by the robbers.

It was my last vacation and I had a good remembrance, of many particular things, which I couldn't tell all. During that time, I happened to see for the first time the famous Padre. The year I turned fifteen, I was in grade nine. I lived in EdagaHamus, five minutes walk to the bus station.

I have to say something that Asmara was for the Asmarini. I am not exaggerating. When it comes to me I am lost. The youth culture was different. I don't mean the Asmarini were more advanced than I was. But I needed to adapt to the culture.

While I was in Asmara, one day my Asmarini friends invited me to join them for a basketball game that was taking place in La sale. Alazar Andai, was his name one of my friends who invited me. I really had a passion for basketball. He knew my hearts desire. I accepted the invitation. I felt very lucky.

It was Saturday evening, the Asmarini were roaming around the main central avenue. The Italian name of the main street "Campo citato", which the Asmarini call it Comuscitato is a vital street, where the citizens and other visitors, satisfy their curiosity and relax their busy minds. Campo citato in English it means a cited area or a camp cited for particular people. The area was only allowed for the Italians. Apartheid in East Africa in the local's land.

For a simple reason of preserving its unique identity, Asmara had continued its colonial beauty, by attracting many tourists.

Built up from the colonial era, Asmara still maintained, the feeling its builders must have intended those many years ago. The setting of the city was very unique. It was a welcoming place a place of tourism and attraction. A center of remembrance were all the deepest territories of love, romance were practiced.

The palm trees are planted parallel to the main avenue. It was our forefathers that planted it. The palm trees were the sign of endurance.

The small cafe's and restaurants along the avenue were full. At five in the afternoon the avenue was crowded. In every corner of the street, you could see people of different age. As they walk along the street 'Selamat', they said and shook hands. Some were heading to the movies. Some were going to the small cafes. Every hour the big bells of the Cathedral, were tuned to tell the time. It was like symphony and followed a certain melody that gave joy and happiness to the citizens and the tourists. On the other end of the downtown, from the main central mosque, the Kadi announced through the microphone to the Muslim believers for the afternoon prayers. The church of Enda Mariam through it's silence, it struck the tourists by its structure and design, that invited peace and tranquility.

People on their way, in a group they chatted, discussed, about many things. Some times, about soccer some times about the political situation. Alternated their discussions according to the situation. Started with the politics, and when they saw some strangers (the government spies), touched their ears to show a stranger was with them, changed their topic to the sport to distract the enemy. They were able to kick the political ball and the soccer ball at the same time. On one hand, the famous teams of Hama, Akele, Serae and Tele occupied their discussions and on the other hand the political situation and the progress of Sewra (the armed struggle). They slightly mentioned about the basketball teams.

I being a stranger to the city, I was not able to catch the Asmarini language. I wanted to know the place and the people. At least, I tried to my best, to follow the Asmarini system of communication. I wanted to wear the system to my bones.

Meanwhile, I started to look like the Asmarini. I had the gift of quickly adapting myself. No matter, whatever it took, nothing had to escape my surveillance. For my full concentration, I must have stayed focused on my target. I needed, mental gymnastics, move creatively, act more swiftly. The Asmarini sometimes the way they talk, was very difficult to understand. To be within the Asmarini community, one must manage to function effectively, otherwise you are going to be labeled.

The next day was Sunday. I was punctual, respected the time. It was 8:30 in the morning and many people most of them Italians were heading to the main gate of La sale. Alazar and me were also heading towards that gate. To get into the compound was not so simple. The gatekeeper an old man wouldn't let you in. Either you have to be an Italian or a student with a pass to enter into the compound. I relied upon Alazar. He knew all the tricks on how to get in without problem.

La Salle School of Asmara, until the year of 1975, was a place for the Italian children or some rich local's who were able to afford and send their children there. The school program was all in Italian. On the lower part of the building, a new elementary school for the locals was opened. The local brothers were allowed to teach only in the elementary school.

By 9:00 am sharp the basketball game started. The team of La sale (Padre's team) were warming up, helped by their couch a little short man by name Berhane. Mr. Berhane who was very friendly, that day he was moving from one end of the play ground to the other. He was waiting the super star Padre. Five minutes before the game to start, Padre showed up on the entrance of the gymnasium. As he put his feet on the play ground, after dribbling the ball for a couple of minutes, he tried his first shot from very distance. He was very accurate and the ball was inside the net. Usually he never misses. Everyone cheered and shouted by saying, "Ni Padre Zitenkefa, fa fa Kulkul Afa" (One who touches Padre would fall upside down). That day the team of La sale won against the guest team. I had good remembrance of that Sunday. Alazar was grateful to me, during all the summer time I was with him.

Alazar and me are around the same age, but somewhat different in our character. If it make sense he is Asmarino and I am Kerenino. I grew up in a small town but he grew up in the capital city.

Kerenino, he called me my friend Alazar, when ever he wanted to impress me. It generated different feeling when he called me by that name. He was a person who had had city life. The portrait that I have traced, about my friend was certainly laudatory. I did not trust the Asmarino way of life, initially. But I used to get familiar with it. My friend tried everything to convince me. Slowly, I was catching up.

Faded promise

I had a dream, a fantasy swirling around in my mind. I wished to move to the capital city as soon as I finished my high school. If I was aware of my wishes that was what I wondered. Indeed I prepared to satisfy my wish. I was told to study hard and my elder brother Norai encouraged me. He had no trouble in concluding. The deal was simple but conditional. On the condition I pass the matriculation exam, I was to join my brother.

I took up the matter very seriously. To succeed I had to study very hard. I knew from the beginning, that the promise would involve a good deal of difficulty. With that in mind I tried hard to succeed. There was no guarantee, but I needed to study hard.

The crucial time of the armed struggle was at its peak. The Asmarini youths began pouring out to the front. In an organized or non-organized way they were flocking to the mountains, to join the liberation fronts. To coincide with my own doubts, my brother Tecle was involved in the liberation movement. He was recruited to be an urban guerilla fighter. Consequently, all the promise he gave to me faded up. Norai left the capital city and he went to join the liberation movement to the mountains.

The year was 1975. My brother Tecle (Norai), before he left to the mountain he used to live in Asmara, in a rented house in Imbagaliano area. He lived more than 10 years at Aya Haile Kelati's house. "Siga Seiti Hassebu" (I swear in the name Hassebus' wife), was the phrase of a swear, Haile Kelati made to any life deal he was making. People in Asmara they knew him by that phrase. Every where they meet Haile kelati, they were calling him by " Siga Seiti Hassebu". Haile Kelati was the best man during my father's wedding and it was from that time he started the famous phrase. The friendship in years they built was inherited by their respective children. Though they were not related they were acting like brothers. One time both my father and Haile

Kelati, got high in alcohol, and while they were returning back home, on the way crossing the rail way station of Keren, they slipped to an open train car, parked in " Forobia Inda babur", (Keren train station). Both of them decided to rest for a while inside the open car train. Since the alcohol level they consumed was above normal, they both remained in deep sleep, inside the car. Early in the morning the car they were sleeping in was joined with the main train that was going to Asmara. When they reached half way they woke up from their sleep. When they saw that they were in a wrong place heading to words Asmara, both of them started to joke. Let us go to Asmara for un planned shopping, Kelati said. It is good chance to see Asmara, said my father. The next day they showed up in Keren. From that day, Haile Kelati had sworn in my mothers name, not to consume any more any alcohol. And he did it.

"Weshin besh", "Bringait", "Fasdel hais", were some of the strange and meaningless vocabularies of my uncle Habtle from my mothers side, which by his nick name we called him "Attuga". He used to try to imitate like speaking in English. Though the expressions in themselves had no meaning, he used the meaningless words whenever he was experiencing a situation of happiness or unhappiness. His nonsense expressions became the center of laughter to all Keren Lalai people. One day, Ande my brother and Habtle my uncle, after drinking enough alcohol in the local bar, together while they were walking home, they got into a fight. As usual my uncle raised his voice, aided by his meaningless vocabulary. On his part Ande intervened to be violent. Some by passers, had intervened and separated them be accompanying each one to his house. After several minutes, Ande woke up from his bed and walked out for another round of fight, by shouting"Aya Habtle, Aya Habtle", (uncle Habtle, uncle Habtle). Instantly, holding back his position ready to fight, "pronto" (in Italian to mean ready), said Habtle, as he recited the usual nonsense words.

It was summer of 1975 and it was that year that I decided to join the De la Salle Christian Brothers in Keren. I cheated my mother. The original promise was compromised. Her desire to join the seminary to become a priest never materialized. Her wish was that I become a priest. But I ended up to be a "Frer", a brother. That time I pretended to be the guarantor of my choice. I did not follow my mom's advice. A different life and a different choice. I transferred the risk to my self. I can't definitely recall my situation at that time. I wanted only to finish my education, to be some one. To reach my goal, I needed to do some thing. The choices were two, either to the monastery or to the forest to join the liberation fronts.

"Tzelot Aboyn Adeyin NeNbeinu" (My father's prayer and mother's are totally different), as they say the Abyssinians. My wish and choice were totally different from my mom's. My mom tried her best to convince me. I respected her, but I tried to maintain my sense of self. I walked until I was sure where I was, but when I found my way, I did not need an advice.

To the opposite my father was more diplomatic. He did not interfere much. His way of dealing was more of libertarian. He lets you to get it over with. There was no psychological pressure. He didn't waste his time. He was quite adorable and gentle. I always approached him with respect.

St. Joseph School

A missionary from Italy by the name Adriano Celentano, in November of 1946, at the age of 63, with the heart and mind of 21 came to Keren. The founding father of St. Joseph School was known by the name Abba Adriano. After 8 months of his stay in Keren he decided to share his dream of founding a school in Keren after which on June 12, 1947, he went to Naples to consult with his superiors.

In Rome, he met with the Superiors of the Institute and the Congregation for the Oriental Church. They encouraged him by not only approving his request, but also authorizing him to study the question of timing and practicality of place.

It was God's providence, after two years, in 1948 when Abba Adriano was in Spain at Premia de Mar, he met a young missionary by name, "Miguel Casiano" (Jose Salces), which the local people were calling him Abba Chahma.

The friend of the Kerenini Abba Chahma after he had served the people of Keren for 20 years he was transferred to Bethlehem in Israel. Immediately after the independence he came to see the old mission and the Brothers. The first love and enthusiasm of his mission came to his mind. He liked his mission already. He thought of what he was doing, back in his youth years. He went far back in his mind and the old memories came one by one. The students, the Brothers, and all the local people came into his mind, he almost cried.

On one hand he was very happy about the independence of the People. This times though he was not able to come physically and help the people, he planned to raise fund for the school together with Brother Pedro Arrambide.

Abba Chahma made a lot of campaigns, in his home country Spain, to raise fund for the school, who once he was the co-founder. After he made a tour to all the De la sale Christian brothers schools, he came to his destination community, where he died of heart attack, while he was on the refectory table. The last word he emitted from his mouth was ERITREA.

St. Joseph School grew quickly as stone upon stone was put in place providing a beautiful new building for the first 150 children who began classes in April 1950. Padre Beyene before he joined the De La sale Christian Brothers he was following his elementary school at St. Joseph by travelling 10 kilometers everyday.

This was the School of St. Joseph. On the other side of the street one could see students flocking to the School. When the northern and southern gates of the school were opened the students scattered on the play ground some of them running, some of them studying under a tree. A very nice classical music accompanied their mind to refresh their day.

At 8 sharp the bell rang and all the students at once they made line in front of their homeroom teachers. The neighbors' anthem in a neighbor's language of Amharic was sung. Three students raised the flag high to the pole. Few minutes but very saddening. How come the locals sing the song of the neighbor. The neighbors wished to make think the locals, that there was one neighbor and the question of the locals as an independent country was absurd.

After this moment of disappointment, the last whistle was whistled, to indicate the students to enter in their classrooms.

With great discipline the classes began their yearly routing. Moral and religious education came first and the other subjects were given accordingly. The classes terminated at four. The school compounds were again in silence. You see people moving to their home. After a long morning of a school day, the students were happy to see their parents. Got together and played the cultural plays. Told stories. Shared their school experiences.

St. Joseph School opened my eyes. I understood how someone could actually be somebody. It was a place where students from different background came together. It was one of the famous schools in Eritrea. Padre was lucky enough to teach in that school. There was a great competition among the students. Studying hard, was so necessary, for achieving the best grades and ranks that eventually became their only concern. It was all about exploring the future.

Keren Lalai

This was how the community life was functioning. The community was programmed for self-sufficiency. To make up a difference without distinction was the mission of the community. As a result local aid organization evolved. Different associations raised their banners. Everyone was committed to join this non profit local organizations. In principle they were social organizations, but they functioned through religious foundations.

They were called "Mahber" (Associations) all those non-governmental local organizations. They were organized locally with a local mind. They were self-insured associations. Membership was the main foundation. It was open to all religions and for all ages above 21. There were rules and regulations and contribution was monthly. The non-profit local organizations were named by Saints. Some of the functioning non-profit organizations were, Mahber Kudus Michael, Kudus Ghiorghis and Kidisti Mariam. The main function of the non-profit organizations was to procure different needs of the families in the community. The non-profit local organization played a great role in preparing and organizing the wedding party, church and state celebrations.

In the community respectance fashioned our daily life. No attention had been paid, to our background differences, which was the foundation of our unity. To become involved, with people of a different background, mentality or profession of faith, was not as such easy.

On the other hand, Keren Lalai located on the southern part of the town, had a powerful remembrance, by many people of its surroundings. I had some self-knowledge about Keren Lalai's life situation before the independence. I am part of the story. To be part of the community was not an easy thing, you have to have a license, authorized by the Keren Lalai male youngsters. These were the rules of the male youngsters of

Keren Lalai into which every body had to conform. No strange person or a guest was allowed to be in that area without the permission of the male youngsters. I don't want to name the action as a gangster. The attitude was neither benevolent. I don't compare with the East Coast and West Coast gangsters of USA. It was only a fun. No one had a gun. No drugs involved. No money involved. No organized violence. They had their own discipline, and their system of discipline stated, no girl was allowed to go with mini skirt, no girl was allowed to come to church with make-ups, no female to go with a stranger male, no relationship has to be made with other county youngsters in either way. If they see stranger putting their feet on the land, they whistle a whistle and gather together to solve the problem.

At the parish of St. Michael, the male youngsters of Keren Lalai had a considerable interference's. When they wanted to employ their ideas, they literally followed the method of criticizing the action and the situation of the anti feminism. To entertain their aim they manipulated the parish priest. They made him think their thought.

The parish priest was called Father Ghebrekidus Meskel. Dedicated and loving Father Ghebre, he always approached his parishioner's with kindness and sense of humor. After the services he liked to play and joke with the youngsters.

The youngsters were able to maneuver anything. One Sunday after the service, as usual father Ghebre approached the youngsters. This time they were ready to inform him about the bad influence the girls were giving to the parish community.

One day, one of the youths by name Yosief Tesfay known by his nickname "Halefom", stood up and said to the priest that there were some young girls, who were wearing the mini skirt in the church. You need to talk and consider this issue on your next sermon the coming Sunday, Halefom added. Father Ghebrekidus after accepting the idea, he made ready himself, for the next preaching of Sunday. When it was time for preaching, in the middle, father Ghebre had raised his voice by saying "woe to you young ladies who are becoming the scandal of the elders and temptation to the young boys", I have seen you with my eyes walking with your mini skirts. You will definitely go to hell naked without your underwears. Everybody started to laugh and laugh especially the co-authors of the sermon. The male youngsters had manipulated the priest's simplicity and they always managed to turn the event, as they wanted.

Another time, after the Sunday service, when all the male youngsters were gathered together talking and chatting, father Gehbrekidus came and joined their conversation. The father doesn't need invitation. His approach was more pastoral, but they abused his simplicity. Kelati Tesfamariam, which they call him by his nickname Fish, had directed his question to the Father and asked by saying, "to go to down town how much time does it take to you?". He promptly answered, by saying "I don't know in hours but it takes me 150 Hail Mary's". While everyone was focusing on the last and to the point response of the Father, Michielai Woldu (nicknamed Chilen), raised a very sensitive issue regarding Ms. Lettu who used to live 10 meters far from the church. Lettu very fat lady all her life never came to the church, but she was always at the back of her house observing, those who were coming to church. She was very famous for gossiping. One day, curiously, Chilen asked Abba Gebre, by saying "why she was not coming to church". The gentle Father always ready to respond in humor, said, "Lettu does not need to come to the Church, since she had a long tongue she can receive the holy communion while she is at her house.

The Monk

In 1977 after finishing grade 12, I was transferred from Asmara to Keren town. Obedience was the lesson I learned early. I left my home to join the monks, not to seek adventures. I joined the monastery only for one reason. To be obedient to my superiors, for the divine service, I had to accomplish for the needy ones. Obedience is not a human assignment but divine. I had enthusiastically accepted the transfer. I knew it was not going to be easy. The spirit of obedience endowed to me, helped me to be courageous, in facing things to be familiar with unfamiliar surroundings.

When I was in Asmara, I enjoyed the Asmarini students. If it were not the voice of obedience, which I vowed to observe according to the religious order, personally I would not accept the transfer. When my superior delivered the paper of obedience, I made my formal appearance once and for all to follow the direction of my superiors, though it was not my choice. Such was the religious discipline, that I had acquired from the institution of the monastery regulations.

For real I did not want to work in my home town. I had enough experience of my home town Keren. After working for two years at St. Joseph school as a teacher, here came unexpected surprise. It was the eve of Christmas of 1979. While I was enthusiastically preparing for the day, brother Ghebretensaie knocked at my door. There is a good news for you, he said, before I asked him what the news was and he started to recite it in plain words. He said, you are assigned to go to Rome, for further religious study.

I had my own dreams. Dreams of being a professor in other fields. I liked science more than any subject. I was good at it. I wished the order would have been re-scanned to words my wishes. You don't negotiate obedience.

"Weldu" I called him and to make a perfect rhyme " Chinka Izi Idu" I added when ever I met him. Brother Weldehawariat a bright and intelligent person as he was, every one in the Institute they were calling him by "Brother Mathematician". There was a similarity and a difference in our characters. Both of us we were sleepy in nature, if I don't exaggerated we had a sleeping sickness problem. We couldn't arrive to a conclusion of a movie we started. As far as our difference was concerned, he was more bright and intelligent than I was, on the other hand I was more creative and innovative. He was reserved and quite to the opposite I was talkative and outgoing.

After supper recreations were taking place, out side of the main office veranda of St. Joseph school Keren. The recreation place, facing to the street of Keren Lalai, was the main spot for a good view of by passers. The time of recreation started around 8:00 in the evening and lasted for two hours. After a busy day of a school, we did not have any TV, or a computer to entertain with. This was how the recreation was taking place, without any moderators. "Mahtsen Ade guramura" (The womb of a mother is made of different colors), as the Abyssinians say goes, in the community some were excellent story tellers, some were good jokers, some were simply humble listeners. The school affair dominated most of the discussions. The social time was a fruitful healing and relaxing time.

Brother Daniel Misghina (the first Eritrean brother by profession), was the most entertaining person. He had always some thing to share and tell the community. You know what happened today, he said, one day, while adjusting his spontaneous and to the point joke, which was the best shot of the day. This morning, he said, when I was coming out from church, I happened to see Mr. Habte passing by the main street. As usual as he started to bow down his head (a sign of a spiritual respect given to saints), coincidentally, I was coming out from the main door. As I saw him, I waved my hand to salute Mr. Habte by saying "selam" (Hi). I thought he was giving me a feedback to my greeting, but to the opposite, he made clear his position by saying " I was not bowing to you the son of Misghina, but to Jesus the son of Mary" he said.

One evening a heated discussion between Weldehawariat, Tecle and Ghedel came to the floor before the gathered community for a judgment. Each one clarified the act of heroism of their respective grandfathers. The whole members of community were curiously following the discussion. My grand father Mengesha, he killed a tiger, from a close range, by one bullet on mountain Lalumba, Tecle said. My grandfather killed a big cobra from a very close range by a spear, Weldehawariat said, when he was given his turn to speak. When Ghedel was asked to present the act of heroism of his grandfather, he said, one day my grandfather Beyan, while coming out from church, he found people guessing to identify the identity of an animal, at a distant standing on the big flat rock of Meshahtito. To make things clear, he added, my grandfather pulled out his rifle and with one bullet he stroke the horn of the animal from a very distant place and the animal was identified to be a goat. After hearing their case one by one, we voted for Ghedel's grandfather with good explanation. All of us our judgment was on the basis of hitting with good tension from a distant. All together with one voice, we decided, that Ghedel's grand father was the winner. Since the killing of the tiger and the cobra was from close range.

During those days of the liberation of Keren town, from June of 1977 to October of 1978 the normal life of the whole inhabitant was changed due to a security reason. The night time became a day and the day became a night. The enemy jet fighters limited the movement of the day functions. Shopping was done during the dark nights. The school system was changed to the night shift. Usually the lessons started from 6:00 to11:30 in the night. Tough days and tough time to remember. The sense of being happy and unhappy became a fifty, fifty deal. On one hand the population was happy because of the liberation of the town, on the other hand there was a sense of unhappiness due to the hard life situation.

When the sun went down and the night was to begin the life started as a normal. In itself, practically the situation was abnormal. It was only the hyena that rambled during the dark night. The night time was good only for those who loved to go to "Bahli" (local parties) and Inda Sua (local bars). As far as education was concerned the situation was bad. It was not feasible to run a school during the night.

Brother Kahsay Ghirmay was the principal of the school. I was assigned to teach in grade one. I was ready and enthusiastic to practice the 101 class management theories I acquired from the start. For one class two teachers were assigned. The principal of the school had designed it wisely, for a purpose of maintaining good discipline. Usually, the student as they enter to their class rooms they started to sleep. Specially, grade one, the one I was handling as a homeroom teacher, the students couldn't resist to stay awake for one hour.

This was the location of the classroom. It was located right at the corner of the long corridor, near the main entrance of the building. At the back of the classroom there was a restroom service. One extra teacher (aide) helper, was provided for me. The novice teachers Habtu and Ghebremeskel were alternating to help me in doing my duty as a teacher.

One night the assigned teacher Habtu was sick and I was alone to handle the class on my own. That night I used my creative mind to deal with the problem. I used to wear an eyeglass. Suddenly, in front of all my students I took out my eyeglass and put it, on my desk facing to the students. In a convincing tone, I told my students, that my eyeglass could see any action of misbehavior or any one sleeping. To test my creative project, I moved out from the classroom and entered to the bath room. From the back of the classroom on the tall painted glass window, I made a small scratch just to help me see all the actions of the students. I left the class only for about 10 minute. As I entered I directed my steps towards my eye glass and put my eyeglass on my eye. Seriously, I asked my eye glass to tell me who were misbehaving during my absence from the class room. When I started to call the names of all those who misbehaved, they started trembling. From that night all the students were surprised of the wise eyeglass. I used the trick for several weeks until I was caught by a student who came to the bathroom while I was doing the surveillance.

To a monk whose all his actions were motherly, I was calling him by the name "Adey", which meant "Mommy". His name was Tensiew Tesfasilasie from Halibmentel a village about 10 kilometers distant from Keren town. In the monastery he was one of my body. His kindness still shined in my mind. In the summer of 1977 we organized a picnic to go to Halhal village north west of Keren town. The day of the picnic, four of us me, Tensiew Tesfasilasie, Hailemariam Ucbagabir and Temnewo Musa woke up around 4:00 in the morning. Breathing the air of freedom, after three hours of none stop walk, we reached the river Beyan in Gengheren Village. We stayed for one hour chatting about our religious life, our students, and other life issues. The steep mountain of Beyan was to be climbed. The road that winded around the mountain was very challenging mountain I had ever seen. The challenging road was named by the name Reagan, (the president of USA who managed to dismantle the eastern block of communism). When we reached half way I was very exhausted and fell down on the ground. Before I joined the picnics I was struggling with a flu. My temperature raised. I was an able to walk and talk. Suddenly, Tensiew remained with me treating me like his child. He gave me some aspirin to cool my high temperature. After I felt good I proceeded with the walk. It was that time that I started to call him by the name "Adey".

A self claimed "Debtera" (a professed Geez Zema songs master), Habtemariam Andu was my competitor in leading the Zema. Because of his excellent voice, he was always the first choice of the priests to serve as a deacon. Every morning of Sunday before the mass was to start we used to lead a "Kumet" (a standing style of singing the Geez Zema) that lasted for two hours. One day me and Wedi Andu without a prior rehearsal we tuned our rival tones, struggling to handle the position of a leading Debtera. My voice was tuned to a low tenor voice but his was tuned to the highest pitch. As he tried to tune a verse of "Shebshebo", (a spiritual short verse of a song accompanied by a drum and a spiritual dance) in a high pitch tone, I was not able to follow with my low tenor voice. I tried my best to coop with the song, but as things were not going according to the song rhythm, angrily, Wedi Andu had lightly struck my head with Mekomia by instructing me to align with the rest of the singers. We were also rivals in beating the drum. Two or three drummers by carrying the heavy drum on their shoulders in a dancing style they beat the drum with rhythm of the song.

I have a surprise to every one in this room, he said, while all the monks were relaxing in the recreation room. His name was Ghiorghis Ghinbot my senior in the congregation. What is the surprise asked Amine Kidane who always acted fast to arrive to conclusions. He didn't wait and couldn't wait. Giorghis after breathing deeply, I composed a new spiritual song so I need your help he said. It was really a surprise to every one. No one expected him to be a composer of a song. His song before it was to be edited he brought it before the floor. The rhyming of the verses was good, but we were not able to manage the song easily. It took us hours and hours to command the song. Despite his creativity, the author of the song was not to be laudable for his voice.

PART II

Padre

What If I continue my work with Padre's experience as a religious member and freedom fighter. Who would believe me? How would I display it? Whom should I have to address to? These were some of the questions that came into my mind. I couldn't imagine how I would be able to hold all these.

Naturally, I didn't expect to write some thing that was out of my experience. I never been a freedom fighter and neither raised a gun. Since I was not one of the freedom fighters I couldn't act as one of them. On the other hand I did not want to limit my self. As a writer I was free to cover things that had fallen on my eyes. An official experience written by inexperienced individual, would never match.

I set my mind to be optimistic to begin with. The most difficult part was not when to begin or where to begin but how to begin. I needed desperately the method and the technique of how to write the content. As far as content was concerned there was plenty of things to write. At the end I guess I should begin. I didn't give chance for a second preference.

The local martyrs wouldn't allow me. I saw them dictating me. I have nothing to loose. I didn't have to refer textbooks. The local's experience was my source. With the martyrs there was always a content to write, a history to tell. My aim was to explore. Use my common sense and avoid very highly scholarly manner.

The content was distinctive. It needed more detailed discussion. I was completely convinced. There was a message to the world. At the end what do I lose?

Something was moving into my mind for a long time. The locals armed struggle, the liberation movement. How to tell the world this magnificent history. My idea was only inviting. Inviting the local scholars to contribute and collaborate in telling the true story of the armed struggle. Not only to restore the locals armed struggle in the world history, but to reclaim this history as a unique history of liberation in Africa.

And then as it comes in my mind, as if I could do something about it, to tell the truth about the whole story of the locals of the horn Africa. Dedicated my time with such a favorable start.

On my part, I tried to discipline my self, to share the true experience of the struggle of the locals. It was an experience, a life of a struggle a whole story of aggression and oppression.

Thirty years of an armed struggle was really a long time for Sewra to stay united and defeat the enemy. It took advantage of its own people unity, and molded the whole system of the armed struggle. It had done it through an engaging system of discipline. It was really some thing to start up and move ahead.

The thing that really attracted me to write about, was the local's heroism in general. In my essay I picked up the name Padre (a martyr to represent all heroes of the land). It was this mutual awareness of my spirit and mind I had that pushed me to write about the local's. And one particular assignment I took, though I had never joined Sewra, was the confidence and the familiarity of the armed struggle, I had, from the conversations with some experienced Tegadelti (freedom fighters).

****

It was last Sunday of June 1977. Padre (An Italian word for Father) was living in a monastery at St. Joseph school Keren. Beyene was his name. A member of the De La sale Christian brothers, he was assigned to teach in a prestigious Catholic School, founded half century ago. Much as he loved the town's charm, the school setting, and beautiful weather, Padre enjoyed teaching in that school. The teaching career was the most important establishment, Padre had at heart above all others. His life had definitely changed beyond all recognition. Those who new him during his career as an educator, and the formative years as a religious member of a congregation, they would exactly be confused. For Padre to be with his students in all time was his first interest, which he considered of the first importance. Until the last minute, he had cooperated with teaching project of his Institute.

As he took more of an interest in his educational career, he made ready everything before entering to his class. In order to take care of his students he prepared himself physically and spiritually. To manage his classes he outlined a strategy. The lesson plan, the register, educational instruments were side by side. One time to correct the homework and one time to organize the lesson plan according to the timetable.

Before he joined Sewra (The liberation movement), his two favorite activities in life were to play basketball and stay with his students in class. The friend of youth and teenagers, Padre measured his time by the love and dedication that were fueled by his zeal. In his native town he served the poor children. He totally gave himself wholeheartedly. Up to now he was well remembered by all his hometown people.

In the monastery life was as follows. At 4:30 a.m. every monk had to get up from his bed. The alarm clock gave its usual right judgment. The superior after getting up from his bed, he rang the community bell, to wake up all the sleeping religious brothers. In a loud voice he greeted every body, as is a religious custom, by saying "Live Jesus in our hearts". From different rooms, some with vigorous and some with a low voice the monks responded the superiors greeting by saying "For ever". That was how the daily religious life function started. Though some one was physically awake the mind will slowly adapt to the schedule of getting up early. Every religious member had to dress up his white or black robe and had to be in the church by 5:00 a.m. for the Morning Prayer. Only 30 minute were given to prepare and clean up their rooms.

The day started with the morning prayer. If you don't begin your day with God, everything becomes confused. Early mornings were for God, since the evenings, without one's wish, would turn to be for man.

The whole night he was busy correcting the student's last examination papers. He was still too weak and dizzy to stand that morning prayer. While all the monks were sitting on their seats, from the back of the chapel a loud voice was heard. It was the voice of the superior. Again, In a loud voice, the superior pronounced the phrase "Live Jesus in our hearts" to begin the day. All the congregant responded in one voice "for ever". The leader of the prayer, with the high pitch tone, chanted by saying "Oh God come to our aid" and the congregant responded "Come soon to our help". The Psalms of the day were recited after which the holy mass followed.

After the religious function was terminated, the monks' went to their own rooms and planned their day.

That morning, Padre came late for the morning prayer. From the minute he sat down everyone was looking and staring at him. He opened his prayer book and tried to follow. He kept reading every word in a very low voice and slightly annoyed tone. Enough is enough, he said, I am no longer fooling my self. He knew, that his status of being a religious brother was a horrible mistake. But how would I ever get free from this preoccupation?, he murmured.

Taking notice of what was going on in his life, one day, he told to himself that he probably wouldn't stay long to live in the monastery. Padre seemed like he lost all taste of life. He felt the same vague uneasiness, for a reason. He was in the middle of crises. A vocational crises. When these crises came to him it was not without warning or a cause. He was experiencing the dryness of a spirit. He was a dead member in the Institute. The perfect legitimate explanation, for his unexplainable status of crises, was the new situation of the local's armed struggle. Everything around him was not going right and not functioning really well. To ensure his decisions and come out with a positive solution for him was the first issue

****

Padre was avid to learn, to know his position as a monk in the Institute. There was no full and ready made answers. He simply needed to sketch an out line and deliver his case on time. In directly, he was confronting his religious duties with different values. There was a religious value and Sewra values that had to be realized in two different environments.

He would go on discussing with his fellow members about the political issue of that time. One early morning, as we were getting ready for a school day, from the next room which was my room, Padre heard the popular song "Agudo Neratni" (I had a Tukul, a house) that motivated many locals to join the front. The locals had developed a fixation on this particular recording. When he heard that song, he put aside everything and wanted to listen the song. He moved to words my room. He looked through the glass window in my room. He knocked the door before he entered but he did not hear any word from the inside of the room. I was having a bath outside my room. After couple of minutes he decided to enter into my room. Sitting at the side of the bed he continued to listen the song over and over. When I came in from the bathroom I saw Padre sitting besides my bed listening to the tape recorder. " Have you finished correcting the home work?" I exclaimed. Yes, he said, by lowering the volume, while his heart was still with the song. The song was not relaxing in its content but more motivational. The words were colored in a way the neighbor would never notice the true interpretation. The mystery behind the words was never totally disclosed to the neighbor's leadership. But the locals related most of the songs to the political revival. In the community most of our discussions ended up in a political affairs.

To this matter I can make myself clearer he said, while he was convinced more than ever that there was no greater contribution than giving oneself as a sacrifice. I would not bargain on the independence of the locals said Padre, who strongly backed his idea. "We are religious people" my brother and we should not mingle with the political affair, I responded. It is unfair and naturally distasteful, to live such kind of life when our people are suffering from the lack of independence, said Padre. It will highly tax my identity, if I remain silent as I am doing now, he added. We need to join the front, he repeated by raising his voice and raising his right hand on the air. After all, Sewra is another big monastery, where some one would really learn to be oneself. The struggle without visible angels, the nature itself disciplines your whole attitude. You have to be there to know everything about Sewra, he said.

I defended my position, as Padre was looking for another offence. While we were in this atmosphere, me staring at him in disbelief, now I am beginning to read your mind, I said. I hope you take the best advantage of the situation and prepare for the results, and the remedy is in your hand, I added. As I see you are just worried about it without any reason. It is a fact that you have to resolve the problem. Take the issue seriously and don't depend on alternatives, case closed, I said. Your well arranged words and phrases wouldn't suggest a thing to change my mind, my dear brother, said Padre.

Likewise, Padre prompted an argument, in which the final result was considerably harmful to his identity. In a self-confident expression, raising my voice, Padre, Padre I said, as though I will convince him once again. You know Padre, I added, the religious life is a straight career if you plan and work on it. Padre, who never grew tired of the argument, asked me, where it came from all these arguments. I, in a flattering way responded, it came from an excellent mannerism.

Padre on his part insisted so strongly to turn down my spirit, so that I no more interfere in his decisions. I wish you better be inspired by humility, I said. By the way I didn't expect from you such contradiction, what is that entire pump, I repeated. To win the respect, I lowered my voice, and once again, though I was not satisfied, I tried to accommodate my feelings. I am very sorry to be the reason of your discontent, I concluded.

****

He finally admitted. He looked like to understand the situation. He had a strong personality, he didn't easily change. Padre's mind was stirred up and started to repeat the last word of mine. Convinced as he was in his decision, he started to revive the entire situation of his people. The continued agitation of his people, due to the lack of independence, would have brought a weakening of mind and depressed his life. So, while I was campaigning to win him back, he took all imaginable precautions to prevent his positions from being destroyed.

Sewra had made him more vulnerable because he had so much more to lose for his people, but it had also made him stronger.

In those days of his religious life, Padre heard a lot about Sewra's progress. He had always delighted, in Sewra's self assurance and many were the moments, when he tried to picture out this progress to his students.

This whole year he had been in continuo crises, or more accurately, dryness of the Spirit. Going to the mountains, joining the liberation front and leaving the congregation where he used to live had caused him a real chaos. It is all being about chaos, about being drawn into chaos.

✳✳✳✳✳✳✳✳

As far back as June 1977, when Padre was totally dedicated in his educational matter, he had reviewed Sewra's progress in the armed struggle. It was in the middle of June. All the classes were preparing for the final exam. All the students were occupied in their studies. Very rare students were relaxed. You can see most of the students studying under the trees and the courtyard.

Behind the mountains the advance of Sawra was heard. The strategy was to liberate the town of Keren from the hand of the enemy. Yet, only Sawra could guarantee to provide the liberation of its people. The first liberating bullets were heard from the southern mountain of Ziban. As the fighting approached near, the students were allowed to go home. It was the last subject for all the classes, some were taking math, and some were taking history or science. The students hurried to wards their home. They did not have time to greet each other. They run along the streets. People from other place were also running to wards their home.

After three heavy days of fighting the EPLF captured the town of Keren, without many civilian casualties. When the EPLF captured the town of Keren, Padre was living in a monastery. He was teaching in the middle school.

It was the end of the school year when the town was captured. The people were very surprised, and the thing that made them more happier was, that there was not casualty. Every night party. The enemy was no more under control of the town. Free to move where they want when they want.

Abadi, Padre's classmate had joined the front one year before the independence of Keren. It was very surprising to Padre to see one of his classmates with Klascinkof. He wouldn't believe it because he didn't expect it. He was not able to remember him. Abadi was an active student when he was in school. He had a very likable character.

When they were students in Asmara they had good time. While they were classmates they were very close friends. They did not have anything in common besides being classmates. Abadi who was born in the city would definitely act as a city boy, but Padre recruited to be a monk came from a village. A week after the fall of Keren town under the EPLF, Abadi who had the chance to be in the town had heard about his old friend Padre. He was very eager to see him and surprise him. And in fact Padre was very surprised to see his friend Abadi. One day a week after the independence of Keren town, Abadi and Tegadalit Senait decided to pay a visit to Padre. On their way, Abadi was telling to Senait, everything about his Friend Padre. He mentioned about all the good old days, while they were at school. Abadi recalled Padre, in many different ways, but above all the supper star Padre, playing basketball came to his mind, .

As they entered to the compound of the school, under the mango tree, a distance of 50 meters from the basketball playground, they saw Padre sitting down in solitude. It was five O'clock in the afternoon. The benevolent sun after shining for almost 12 hours it was sinking down behind the mountain of Senkil. Padre had always spent his time after school, relaxing, having mental refreshment and meditating. Though sitting down for a long time on a concrete seat was not comfortable, he always managed to do so for one or half an hour just meditating. Some times some brothers joined him and shared their experiences. The only topic that occupied their discussion was the class management. It was also most common to talk about the war situation, and the political issue of that time.

While Padre was in the atmosphere of peace and tranquility a small kid approached him and said that there were two guests Tegadelti (Freedom fighters) to see him. From a distance a voice came saying "Padre Beyene the suppers star." Padre looked very surprised. It was dusk. It was becoming a little dark. He could not recognize him at once. Abadi started to smile but still for Padre was a great puzzle. Do you know me added Abadi in a low voice? Yes, you are one of the Tegadelti said Padre, but he added if I am obliged to pay attention and figure out who you are I think you need to give time to solve the puzzle. Do you have any clue of who I am, asked Abadi? No nothing, I don't have a clue, said Padre. Have you ever heard the name Abadi?, asked Abadi? I think I have heard it in Asmara. Can you recall the Abadi Asmarino, from Asmara playing with you basketball and going to the same school? Padre shook his head. I can not recall you in this condition. There is a big difference, I didn't expect like this, he said. The Abadi, I knew in Asmara and the one I see, are totally different, he added. It was a long time, and my mind refused to reveal. Padre grabbed Abadi and hugged him. They sat down for a while talking under the mango tree. Padre invited Abadi to stay with him for supper. I just came to see you, right now I can not accept the invitation, since I did not take permission from our line leader, Abadi said.

There were no Generals, Colonels, and Sergeants. The system of the leadership of the EPLF was totally different. Nothing you can do without permission. Limited vocabulary but fruitful obedience to the up line leaders. You have to be ready for any orders. Whenever the introductory words of salute "Selamat Bitsot" (Hi comrades) were pronounced, the readiness of the Tegadelti (freedom fighters) was always there. "Awet N'Hafash" (Victory for the masses) follows after every conclusive meetings. In a vigorous voice everyone repeated the same word after which the daily-armed struggle task began. This system created a climate of harmony and unity between the freedom fighters.

Pulling down his Klashinkof Abadi sat next to Padre. They started to talk about the past experience and the war experience. Padre's attention was with his old friend and classmate Abadi. He started to ask many questions, he was infinitely curious to know about every thing. Abadi on his part was very selective in his answers, because Sewra taught them not to give any information that will damage the foundation. The restrain was for a political reason.

I am glad to see you again said Padre. So am I, said Abadi. While seeming to be following the discussion, St. Michael and Mary have made a great help in liberating the town of Keren, commented Padre. To give a religious backing to his statement, it was a great miracle, added Padre. Abadi though he was following Padre's thought, instinctively interrupted him, by saying, " did you see St. Michael or Mary holding a Kalashnikov", It was, we by our hand that defeated the enemy. Padre saw some thing different in Abadi's face.

He had changed a lot since he joined the liberation front, said Padre. He noticed greatly of his change. The way he used to talk when they were at school and after he joined the front there was a big difference. The Abadi, Padre used to know was an energetic and enterprising one, but once again, he saw a different character in his old friend. He was very calm, and with great reflection, and did not raise his voice as he used to, but he rather became a listening person. He was very disciplined. I think Sewra might have done some thing, to change Abadi's behavior, said Padre. I was not expecting him like this. I would like to know from Abadi, the reasons of his change of character, if ever I get a chance, said Padre.

****

One evening, as usual, when Padre was sitting under a mango tree, he heard from a megaphone, that there was a "Bahli" (a cultural party), big event taking place in Keren town. Very an noted and famous singers were around Keren town, so the people were anxiously waiting for this day. Usually, there was almost every day, a special occasion that motivated the people to get together.

That evening thousands of people were flocking towards the show place Joko. On their way every body was singing a revolutionary song. The whole night the singers entertained the whole population. Some known leaders of the EPLF were giving political speech and revolutionary enlightenment.when Padre decided to go to the show. He totally forgot for the time being the community commitment. He was unexpectedly lifted up, by the big success of the EPLF. All his publicity as a basketball player, and the good reputation he had as a teacher, had considerably lost their tone. Most of the people and the students, they diverted their attention to the politics and the struggle affairs.

I have being for long alone, now I need a break, so I better go to Joko to see what is happening, he said, to himself. He took off his religious robe and became simple in order not to be recognized by his students. It was seven o'clock. He hurried towards the northern gate. He saw left and right and joined the large crowed flocking towards the show place. From across the street one of Padre's friend, Berhe his name joined him and started to walk together. Many of his students were also going to the show place. While on their way he shared with his friend Berhe the surprising meeting of his classmate Abadi. My meeting with Abadi made me very much encouraged. Abadi used to play basketball with me while we were in Asmara. I know that is very surprising said Berhe.

While they were watching the show at some intervals they were discussing about Sewra's undertaking of the armed struggle. All in all, I am very much interested about all the liberation movement lead by the EPLF said Padre. What surprised me more, was the meeting with Abadi. He gave me a lot of information's, regarding the system and the leadership of the EPLF.

As follows was, what Abadi shared with me about the liberation front system and strategy. From the start, the system of the movement became clear to every body. The leaders themselves became the models of the struggle. The outstanding reputation they had, came from their sacrificed and the disciplined life. You see, when I first saw Abadi and related the past experience, I noticed a big difference. From what I understood, and from what Abadi had explained to me, I thought that discipline was number one means to arrive to their objective. And it was this discipline, that has created a constant union among the freedom fighters. To add an opinion to his idea, in the middle of their conversation, Berhe said, that our Tegadelti, they completely set aside everything in their clothing's, food and exterior deportment that might have suggested the air of division among themselves. No one needs to tell us, Padre said, we have seeing them, their food were the most frugal, you can not eat it with appetite. Every day the same menu. Ades with Wed-Aker were the main dish. It was very mortifying. I think that Sewra had commanded them anything which would have put their life to a sterner test, said Berhe. I myself can not imagine some one going against ones nature and modify the usual manner of being a sacrifice, said Padre. It raises a question, that how the Tegadelti carried out, such an honorable duties, unless they possessed uncommon power of discipline, said Berhe.

"I am very much preoccupied for the situation our people are living" murmured, Padre, as he pushed back his chair, to sit down. I am being strangled to live without any compromise, with the enemy, he said, wishing to go elsewhere in search of breathing space. I decided long time ago to channel my energies, to keep my own people safe and happy, concluded in his mind.

****

Through his bedroom window that faced to the east, he started to see the barren mountain of Etabir. Mountain Etabir, once the place of wild animals, after several years it became a place of snakes and mice's. The sun was shining brightly. He accompanied his solitude, with a revolutionary song, composed far away on the mountains.

In the morning, he was tuned to the edifying religious song, that gave him a certain inner sensation. Naturally, with out any conflict he adapted to Sewra's songs. He was playing on the tape record over and over. In 1970, when the neighbors soldiers destroyed the village of Ona, by massacring and burning the houses, he was living in the religious congregation of the De La sale Christian Brothers at St. Joseph school Keren. He was preparing to be a religious brother. At that time he was doing grade nine. Abadi his closest friendm had joined the liberation one-year before the capturing of Keren town in 1977. Abadi was an active boy when he was in school. He was the opposite of his friend Padre. Abadi was living with his family before he joined the front.

That night, the show terminated at three in the morning. He had only two hours of sleep, before he was going to join the community for the morning prayer. That day, he skipped the community prayer service. He had no time to prepare, but he had to get back to the classes. Looking down on his table, he saw the piles of his students exercise books, to be corrected and be evaluated. I am screwed up, and my day is screwed up, he said. He had never been to class without being prepared. He preferred to remain in his room, and ask for sick leave, but he had to be there with his students.

Padre did not share with any one, the apprehension he had, about the current situation of Sewra. However, he remained firmly resolved, to keep everything secrete. He no longer had much to do with his own congregation and seemed to have lost all confidence in the Institute. His perception of living in a community with monks had dried up. His superiors became suspicious, when they saw Padre changing his character, in regard to the congregation's habit and regulations. His superior attempted to penetrate to the secretes of Padre's mind. He wanted exact account of his life, so that he wanted to be informed directly from Padre him self. One day the superior called Padre, to his office, and asked him what was going on in his life. What is happening my brother Beyene? Said the superior. I see a big change of character in you, added the superior, though he did not get any response.

Padre preferred to remain silent. With this attitude he was so apt to reduce the superior to silence. For the time being he wanted to say nothing, and let the event speak by it self. Padre did not look upon the cause of liberation, as one that concerned him personally, but as one affecting the whole society. So he felt that it was not up to him to give answers, at least for the time being.

On the advice of his friend Abadi, Padre remained in his native town. He extended his stay in the congregation for two weeks. He still was hesitating of joining the front. He wanted to commit himself, wholeheartedly, for the cause of the independence, but the main obstacle of not doing so, was his status of being a religious brother. There was not any raise of voice in the community. Everything was kept secrete. Padre and the superior for the time being they wanted to keep it that way.

To be an instrument of liberation, for Padre was not a simple task. He foresaw many obstacles, in pursuing the path of being an instrument of liberation. Another war another battle of thought. Divided between two goods, between two preferences. He persistently pressed, for joining the front, but on the other hand he audited, what he was accomplishing in the religious institution. He said, I don't know where I am heading? He started to be a little overwhelmed. I know this might be hard for me, to be divided in to two state of mind. What I was accomplishing then, as a religious, it was productive, said Padre. He had to struggle mentally hard, to make himself overcome the situation.

The moment I decide to leave the Institution, my desertion will make a good deal of noise, and every body will speak about me, said Padre, to him self. On the other hand, not to decide for a long time,

81

would deteriorate my identity, he concluded. In un affected tenor, he said, he would not bargain on the cause of liberation of the locals. He added, It would be unfair prejudice, to disclaim the good outcome of the apostolic work he was doing. For any reason, if I do so it would highly tax my identity, he said.

Immersed into deep thought he started to conclude that it was not possible to combine his presence to the Institute and join the liberation front. Giving his fullest approval, to the matter of leaving the institute and further delay might cool off his decision, he organized himself to approach the office.

One day he took up the matter, to discuss with his superiors, so as to conclude his career of being a religious Brother.

After several days Padre decided, to meet the Superior. Upon Padre's request, a week later the superior accepted the invitation. At this time, he was very ready to express him self before the superior, because the situation in which he now found himself invited him do so.

Padre was deeply thinking about the visit for a while. At last he did it. Finally he was able to confront the situation by himself. On his part the superior was surprised about the visit. With this in mind, he gathered together all his opinions and ideas, and spared nothing to win over, to make his Superior accept his point of view. In order to convince him, he adopted a more familiar and engaging attitude. The Superior, at first, expressed his surprise over the fact and remained perplexed since he did not expect it from him. Padre in his Institute was a very promising member. Every body liked him.

However, when Padre began deliberately, to share his idea of leaving the Institute, the Superior tried to soften the prejudice he had in his mind. The solid argument he used to advance, suddenly interrupted. He pointed out, that his decision would not be a burden, but how difficult it was for him, to make such a choice, when the time came to do it. I don't want to dictate your choice, I rather prefer not to interfere with your liberty, added the Superior.

His good intention gradually brought him, to where he wished to be. Padre in all manners tried to be good, and at the same time present his case. He said to the superior, you know I have to base my choice, not on what my life might become later on but on what I am at this time. Choosing life is historical and mysterious. I have to prioritize my choices. Right now the public good is the independence of locals. Without freedom, whatever we do or act is baseless, expressed Padre. It is true, said the Superior just to conform his acceptance, but tried to make him understand that the choice he previously made, did not turn out as well as he hoped.

You know, every day I am weeping fresh tears, over the situation I am living, said Padre. My patience has reached to its highest limit. I don't like this kind of situation, making me suffer for too long, added Padre, while negotiating with his Superior. On that part, I don't think, I did any wrong to you, answered the Superior. I still want to help you and I don't want to convince you for long. As I see and imagine, you are terribly exposed to the situation and I don't want you anticipate any failures and more of the same sorrow. But to be fair with you, there is still chance for the prior decision you made, to acquire the life of being a monk, said the Superior. By defending himself, he added, don't get me wrong, I am not taking any pleasure in convincing you, to stay with the congregation, but you have to consider the matter carefully.

I am certainly aware, that I was well instructed and brought up in this Institute, said Padre. By the way, I am not comparing at all, but prioritizing, he repeated. Right now, I don't feel good and fully satisfied on the account of the choice I had made.

Any way, let us go to the beginning of our affairs, insisted the Superior. Padre as though he wanted to disregard the initial discussion , "what affair?" he exclaimed. The affair you made a contract with God, answered the superior.

The change of mind, had very much disturbed the Superior, who had expected a lot from Padre. Suddenly, he took an aggressive approach to wards Padre's decision. There is still chance for the prior decision you had made, said the Superior. You mean the option of choosing a career to be a member of the Institute, asked Padre. Yes, exactly for the decision you made to acquire the life of a monk, said the Superior. You are just defending yourself, and I am not able to furnish you enough answers, added the Superior while pretending to admit Padre's proposal. I don't get much satisfaction and joy on account of the choice I made, replied Padre. The Superior, as he saw, that he was really running for a risk, he restrained his feelings, and said, I am very sorry to be the reason of your discontent. For the time being Padre resolved to remain silent and say nothing. When there was no feed back, the Superior in an angrily manner said, I don't think your silence is the sign of innocence. I think, said Padre, (to defend him self without contradicting his identity of being a monk) you are very much hearted by my situation. I don't know, whether my decision is wrong or right, I am not preoccupied to discover my true identity, in the harshness of the conditions imposed to me, and I will never draw back. I can not influence your will, but I would rather advice you to see back to the first promise you have made, said the Superior, while presenting a motive, that would justify his opinion of rejection, to the decision made by Padre.

A week before his departure to the front, he was making ready himself by being in close contact with his old friend Abadi. Life is short so I have to hurry up and get it done, he said. The armed struggle was the only thing in his mind, and the last thing that remained to him, was to say good bye to the Institute.

The time that we managed to spend together, seemed very short, but I realize that it was a treasure, and both of us had taken advantage out of it. The opportunity of having dialogue was good for both of us exclaimed the superior.

In order not to miss the dialogue, for a while the superior resolved to remain silent. Trying to win Padre back and convince him was not easy. Padre, so secure in his feelings, managed to cross through the fire of contradictions to make better his positions. On the eve before his departure to the front, while most of the monks were at recreation, Padre approached his brothers, to say good-bye to all. These were the last words of Padre before he joined the liberation front:

No matter how hard it will be, no matter what the future will be, the liberation of the locals had taken precedence to all my previous decisions. I deeply love my Institute, my students and my profession. My life might not be with the Institute. For the time being my rosary would be changed into Klashinkof, but after the independence I will knock on the door of my Institute by hanging my klaschinkof at the gate of the monastery.

It never happened like that. Padre didn't come back. He didn't join his beloved Institute. He remained on the mountains of Sahel. He became a sacrifice in 1982, during the 6th offensive campaign (the red star campaign), as was known by the neighbor.

I didn't hear about Padre since he departed to the front. The first time I learned about Padre's martyrdom, was during the official announcement of the EPLF administration in 1991. That day I heard the name of Padre on the list of the martyrs.

On the day of the martyr's name announcement, I was at Saint Joseph School Keren. I was there, but I was not really there at all. I felt as though my head was upside-down. I had no idea of what was going to be. I simply waited. The whole day I was listening to the radio, sometimes sitting and sometimes standing. The martyr's families were with me in my mind, since I knew how this would feel. I thought of how many times the families were waiting the return of their children.

Of course, I didn't actually accept the situation, but I expected it would be so, since the nature of the struggle was like that. With out paying life nothing would come out, that I learned it from the beginning. It was this reality and my expectation that clashed. I would have liked that Padre wearing the black robe and the white robbat. I would have liked, he entering in his class and giving his lessons. I would have liked, he dribbling the ball and scoring many shots. I would have liked, I holding him near me. I would have liked, many good things to happen.

After all I realized the fact of the armed struggle. The fact of dying within the process of the struggle. I was not able to stop trying so hard to accept the fact. I had a strong picture of the struggle, but my own weak sentiments and feeling wouldn't help me, since my mind was not that enough to handle it.

I invited my mind to rewind to the old times. The good times we passed in the monastery. In the monastery we found our common interest of being brothers for the service of other people. Over the course of the years, after Padre left to the front, things had changed for worse. A friend and a companion of Padre, Fitzum Gebrezabher (a freedom fighter) who survived the war had told me a lot of the armed struggle experience. He told me that Padre did not change. He was the same Padre with all his dedications and full energy. He was always the first to help. To the last day of his life, he had the role of leadership. An exemplar Padre he faced everything with courage. The discipline was different since the field of the commitment was different.

I attributed our past experience in the monastery, at least in part, the life history of Padre before he joined Sewra. **THE STORY WOULD HAVE ENDED....** here, but I did not want to conclude it here. I would have continued trying to imitate. Finish my work for the sake of finishing. There is a content to be told but some one has to tell. I can not tell it. It is out of my experience. I can not recount the life of Padre when he joined the front. Some one might help me since I was not physically in the armed struggle

PART THREE

Roma

"**R**oma bella" (The beautiful Rome) was my destination for my continuing formation, from 1979 to 1984. On July 21st of 1979, I landed at the air port of Fiumicino. Brother Bartolo Parisi was the one who came to pick us from the airport. Me and Tecle Meconnen after being introduced, we headed together to the collage of Colle La Sale in Via del Imbrecciato. I loved Rome. Asmara city, the second African Rome, was to be substituted by the real Italian Rome. Colle La Sale besides being a high school, it hosted the senior and disabled brothers from all over the country. It was a home for the retired brothers. At the begging of September of 1979 we were registered at the university of Teresianum. My Italian language ability was a beginner one. I did not go to Italian language sessions to upgrade my Italian language. As I came, only by speaking I had to learn it. After three months I was able to command the language fairly.

It was Christmas eve of 1980. I was serving at the Geez mass, held in Vatican city inside Collgio Etiopico. As the mass was to end, before the priest was to greet the congregant, with the liturgical greetings "Go in peace", I was greeted by a smile from a female, who was sitting in the front row of the Church. I gazed at her. The face was common. She was still smiling, obviously impressed. My mind wondered to identify the strange female. I acted like I was not looking at her. I didn't want to stay longer where I was. I hurried to the vestment room to take out the liturgical vestment I was wearing. All the congregants left when the mass was ended, but she stayed behind, still sitting where I saw her. She was waiting me to come out from the vestment room. As I came out, she called me by my name twice. My mind started to catch up. Though I gave no sign, I tried to hold her in my focus. All at once, my remembrance level started to rise. All her look was totally changed, but I recognized her voice. Are you Nardos Kinfe I said, looking towards her face again. Yes I am, she said to make things easier. All I knew about Nardos was, when she was living with the nuns of the Orsoline Sisiters. Besides her beautiful face, which my mind was acquainted with, to describe the whole look of Nardos was impossible. I used to see her, wearing her religious vestment, everything from covering her head to the tip toe (a long heel garment). My mind couldn't connect easily. When I was sure about her identity, I hugged her. My eyes began to click. I turned my eyes towards her. Like a camera man, I started to take the new picture of Nardos. One time taking the view from up to down, and another time from right to left. Once she knew, she was being photographed by the hidden camera of my conscience, she controlled all her outward physical expressions. She looked like the last copy of an artist, ready to be exhibited. Her beautiful opened wide large eyes, her hair well trimmed in afro style, her lips extended in a "C" shape, accompanied by her inviting white teeth, had dominated my mind.

I leaned towards her, to place the exact picture of her in my system. Sweet things come from sweet souls, I said, while covering distinctively the fresh live picture of Nardos. Her gentle voice started to flush my mind with wonder, like a child at his mothers breast. To enjoy her more and perceive her prettiness, I invited her for a coffee, at Piaza del'Independenza, a coffee shop where most of the Habesha immigrants get together. She accepted my invitation. She couldn't have believed that she found me in Rome. That was what I learned from our conversations. Her presence some what confused me. We exchanged our phone numbers. The preordained environment of being a monk for the time being was put aside. See you next week at church, I said, when I was to go home to my collage.

The next time we met at Church, we agreed to meet one hour before the mass was to start. Seated in front of the Vatican garden we were chatting about our past experiences while back home. The stocked stress in her mind one by one started to come out. Nardos was emotionally complaining about the immigrant life she had started in Rome. I did not expect that Rome would accept me in this manner, she said. Caught by her interminable crises, she was looking some one to stand besides her. One day she called me to see her at her house. As I came to her house, she was sitting on a sofa alone in front of a TV. What is all that after being in a status of happiness suddenly I enter into a status of stress, she asked. How come two identity in one personality, at the same moment would act, she added, by expressing the change of behavior from minute to minute, she was experiencing. This time I considered my self like a counselor. I let her finish. Never interrupted her. I restrained from giving her ready made solutions. My good understanding protected me from interfering uselessly. The more I listened her the more she confided me. I did not need to instruct her on trust. She already trusted me. To approach her problems as a counselor professionally yet it was not my time. I was only a student. "Little knowledge Kills", as the saying goes, I was to keep to my self the little knowledge I had.

When Nardos was certain that I had been considering her problems as mine, she decided to turn over the relation from a counselor to a lover. Her tone changed 180 degrees. My presence became a source of her tranquility. Naturally she would have spoken to me about this new love development. She was driving fast in that matter. Some times our phone conversations turned hot. On her part she was clear and simple, but on my part there was an obstacle. Despite the on going situation of attractions it was not the right time and the right place. I retreated. Her insistence on the subject continued.

She devised a wise idea of an offence to involve me in the field of jealousy. She started to date an Italian man, while her heart was still with me. I knew her action. She was doing it out of desperation. She openly was sharing with me about the new relationship she started. I assured my self and assured her that I will take care of her only as my sister. This was the very most I could do, I said when one day she met me in the Church after the mass. Consequently, when she began to repeat her self that she was in love with me, I made clear to her that things were not going to function this way. Her mind couldn't cope with my stand. She took it as if I was trying to run from the situation or ignore her. In the middle not to depress her I shared my appreciative glances.

In May of 1996, after 13 years working In Eritrea and Ethiopia, on my way to Chicago, I met once again Nardos in Rome. The day she learned my being in Rome, she immediately called me. She was married and got two children. She came to the collage where I was staying and the next day she invited me in her house. Now was the time, the then counselor to be counseled (being in the middle of crises, I myself), I said by reciting in my mind the biblical verses of the prodigal son. The conversations of years ago came out one by one. I found her as I had left her. On my part I was totally changed for her.

Bashay Teclemariam was his name, an x-freedom fighter of the ELF, who came for brain surgery to Rome in the Summer of 1980, from Saudi Arabia. He was injured in 1977, at the war of Barentu. When an enemy bomb exploded near him, some fragments of the bomb had penetrated his skull. At his youth age, one thing I can remember about him was his fearless attitude. Generally he was cool and calm. He didn't initiate any argument by himself. We were calling him by the nickname "TriuKriuK". By the way through all my essay I bombarded my readers with a litany of the nicknames. To defend my thesis, for the youth's of Keren Lalai, a nickname was a second name given to individuals without a baptismal celebrations. The practice of nicknaming was a spontaneous one, and some times to the point. No one chose his nickname. Everything came from the community members. A repeated move or act of an individual would lead to a possible nicknaming.

Bashay's older brother usually called by his nickname "Sheitan" (the devil) was the group leader of the Keren Lalai youth community. He was very well known by his bravery. People from other counties as they heard the name of Medhanie Sheitan they get scared. Around 1975 he was recruited by the ELF (Eritrean Liberation Front) as an insider informant. He was working for the government at the airport of Asmara as a security agent. He was the source of all the information's (to feed the liberation movement) by going through all the airport facility.

One day to refresh his mind, I invited Bashay, for a tour of Rome city. Early in the morning to elevate his spirit "Nebsi" (to mean my body), I called Bashay to give him a sense of my closeness. That morning he saw me collecting the Italian coins of lire before we were to go to see the old Rome. To make a phone call, to drink a soda, to play games, to check the weight, to ride a bus, the need of the coins was very important. He saw me everywhere we went putting coins. At last we entered into a big Cathedral. Bashay I said, as we entered inside the Cathedral, put some coins to light a light. He did as I told him. When he exclaimed, "even in the house of God gambling"! to my surprise he became the source of my laughter.

****

I left Eritrea at war. The six military campaigns known by the name "Werarat" (Red star campaign), one after the other, successively were fought on the mountains of Sahel, form 1978 to 1982 . The military campaigns had empowered the resistance. As the military tried to crash the resistance none stop, the mountains of Sahel the strong hold of the resistance said no. The sixth's "Red star campaign" , big in its size and its preparations, publicly announced to the world, by Menghistu Hailemariam, was completely destroyed. How many enemy soldiers remained on the mountain. As the Abysinian saying goes it was like, " Adiom Tiquzerom" (Let their mothers count them). The last big military campaign was the un anounced 7th campaign "Selahta Werar" (the secret campaign). After 10 years of trials and retrials, the mountains of Sahel, became vocals. They raised their voice for offence, and in 1988 the first counter offence was accomplished by the EPLF. "Nadow Iz" was completely destroyed within 49 hours. The big snake was struck on its back. Though it was moving hopelessly for several years, at last in 1991 on may 24, it was struck on its head, to open the door of the independence.

While I was in Rome I was following all the current affairs through the world media. I never had doubted for single time to the success of the Eritrean resistance, in defeating the enemy.

****

At the age of 27 I composed a drama. And I realized it with the youth association of Dekemhare. That summer of 1987 we made a tour to show it in Asmara and Keren. It was my first adventure, on the field of authors, and I was confident in what I accomplished.

Most of the actors of the drama have joined the liberation front . In 1991 after the independence I was lucky enough to meet some of my students back alive with their Klashinkof. My mind started to flash in a random pattern to recall my x-students. I was relating their faces with their names and suddenly my mind underlined their actions. I totally forgot the content of the drama, but they recited it for me from the beginning to the end. I wished all the actors were alive to show it again, I said.

Theater had always been my hobby. I enjoyed directing rather than playing or acting by my self. In my mind I creatively played the different roles. I was good at it. The title of the drama I composed in that year read: "To day we won't show the show". As far as I remembered and tuned my mind to the recitations of the x-students I started to rewrite it like this. I will be very brief. The whole message of the show was political. Unless one deeply analyzes it, one can not enter into the main massage of the show. I doubted even the actors knew about it. The drama reflected the situation of 1987 the historical year of the unification of the Eritrean Popular Liberation Front and Eritrean Liberation Front.

As follows was the content of the drama. Behind the curtain a loud and angry noises was heard. It was a bad noise, very disturbing in its nature, the actors were fighting and exchanging bad words. On the other side inside the hall people were anxiously waiting to begin the action. Everyone seated on his seat was watching the time. They were really worried about the situation. All this happened while it was remaining five minutes to begin the show. After a couple of minutes, Beremberas a short guy with his tie came out from behind the curtain. He was the announcer of the show. People from inside they shouted to start the show soon. But the announcer started apologizing the audience. He said, sorry, today we are not going to show the show. The audience didn't give him chance to finish his sentence. The argument between the announcer and the audience it continued. The announcer couldn't handle the problem. While they were in this situation all the actors one by one came through the other door and systematically joined the audience. In the middle of the fighting and argument one of the actors Hidru, stands up and goes towards the stage and he said I could save the day if you give me chance. The announcer said if you are able to do it do it please. Hidru walking towards the stage he started to ask for the audience's collaboration to calm down. He said, looking right and left, "you see if there are not horses to pull the cart, there are donkey's available", and one by one he started to call all the actors from within the audience, and then by being united they showed the show. They sang a song of unity, accompanied by the lead guitarist Kaleb, the base man, Weldegabir and the pianist Petros. At last the show finished and the audiences were very happy.

Shinara

Marradona I called the white Rify donkey (a desert donkey usually used for long distance transportation), I used to have when I was assigned to teach at "Lideta Mariam" (Nativity school of Shinara), a windy village, located on the western part of keren suburb. It was about 9 kilometers distant from keren town. The majority of the villagers were farmers. By faith 95% were Catholics.

The De La sale Christian brothers were running the school, from the early 1980th. I was running the elementary school as a principal, from 1989 till the independence year of 1991 . The first day I was assigned to join the community of Shinara was on the fall of 1988. I grew up in a town and I had hard time to adopt the villagers life.

It was the harvest time of 1988. The villagers were engaged working on their fields. The year was a year of abundance. One could hear in every corner a harvest song being sang by the villagers. The harvest song made the farmers to work fast and efficient. They were singing Bilen songs. I wish I knew Bilen language at that time to be the immediate family of the villagers.

One day while I was going down to the school, one of the villagers by the name Woldemicael Jimi approached me calling me by a strange name Bicar. The name Bicar resonated in my inner most soul. I was astonished, when he called me by that name. Frankly, the new nickname I did not accepted it, since I had good reputation of the founding missionary father Ficardi from France. Almost two centauries ago father Ficardi, (very well known by the name Abuna Bicar), was living with the people of Shinara. He was very fluent in the local language of Tigre. With all respect he had performed an outstanding missionary work among the villagers. He was everything for the villagers, a father, a counselor, a mediator. He became a center of all their life references.

The holy missionary lived a simple life. Until now his name is referred in different circumstances. The gracious missionary, a true messenger of the church had left a historical legacy.

Though I was the principal of the school, I assigned my self to my self, to teach at the lower level. I was teaching English to grade one. My decision to teach English in grade one was for two reasons. On one hand to learn the Bilen language, and on the other hand to teach them English. After many years of thinking creatively about how to teach children English, I came to a conclusion of doing it differently, from the usual way of teaching. I actually did it. I finalized that in three days time, the students should be able apprehend the alphabets. I manipulated the Bilen songs and dance. Belen's were crazy in it. It was part of their life. They created an occasion to be together dancing, some times dancing none stop the whole night.

I did not waste my time teaching them counting the alphabets. A new way a new strategy. I prepared the lesson plan my self ahead of time. I arranged all the consonant in my way. Separated the consonant from the vowels. Not the traditional way. No fixed chronology to follow. One alphabet at a time. Every thing was accompanied by song and dance. I came with a design of an alphabet and put in front of the students. In Bilen language, I asked them " Wre teketi" (what does it look like). I left them figure out by themselves. Their response was environmental. They tried to relate the alphabet with any thing that they were in touch with. They never explored out of their surroundings. Once I was sure about the majority response, all together we baptized the alphabet. After the acquaintance of three alphabets, we composed a Bilen song after which all the students danced and chanted. It took me three days to teach all the alphabets, which generally took three months to count the English alphabets.

Bicar became crazy they said all the family of the students. I became the center of the villagers discussion. They never suspected my profession as a teacher. It was a new idea a new fashion. After school when they were in their houses they were singing the English alphabets at times dancing.

It was Anter "wedi Jimi" (son of Jimi). I saw him coming towards me. As he came near me, Bicar, he said, you know you drove all our children crazy. I did not take his comment personal. His question was neither malevolent. Instead of answering his question, I jumped to conclusion. That was why I came to Shinara, I said, underlining his comment of driving crazy the whole villagers.

The center of the villagers entertainment, Deki Jimi, they had their own share in my life. A screen less live jokes of Deki Jimi, maneuvered the daily life of the people of the villagers. In any conversations if they saw a strange attitude the conversant disclaimed by saying " Zereba Deki Jimi", (the talk of Deki Jimi). Of course everyone in the village knew the popular figures of the entertaining ability of Deki Jimi. Their jokes were to the point, some times dangerous. For what ever it was, it made the villagers to forget what they did not want to remember.

Inseparable bodies, as they were they entertained the people during the crucial war time. Their jokes were local and at times unexpected. The whole jokes of Deki Jimi would have been a book in itself.

Let me share one, with the readers. One time both, Weldemicael and Anter, while they were walking from Keren to Shinara, they met an old woman heading towards Shinnara. It was dusk, and the way she was walking was very slow. As they saw the woman on their way, they made a trick. They did not want to leave her on the road alone, and neither they wanted to be slowed down by her walk. Instantly they invented a false news. As they approached the old lady, they told her, "today your son Ghebrai and Andu were fighting to death in Shinara".

The old woman as she heard about her son's involvement in the fight, she started to speed up and walk fast.

Keimet was her name a quiet and a shy girl from Rora bet Ghebru. Her innocence was easily read on her face. She was down psychologically because of being fatherless for a number of years. It had affected her life. As she was the oldest daughter she was helping her mother to take care of her young brothers and sisters. She went to Lideta Mariam (Nativity) school of Shinara from grade one to grade six.

After many years of being absent from her life, in 1990 her father showed up from the neighboring country of Sudan. He came from Sudan with a new religious conviction of Islam. The new religion that he had embraced was called by "Wehabiun" (one of the Muslim religion branch). His view of the original faith of being a Muslim had been totally changed.

At the age of fourteen, when her father came from Sudan, he immediately made a wedding arrangement for Keimet. The unexpected decision of her father had surprised her, because the new imported situation was far from her mind. Her mother's desire was that Keimet continues her education. Both parents went to a deep arguments. "Kab Zizarebu TZomom yhderu" (instead of arguing better stay hungry) as the Abysinian saying goes, though her mother assumed the job of defending her daughter's right to go to school, she was not able to confront her husbands extremism. The essence of the litigation, that was going on, was the result of the view of the new faith, her father had acquired from Sudan.

A voiceless Keimet, remained a victim of her father's agenda, of getting her to be married, to a stranger at a very young age. A defiant father, abusing his daughter at her young age for me was unacceptable. One morning before the school day was to begin, Keimet's mother came to see me in the school. I heard her sigh, she must have had it, the whole night arguing with her husband, I said. After all those years, living alone with her children in loneliness, to be alarmed by her husband's decision, was not fair. At the beginning, the no of Keimet, it hurt her father's pride. As he saw less and less cooperation from his daughter's side he planned to kidnap her to a distant village.

With his new way of life he couldn't tolerate to live in peace with the old friends of his villagers. He was never close to the men of his village. The new supply of religious sentiment he bought it from the neighboring country couldn't make him live in coherence with his old friends. The good old days and the old stories had been forgotten.

May 24, 1991

Once again behind the mountains of Sahel, Sewra was reorganizing it self. The year was 1987. The struggle marked a turn over of the situation. It was the year of transition, from defense to offence. It was the year of unification, where attention to the political and the armed struggle were given. It was the year of political recollection, that directed the armed struggle to the final victory.

That time Sewra was officially twenty-six years old. Everything was happening so fast.

On March of 1988, the first offensive attack started. The enemy soldiers were completely destroyed in 49 hours, and were forced to retreat towards Keren. The town of Keren became the center and the stronghold of the enemy's soldiers for almost two years. It seemed that the enemy's war strategy was in a terminal decline. More than 40,000 civilians were hostages for more than two years. The town was surrounded by the EPLF (the freedom fighters). It was like we were in a big concentration camp.

This again, was what greeted the enemy soldiers. Masawa the sea outlet of the inner land, in 1990 fall under the Freedom fighters. The enemy as they were driven out from their strong holds everything crumbled.

There was no food to eat. The daily family ration was diminishing day by day. The people of the town were dependent, on the relief food donated by the international food aid organization. The enemy occupied the agricultural lands. They people were not able to cultivate their land. Two-rain season passed with out cultivating their lands. All over the place you see the enemy soldiers with their green jacket. Prostitution had enormously increased. The soldiers became themselves starved. They started to steal food from the civilians. At last the freedom fighters had agreed to access food to the towns and villagers.

Little by little we get used to the enemy's desperation and the ineptness of their counter offence.

The local's wondered how it is going to end. The only fear of the locals was to be a target of the enemy's revenge plan. Almost 15 months after the down fall of Masawa the EPLF were able to brake the enemy's last stronghold of Dekemhare, by triumphantly entering Asmara the capital city of Eritrea.

I wish I was a martyr like Padre, I said when I saw the locals enjoying the independence in 1991. Yes I was very jealous to be one of the freedom fighters, who realized the independence of the people.

✶✶✶✶✶✶✶✶✶✶

Before the independence I was totally in solitude. It was this solitude that I was experiencing. Or at least this was what I was feeling. I was scared how all this things are going to end. The fear did not come right away. I had to spend all the past eleven years in a desperate situation but very much controlled. I have some what complicated the power of the armed struggle with that of 1977. I reminded my mind to those testing years of Sewra's retreat to Sahel. Slowly, I was entering into the whole picture of the struggle. I ultimately, concluded that this time would be different in the end.

1990 was the darkest year for the local's who were under the enemy's control. The minutes became hours, the hours became days and the days became years. Sewra's accomplishment and the strategy were totally out of the mind of the local's. Everyone was waiting the day of the independence to be the next minute, hour, or day.

I heard a voice telling me from above. Here you go. This is the independence you were waiting for more than a quarter of a century. Do you like it like this? If you do so enjoy it. It was the voice of the martyr Padre. All right I said, though I was a little bit distracted by the vision. Then I looked to the right and left, and as far as my eyes can see only the local's were at my sight. The joy and happiness they were experiencing was an imaginable. People were on the main roads of the city day and night. Finally we are independent, history had been made, the people exploded, with laughter of joy and cheers.

Home discipline for the time being was forgotten. No one was at home. I couldn't believe it. If I said they were crazy I didn't exaggerate. I walked around the city and took in all the scenery. You have to be there. Why do people act like that I said if I was sure enough to identify the situation of their happiness.

****

I happened to be in Shinnara, during the independence day. Two days before , I was tuned to the radio of "Dimtzi Hafash " (radio of the masses). For two days there was a complete silence, even the only source of hope the radio station of Dimtsi Hafash was silent. Three days before the independence the radio had announced, that war was gong on, on the Dekemhare front line.

That day I got up early. It was around five o'clock in the morning. I began with the usual morning prayer, before it was to start, a normal day of a school day . I took time to take my breakfast around six o'clock. When I tuned to the 7 o'clock radio program, I heard a monotonous news repeated on the radio. "At last the land is liberated". I jumped and danced like crazy.

The front of Dekemhare was broken after heavy two days fighting. The freedom fighters after liberating the town of Dekemhare, they marched towards the capital city without any resistance. The enemy soldiers started to flee towards Sudan, the majority of them surrendered to the Freedom fighters.

That day I was supposed to go to the school, but the event wouldn't allow me. All the villagers in groups were heading towards Keren town. Instantly I canceled the school day program and joined the people.

Let me have my share, I said. Went back to my house. Made ready my only transportation means Maradona and left for Keren. Half way when I reached the natural water fountain located under the Lalumba mountain, I stopped to drink some water to quench my thirsty.

From far, as I was nearing the water fountain I saw a female freedom fighter, doing her chores. Selamat, she said, in a happy face with her Klashinkof laid on the ground, on one side. There were other freedom fighters of her unit relaxing and rejoicing, distant from her. After we exchanged a hug, I sat down near her. She interestedly was observing me, after which she asked me my name. My name is Hiabu, and I am a member of the De la sale Christian brothers, I said. Her mind was not able to register my name. It was a strange name for her. Any way all the freedom fighters when they joined the armed struggle, they were named by a different nicknames. What is the meaning of your name, she asked. "A gift", I answered, while waiting from her to tell me her name. Nice meeting you, my name is Hiwet, but I am well known by the Sewra name "Gual Mussie" she said. It was her first time to see a monk. Because I was wearing a white rob, which looked like the Muslim cloth, she suspected my identity, and asked me if I were a Muslim. No I am a Christian, I said, to explain what was absent from her experience. During the armed struggle the mention of religion, race and ethnicity was prohibited. A perfect balanced discipline that had dictated the mind of freedom fighters, in order to keep their unity. With that system all the fighters were feeling at home.

Her innocent smile attracted me. I was eager to follow her discussion, about the life in the armed struggle. She too was eager to know about "Gebar" (tax payer citizen). There was no sense of bragging. All her words were simple and calculated. Humility was shining on her face.

Originally I am from Dekemhare, and I joined the liberation front, when I was 10 years old, some time around 1978, she said, feeling uncomfortable about Sewra's indoctrinations. We were both caught by our experiences. As she explored from my discussion with her, she came to a conclusion, that Sewra's life was like a religious life. I joined her idea to a certain level, with an explanation. Sewra's life was without angels, a struggle to a level of giving one's life as a sacrifice, I said.

Two weeks later she came to St. Joseph school to see me. I was very glad to see her again. The interrupted discussion I had earlier with her started to revive in my mind. The innocent story of a struggle, re-told by an innocent female freedom fighter renewed my spirit. Though my way of discussing with people, generally was philosophical, I tried to restrain, with her this time.

She whisperingly approached me by attempting to tell me about some good news. I got a permission for two weeks to see my family, she said, happiness flowing from her face. Good luck, I said hugging her and giving her a cultural kiss on her cheeks, three times.

As she left the compound of the School, I returned to my room. While sitting in my room, I started to revise our conversations. Good lord, "keep safe and alive the parents of Gual Mussie", I said in a prayer. I did not escape from what I feared, both of her parents and her two elder brothers were killed by the enemy soldiers around 1984.

The testing time of a guiltless female freedom fighter started. Her long desire of meeting her family safe and alive was shattered. As she approached her village, from far she saw her house being demolished. She came to a near by house. With great fear she introduced her name. The old lady as she knew she was the daughter of Mr. Musie, she automatically tried to divert the situation. All your family were relocated to Bahri (a farming location area along the southern red sea coast), she said. To backup the wise and temporary mis information, "we are going to surprise your family", but till they come, you are welcomed to stay with us, the old lady said. The toughest of all for the old lady, was how to tell the truth about the where about of her family. To be up front and tell the situation, was not the cultural way she grew up with. Until she found a comfortable situation she preferred to stay silent. "Merdii" (the announcement of death), it should never be a surprise, but it had to follow a certain cultural way. When it was the proper time, the old lady decided to tell the where about of her family. To get through the business of telling of her families death, as it was a culture she invited several people from the neighborhood. In the middle of the social gathering, Hiwet was told that both of her parents and two of her older brothers were being massacred by the enemy soldiers. Gual Musie remained un movable and speechless. Tears won't come out. The news tiered her life. She wanted to know the where about of the two surviving younger brothers. Her two brothers were living with an old widow about 14 kilometers far from Dekemhare. She decided to see her two younger brothers. The next day she traveled on foot to the village. When she approached the village she saw many children playing local games. By chance she spoke with one of her brothers. She asked to the boy if he knew the address of the widowed woman. She is our mother, he exclaimed. Where is your brother, she said. By pointing his finger that is my brother, he said. On the way, until she reached the destination, she did not reveal her identity to her brothers. When she felt it was the right time to reveal her identity, she did it in front of the old lady. I am your sister, she said. After thanking her for what ever she did for her two brothers, she wanted to share with the her, the plan of a family reunion.

I wish I died, I was a martyr, she said after she learned the horrific killing of her family. In that moment, she entered into a deep thought. With her mind she began to revisit the experience of war and survival. This was Sewra. Sacrifice was particular in kind. Death was a common denominator. As one joined one died. No organized funeral. Buried where one fallen. "Awet Nhafash" (victory for the masses), followed the last honoring farewell phrase. After any military operations, there was "Bahli" (A party accompanied by revolutionary songs and cultural dance), organized without any rehearsal. A tuned "Krar" (a five string local guitar), with all its melody revived the spirit of freedom fighters. The after war shocks and traumas were handled around a tuned Krar and beat of "Kebero" (a local drum). No need of professional counselors. The healing process was a participatory in its method. All were involved to encourage each other. The problem for every freedom fighter was common. "Tebeges" (ready) was the word that broke the routine of the day. Besides "Zihazka Hizka Tebeges" (ready to move, with whatever was in your hand), the freedom fighters never knew until they reach at the threshold of the military operations. Any military engagement was kept secret for the fighters. No chance for any leak. Secrecy was number one tool of any operation. "Higem" (Go attack forward), the enemy position until they surrender or die. At times there was " Tetzabeo" (a resistance), from the part of the enemy. If the situation was against us we were forced " Ansehab" (Withdrawal), to make a strategic withdrawal.

I waited patiently until she returned back from the subconscious level. The touching moments of her past experience as a freedom fighter had begun to emerge through her sensual channel. She was mitigating the status of being a "Gebar" (an ordinary citizen) and a "Tegadalit" (a freedom fighter). As I knew she was in the middle of stress, I backed up from my brilliant academic counseling. I was only acting as a conveyor to facilitate all her disappointments.

When she came back from Dekemhare, she immediately came to see me. The happy and charming Gual Mussie was totally changed. After greeting me in a low voice, she turned down her face. My mind started to read her situation. Something might have happened, I concluded while inviting her to come in to the guest room. In the guest room, I glanced at her to have some attention. I did not want to enter into her emotional status immediately. I brought some thing to eat. She tried to eat but she couldn't easily swallow. Her entire digestive system was blocked. Gual Mussie, please eat, I said seeing her appetite was not normal. After consuming little food she said enough. Once again to relax her, I brought her some tea. While drinking her tea I started to deal with the situation diligently. To begin, how was your trip, I said. As I raised my question, tears came from her eyes. Some minutes later, she broke up her silence. She began to speak to me with confidence. She covered the whole story of her trip to Dekemhare, un interruptedly, while my mind was searching for a solution. "Perhaps you could help me" she said, adding her usual convincing smile. Her plan of her trip, to stay for two weeks with her family, abruptly, was changed. She decided to go back to Dekemhare to bring her two brothers with her in Keren, but financially she was unable, since she couldn't afford on her own. Her only income was only the monthly "Mesarif" (food coupon) that she was dependent on. On my part, I knew what was needed to help her. After I assured her, she started packing her things and the next day she left for Dekemhare to pick up her two orphan brothers. After staying two day's in Dekemhare, she came back from her trip. In 24 hours I made ready a rent house all furnished. When she saw the surprise, she got very happy. A different book a different story to write about, I wished that she was still alive, to re-write her story. Only three months after enjoying the air of independence that she learned about the horrific news of her family massacre. After all, she had a soul despite the Sewra discipline she acquired from the armed struggle.

After the independence

It was somewhat around December of 1992. I was in the capital city for a business to buy paintings and remodeling items. St. Joseph School started to be remodeled to accommodate the martyr's children.

On my way back to Keren, when I was standing and waiting for a bus in Edagahamus bus station, Felati the x-administrator of Keren Lalai came for a ride to Keren with me. Felati had been working in a "Kebele" (Keren Lalai district), as an administrator. Before he became an administrator he was selling tobacco in the down town of keren. "Min Timbak dib Abo Member" (From selling the tobacco, to being the administrator), they teased, the people of Keren Lalai, underlining his commitment and dedication. He was not very literate in the local language of Tigrinya. He was fluent in Tigre and Arabic languages. He retired from work for more than fifteen years. He started other business. While we were chatting, suddenly I was flooded with past memories. This time we seated together. The bus was full. Everyone had his or her place to sit. On the other isle of the bus opposite to our seat there was one lady who was whisperingly talking through the window of the bus to another lady. Before the bus started to move the lady who was standing out side the bus in a loud voice told the other lady to tell her sister to come in Asmara to give testimony in the court hearing. She said by tomorrow morning my sister should be here in Asmara. I cached up the last word and compared it to the past experience of the war. During the war movement was very restricted. Touring along the past experience of war and comparing with situation of freedom our people were living I had to awaken my memories. I was simply exited. This is really freedom I said when I compared to the past experience.

While Felati and me were talking, I asked him why so many people were moving very frequently to the capital? You know, since the independence people got the chance of moving. They got time to open files and cases. It is another war front. The situation was contrary to the martyr's wish, he said. I could imagine, before the independence, the Churches used to be full but now they are almost empty, I said. What do you think the reason was? I added. People have no time to go to church Felati said. Why? I said. Because they are occupied to go to the courts, he said. God protect us, are we not really free? I said. After repeating the word over and over in my mind, I said are we no longer appreciating the true experience of the independence?

After three month the work was finished and 103 war orphan children came from Sahel to St. Joseph School. I assumed the responsibility. Those days were the happiest days of my life. I was totally a different person. I felt something new in my life. The day the war orphan came to the School, It was the time I felt to sense an interior joy.

Padre came into my mind. The last conversation I had with padre became vivid. I started to repeat in my mind the last words of Padre. The picture of Padre with the rosary and klashinkof came into my mind.

The Martyr's Children

It was 1992. The rain season was coming. It was almost three months since the war orphan children came to the School. To adapt to that kind of life was not easy. The mentality and discipline was totally different. The same language but different experience, to understand them one had to be there and listen them.

I had plenty of remembrance of the martyr's children. They are very open and they spoke their mind. The values they had been trained on, while they were on the mountain of Sahel were different. Their classes were out door under the tree shade. There was no need of building, four walled classes. The situation wouldn't allow them. Everything was in common. The system trains you to be self-sufficient. There was a common sense of altruism. Their mother and father were Sewra. They never had chances to hold money on their hands. The system would never allow them. The only thing they knew was "Mesarif" coupon.

One time, the uncle of Sewrawit who happened to be in St. Joseph School he tried to give money to his niece. It was the first time Sewrawit saw the coin and money note. Sewrawit refused accepting the money. Her uncle insisted her and told her that she needs the money to buy something. She on her part resisted to receive the money. I don't need money I have "Mesarif" (Coupon), she said.

One day while Ghirghis Amine the principal of St. Joseph, was passing by, several of the Orphan girls were chatting in front of a status of Mary. One of them by name Finan asked him what it was. He frankly told them that it was the status of Mary. Is she one of your members? Finan asked. He said, no she is not a member, but she is the mother of God.

In St. Joseph school as was custom all the lessons begin with moral education. The moral teaching period, nurtured the spiritual growth of all the students. One day, when the moral teacher brother Hiab Ghebresilasie, was explaining to his students about the meaning

110

of resurrection, one of the orphan boy, by his name Fithi raised his hand and asked the following questions. Are the martyr's goings to be resurrected? Was the first question he asked. And the teacher affirmatively said yes. Are the enemy soldiers going to be resurrected too? Was the second question of Fithi. Though the question was not that easy to answer, and he knew he was trapped, he affirmatively answered, yes the enemy soldiers too are going to be resurrected. At this time the orphan boy who was not happy of the enemy's resurrection he said "well we will see each other and we will show them".

On another day, the teacher, while explaining the death of Christ, he said, " Christ in order to save us he died on a cross and saved us". He practically brought in the class a big cross to show the students how Christ died on the cross. Their eyes were fixed on the big cross. Denden who was sitting together with Ginbar in a low voice he said 'can you see the long Plus' (while pointing to the cross the teacher brought) in front? Yes said Gimbar. You see Ginbar the Plus we used to see in Sahel, was not like this one but very short one, he added.

Denden who was sitting in the middle of the class, in a loud voice he asked the following questions. Who is this Christ? Is he one of the Tegadelti (Freedom fighters) martyrs? He asked. The teacher had answered no. The only martyrs, the children of the martyrs were aware of, were only the Tegadelti (freedom fighters). The teacher tried to explain the difference between Christ sacrifice and Tegadelti's sacrifice, and he explained the purpose of Christ's sacrifice, which was to die on a cross to save the world, while on the other hand the purpose of Tegadelti was to die to liberate the country.

The culture the martyrs' children had been into, was totally different, from the culture of the other students, who grew in the town. The discipline was different. For a quite some time, for the teachers to adjust the two experiences and deal with their classes was not easy.

Anyway, here's what the sainted nun who was taking care of the martyr's children told me one time. We needed to be very strict about some relationships the martyr's children were practicing, she said. What relationships ? I said to be clear about the situation. The situation of love affairs, she said. We have to stand up with clear discipline that they should restrain from acting so, she added.

Since I wanted to know her intention deeply, I asked her what is going on. You know, she told me, that Samrawit is in love with Gimbar. So what, I said. We shouldn't allow them to do that, she said. I was able to figure out from her conversations of do and don't, that she wanted to discipline them in her own way.

She always liked to tell me, whenever things were not going according to what she had planned. Her mind was in a continuo conflict. She had totally forgotten, about the past experience of the martyr's children, while they were on the mountains. She was focusing on the discipline she had acquired from her convent.

I was concentrated in nurturing the good experience of the martyr's children, rather than contradicting with my ready-made discipline. The experience into what they have been was the real presence they were experiencing. I decided not to teach them an absence. It doesn't feel good. It will only hurt. I didn't want neither to embrace the complications of the nun. This whole year I've been trying to make her understand. Most of the complications she had, were not of her own making. I said, that was how she was formed.

From Ohio to Keren

I was so fortunate to meet Mr. Brad in keren town, working as a volunteer. An innocent gentle man from Ohio state, came to an innocent people of Keren, to do a voluntary job as a teacher in St. Joseph school some time around 1993. I met Brad when I came back from Meki town in Ethiopia after working one year in the mission. I was assigned to teach Pastoral theology at the IRS (Institute of Religious Studies) in Asmara, run by the De la sale Christian Brothers. The first time I met the simple soul was in Keren town. I came for a visit for two weeks to stay in St. Joseph school. It was summer of 1994. The day I saw him I got acquainted with him. As we were chatting I started to read his simplicity. Brad was living inside the monastery. He was getting ready for the next school year classes. He enjoyed my company. He never exaggerated to mention about the affluent country of USA. He was totally immersed into the new challenging missionary work. I am lucky that I came here to do different things and to live with innocent people, he said to me. You have something to give and something to receive, I responded. I wish and pray these people would never change, he said, recalling in his mind the complicated life in USA. The community in itself distributes joy and happiness, he said. I wish I knew the language of the people to communicate effectively, he said. Never mind as long as you have the language of love, everything will come, on its time, I said. At that young age to leave the comfortable life of USA was not easy, for him. He started to compare the noisy, very busy, hectic life of his country, to the simple life of the people. He never saw in his life a live donkey, camel, cow, goat besides seen them in TV. He felt close in touch with the nature. He liked to go out for a walk on his own. He was going to the suburb villages. One day he told me he was invited by a family from the village to join them for a coffee celebration. While he was training his mind to adopt to the simple life, he began to adjust his imported stomach to the local food. Brad liked all kind of the local food, like Ingera (the flophy bread) Tzebhi (a hot sauce) Shiro (a grinded peas) Alicha (a vegetarian sauce). There was another favorite food of Shehanful that he was in love with. Since the food was not available in the community he was going to Inda Shahi (tea shops) for consumption of the food. One day he told me that he ordered two plates of Shehanful with two Cokes. I was totally astonished and began to laugh, since it was very difficult to consume more than one dish of Shehanful, at the same time. Shehanfull it had the power of staying in the stomach for hours and hours.

A year later I was about to meet another gentle lady from Minneapolis Minnesota. Her name was Sarah Hansen and she was the soul mate of Brad. After one year of being in touch, both decided, that she come and join him in Eritrea. He was telling me about Sarah's desire to come to Eritrea. I was eager to see the beautiful lady from Minneapolis. The coming of Sarah to work as a volunteer, was a great compensation for Brad. He was too good to get that kind of an award. Actually he needed some one besides him to spend time with.

The day of her arrival, I was the one who went to pick her up from the airport. I had already traced her looks in my mind. Tall, with blond hair, wearing an eyeglass was the description given to me. The plane landed at the airport around mid night. While I was waiting in the waiting room suddenly, I saw a white tall woman coming out from the main gate. She was not a blond hair, with an eye glass whom I was expecting for. I approached to her and asked her if her name was Sarah. She hardly could understand my English, since she was from Germany. Right after the German lady, Sarah was on line picking her bags. As I saw her all the descriptions fitted. I approached her with confidence and asked her name. Yes, I am Sarah she said smilingly.

The first night she was to stay with Daughters of Charity at the convent. As instructed I drove her to the convent. The convent door was closed and all the nuns were sleeping. I tried to ring the bell, but there was no answer. I had two choices either to take her to a hotel or take her to my brothers house. At that time I didn't have enough money to take her to the hotel. I took her to my brothers house to stay for the night.

My sister in law she got up early, to prepare the local coffee for the guest. Sarah was curious about the activity that was going on for the coffee celebration. Every meal in my country is celebrated. There was always time. No rush, everything was done in calmness. I started to explain the whole procedure of preparing the coffee. Pointing to the coffee pot, I said this is Gebena (a local coffee pot) a round shape made of clay. This is Menkeshkesh (a coffee roaster) and these are Fenagil (tiny coffee cups). I tried to philosophies in the middle of my instruction. You see, I said one time to catch my attention. Usually the word co**ff***ee* has two F's and two E's, but the special coffee that you are drinking is made of three F's and three E's. It took us two hours to consume the coffee.

Brad showed up in the afternoon on the day of her arrival. The reunion was formidable. I left them alone. After five months of working as a volunteer Sara and Brad planned for a weekend picnic crossing the border in Ethiopia. It was at that time that Sara got infected by a dangerous insect on her lower feet. The health situation forced her to live the country. She was sent back to USA for professional treatment. In 1997 I met both Sara and Brad in Minneapolis at my cousin house.

The Mid-Crises

Accumulated small sins in time become big sins, and accumulated small stresses turns to a depression. That was what I was experiencing. The plus and minus of my life experience dug deep inside my conscience. I was to listen to a different voice. A strange message dominated my mind. At last I noticed I was in the middle of crisis. My age was almost to reach two twenties. The ample period for a middle crises. The seemingly happy Hiabu was no more to function normally. The environment controlled my situation. The local counselors were not available. The wise elders were out of my sight. No one to mediate on behalf of my life. There was no short cut or an easy way out. Mommy my only counselor was in bed suffering from an incurable disease, lung cancer.

The original wish of my mother, of becoming a priest, was ringing in my conscience for more than two decades. It was in 1996, some time after the new year, I went to visit my ailing mother, before I was to leave for USA. Mrs. Barhet best friend of my mother, was with my mother sitting near her bed side, reciting the rosary. As she saw me from far, "Iquar" your son is coming, she told my mommy. You mean Paulos, my mother responded, since the name she could only pronounce was that. I pulled a chair and sat near my mother. Make a tea, my mother ordered to Mrs. Barhet. I did not want to interrupt their prayer. I joined them in reciting part of the rosary. As the rosary was finished, the house became quiet like a tomb. We all looked at each other. I was a kind of scared to tell mommy about the new offer the congregation gave me to go to USA for my sabbatical year. I carefully picked my words, before I was to read my thoughts to mommy. At the beginning, I kept it as much as possible to my self. It didn't seem fair to keep it for long. As I started to reveal the secret, she looked at me sternly. I thought she was going to be mad at me. The energetic mother lying on her bed like a weak it didn't resonate in my mind. I paused and started to accept her situation of staying on her bed. Then came in my mind her dedication, the love, the childhood attention she gave me. The first and the last pioneer of my life to leave her in a situation of incurable disease I felt desolate. It was a farewell the last visit before she died. To catch sight of the old days before I joined the congregation, I waited for her spontaneous smile. She spoke very calmly and said, Paulino this time I hope you become a priest, at least upon my death your prayers and the holy masses could rescue me from going to hell. I didn't want to share my current crises, of a vocation change, I was planning. I withheld it on purpose. Though my mind concluded, that I was never to fit into the dream of my mother, let it be the will of God, I said. After two years, three months before I was getting to be married, in 1998 she passed away.

Almost for more than twenty years of staying as a religious member, the intimate life and all the ideals I had started to crumble. The fervent hope began to fail. I was in a complete darkness. Suddenly the situation became my enemy. Absorbed as I was in my situation and my future life, I entered in to a deep silence, and kept repeating those puzzling questions regarding my status of life. Centered on the decision I was going to take, I was wondering whether it will justify my doubts. The present life as being a professed religious brother or to join the world as a lay person maximized my doubts. In order to compensate my decision I said, the life I am actually living in it self is not an obstacle to good works and it demanded great sacrifice but I have to see the actual situation of my life.

Dis-satisfied and left alone, it was difficult for me to seek the way of my life. When hopelessness was still shining on my face, one day I got a letter from Dominc Ehrmantraut from USA. The letter energized my inner most life. Around Christmas of 1995, when he came from USA for the annual visit, I had a chance to meet him personally. During all those times no one had understood my situation. You need a brake, said Dominc after observing my situation deeply. He came with an idea of giving me a sabbatical year to help me and confront the situation professionally.

The endeavor to please my mom, to fulfill her expectations, to fit in where I knew I didn't belong, couldn't work at all. I did not like the tryout tactics. I preferred to be sincere. Ultimately, I urged my conscience to collaborate. When the proper time came I quit. The year was 1997. I decided this because I was not comfortable where I was in the monastery. I started feeling this way back in 1984 when, I came back from my studies from Rome.

Brother Amilcare Boccucia the superior, of the De La sale Christian brothers, noticed my situation. At the beginning he did not accept my new situation. During all those time he saw me flying every where to serve the poor people. He positively, used to qualify my dedications. I was under his assessment. He never suspected, I was to fall in that kind of life. I started to close my self socially. I became a target of scrutiny. Every one noticed my new situation. The desire to reach a higher and a better place, through the religious training I acquired little by little, it lost it's definite reality. Ultimately I came to the end. The religious standard values were obscured. I was accountable to that.

To cover up I was accompanying everything, with a smile, the only natural virtue I possessed. I was not ignorant of the present responsibility of being a religious member, but the challenge I was facing, completely darkened my conscience.

The reality that was ringing in my mind began to disturb me. If I was clear with my life, the one disturbing me the most was the other choice of life, as a married person. I was caught in between two significant facts. The one I embraced by promise and vow, to be poor, obedient and chaste was compromised by the secular world, to be a lay person. The secular intention overpowered the religious status, which previously I was influenced by.

Deciding was not so easy, I would have to prepare mentally. Engage with urgency. I did not chose to live as a dead member. The new found choice, I was experiencing might affect my mind. I never gave a second thought after all I didn't have any legacy to live behind, besides what I invested to educate the most disadvantageous people.

****

Chicago

"**W**hat you stepped on belongs to you" as my mother used to say, for me Chicago was the best place of my choice, when I was given the chance of the sabbatical year. On July 17, 1996, I landed at the airport of Newark, New jersey, after which I was connected to the flight going to Chicago. Everything was ready for me. I was to be all alone by my self. I was living in Hyde Park near the university of Chicago state university. Only three blocks from my residence there was the congregation of the Combonian fathers. The director of the community was father Menghisteab. I used to know father Menghistab while I was back home. In the community there were other two combonian students from Eritrea, following their religious formation program. I felt like I was at home. I was treated well. Father Menghisteab which later he became the bishop of Asmara Eritrea, was my closest friend and counselor.

On September of 1996 I was enrolled to the Catholic Theological Union, which was a walking distance from my place. I took part time classes to refresh my studies. Medhanie who used to be my student became my friend. As the Tigrinya saying goes, " Meseta Kedamot arki Dahrewot", (Peer of the first generation becoming friended to the later generation). In age wise there was almost 15 years of gap between me and Medhanie. Medhanie helped himself to be in my level and I tried my best to disregard the age gap. In 1998 when I was getting married Medhanie was my best choice of a best man. With his humor he made my wedding, the best I can imagine.

For one year I was following a professional counseling program. The attitude of "let me face It", started to reign in my soul. The lost confidence of self, which had accompanied me, for more than two decades, was terminated. Living with the De La sale Christian brothers became odder interest. At last I saw the end of my career as a religious person.

****

It was an eve of valentine day of 1997. I was busy doing my studies in Chicago. The sabbatical year taught me a lot. It was my first time to live as a single in my own. Doing my chores, cooking and shopping became my first duty. The easy menu of spaghetti was the main menu, I was expert in cooking it. Almost I was cooking it daily. I was never tired of it. After all, what can I do about it.

At the corner of South Cornel street five blocks from my house, there was a small grocery store. I was the favorite customers of the grocery. A Spanish speaking lady by name Anna was working at the grocery. She was the one who opened the page for me, to learn Spanish language. Her beauty was on her face. She barely spoke English. I was always trying to speak to her in a broken Spanish. I was accumulating common spoken Spanish words, from Anna, whenever I was going to the grocery. The other part of my vocabulary, I was building it from the Spanish TV program of Tele Mundo.

Anna knew my grocery orders by heart. She was always making ready my groceries, ahead of time, even before I reached the counter. My broken Spanish was always entertaining her more than any thing. Teach me English and I will teach you Spanish was the consensus deal we made with each other.

I missed the local food of Ingera with Tzebhi, Shiro and Alicha. At that time there were no Habesha restaurant in Chicago. Lucky enough I had several family friends from Eritrea who were treating me like a king. The family of Damer, Ghenet (who is deceased), Rigat were some of my country fellows who protected me from being lonely. To Ghenet, I owe her my prayers may the Good lord give her the eternal peace and to the family of Damer and Rigat let my respect shine into their face.

That day I was not aware of it. The event was new to my experience. New word new vocabulary. Calender wise it was 14th of February and the year was 1997. I got a valentine greetings, via phone connection, while I was busy doing my paper work. On the other end of the phone, whom her voice I couldn't recognize at first, said Hello. I said, hello to the strange voice that challenged me for a while. I couldn't recognize the voice besides being a local voice from my own home country of Eritrea. Happy Valentine day, she exclaimed, while my mind was trying to catch up with the caller's identity. Who are you I said, to reconstruct her identity again. Guess who am I, she said, by putting a none negotiable quiz in my mind. Another home work without award, I said, while following the flow of the conversation. I altered my conscious level to the degree of recognizing, the strange female caller. I did not want to enter into a guess play. I did not want neither to be a victim of name analysis, until I figured out correctly her name and her identity. At last she gave up and I gave up. She wanted to finish the drama. I, too. To give me a clue, she said, think of the first girl you were in love with, almost 20 years ago, while you were back home. I stepped back in my mind and after few seconds of deep thought, I got you, you are Hiwet Fesehaie, I said. Both of us started to cry.

In my mind Hiwet was dead. How come dead people speak, I said. I, couldn't believe her. Her voice never changed. Where from are you calling me, I said to locate her address. I am in Kentucky state, she said. Where in Kentukey, I inquired, again to know the exact address. In Louisville, she said, still crying. She never stopped crying and her cry was making me cry too. We exchanged our phone numbers, and from that day on we were calling each other every day.

The last time, I lost contact of her was in 1980. I was studying in Rome, Italy. The last letter she send me, was at the beginning of 1980. I remember the photo she send me, before she joined the liberation front. She sent me about four letters, before she joined the liberation movement . Things didn't work according to our thought. Almost, for four months, I did not receive any letter from Hiwet. Her silence made me think bad about her situation. The last letter I send her she did not receive it. Our communication interrupted right then.

In her last letter, I was communicated that she had completed grade 12 and she was heading for a national service to teach in Adi Hawsha a village in the suburb of Asmara. That summer the EPLF raided the village and after a heavy fighting they were able to control the village for a couple of hours. After completing their task, they took all the teachers who were teaching in that village. Hiwet was one of them. She joined the liberation front.

In 1991 after the independence, I was eager to see Hiwet alive marching on the street of Asmara. It did not happen like that. My mind was curious enough to ask about her where about. To every Tegadalai or Tegadalit (freedom fighters), who survived the war, I asked, there was no trace of her. Finally I waited patiently until the official announcement of the names of the martyrs. During that time I tuned my self to the national media. When her name was not on the list of the martyrs, I was put into dilemma.

The next guess, that came to my mind was, that she might be some where in the neighboring Sudan. Some time before the independence, Hiwet escaped to Sudan, though I didn't know the exact day, month or year. I wish she would have recounted her whole story to me to write her story.

Our connection in USA was all via phone until I decided to see her one day. In Louisville I had a distant cousin and her name was Hidat. She came to USA when she was very young. She was living in Keren town, one block far from my house. Hidat was an open minded gentle lady. Her openness in a conservative society of Keren Lalai couldn't function normally. When first I saw her, I never found any difference. The Hidat I knew, years ago, during my child hood and the immigrant Hidat were the same. I was glad that she never changed.

In Louisville, Hidat and Hiwet became close friends. I had good opportunity to see both of them at the same time. Both of them were the center of my childhood remembrance. Killing two birds with one stone, I said when I decide to visit both of them at the same time. Hidat was married to an African American guy, with no children as far as my knowledge was concerned.

During the three months of phone connections with Hiwet, on my part I could say, I fall in love with her. Our phone connections lasted only for three months. Hiwet shared with me a secret of her love engagement with Ande. Ande was one of my youth friend who became a Capuchin priest. He came for his studies in USA almost one year before me.

The river begins from the mountain, flows on the plain and it dissolves to its last destination the ocean. Not all rivers dissolves in the ocean, some also remain in the desert. Though my connection with Hiwet was historical, I didn't want to confuse her situation. I backed up since I respected her and my friend Ande. Hiwet was so divided, and her good soul couldn't accommodate two loves. It neither was natural thing, to her.

On my part connecting historical dots for the sake of self fulfillment was not practicable. I wished she was free and on her own, everything would have gone smooth. Since I knew how to make a relation and when to break it, I decided to call Hiwet to come to Chicago for a spiritual retreat. To calibrate her self spiritually, I had asked her if she had a break from her job. She agreed on the proposal I made and one day she came for three days to do a retreat in Chicago. She was staying in the retreat house all those three days. When the retreat was to end, I came to see her and told her one final thing, I wish there was one Hiwet with two identical original copies of her, one for me and one for my friend Ande to share.

****

Three major decisions

Eight years after the independence in 1998, when I was living in DC, something came in to my mind. It was a strange thing. All my life I had been listening to people, to events and circumstances without being able to see with my creative mind. I learned to meditate, on the meaning of life, from the career I had as being a religious person. Suddenly I opened my conscience, everything was there. I needed only to concentrate.

The counseling sessions, that I was taking, while I was in Chicago had helped me a lot. I was very much inspired by the program. Until then I had considered myself, as some kind of richness, I had acquired from the program. The previous loyalty to my congregation was to give up. Things had started to change in my system. I began to look at the entire course of my life, as a religious member. I had seen all my religious accomplishment crumbling in my eyes.

At the end of my sabbatical year around the beginning of September of 1997, I decided to leave the congregation. I did not want to stay, where I had no hope to grow.

Dominc Ehrmantraut, who was closely following my situation, advised me to write a dispensation letter to Rome. I deed as instructed. After three months I received the dispensation reply from Rome. At least I was psychologically relieved. My next step in life was in my hand. I was responsible for whatever choice I had to make. Living in a congregation was like playing a soccer. In a soccer game, a team in order to win, all the eleven players must play well enough in cohesion. On the other hand the married life is like playing ping pong, in which the two couples had to play coherently to maintain their marriage life.

While waiting for the response of the dispensation, I decided to move to DC. It was in DC, the first time I met my x-wife Ghennet. Gabriela my cousin made the arrangement. She called Ghennet to come to Woodbridge, Virginia to see me. Ghennet respected the invitation. It was around the beginning of September, 1997.

It didn't take us long to start our relationship. At the beginning, I was a kind of scared not to lose the future. A new life a new field. All my actions were fresh and candid. I needed a new vocabulary of a relation. I was acting as I knew my self, in the words my religious congregation taught me. Indeed, I needed a new strategy for a new challenging married life.

Me and my x-wife, lived two different lives. Two different experiences started to clash. I came from a monastery where the discipline of a religious life dominated my mind. She came from the other order of life, a settled lay life that disciplined her differently. The time we were together as married couples most of the time we were at odd. No one to be blamed, may be I had to change since I was the one who was changing a different life discipline. May be I was too slow to adopt the new life I was to embrace. Yes, I knew, I was as proud as ever, coming from a religious order that shaped my initial way of life. I was part of it. I don't regret. I was not able to reform the old materials. To make something new out of it, to protect my marriage, I should have done it differently if ever I had a chance.

In three years time, I have undergone through three major life decisions, one after the other. In 1997 I quit my career of being a religious brother. In 1998 I got married. In 2000 I was separated from X-wife. After two years I was divorced. I said something was going wrong in my life. I looked like empty jar. My decisions went against me. I left the Institute in the hope of doing better. But things became worse. As the Tigrinya saying goes "Zighedede Mahber Inda Aboy Ghide" (the worst of it, was to associate with the association of father Ghide". From this, that was worse. I wondered around feeling sorry for my actions. I couldn't explain all my actions, besides being in the middle of crises.

On March 19, 1999 my daughter Saron was born. It was great blessing for me, to have such a beautiful and adorable baby. I baby sit her for 9 months. To be the real father for my daughter, I needed a security of a status. The new scene of being a father contradicted with my status. On one hand, in my mind, I declared to be the good father, and on the other hand, I was suffering for being a status less. My leave of absence from my beloved daughter was so distressing. I felt the feeling of culpa mia, for being absent from her life for so long. As the Tigrinya saying goes "Zemen gebel zihabuka tekebel" (in the era of the Cobras, accept what the Cobra gives one).

When I got a rejection notice letter, from the immigration office of Maryland, I was totally shocked. The situation turned me down. It greatly disappointed me. I couldn't take it all. My frustration grew to a level of stress. I understood that the game was over. I was all on my own. Loneliness became my breakfast, dinner and supper. Everything was a grievance to me.

This was what America gave to me. I remained status less for more than 10 years. I wished America would have acted with a common sense rather than intelligence.

Maryland

The day I learned the death of Aster Fitsehazion I remained motion less in front of my computer while browsing the current affair about Eritrea. This was the free Eritrea every body was expecting? I said, her tragic death emotionally disturbing my mind. The rumor of her death was circulating for quite a number of years. I was hoping that she was going to survive the awful prison of the regime.

In years, a built up false praise to Isayas Afewerki (the president of Eritrea), made him confident and to be in power. Practically, he pretended not accepting the praise, because his own picture of himself was quite different. The everyday praise of the president, by the people, had resulted a status of tension. The destructive wishes, to ruin a whole society, to the point of eliminating the people, these was very ridiculous. Eighteen years as a king of the locals, I said, while comparing to the previous regimes. What was the difference between Isayas and emperor Haile Silassie? the open question that came into my mind. Un elected president, he was moving swiftly to gain power. He was Idolized by the people, to the point of being worshipped. In time it was the people who had become the victim of these vicious circle of suppressions.

This was the dream of the martyrs, I said when the country was turned, to a lawless state, young generation deserting the land, the local elders being jailed, the escapee killed in a cold blooded, the educated individuals being hunted, the farmers being confiscated their farming land, the reformist being targeted and jailed without reason.

In the middle of my deep thought Aster came to my mind. I mentally parked where I was. Sitting speechless. I didn't expect her interruption. I began to follow her. She was very collected and calm. I could see in her face. After a couple of minutes she continued to talk. I definitely accepted her interruption. She began to instruct me out of her experience as a freedom fighter. We know who we are and we know how we came to power. The other face of Sewra that was hidden from the eyes of the innocent people was awful to tell. The big fish eating the small fish. How many freedom fighters we buried in the mountains of the beloved country. Facts will tell. Till that time grow your tolerance.

Me and Aster knew each other since our childhood. She was coming to pass her summer vacation in Keren town. The last summer I saw her was probably around 1974. Her mother Demekesh and my mother were close friends. Though our families were not related, they acted like a family. They were " Melaminti Hawi" (a Tigrinya saying to describe the closeness of a relation between two families).

How hard it was for me to accept her death. How hard I reasoned with my self to reach the atrocity of the regime. Out of desperation my heart kept racing. Unwillingly, I was pushed to enter into preoccupations. In my mind I have traveled back and forth. Too many questions were coming in to my mind. A voice whispered to me not to ask too many questions. It was the voice of the martyrs. As always I was encouraged by the martyr's good advice. I no longer felt afraid. This was not the first time that the martyr's had made me feel so strong, so safe. My inner self told me that I would never bow under pressure and I would never allow any one influence me.

A terrifying dream that controlled my conscious level, the whole night, when I was awakened from my sleep, started to disturb me, terribly. It was a unique dream in its kind, from all the million dreams my mind composed, during my life time. The dream that so overwhelmed me up to this time, was not about the strangeness of the content, but about the message of the dream. I wish I had the wisdom of interpreting a dream. I fought to draw my mind together at least to recite the content of my dream. This was how the content of my dream went on: *I saw a town surrounded by four big mountains. As I was walking from a suburb village towards the town, I saw two male individuals, tied their hands and being escorted by two armed guards. Once they were on their way, I asked one of the guards, why were they escorting the two individuals. These are the criminals of the town and they are sentenced to death, by hanging, he said. If they are criminals "Idom Rekibom" (they got their hand), I said walking towards the destination where they were heading. On the way, while I was discussing about their criminal act with the guards, one of the criminals untied himself and started to run. I followed him running after him. Before I reached him in front of an old "Tukul" (a hut) he stumbled and fell down. I fell over his body by grabbing him tightly. When one of the guards came, he pulled out a pistol and shot both of them on their feet. I said, why don't you shoot them on their head. They are sentenced to die by hanging not by bullet, he answered. It is the same I contested, angrily by saying what was the difference. People have to testify their death in hanging, he said to calm the situation. When we were nearing the destination of the hanging place, I started to drag backward. Thousands of the town residents were following the scene. It was like a procession. On the way no one was crying to the opposite there was laughter of joy everywhere.*

When I opened my eyes, I heard my clock ringing, at intervals at the time I set it up. Though I wanted to continue sleeping and I wanted to take my day off, I decided to wake up with my mind, full of preoccupations. When I thought about the interpretation of my dream, there came Adey Kidan. I called her to explain the meaning of my dream.

As follows was the interpretation of my dream. *The image of the town surrounded by the mountain was the image of a country. The image of the two criminals was the image of the current leaders of the country. The image of you was the image of justice seekers. The image of the people was the image of the oppressed residents. Since no one was crying everything will be turned for the good of the people,* she said via phone.

The Verdict Day

It was 1998. The whole world was occupied with the soccer, the World Cup that was taking place in France. But in the remote land of East Africa, at the time the soccer games took place, a war broke out between Eritrea and Ethiopia. Badme became very famous. It became the main battle-ground of the conflict. The neighbor's regime tactically found supporters who easily cheer without any foundations. The two regimes as a cheer-leaders directed the sisterly country, to a situation of war.

I heard a voice calling me from above. It was the voice of Padre. The martyr Padre came this time to dialogue with me. I was totally occupied, I did not expect that Padre descend to the world. He caught me by surprise. It doesn't work that way, we go to them but they don't come to us. It was not natural.

In our open discussions, there were things that Padre wanted to know, about the situation of the recent war with the neighbor. Padre and me we stepped out for a conversation. As usual we entrusted our conversations and Padre was very focused.

At the time, when we were enjoying the freedom and peace, exactly after seven years, unexpectedly, war broke between the local's and the neighbor's, which took some time to identify the real cause.

It seemed particularly odd for us, since it was not in our mind. As the Abysinian saying say, "Dihri may ab beati" (after the rain to the cave), the local's and the neighbor's people, had become victims of the unexpected war.

I think, the one that caused the war, was the dual insistence of the two regimes, under the banner of think our thought. A revision of war history, that wounded the two neighboring countries, It greatly wounded us once again. People's thought couldn't be their thought. Both of the leadership were scared of losing their respective future. They limited our co-existence as two countries living side by side.

A dawning political awareness blinded the leadership of the two countries. To get attention and understanding they legitimized violence as an only means to destroy each other. There were two opposing dreams that they were tuned up from the beginning. They were reading from right to left and we were reading the opposite. They engaged their mind suspiciously. No one was able to monitor the situation wisely. They were not ready for a solution. At the end the population of the two countries were the one who paid the price.

History is not some thing spoken about some one, but it is about what one becomes, and what one is. What they were and what they are now was totally different. They had totally forgotten the previous wars. It was possible, and one might go to assess mentally, the malicious agenda of destructiveness they planned to go to war. To know the exact cause of the war, It needs a kind of social and political analysis, to be detected in time.

It was a confused agenda of war. Various agenda of war were shuttling between the minds of the two leaderships, which somehow, had disrupted the attention of the mediators. One time it became a border issue, another time it became a security issue; one time it became an inferiority complex issue and another time it became an expansionistic issue; one time it became political issue another time it became a threat to their establishment.

The causes of war could be varied, mistakes and miscalculations could be accepted, but one thing unacceptable was to proceed with their agenda once they knew it was not the right thing. A U-turn would be a wise decision, instead of proceeding in vain by contriving intrigue after intrigue.

Before the declaration of the war both leaderships were fanatically devoted to the Marxist philosophy. They had been exhilarating the fallen philosophy to make it happen in the their respective land. But their leadership had totally gotten out of their hand. The imported philosophy, was not able to sustain the culture of coexistence, that virtually respected humanity. The political gratification, that was usually granted as a blessing, by their people turned to be a curse.

War and conflicts were always possible, the dangerous part of it was when there was no cause. As a matter of fact, the main cause of the war was the continuous preoccupation of both leadership about the fear of loosing their future. In order to spare the political status and not to loose their future, both the leaderships, brewed a tactic of war engagement with each other. They started with a border issue just to confuse the international community.

The illusionary dream had separated the leadership into many bands of personalities that contradict each other. On one hand, they present them selves as guarantors, of defending the sovereignty of their respective countries; on the other hand they accused each other as invaders. Really it was a confusion of identity, facts will tell, in time the people will know the real cause of the war.

The initiative taken by the international community, were many, but there was not a substance of mediation. For some time the international community had been deceived by the neighbor's campaign of intimidation. Fortunately, the falsity of their political and war deliberations was soon discovered by the world, which they have previously convinced diplomatically. For a while they have been telling barefaced lies and were extraordinarily adept at deceiving the international community.

There were two facts one was to reject with truth which was something positive, and another thing was to accept with deception. This was what the stand of the leadership of the neighbor's from the beginning was. Their tactic was centered on know how to refuse while appearing to accept or agree. What was an issue yesterday, today becomes non-issue. Their claims changed one hundred eighty-degree. A continues ritual of refusal accompanied their claim. One day they accept the next day they refuse. For a simple non-sense reason they resume their assault. Tactically they press on it even if they know they are wrong. They rallied their dreams one after the other through a deceptive agenda

It was April fools day of 2002. I kid you not. I don't lie you. After two weeks it was the arbitration day. Every body was looking for that day anxiously. The court was in Hague. The case was open. No plaintiff no defendant. For the locals the real issue was only about demarcation. But for the neighbor it was a confused claim.

I couldn't stop my mind, from racing wondering where all this would lead me. The day of the verdict was coming. For the locals it was the day of victory and triumph. To win one has to pay a price. We paid more than 65,000 during thirty years of armed struggle for our independence. We also paid 19,000 during recent war of 1998-2000 to keep our land from aggression.

When it was a skirmish before it turned to be a conventional war, I denounced and condemned the war. My position in regard to the first mediation of the Rwandan-American, though in itself was not 100% satisfying, it would have being more effective if the Eritrean regime had accepted it. The day the Eritrean regime rejected the content of the mediation, I voiced to the opposite. The dialogue at least would have began right at the beginning of the war. We wouldn't have lost all those innocent souls.

The martyrs don't have computer and they can't access to the Internet. They couldn't stand being left out any longer. They didn't want to lose the last results. They needed to get informed On-line. Everything in the world was on the Internet. They needed to be informed after all it was their sacrifice that made things happen.

The day was April 13, 2002, it was the day of the verdict. I was counting down, Ten, Nine , Eight, Seven...One, Zero. And then came the last day of the verdict. Twelve days after the April fools day. The neighbors were getting more nervous.

Abba Tesfamariam (the priest) in DC stood out to defend a dead case. It was too late. But it was his character, he always thought last and felt bad the last minute.

At first when I read the Abba's concern, I thought, well, may be he was just going to give his last sermon, which would be embarrassing but not that embarrassing. He used over and over, the same vocabulary, the same expressions we used to hear from him during his last sermons. He used always to be loud at the end of the day.

Facts don't count on him and he can't hide himself from the truth. The deal was between two countries and there was no third party. The case can't accommodate for another party. The demarcation was between two countries. The result would be either you are here or there. A country might be a matter of choice. You can't chose two. The opportunity was one. If there was a need there would be a kind of referendum just to give chance to the decision of the people.

As far as the philosophy of Abba Tesfamariam was concerned, I had no doubt, it was only ignorance. I tried to locate his position. He was always there, he did not move an inch. He spanned around the same interest. If there was no self- interest he would never start another case. I doubted his career, not his priesthood. He was really messed up. I was thinking, may be he would learn from his past experience. But I never saw any change. The more I thought about him, the more I thought that his personality was in danger. I would like to give him an assignment. To keep his vocation as a priest it would have been good that he focused on the word of God, rather than mingling with politics.

It was Friday April, 12 2002, the eve of the verdict day. I had a call from long distance. I was not surprised by his call since he often calls me. After chatting about different affairs, he told me to buy a lottery ticket for him, since it was 250 million worth the Big game. It was six o'clock when he called me. 10 hours were remaining for the verdict. I already started to count down. I went to buy a lottery ticket, to a near by Seven Eleven run and owned by a lady from Eritrea. I often go to take my coffee and have a little chat. While I was driving towards Seven Eleven, in my mind came, the other big lottery-taking place in Hague. Hi Nighisti, I said, to the owner of the Seven Eleven and asked her to give me two lottery tickets one big game for Friday and the other for Saturday morning. To satisfy my order, we have only that for Friday, she said, by instructing me to buy the other power ball ticket, by going to DC. I am asking you the lottery ticket for Saturday, I said, by indicating the verdict that was taking place at Hague. We don't have that of Hague, she answered. When she understood what I meant, Oh that is the biggest lotto She said. God knows at the end justice might be done to our country and we will definitely be the winners, she repeated.

That day, no one won the Big game of Maryland so it was valued to be 300 million dollars the next mega million lotto. But we won the lottery of Hague, it was the greatest victory in our history.

As soon as they heard the court decision, the neighbor's regime decided to approach their people with a sense of victory, which after two weeks of the decision they had practically denied, to begin all over again. The demarcation case already stirred up more confusion onto the neighbor's leadership.

At last, the country Eritrea was defined on a map with all its boundaries.

All right, *Alleluia, congratulations,* let us celebrate.... I said.

✱✱✱✱✱✱✱✱

Millionaire

I wish, I could have eaten the excitement, said my lonely soul after lingering for months to be the millionaire. At that time I was living in Gaithersburg Maryland at a townhouse 8641 Watershed Ct. I quite my job as a counselor to own my own business as a courier. I bought a used van for $ 6000, in cash.

It was October 17, of 2005. Around 8 o'clock in the morning I heard my door being knocked gently by my room mate. His name was Ashok, from India. That night I spent dreaming the whole night. There were many images in my mind. An image of being a millionaire. An image of owning a business. He was into the business of a courier for more than 5 years. He was the one who convinced me to start the courier job.

As I got up from my bed to open the door, I saw Ashoke standing, right in front of me. Good morning, he said in a low voice, when he got him self together. "Good morning to you", I responded, while rubbing my eyes. Sorry to wake you up early, he said, while up loading his mind for the first move. It was time to wake up any way, I said, comforting his mind. May I ask you a favor, he said. Sure I said, though I was not aware what kind of favor he was going to ask me. May I use your van to transport customers for today, he said. Since his car's cooling system was not working, he wanted to use my van. After giving him the car key, I went to bed to cover the remaining hours of sleep. As I laid on my bed, I tried to close my eyes. I changed many sleeping positions, to surrender to the unconscious level. But I was not able to lose my conscience. I entered into a deep thought.

A week before my van vanished, I made a contract of a false transaction. Suddenly I heard, my phone ringing. I run to pick it up, but when I saw in the screen a strange number, I let it finish up. Five minute after the phone again rang. This time I decided to pick it up.

A strange voice from the other end, politely greeted me. My name is George, he said, on my part giving him a green light to identify himself. I am calling you from Canada, he added. It did not take me time to locate the voice. The voice was a Nigerian with Nigerian accent. You are a winner, he said, trying to put me on track. Specially, when he told me that I won five million dollars, my excitement level grew very high. To calm my doubt, your e-mail number was found as a winner, he said, before I asked any question.

I was intoxicated to the maximum. I started to fortify my simple conviction of being a millionaire. Within the process I lost the sense of common sense. I really was dominated by the strange surprise. An empty battle ground between the common sense and the excitement. In between I was caught.

He was trained to handle the situation on his way. I never had any suspect of the mastermind. He calculated the degree of my excitement. Once he observed the weakest part of me, he started to manipulate. I said, "let me follow the river". I never had any surprise for a long time, besides the years of depression. At last those days of loneliness are gone, I said.

To cover the content, in detail he advised me via phone to see my e-mails. I was totally astounded when I read the message of the e-mail. Still swimming in the ocean of excitement, I asked my self to my self " how can one be a winner without ever buying the winning ticket. That was not the kind of miracle, I was expecting. Let the situation stay for tomorrow, said my mind.

The next day, early in the morning when I got up from my bed, a phone rang. The familiar voice of deception, was once again, on the other end of the phone. Did you receive my e-mail, he said, with a convincing tone. I was on my way, to walk out side, to buy my groceries. While chatting with the stranger, suddenly, I made a glimpse on the sky. Big birds flying on the sky fell into my eyes attention. To enjoy the bird's sky acrobat performances, I sat down on a concrete platform. I could see the birds flying in geometrical figures, such as straight, curved and circle lines. Before they were to disappear from my sight, one last time, the birds performed a question mark symbol. What is this sign? I said, entering into a deep thought. I was still on line with the stranger to discuss on how to recover the big money. The stranger first he asked me, if I had four thousand dollars to pay for a processing fee, in my bank account. I said, No I don't have. To keep me on line and follow the drama he changed his tone. Don't worry I am going to send you 40,000 dollar check, which would be deducted from the principal money you won, he said.

Five days later via express letter I received the check. Since I came to America, I never had such a big check in my bank account. Again the symbol of a question mark came to my mind. That day, after grinding enough the excitement, I went to deposit the check as instructed. As I approached the counter, a female bank teller from Guinea Conakry, smilingly greeted me in French, by saying "bon journe". The only time, I practiced my French was, when I meet that beautiful African lady. As she saw the big check, she saw me in my eyes and said "Enchante tu est rich" (be happy you are rich).

As I returned from the bank, I started to experience an ecstatic life. A life I used to experience, while I was living in a religious life as a monk. I was completely out of the reality. The conscious level totally was over powered by the unconscious. A day dream in a broad light.

To distract myself from the situation I put my TV on. While I was watching the TV news, suddenly from outside I saw my room mate coming in to the house. Trembling he stood in front of me, motionless. He tried to express himself verbally, but he remained speechless. His eyes turned red. He was breathing abnormally.

What's up, what is going with you, I said. Unable to speak, he just turned his back and started to cry. I jumped from where I was sitting and stepped towards him. Gently from behind I tapped his shoulder, by repeating his name, Ashok, Ashok. He really felt my hand

and started to open up his mouth. In a low voice leaning near my ear, he said " I was a victim of robbery". All his body was shaking. The communicative attention slid away from him. To cut off the line of my questioning, he remained silent. Deep in his mind, he heard some thing accusing him. I intervened diligently, to win his attention and confronted him with a generous attitude. When I touched the territory of his heart, he opened up. The time he felt sure about my approach, he started to recite the story. He moved his head down, still less settled. Again to change the game, I started to gaze at his face smilingly. As he felt energized, by my approach, he started to explain of what had happened that day. "Your van was gone", he said. You mean stolen, I responded. Yes, he said embarrassedly. My mind couldn't easily tolerate, but my conscience decided to follow the whole story. I made up my mind instantly, not to jump into conclusion. Thinking of the harm, he already got, I preferred to stay stand and neutral. In the meantime I stayed cautious, to let him finish. He said, as I was driving from Dallas airport to Silver Spring, when I was dropping the last customer, I became a victim of robbery. Three Spanish speaking guys, approached me with their pistols, pointing at my head. They dragged me out of the van, after which they tied both of my legs and hands, by taking me into un abandoned room. They took all my wallet.

In my mind I was ready to console him. The forty thousand dollar check I deposited earlier that day became my guaranty. Truly, I was not stressed about the situation, for a simple reason of being a millionaire. I enjoyed that title for almost three weeks. Not to break the story, I asked him if he had reported the incidence to the police. He said, no, in a restless mood. I was not in a position to examine the incidence, and it was neither my profession. I immediately called the 911. I took as my career to relax him before the police showed up. It is not your fault, things happen, I said to calm him. 10 minutes later two copes showed up into our residence. As they were entering to the house, by chance his wife came from out side. When she saw the police, she started screaming. To draw her mind to calmness, I took her out and tried to explain her the situation. She couldn't accept the situation and started to raise her voice. Damn, she said.

In three days time, I became a car less, jobless and fortuneless. The fact of being a millionaire became only a day dream. I learned about it the next day when I went to withdraw the money, that the check was a fake check. My van vanished from my eye just the day I deposited the fake check in the bank . The three life misfortunes tuned up to raise my stress. It was very tough. No money in my bank account. No immediate job to count on and no car to move with. For more than two weeks, I stayed at home just chopping stress.

Three blocks from my residence there was an auto sale dealership. I bought my van from that company, three days before it vanished. After navigating jobs for two weeks, in the internet, I planned to apply for a walk in, job application. One day, dressed up in an attiring dress, I showed up to the dealership complex. The manager by name Greg, as he saw me coming in, he greeted me as a customer. What can I help you he said, after introducing himself politely as was the business custom. As he saw me he recognized me. How is your van, he said waiting for my response. The bad news that I kept for my self I started to reveal it. My van was stolen, I said. This time, I came not to buy a car, but to get a job, I said. From the way I was dressed he figured out. Do you have your resume with you, he said. Taking out from my folder I said yes. As he started to go on reading my resume, he jumped to my language skills. Mr. International, he exclaimed, seeing that I was multilingual. Still swimming in the ocean of admiration, how did you study all these 8 languages, he said. Did you go to school for all of them, he added. Accept for the English and Italian all the other were self learned languages, I responded. He started to underline the positive inner inspirations, I possessed. On the spot he hired me.

This was a high time for me. The testing days were to be compensated. After being trained for two weeks, despite of being un experienced as a salesperson, I was optimistic enough that I could handle the job. Naturally I am a smiling person. I never shopped the artificial man made business style smile. This was what other people tell me. My linguistic skills helped me a lot. I did not doubt about that. The abc of relating with people was my warranty. The sense of humor and story telling became my business corner stone. I negotiated my way. First comes first. The self description came before the auto description. Once I was sure enough about my customer status of buying a car, I easily slipped into the business deal. My style helped me. My style was my style, I had it all to my self.

Garrison Blvd

After five months, my stolen van was found, by the police parked in a residence area in Columbia Maryland. To my surprise I found it clean and in good condition. Out of joy I screamed, by saying "Mariam Deari", "Kidus Antonio", calling the names of the local saints, to appreciate the miracle.

It was around February of 2006. I came in Baltimore city to live with my friend Hiab. At that time I was jobless for almost the duration of three months. The day I found my van I entered into a temptation of using it to work as a courier. Back to square one, I said. There was no other choice.

I applied to be accepted as an independent contractor, with Laser company, (a courier company in down town of Baltimore). I had no knowledge and neither experience of the carrier. My map reading ability score was F. Once again, I was to be on the streets of Baltimore.

Equipped with walky-talky, the next day I was to start my Job. As I was trained I said, "Ten Four", when the dispatcher instructed me early in the morning, for a pick-up order. It was my first day of work. To locate the address I engaged my mind. I opened the pages of my map. It was an ugly day. It was raining and the visibility was horrible.

It took me almost half an hour just to locate the address on the map, and it took me another half an hour to reach the destination of the pick-up order. I hated long distance drive. My concentration level fall down. What a challenge, I said, the day I shopped problems by my self.

Once again the dispatcher " Driver 392" where are you, he said. I am on my way to the destination of the pick up, I responded. Are you riding a camel, he said, teasingly concluding that I was not fit for the job. I wish my ride was that of camels ride, I said in my mind entering into a deep thought. To feel comfortable, and give sense to my response, I said you see, when one rides a camel, the ride is free, enjoying an open view, free from carbon monoxide, no insurance to pay, no tag fee, no traffic, no congestions.

That day was not my day, I did nothing, no commission to claim. I wasted my money and energy for nothing.

****

After driving 10 hours none stop, I parked my van at 3300 Garrison Boulevard. Berwyn street and Garrison Blvd meet at an angle, where the strategic BP gas station was located.

A well barricaded Gas station as it was, the area of the compound formed an isosceles triangle. As I approached to a very tiny rectangular busy store, fortified by an extended bullet proof glass windows, I saw the gentle man from inside the window.

Exhausted from driving slowly I stepped towards the window. From inside it looked like a prison cell. There were many customers waiting before me, in line to be served by the gentle man . It was in the middle of August of 2006. The time was around seven o'clock in the evening. When it reached my time to be served, I made a quick glance at the gentleman. As I knew from his face, I concluded that he was one of my countrymen. On his part, he also figured out that I was a Habesha (a common ethnical denominator for Ethiopians and Eritreans). As I greeted him in the local language of Tigrinya, he started to smile. He let me in to the store and I accepted his invitation. He invited me for some soft drink, while serving the long line of customers. His kindness attracted me. I did not want to disturb him while he was working, since the Abyssinian saying goes "Ab Kidmi Sirah Aitiznah", (don't stay before a work). I rather let him finish his shift. One hour later when he finished his shift I asked him if they were hiring. Yes, there is one opening for night shift, he said. Could I apply to work with you, I said. "No problem", he said with a smile. By his smile I felt a spiritual fulfillment.

His name was Michael Giotom, the gentle man who was working as a manager of the BP gas station. At the beginning the job was tough for me, but in two weeks time I got a control of it. As we got close and very acquainted, he started to call me by the name " AYA" (a name given to an older brother).

Our relation, age wise was like a son and a father. He was working as a manager of the store. Before he immigrated to USA he was a known business man. He started to count money at his early age, while he was back home in Eritrea. At the age 17 he took a responsibility of running a family business. As he was growing he turned the small family business to big business of his own. In 1995 he opened a business of import export named by his name. He started to make an international business deal. China, Australia, Arab emirates, Kenya, Ethiopia, Djibouti became the center of his business deals. Language wise though he was limited he was able to manage his business skillfully.

I looked around the store, which was 3X6 meters. Movement was limited. No physical contact with the customers. Connections was via microphone. Transaction was done through the small hole. The deal was "Give us your money we will give you honey". We sold legally different kind of guns of Dutch Master, EZ-role, Philly blunts, Cigarillo. The customers were getting the illegal bullet of Marijuana, Dopes, Cocaine out side of the store.

****

Saturday after Thanksgiving day of 2006, I was alone, working at the gas station. It was very busy night. At mid night robbers were attempting to break the main gate locker from out side. Since I was very busy I was not attentive to what they were doing and since there was no direct visibility of the main gate I couldn't hear at all. In the morning, when I was getting ready to close the shift around 6:30 in the morning, the robbers in an organized way they surrounded the store. I was totally distracted from their action. I didn't suspect any and my mind was absorbed to close the shift only. While I was counting the last drop suddenly, I saw from far a red pick-up truck backing up in full speed. After a couple of seconds I heard a big blow. The noise was so frightening I backed up and as I noticed it was not a simple accident I went to the bathroom and locked my self. Through the key hall I saw about four of them breaking the windows. They were able to knock down the bullet proof after which they were able to enter inside the store. They took all the money that was in the register.

✱✱✱✱✱✱✱✱✱

It was around May of 2007. It was one Sunday. The sun with all its power, was rising from the east. The bright day was praised by all the customers, as a nice and gorgeous day. Every body was wearing a light summer cloths. My immigrant mind used to recon all days as beautiful and nice. I wish I would have given, the sun of my country to all my customers, I said.

At seven sharp, I reached the destination of the BP gas station. An old lady, before heading to her church, she parked on one of the pumps and showed up in front of the counter to pay for the gas. After a warm greetings and convincing smile, she demanded to be served. Peace gushed out of her face.

It was very rear to hear the word "thank you". Respect ion had run from the area a while ago. To be polite was seen as a weakness. The word "Yo" and "my man", some how they became the dominant expressions of their daily life. Good manner was not its location. Forged money circulated on a daily basis. The police chased the drug sellers. But as the Abyssinian saying goes "Mohamed Inte keidu Kalii

145

Mohamed Ymetzi", (If Mohamed goes another Mohamed will come). They put them into jail but other came to replace.

As they curse you are forced to curse. Argument was a normal process. Fighting was a spectacle to be viewed. It was a live movie.

"Good morning" I said to the old lady, by launching the rare expression I emitted to particular people who deserve, my greetings. While I was serving the lady, a guy who was next in line, started to raise his voice. He was yelling from a blue moon. I read his frustration through the window glass. I was not able to detect his motivation. The drug he consumed the night before might have lost its spiritual flavor. He needed a refill, but he had no money to buy one. He approached the lady and asked her for some money. Sorry, I have no money, she responded politely. She offered him a smile, the only thing she possessed. He couldn't buy her smile. Un wanted transaction. Again out of frustration he started to curse. He couldn't control him self. To calm him, she entered into another deal. I would like to share with you the power I have, she said, once again, glancing at his face smilingly.

while I was following the whole discussion, my mind clicked to the past experience of my life as a child and teenager. There was none to compare. Different world different experience. In my country we celebrate the greetings. Greetings was not an exchange of words or phrases. It goes on and on until one of the greeters closes by saying, " to all those whom we have never mentioned".

I wish he accept the deal, I said. Closing his eyes and gasping voice less, he asked the old Lady, "what she was going to give him". It is an everlasting happiness, she said once she saw him calmly following her views. Give me now, he said, frankly jumping to the deal. She took out a note book from her purse and wrote the address of the Church after which she invited him to come to the church.

✱✱✱✱✱✱✱✱

"**J**ambo" I called him an African American, who never missed a day without coming to the store. When ever there were no customers me and Jambo chat via microphone. I gave him a part time job to clean the compound of the store. After collecting enough money from the customers, he used to leave me on my own just to consume drugs. The Jambo I saw before taking the drug and after taking the drug, there was a big difference. Things changed in a matter of minutes.

Some time in August of 2007, Jambo was shot his two legs by individuals who wanted to robe him. That morning we were chatting for the whole morning. Before he was to leave me, "I am going home, see you later", he said. Few seconds after he left, at the corner of the gas station before he crossed Garrison he was shot. I heard about three gun shots.

I called his name, via microphone. It was Chief who was passing by, riding his bicycle. The exact translation of the name " Chief" in Tigrinya language is "Chica". I always called him by the name Chica. He liked it. I felt comfortable.

What's going on, I asked Chief to know of what had happened outside the gas station. "Jambo" by calling his real name Eugene was shot, he said. In America you die on your own, I said, feeling sad about the bad news I heard. My mind aligned to criticism, started to judge wisely. I grew in a war torn Eritrea. I saw people dying. Death was every where, but heroism was the common purpose that kept well sealed the struggle. When I heard about the senseless death's of innocent people, in churches, schools, work places, parks, recreation places, I said, bad management. To mention some of the mass killings, that had occurred in Columbian high school, the Virginia Tech, the DC sniper, were all the result of having uncontrolled bullets in the hands of the crime perpetrators. Isn't that because of the millions of bullets sold to people legally that put the innocent people into trouble? My innocent mind was bothered by the undeclared war. A war in which bullets had no politics. The word "I will kill" you was a fact to be dealt. Whether they act or don't act the word was expressed every time, anyway. Don't stay in a wrong place.

A place where you don't know your enemy, I murmured by saying "Aitikedem" (never give chance to be a victim of any one). Back home it was easy to figure out who was your enemy and who was your friend. There was only one social class. No millionaires and no billionaires. I wished I was an American citizen, I wished I had a voice, I wished I was a congressman, I wished I was a president of the USA, to change the rule of all gun holders. For years America defended the deal of owning a gun, for a simple reason of protecting oneself. In fact in my mind I came with a new bill that of banning the bullets. A new idea, a creative thought. My new bill would have been as follows: collect all bullets that were in the wrong hands, pay for each voluntarily returned bullet, forbid any selling of bullets, campaign for bullet ban bill under any circumstance.

✳✳✳✳✳✳✳✳✳✳

Hey, Mike she said since the majority of the customers call me by that name. I never told my true name to any one. Every worker was Mike. Even when they sneethed, the word that came out from their mouth was "Mike".

Her name was Kelly a white lady rambling on the street of Garrison blvd. She had a bad tendency of taking the cocaine. I got to know her as my customer when she was down in her life. She looked very sick, like she was suffering from incurable disease. For years she was leading irresponsible life. After being pregnant for 9 month some time around January of 2009 she gave birth to twin babies. When she was pregnant she was coming to the store to buy food and drinks. I wish we were given the chance of choosing the womb, from which to be born I said. My mind started to move here and there from a pro-life to pro-choice. When I was doing grade 9 I read an interesting book circulating in Amharic language, back in 1973. The title of the book was "Alweledim" (I won't be born). The author of the novel book Abie Gubegna was libertarian in his view. I read the book from a conservative view which I grew up. The content of the book was dealing about an entire conversations, between the fetus who refused not to be born and the mediators who insisted the baby to be born. The main reason of the fetus to resist not to be born was because of the social misbalanced life, inequality, racism and poverty. The fetus inside the womb represented the pro-choice attitude, and the mother together with the mediators represented the pro-life.

I never saw Kelly for almost a week. I went to my usual conclusion. She might be in the hospital, giving birth to the twin babies. I never saw her taking vacations during all those times I was working in the store. That was how things were going at Garrison boulevard and that was how it was made. As far as drug was circulating on the area she would always be there. Because of the drug the in and out of jail became a custom. If one was out of site the probability was that he or she was inside the big house or sick.

✳✳✳✳✳✳✳✳

I bought your book, I need you to autograph for me, he said, a gentle man who comes every Tuesday for a delivery inventory. His name was Mr. Dave. He called me Mr. professor. I really didn't like the title, but I respected his appreciations. When ever he came to the store, he always wanted to chat with me. Our chats at times were political, current affair, cultural exchanges. His eagerness to know about Africa made our relation better. One day he raised a question on how to deal with unification of Africa. To unite the big continent of Africa into one country or state is not easy, I said. Spontaneously, I said the day the out side influences stops then Africa for real would be united. Mr. Dave after following my opinion of the deal, he nodded his head, by saying it was an excellent deal.

Poetry was the field I very much handled good, since my childhood. I used to recite, a self composed poems, in my mother language of Tigrinya. The whole content of my poems used to be spiritual and moral in their essence. At different events I was reading my poems to the local audiences. The creative field of poetry had created infinite surprises in my life. It was my uncle, Aboy Elama that convinced my mind to be a poet. The artistic oral recitation, of his poems, in different occasions, had strengthened me to be a poet. All his oral poetry had transcended the bound of ordinary thinking of the time. The different political, social and religious events shaped his poetry. His way of interacting with the local people, was always in short phrase of poetry, that targeted the occasion.

In 2003, I tried to check my poetry ability, in composing poems in English language. After so many trials and re-trials, I saw my creative mind was fit for it. My style of rhyming was totally local. I was only interested in sending the messages. I was poor in the language management, but to the point in transmitting the message. My style was the style of parallelism.

✳✳✳✳✳✳✳✳✳✳

Since 2005 up to the present time, I had to deal with a mysterious number. Still unrevealed the number followed me for more than four years, from day one. The number was **"44"**. In my culture the number was a bad luck number. It was a number of the "Ganen" (devil). The unrevealed number was repeatedly, every hour coming to my mind. It came every where, while at home, driving, at work, at recreation time. At the time I was writing this part of my essay, the number came. I hoped that the number would be a lucky number. The day it is revealed I promise I would share with every one and every body.

After each revelation a short prayer followed. At times I was reciting a part of rosary. To say it was a kind of hallucination, I never had the bad practice of any kind of a drug. I was always silent, I never shared with any one.

One time on January 20 of 2009 the number came. It was the inauguration day. Barack Obama was to swear as the 44th president of America. As I was following the event of the inauguration being alone in front of my TV, tears of joy came out of my eyes. The historical event a black man to be a president of USA, was a dream for me. The campaign with all its colors had passed, taking the energy, the money, as usual.

The inaugural speech presented by President Obama was very touching and historical in its kind. I am very proud of him. I hoped the old political games were to discontinue. A new era a new history.

I saw the trio Eriam sisters celebrating success in a TV. For me it was a surprise. While I was watching the NBC news, right after, the show of "America got talented", aired. The umbilical cord of both their parents, that had been buried in the local land of Eritrea be blessed, I said again thanking from my deep heart the hosting country of USA. When I compared the culture of "HUH" (a culture of Don'ts) that I grew up with, against the free culture and free world, I got confused. I never ever expected American born of Eritrean origin to act like that.

Let me tell you immediately what I felt, the day I saw the Eriam sisters on the TV show. I felt free since I had been chased for a number of years by the insecurity of life. I felt happy because of seeing the extraordinary souls being performing.

In 2009 I was surprised by three things, the election of a black president Barack Obama, the Eriam sisters and the completion of my book.

Case Writer

My writing skills made me liable to help other immigrants from my country. I volunteered to compose stories about their cases of immigration. The access to different languages I possessed was a plus that decorated my resume to be a case writer. The immigrants from Eritrea whom I was in touch with, always had stories to tell. As I revised the core problem of their plan to immigrate to USA, was the endless war situation and the religious persecution they faced. Most of the immigrant from my home country, they sing the same song, some tuned to the war situation, some to the religious persecution. Murder, tragedy, imprisonment and the uprooting of people, due to their faith and political views were the main content of their case to immigrate to USA. The only freedom of land they had known was gone. The people could not live without freedom. Things became intolerable. The only choice was to escape.

In that blessed country, my home country "Sidet ab NigDet Telewitu", (migration is changed into an open pilgrimage), I said when the whole population from all walks of life started to flock to the neighboring country of Sudan and later to their last destination to USA or Europe. Back then the way I knew life was different. The new experience of being an immigrant for me became a strange thing to grasp. Remembering the good life I passed in Eritrea, I said " TiUm KeyBelNayo TiUm Gizie Halifu" (the old good times without appreciating it passed).

My mind still navigating in the past, the generation of farmers with abundant rain, the generation of simple people, nothing to complain, a cooperating generation where no one left alone, a compassionate generation where the sense of altruism reigned, how in the world suddenly changed I said, remembering those old good days which I wouldn't trade for anything.

I remember all those times during my childhood, when the elders were respected and we were tuned religiously, always to help the most disadvantageous citizens. I remember the wisdom of the elders, that strengthened us how to live in a community harmoniously. I remember the law of the land being applied to mediate without lawyers.

Rahwa was her name, the gentle lady who introduced me to Aya Makonnen Solomon. As I came into the Gas station where she was working, there I saw Aya Makonnen chatting with her. Hiabu "Shikor" (sugar sweet) I have a surprise for you, she said, smilingly. The good mood of their conversations, I could tell from far. Age wise they were like grandfather and granddaughter. Relation wise both of them were able to manage swiftly despite the age difference. A different view from the view he grew up, a different belief from the belief he was used to, Aya Mekkonen was swiftly interacting with Rahwa. As I observed, I saw him blessing the young generation, without giving up the old good times. He couldn't be both at the same time, but at least he tried to represent the two generations.

I found for you a "Zemed" (relative), Rahwa said, as I was waiting eagerly for the surprise. To make the relation robust, he is from Keren Lalai, he is from the Bilen tribe, she said. I wish it is not "Zemed KoTzirca" (counting generations of being related), I said.

I listened intently, while Aya Mekonnen was recounting the historical connections, of being his relative. In fact on his father side we were from the same clan, the same family root of Adi Idekel.

He started to lead his own life at the time of his retirement, in Baltimore city working at Wal-mart. One day while exchanging our immigrant life issues, I heard Aya Mekonnen complaining about his being immigrated in his old age. Aya Mekonen when he came to USA he was in his early 70th. He shared with me about all his life in Eritrea. When he was thirty years old he tried to be elected as a candidate for the house of representative. In fact, in his jurisdiction, though he won he was cheated by the elders, by saying he was too young and not fit for the position. He became an entrepreneur at his young age. He opened a car leasing company. He became the head representative of all Ethiopia's health care department. At last he opened a publishing company in Mekele Tigray . A strong spirited man as he was, I was trying to help him to succeed in bringing his family to USA. Family reunion was not easy he waited almost 6 years. It was really a struggle. Two fronts to fight one with the immigration authority and one with his age. At last his case of being reunited with his family was approved.

PART FOUR

The Interview

I became a writer constructing the story back from my mind. Having been virtually not experienced regarding the armed struggle, I decided it was time to build with my imagination the true story of the local's life struggle. Sometimes I couldn't quite remember where I was. It was a kind of ecstasy, but there was a real contact with the martyrs.

I had to write about the martyrs, I said. I started to recall all the martyrs. It was 1991 after the independence. I did realize that Padre was in the other world, in the unknown land. I knew how tough the work would be. Connections would not be easy. I did not want to voice an opinion that was not to my level of experience. The only power I managed to have was the power of imagination. I set up my mind and organized a long trip of imagination to the land of the martyrs.

My reflections, I borrowed them from the local's struggle. I made a trip in my mind to review the armed struggle experience of the locals. In my memory, I climbed the mountains up and down, crossed the barren land, always monitoring my remembrance level.

Surprisingly, I could produce a strong argument, which could highlight a lot of untold mysteries of the armed struggle. To do this I freely wondered through all the past experience of war. With my mental compass, I spin around the same experience, that experience of a struggle.

With the same promptness, hoping to make use of my common sense, in relating the local's struggle, I afforded my whole faculties in advance. To make my self feel better and interpret the true sensation of the struggle. I decided to interview the martyrs. I asked the martyrs to call in and tell me what it was in their mind to be a martyr. I expected an answer. And all their answers were unique.

To give a solid foundation I completely depended on the past experience of the local's struggle for the independence. Consequently, I have nothing more at heart than to make the hero's contribution to be known by the world. It was the martyrs that have inspired me. I my self would have labored in vain, if I did not inquire the martyrs contributions. And it would be impossible to read the facts of the struggle, without the martyrs.

I don't think there was any thing I would rely upon, besides the local's experience of a struggle. The heroic reading of the armed struggle through the eyes of the martyr's view required a transformation of minds.

The fervor of the struggle that filled my mind during those years of struggle made me to do a long trip of imagination. The martyrs accompanied my thought to the table.

The local's armed struggle for the independence, had been urging me for so long time. In fact, for the time being my time limitation made it out of question. Working so many hours in a company, and having very little time to write limited my approach to provide it in time. Though I was busy making my life to exist in a foreign country, I tried to my best to give the necessary attention to the locals struggle.

I believed in my self and wondered if I could support my self by my pen. I told myself and believed in my own sense that I was totally indebted, to share the struggle experience of the locals. I escorted my idea with deep conviction, ready to tell about the forgotten struggle. The unique struggle in Africa. It seemed, likely, that I invested my leisure time in something better to write about the locals. I started with great sympathy; it was my first exposure to the world of writers.

From all the local martyrs Padre was the one who volunteered to be interviewed. The other martyrs clocked their movement with their eyes and followed the interview with great attention. I slowly approached Padre, as if moving through water. I raised my hand and greeted him. He returned my greeting with an angelic response. Serenity was flowing on his face. His eyes were looking into mine, and I was about to start my interview. The year was 1991 immediately after the independence.

Icquar: What were the main ingredients that fueled your life to be martyrs for your own people? Was my introductory general question.

All the martyrs: From corner to corner with the same voice and clear words, they exploded and defined the purpose of their martyrdom, by pronouncing the words Discipline, Self-Sacrifice and Self-reliance. These were the only triune power we possessed during the armed struggle, they said.

Icquar: What do you mean by the triune power of the struggle? Was my second question?

Padre: The triune principles of the struggle, were the three powers in unity, that made the martyrs resist the enemy boldly. We clearly identified ourselves with the triune principles of the struggle, with the risk involved in giving our life. During the time of the armed struggle, these defining attitudes created an explosion of consciousness, breaking the social, cultural and political boundaries.

Icquar: *How did you familiarize these triune powers in the struggle?*

Padre: Through a mental gymnastics and practical exercises we were able to internalize them little by little to our system. The triune principles themselves became a culture and a life style of all the Tegadelti (freedom fighters). We internalized and demonstrated them in our daily accomplishment through the living experience of the struggle. No one would understand Sewra without understanding, the liberating values and vision it had, during those years of armed struggle. The triune principles were a liberating value. They characterized most of the movement's undertakings.

Icquar: *What do you mean by self-sacrifice?*

Padre: It is a heroic act that led Sewra in its struggle against the enemy. No doubt, all the resistance for the independence of the locals was the act of a consent to be held in a disposition of heart. Through this excellent preparation of self-giving, we were able to shed our blood that has demanded our precious life. With this great involvement we went ahead to foresee the goal and the process in which we were sure where it would lead and end the struggle.

Icquar: *What is Heroism from the perspective of your experience?*

Padre: It is unusual life giving spectacle that some one offers to the others. A hero does not recite his story but some one will say some thing about him or her. The local's heroes they died, but their deeds are vivid with all honors in the heart of the locals. The locals became the place where the heroes gave proof of their heroic commitment. The local's heroes, filled with courageousness and entirely devoted to the liberation of the locals and the welfare of the people, they wished to put the crowning touch through their self-sacrifice. The impression of heroism was the fulfillment of the principle. No one was born hero but we became within the process.

In the west it is manufactured for a purpose of business in the movies. It is fantasized, exaggerated and incapable of sustaining the true concept of being a hero. A hero was depicted as one who destroys and demolishes the surrounding. It had lost its true meaning. A hero was one who tolerates to celebrate the weaknesses and the successes accordingly.

Icquar: **W***hat was the degree of tolerance?*

Padre: **C**ompared to the time, the resistance for the independence was almost, a life journey. The aim of Sewra was only the liberation of the locals. Every step we took for the cause of the independence on the other hand brought us every now and then fresh difficulties and numerous obstacles. As long as we remained faithful to the liberation of the locals, we gave no thought to any thing, except advancing with courage to further our aim of liberation.

Icquar: **W***hat was the discipline in the struggle?*

Padre: It was the first requirement of the armed struggle. It created a constant union within Sewra. However, Sewra who had learned the discipline of struggle, at the cost of its life, realized that all the difficulties, oppositions, bear the mark of its resistance for the cause of the peoples liberation. Only Sewra, could carry out such an honorable duty of liberation because it possessed uncommon power of discipline.

Icquar: *To what degree was the discipline exercised?*

Padre: To the degree of going against our nature and modifying our usual manner, which the struggle had brought about. From the start, Sewra appeared to be a model of struggle. We were very careful for every thing in our clothes, food and exterior deportment that could suggest the air of division among ourselves.

Icquar: *What was Sewra for you?*

Padre: Sewra was a political convent where every one and every body joined the movement voluntarily. It was a place where gender divisions and sex obstacles were overcome. It was a situation of equal opportunity in the struggle. It was a brotherly and sisterly managed struggle.

For the sake of unity the ethnic and religious background was repressed though it was vivid in our inner life. Sewra was growing at once more detailed and more unified everyday, with an epic resistance in all events and circumstances, all held together through a mysterious system of discipline.

It was this discipline that had balanced our different characters, backgrounds, beliefs and social status in the struggle. The past experiences, the family, the neighborhood and the place where we came from was tactically disregarded. We became part of Sewra within the process. To become part of it, we needed to pass through a struggle.

Icquar: *How do you explain the role of discipline in relation to the struggle?*

Padre: Discipline was the guaranteed road that empowered the struggle to succeed. It was a mortifying experience, swimming against the tide. We determined not to live for ourselves but for the others. How many remarkable Tegadelti (the patriots) gave their life to keep the reputation of the locals as a free people. The decision taken by the individual Tegadelti was the outcome of the discipline. Their aim was to liberate the locals. It was not a simple kind of character, which would allow our sensitive life to be exposed to the harmful experience of war. Our preference was the liberation of the locals and our unique and constant occupation was the salvation of our people. As long as we remained faithful to the liberation of the local, we gave no thought to anything except advancing in courage to further the struggle to word its completion.

Icquar: **D***id you have any backing during the armed struggle?*

Padre: **T**o consolidate the struggle undertaking we needed no authority, influence, and human backing, but a sole courage that set our course and directed us through the dark and stormy nights, so full of difficulties and obstacles, which the enemy threw into our path.

Icquar: **W***hat made Sewra so different from other movements?*

Padre: I believe it is the discipline in all its political, social, and moral dimensions, which Sewra ought to pursue by all means, and which it could neglect only to its own great disadvantage. The revolution for the independence had awed a large part of its success in the discipline of Sewra, which had strengthened and prepared us even for self-sacrifice of our life. This exceptional degree of self-sacrifice led the revolution to proceed in hope and conclude in victory.

Icquar: **H***ow was the discipline accomplished, based on your experiences?*

Padre: It was the fundamental principle, which Sewra had managed to organize it self, right from the beginning. Every one had to conform to it completely. It was a grievous struggle, an agonizing experience.

In such occasions Sewra trained it self to overcome the threatening struggle of war by doing violence to its natural feelings. For in such occasions, exaggerated efforts often by human terms difficult to be explained lead the revolution to words the independence. Through discipline we became our own executioners at the cost of our life. The armed struggle discipline was so difficult, that we were not able to follow our own inclination. We did not have the chance to show the likeness and dis-likeness as was natural to human being. No one inherits discipline but it growth in ones nature through certain mental gymnastics. It is true when some thing opposite happens every one finds it rather strange. The future, the independence of the country, surpassed this entire tendency in the mind of freedom fighters. We store up in our memory, the awful experience of war, in which no one would be ignorant to know and which it was more appropriate and more difficult to forget than to learn.

Icquar: *How was it managed?*

Padre: It was managed by putting an intense focus on the unity of the freedom fighters. Discipline was the cornerstone of all the system of the Liberation Front. We managed to get all alone and build our political and military strength. Indeed, the main concern of the system was, to continuously maintain and cultivate this union and solidarity among us. However distasteful it may have been, for us to lay aside our preoccupation of the liberation of Eritrea did not give up hope. It was true when some thing opposite happened, every one found it rather strange. To counter it and as long as we remained faithful, to the liberation of our people, we never thought any thing, except advancing with courage to reach our goal.

*Icquar: **W**hat was the main challenge of the armed resistance?*

*Padre: **T**he* main challenge was the interference of the supper powers one after the other. Within the course of the struggle every time Sewra returned with new courage and renewed spirit of resistance. All times were very challenging ones and there was time of almost total distress. The neighbor with the help of the eastern Abisha (Russia) in the late 70th has changed the course of the struggle. The locals struggle for the independence had to start all over again each day the same struggle but with different strategy. There was not only one enemy, but also many and the struggle was against such long standing enemies, to ensure a certain victory. In it self, the resistance against the neighbor and its allied western and eastern Abisha's had proved the most effective organization of Sewra, living in extreme unity despite the lack of alien Abisha. If the struggle was hard one, the victory was complete for the triumph we won over the enemy after 30 years of struggle is appreciated.

In this way Sewra managed to get alone with discipline to rebuild it own strength some what by resisting the exhausting struggle always with a new spirit.

*Icquar: **W**hat was the valuable result that discipline promised along the course of the struggle?*

*Padre: **I**t* was the unity of principles and minds. Moreover, Sewra's continual patience was not a state of weakness, nor unmindful to the act of atrocity of the neighbor. Its esteem for the armed struggle, was so great that it judged its own steps, on the progress it made within the process. In the course of its struggle life, it cultivated the spirit of unity, that yielded place to independence. The only means it recommended was a continuos discipline, that can awake an attraction of the locals to join Sewra. It considered discipline of the first importance and became well disposed towards all social, political and military undertakings.

While conforming to the situation of the struggle it had more reason to feel satisfied when it saw the unity of the locals. The good results of the discipline were even more evident, since they were able to win over all the minds of the locals.

Icquar: *What is self-reliance?*

Padre: *It w*as the second needed weapon that we obtained through the full cooperation of our people. We relied to this principle from the beginning of the struggle. The fact was, out side of our own people, we had no other resources to count on.

Icquar: *How did this principle functioned?*

Padre: Right from the beginning, at the start of the struggle, we instituted the philosophy of self-reliance, which have matured during the struggle. In the long run the hidden strategy of the struggle was certainly acknowledged and accredited as a unique stand of the resistance, which became an example for the entire world.

Icquar: *In what way you demonstrated it?*

Padre: We demonstrated it with our own life. There was no model or a style, to refer to, out there as a reference. We pursued this goal and its reasonableness within the process of the struggle. Our struggle had been shaped by this principle. The principle of self-reliance before it became a reality it had undergone through an incredible test of war experience. We were tested and refined during the struggle, as we walked in unity.

Icquar: Did it become a lesson to any one?

Padre: Yes indeed. In time the local's struggle for independence had shown the world that we were alone in support of our own-cause. Based on this principle we were able to hatch a successful plan of an armed struggle. We equipped ourselves, sufficiently against the potential enemy backed by the supper powers, one after the other.

Icquar: How?

Padre: By simply pressing on, in a battle and determining the liberation of our peoples day by day. Since we understood the principle of self-reliance in time would make sense, we definitely resisted to the end, for this holy cause. We made self-reliance as our first choice. We were very consistent to this principle and exploited it to the full, since we knew the outcome will be the welfare of our people.

Icquar: In what ways?

Padre: It was on being united that we defeated our enemy and we were careful in cultivating the roots of unity. Our perspective was the liberation of our people and for this purpose we were ready to die. We believed that the fulfillment of our ideas and principles would come true only if we struggle in unity. This, we did it out of necessity for the sake of our people. Unlimited consciousness with limited life, the life of a struggle that is supposed to be compensable, created the main goal of the resistance. We saw things differently.

Icquar: What was your goal?

Padre: Our goal was to live and die with honor, to make a difference. We never thought for a minute about surviving the war. Our only concern was to create a new country and a people with a history.

An absolute commitment to liberate our people was our stronghold. Dedicated to our peoples cause we became more confrontational and committed rather than compromising. We preferred not to sail with current but against the current, though it may cost our life. We conditioned our life with a principle, and willfully subjected our life to all the suffering and pain of the struggle.

Icquar: *What was the claim of the neighbor*

Padre: I guess it was the claim of three thousand years of existence as a country. I believe they had started to deny the whole true story of the locals. They had already invented their story. A story written by them, the authors were the neighbors. They spoke about existence, presence, and they counted years, they united and disunited concepts. They used a plain propaganda that was consumed only in the land of the neighbor. A time may come when they will accept the reality. It was not about a false or true narration, the neighbor did exist only 100 years ago.

Icquar: *What was their perspective in doing so?*

Padre: They didn't have any perspective other than to mislead the people. It was somewhat misleading one. It was a home made. It discomforted the position of the people, because they perceived it certainly in a twisted way. For the time being, they succeeded in setting up a vast and buzzing information network, for their own defense. They quoted the bible, recited it to the people. They had their version as a proof of their biblical genealogy. Before Christ the neighbor existed with the same boundary. To protect the home assembled excellencies, they presented a better historical demonstration of their legacy to Israel.

Icquar: Would the account of this claim of being a country since the time of the Old Testament would actually violate the state of good reasoning?

Padre: Yes it would certainly does. A legend made up of fantastic story and told as if it would give a common sense, could mislead people. It was, therefore, a matter of supreme importance for the neighbor to make sure of its existence as country and claim the local's land as its part. But that was as difficult to accomplish, as it was important. On the one hand, the distorted history composed by the neighbor, on the other hand the reality of the African states after the colonial dominance, made unsatisfactory claim that has caused so much trouble to the neighbor.

Icquar: What did they do to make this legend true and believable?

Padre: What they did was perpetuating their legacy, in order to construct the claim of being a country, before any country in the world. They insisted us to repeat the same history, the way they did, a simple tale told by our enemies. The priests expound in their most evangelizing method of "Kene" (a spiritual or cultural poetical song) by saying, " The neighbor raises its hand to God." King Solomon and queen Sheba, the main reference of the legacy, were quoted to demonstrate the long history of existence as a country. Out of this legend they had made an excellent history. They were very insistent, to tell a story of a neighbor as a country, with the same boundary and the same people, but their idea was very flimsy. They inclined to twist every thing to their advantage. Home-fabricated story intoxicated the neighbor and as long as they told the same story, they remained the show place of all contradictions.

Icquar: *It seems that the neighbor's historians had lost their common sense?*

Padre: You are right. If it is not common sense it is non-sense. They never grow tired of reciting the same story, their version didn't surprise us, they sing the same song and in time it covered them with confusion. Hundred years from now, nobody will be able to tell for sure the same story and no one will listen to their distorted claims. They told a story that didn't follow a sequence. It usually was a disjointed story that changed often. They won't be able to distinguish truth from fiction. Always reciting the same distorted and misleading story, of being a nation since the time of the Old Testament. When the locals claimed only one hundred years of existence as a country what hindered the neighbor to accept the fact if not to mislead people.

Icquar: *What main reasons did you have to doubt their story?*

Padre: There was a fact of African history as people living within the continent without boundary. And there was a fact of colonialization. The first fact can not categorize the second one. You become people only to your surrounding. To go out of your surrounding was to enter into the boundary of other people. As a matter of fact language, culture, religion was the boundary of the people. To go beyond was to conquer or evangelize. How can the neighbor tell the story of the locals unless they wanted to conquer? How come the local became part of the neighbor.

Icquar: *What was the background of their reasoning?*

Padre: I think as the Italians say, "chi si alza presto comanda", (one who gets up early commands), it implied to the neighbor's reasoning for the fact they had started to tell the story ahead of us. The thing was not about who told the story first, but how the story was told with a character of sincerity. The neighbors had totally lost the sense of relation and created their own system, around which they could revolve, reciting the same legend. The legend was carefully contrived to make their story look true and innocent.

The stereotyped way of reciting the history couldn't come out with a result. The locals did not give ear to the neighbor, telling the same lie over and over. The never-ending story of a legend had created a sentiment of fatigue, frustration and illusion.

Icquar: *What was the logic behind their story?*

Padre: I didn't see any logic that satisfied their claim. On their part their logic were many. They claim as the only African country that had never been colonized. A chosen people with a particular history. They bridged the antique history of the Old Testament to the New Testament all the way to the present. They magnified a little event to make it big and credible. Motivated only by the events but never disciplining themselves by truth. The cultural pride, the defense mechanism they bought cheaply, they sold it at high price, while on the other hand they were losing reputation within the global community.

Icquar: *The historical bargains of a country as one neighbor and as one country for three thousand years would it be profitable for the neighbor?*

Padre: I think it was like trying to give substance to its own claim and lend them semblance of truth. They speak about kings and kingdoms, about land and boundaries. When no country in the world started to exist less than five century ago, the neighbor's claim of existence as a country, three thousands years ago would give no sense. The neighbors they disliked to be called neighbors. They never invested their time and skill for the sake of being neighbor. The only voice they could pronounce was one neighbor one country. They created a story with the content that satisfies their claim. But as time passed everything got into focus.

Icquar: *How did we demonstrate the true fact of our position?*

Padre: At the beginning we demonstrated our position diplomatically, but later when our voice was not heard by the international community, we started an armed struggle that cost our life. The entire struggle was on how to be a people and tell the neighbor that we were only neighbors. From the beginning it was clear for them that there was no ground for accommodating with the neighbor. All those years the neighbor did not pay attention to the question of the locals. Bullets were not our choice, but they pushed us to act so. They preferred to provide a violent agenda to the case, while we tended the none-violent.

Icquar: *In becoming violent did they gain some thing?*

Padre: Indeed they didn't gain anything, in fact they became losers. The neighbor on one hand, in vain had exhausted all it's violent agenda against the locals, on the other hand the awareness and unity of the locals, would never allow a gap of discord between the people. The frequent and dangerous visit of the king had greatly wearied the locals, and put their patience to a severe test. For some time the locals showed their stand peacefully.

Icquar: *What was the effect of the legacy of Western Abisha (USA) and Eastern Abisha (RUSSIA) to the neighbor?*

Padre: Right from the beginning, though the local's choice was to be one and independent country like many African countries, Western and Eastern Abisha one after the other they tried to hamper the peoples desire. At the time of which we speak, when most of the African countries were given the independence after the era of colonialism, for the locals it only remained a dream. The status of being an independent local had been urging its people for a long time, but they had not been fortunate to get is as they intended peacefully.

In fact, the Western Abisha, the near friend of the neighbor complicated the situation, for a simple reason that the local can not live on its own. The locals from the time they first acknowledged, that the things were not in their favor, they first tried to solve the problem peacefully and diplomatically, but the influential neighbor succeeded in getting hold of dominating the locals land by force. The locals criticized Western Abisha's misleading influence and political shortsightedness. As a devoted friend, Western Abisha, though believed that the historical reconstruction of the neighbor, was not true, for a simple reason of self-interest it had accepted the claim. Western Abisha, it complicated the situation only for self-interest and enjoyed more influence and authority to help the neighbor, within the process. They pretended to be ignorant of the fact for so long. When it saw that Sewra was born in the land of the locals, it took all necessary means to repress it.

Icquar: *What was the reason behind the legacy?*

Padre: The only reason that drove Western Abisha was the self-interest to have a permanent military base. To do this it approved the annexation of the local with the neighbor to be one country. Western Abisha did not dare to approach the matter in a rightful way. However, the locals though despised and neglected by western Abisha, maintained their struggle in solidity and unity. Sewra might have found difficulty, in its course of the struggle because of its isolation from western Abisha

It was very ridiculous, for ones interest to bargain the land of the locals and on the other hand practically recognize the independence of many other African countries. It wished to go on record for favoring the friend neighbor. Distance did not prevent for Western Abisha to do so. To keep the friendship, the neighbor presented it self with a tactful manner, to make believe her Abisha. The most often repeated predicament of the neighbor, was its presentation as the only independent country since 3000 years and with a long and unique

171

history. Before the existence of Abisha the neighbor was a country. At such time western Abisha forfeited her attraction in self-interest, for she showed favoritism to the neighbor. She stood firm, to gain a momentum from this relationship.

Icquar: *Why was the agenda of annexing the local land became the priority of the Western Abisha?*

Padre: The pernicious agenda of annexing the local land, with the neighbor, was born of the malice or at least dreamed up by the Western Abisha for a simple self-interest accommodations. This attitude in it self created turmoil.

Quite soon, the annexation of the local, through a military action by the neighbor was accomplished. At that time the locals since they lacked an influential Abisha, to defend their right they subdued to the situation unwillingly. The decision of federation of the locals with the neighbor, which at later time gave a way to comply in annexing, caused so much complications.

However, when the locals saw this action was not for their interest, they remained convinced that the only means to defend them selves, was by means of an armed struggle. Of course, the tricks involved by western Abisha and the neighbor was not so easy. Great as was the influence of western Abisha on the other hand the locals were not intimidated to defend their case.

Icquar: *How could you explain the local's historical commitment of the struggle?*

Padre: If one was permitted, to recite the heroic days of the struggle, he or she would definitely mark it differently, for whatever may be the truth. We who had given our life for our people, would definitely recited it differently. The struggle was particular and unique in the history of the world. To tell it to the world it needed a particular vocabulary, in which the world would never understand. We, the martyrs had given the proof of our heroic actions of giving our life for the sake of our people. We passed through the struggle and sensibly provided the locals the independence they longed for three decades. We did accomplish it, with our own life.

Icquar: What inspired you to be confident in the struggle?

Padre: To my best knowledge to answer your question, I need to recount the whole facts of the struggle, which you would not have time to listen to me. No doubt the struggle for independence, in its course, had always remained flourishing, in spite of all the storms that shook it. It was quite evident, and no one could reasonably deny that fact of a struggle. The more we were attached to the principles of liberation, the more our commitment grew day by day, to make the world believe. As long as the struggle was within the process, Sewra granted its protection to the locals and it was the same struggle that led us to endow liberation to our own people, to inspire the locals, with great confidence to support our people.

Icquar: Could you briefly recount to me how Sewra was born?

Padre: I am ready to tell the true story of Sewra the daughter of the locals. The centrality and the focus of the story is about the exceptional struggle of independence participated by all ages and category of people. Sewra was born and raised in the local land and its first exposure to the locals did not come until the beginning of 60th. Before that time Sewra was heavily engaged, to deal with the problem of the locals, in a peaceful way, fundamentally, concerned about the future and the independence of the locals.

Brought up within a disciplined culture and people, in time it deeply influenced its own people. With altered consciousness it stepped before its people, when unrest began to stir in the land of the locals. A number of the locals got fed up, with the intended malice of the neighbor and organized a protest within the cities and towns.

Sewra had placed the largest share of its commitment, in reserve to its own people. Though, the struggle was not easy, it had shown an outstanding sacrifice, for the liberation of its own people. Indeed, as soon as it learned from experience, it let, that these experiences monitor, the whole undertaking of the struggle.

Icquar: *Would you share about Sewra out of your experience, since I consider that life experience was a subject to all the prescriptions of historical facts?*

Padre: To start to tell a story was to begin a journey. Life in it self was a journey; a process in which learning took place and even if there was a mistake or a false start a correction was possible, if we believed and understood where we were. There were different ways of telling a story. The thing was where the place of the storyteller was. The winners tell about their success. The loser on the other hand they would never admit their loses.

While we are within the process of the struggle, we had to be conscious to what we share, with whom we share the space we had. The coming to be in a culture, grow in a society demanded a struggle.

As I see it now, Sewra's prominence in the struggle was related to its dedication of its political, social and popular undertakings. Sewra's movement in all its dimensions was worthy of recognition. It became a recognized authority with all its principles in east Africa and the whole of Africa. There were many liberation movements that had arisen in Africa after the era of colonialization. Some of them reached their goal but were not able to discipline their people to words the goal they had achieved.

Most of the political, social and human undertakings of a struggle were measured by the success they produced in the people's life. Many revolutions as they started they placed their foundation on a particular problem for a particular solution. They forgot the illusive quality of communizing their solutions for the problems. Some of them moved to solve the problem, through military action only, without motivating their people. They focused only on the military might and capacity of eliminating the problem. The social, cultural and human dimension of the movement was totally forgotten. The locals armed struggle in its kind had hired the global sense of a revolution, which they placed a greater importance in holding all the dimension of a revolution.

Icquar: *What was Sewra's primary objective during the armed struggle?*

Padre: Sewra's primary objective was to share a common experience with uncommon power of struggle. We had noted, that local's armed struggle depended heavily, on the unique experience of Sewra's undertakings. It was obvious in all the struggle experience, for Sewra to come out with the formulation of resisting the enemy in all cultural, social, political dimensions.

Despite everything, Sewra's influence and prominence still continues to our day. There were two main objectives Sewra used to explore the whole foundation of the armed struggle. The first, was an attempt to base the armed struggle as sole means of liberation in the local's history of independence. Secondly, was to perform the armed struggle from the context of the local's life experience . The content of the armed struggle was intensely local. Sewra's claim was, that the whole struggle, had been a radical exposition of local's principles, in relation to their experience. Sewra considered the armed struggle to be one of the main concerns of all the local's. In its message the address of Sewra's concern regarded all the local's. It set out, with a deliberate intention, to construct a home made struggle, by raising this complex set of historical, theoretical and pragmatic consciousness. In its kind, the armed struggle would be of great value, in relation to the cultural, social and political dimensions.

Icquar: How did Sewra organize itself politically?

Padre: To secure the enthusiasm of liberation and uphold the primary motives of the struggle, Sewra had displayed a strategy of a struggle. This well-designed strategy, launched by the local's, against the neighbor's successive campaign of intimidations, was the unity of the people. It did not take long, for Sewra to organize it self politically and restore the unity of the locals. Since it believed its own people, it knew better than any one how to assume responsibility when necessary. Desiring with such laudable eagerness, to see the local's assume their responsibility, Sewra insisted, so strongly that the neighbor could not turn them down.

The neighbor had highly incensed its project of destruction. Announced, war campaigns one after the other. Baptized the different campaigns with different names. When ever it lost, it adopted the profession of mass killing, threatened with prison, counteracted with terrorism.

Sewra, who occupied the center of the locals' struggle, despite everything did not change its mind of liberation. During those time of liberation, it foresaw the storms that would arise against it. Every time, it strengthened it self, with courage, to withstand the enemies successive attempt, to destroy the locals.

Icquar: How did Sewra's plan of liberation found adherence in the local's mind?

Padre: Not surprisingly, Sewra had at first offered to its own people a deep sense of a revolution in all its dimensions. It has the highest record in the history of our modern world. The people, the greatest blessing of the land, believed firmly to their case of being an independent local in Africa. The struggle was the only foundation of Sewra, in which it considered as the first importance; hence it was the only means to reach its goal. So, being well disposed towards all undertakings, it cooperated with its own people.

It is indeed amazing, the world's position, in disregarding the struggle of the local's. It is even more amazing to qualify the neighbor's claim of the local's land, as true and historical one, while disregarding the African history of colonization. The most amazing of all, still the western Abisha (USA) does not accept practically the independence of the locals.

The locals needed a leader, to direct them and communicate the struggle's influence within the process. The struggle seemed unbelievable. One would hardly dare affirm it. If there was any thing, that seemed extraordinary was the unity of the people. Sewra proceeded in everything with the greatest precautions. It had brought the local's up, in the course of the struggle. Addressed its own principles of the struggle, the only principles of liberation, since it was convinced that the liberation of the local's depended on the commitment of the local's. Still the martyr's presence, was the most felt, in the heart of the locals despite their physical absence.

Icquar: How were the beginnings of the armed struggle?

Padre: Right from the beginning in 1961 Bretawi Kalsi (Armed struggle) was conceived, in the mind of the local's, which in time became a realty of a struggle. Before Sewra gave birth to Kalsi (the struggle), it hid on it's own inner self. It's own people noticed its pregnancy. Sewra did not want to disclose its secret. It rather preferred the solitary life. The neighbors were greatly surprised when they learned that Sewra gave birth to Kalsi.

The mountains, rivers, and the valleys assured Sewra, their collaboration and encouraged it towards future undertaking of the armed struggle. As far as Sewra granted its protection to the locals they promised their collaboration. To attain its end it had tried the path of secrecy. It climbed the high mountains to foresee the need of its people. Until the local's desire of being a free people and country was totally accomplished, Sewra did not relax for a single time. The neighbor simply in vain strive to destroy the existence of Sewra.

Icquar: *What was the counter reaction of the neighbor when it learned about the birth of Kalsi?*

Padre: At the beginning the neighbor did not accept the reality of the birth of Kalsi openly. But after some time, when it was not able to hide the fact, it tried to cause the genuine struggle to be ill thought by the people. It brought down, to discredit the locals undertaking of the struggle, by using fanatic measurement, such as referring the struggle as an aggregation of bandits and the outlaws. Their radio preferred to criticize and ridicule the local's leadership.

False propaganda was another battleground, where Sewra had to vanquish, the same powerful enemy. During the years of the struggle, we grew so accustomed, to these false propaganda and never gave an ear. The successive regimes of the neighbor, used this false propaganda, as a discipline, to wage a war, in order to suppress the resistance. No one, could ever forever flatter the people. On the other hand, the resistance grew stronger day by day, in the heart of the freedom fighters, and to the opposite we added courageousness after courageousness, to present our true representation of our people.

The locals beside Sewra, they never practically expected any one to collaborate. The world in itself has taken, the tactic of silence or compliance with the enemy's strategy.

Icquar: *What were the degree of your resistance and the tactic of the struggle?*

Padre: Secrecy was number one means for our resistance to the enemy. Kalsi was moving from place to place, without any notice of the enemy. Its own people were its protectors. They believed only through Kalsi would come, the security and the freedom of the locals. At the beginning, it preferred to be alone and moving secretly. It became the friend of the mountains, cliffs, rivers, and valleys, calculated its steps and when necessary it changed directions. Kalsi was forced to act, design and underline its strategy, in a hidden and secrete places. Yes, in that segregated place, when stomach was without any food, the rule of fasting was spontaneously observed, when the lungs respected to breath the warm fresh air, a chosen life of hermits on the mountains of Sahel, organized Sewra, to discipline itself for the undertaking of the armed struggle.

It was a grievous struggle an agonizing experience, which for a better reason of being sacrifice, every one had to conform to it completely. For such occasions, all of us trained ourselves, to go against the threatening situation, by doing violence to our natural feelings. For in such occasion, exaggerated effort, often by human terms difficult to be explained, the system of the liberation front, lead the resistance for the future victory. It was not a simple kind of character, which would allow their sensitive life, be exposed to the harmful experience of war. Our preference was for the Eritrean people liberation. The exceptional degree of our sacrifice led us towards martyrdom. We ourselves through discipline, set the front of the liberation on a solid foundation.

Icquar: *How helpful was the strategy of secrecy in the undertaking of the struggle?*

Padre: Kalsi at the beginning, in order not to attract the enemy's evil attention, was very careful, to remain for a while in obscurity, though its attitude in principle betrayed it. Its radical version of the liberation of the locals, would not allow it to remain in secrecy. Kalsi knew, it was fighting for a cause, therefore it accelerated its movement. It did not leave an open door, for the enemy that can be fatal. It preferred, the struggle to be the common means to its final goal. It devised, how it could win the war amidst all the enemy's strategy.

It presented it self to the locals as the sole instrument of liberation. The locals did not take long, to notice the beginnings of the struggle. Discipline, self-sacrifice and self-reliance accompanied her for the undertaking of the struggle. For the locals it was the symbol of unity. That was what made the locals eager to join the front. Its original wish was to depict the armed struggle for the independence and that was why it withdrew to the mountains. Since it could not trust any one, except its own people, it chose the strategy of secrecy. The great majority of the local's population remained faithful to the end, but some anticipated failure by joining the enemy. The only relief it could find, during the process of the armed struggle, was within its own people. It believed its own people, with unfathomable character of dedication and its resistance against the enemy, made it's commitment grow day by day, by redoubling the effort of the struggle.

It withdrew to the mountains in order to calculate its strength. On the other hand the enemy was taking an advantage of diffusing a false propaganda, what they broadcast at breakfast (in the morning) they contradict it at dinner (in the evening). Their mouth uttered what their heart dictated. To have been born from those people, (the locals), was the greatest ambition one can have. Kalsi way of dealing its case, through an armed struggle, little by little became evident, in the mind of the locals and with time it became so strong and clear.

Icquar: During the course of the struggle what happened to Kalsi?

Padre: As it is a fact, that the hope for the harvest is in the seed, also the duration of a struggle for independence depended on its foundations. It was true, that the freedom of the entire population, would cost a lot of lives. Kalsi's dedication, for the cause of the independence was not an easy task. For this reason, beforehand it had calculated the enemy's hardness of heart.

While Kalsi was building its strength of offence, the neighbor declared a total destruction of the foundation. It had deliberately chosen, the strategy of lying, to give moral to the soldiers that it recruited. On the other side, over the mountains of Sahel, Kalsi had established its defense and took all imaginable precautions to prevent the enemy move in any direction. It took the advantage of discipline to bring back to the initial undertakings always accompanied by sacrifice.

Indeed, its main concern was to maintain and cultivate this union among it self. The neighbor on the other hand, right from the beginning, with its intoxicating propaganda tried to manipulate the situation. Their real target was, to dismantle the struggle and at any cost they tried, to twist everything to their own advantage. After almost a decade of "Kalsi's" (struggle's) birth, it was forced to reveal the division it had in itself. Though at the beginning it refused to reveal the division, the position of secrecy lost its aim. Since the new circumstance of division, were presented to the locals openly, the local's found a way out to mediate the situation. The enemy in the capital city, by taking the advantage of the fact of Kalsi's division almost succeeded to divide the locals by means of soccer. It approved ethnically soccer team clubs.

Icquar: What were the leading mottoes of the armed struggle?

Padre: They were many, but there were two fundamental ones, that had characterized, the entire movement of the armed struggle.

The first one was "Heroes, don't live but their history is inherited". And the second one was "the struggle will be very long but victory was for sure".

Convinced enough, Kalsi trained us, to unite our effort to destroy the enemy at any cost. It encouraged and comforted us in the struggle undertakings. Day after day, we possessing superior military and moral capacities, we were able to defeat the enemy.

Kalsi knew its duties. It was loyal to the locals. It believed in what it was doing. At the time, when the neighbor was constructing a whole edifice of lies, to divert the flow of the liberation movement, Kalsi ensured its people by defending them wholeheartedly.

Icquar: What were the main strategies that influenced the armed struggle?

Padre: They were three, the first was to enlighten the local's politically, the second was to arm the local's for a cause and third was to unite the people as a party.

However, practically, the armed struggle, had used this strategy to its maximum, by following the sequence, to enlighten, arm and unite the people, for one goal for the independence. Within the course of the armed struggle, how distasteful it may have been, we did not lay aside our preoccupation of the liberation of the locals. These were the main strategies we introduced into our life. This strategies we had taken them from Sewra, which became our portion forever and that we desired no other inheritance.

While, so usefully occupying our position of liberating the local, we learned to our great advantage, that the struggle would finally bring a solution and consoled our selves.

Icquar: *Did the two Absha's learn something during the course of the struggle?*

Padre: No, I don't think so. Still they did not learn from their past engagements. They don't want to learn. The independence of the local's was not to their interest. They had accepted the reality only because they were forced by the situation. It was this cycle of continued engagement of the super powers that had energized the locals to defend their rights. The locals coordinated their efforts. The only weapons were its peoples. The unity of the people made the resistance more a matter of reality, which in time the breaking point finally came.

In deed, the direct influence of the supper powers completely disregarded or at most limited the movement of the struggle. One after the other, western and eastern Abisha helped the neighbor to continue its warfare against the locals. The local's resistance was against the said supper powers and the neighbor. Western and eastern Abishas became the losers in time.

As soon as I concluded my interview with Padre, I headed to words the local's land Eritrea. All the martyrs in one voice invited me to come again. I accepted their invitation but never promised any thing.

The imaginary interview was done in 1991 immediately after the independence day of May 24.

Archway Publishing books may be ordered through booksellers or by contacting:

Archway Publishing
1663 Liberty Drive
Bloomington, IN 47403
www.archwaypublishing.com
844-669-3957

Because of the dynamic nature of the Internet, any web addresses or links contained in this book may have changed since publication and may no longer be valid. The views expressed in this work are solely those of the author and do not necessarily reflect the views of the publisher, and the publisher hereby disclaims any responsibility for them.

This is a work of fiction. All of the characters, names, incidents, organizations, and dialogue in this novel are either the products of the author's imagination or are used fictitiously.

Cover art is by permission of Fr. Christopher Klitou

Scriptures taken from the King James Version of the Bible.

ISBN: 978-1-4808-6381-1 (sc)
ISBN: 978-1-4808-6382-8 (hc)
ISBN: 978-1-4808-6380-4 (e)

Library of Congress Control Number: 2018949858

Print information available on the last page.

Archway Publishing rev. date: 11/09/2020

CONTENTS

CHAPTER 1

Bethlehem

"He could have done better for you," repeated Leah, with a look revealing her contempt.

Jerusha glanced around. This house and its contents were all her husband left her — all the worldly possessions of a recently widowed young woman with three hungry boys to raise. A one-room house with sleeping loft. Limestone walls, except for one area of patchwork with sticks holding back wattle consisting of everything from broken chunks of Roman-made concrete to mud bricks and dried dung, all lightly white-washed. Parts of the wall stones were smoothly hand-finished, indicating the structure had once been a rich man's stable, before Bethlehem had crowded this far north. Maybe in Solomon's time? But nowadays, most stables were caves in the cliffs outside of town.

Her house wasn't in the airier parts of Bethlehem. Although there were several hundred families in the town, most lived close together to save on land valuable for grazing and cultivating. Jerusha lived in the northwestern quarter, in a despised warren of narrow and odoriferous streets and alleys, but not far enough north to receive any of the country air from the five miles of open land between Bethlehem and Jerusalem. Air fragrant at times of the year and cold at others, but always fresh. This was denied Jerusha's family.

At least she had a house of her own, and no male relatives likely to contest her possession. Unlike most dwellings in Bethlehem, which opened into courtyards surrounded by tenements or small houses crammed together, thus offering more security from the street, but less privacy, Jerusha's house opened directly onto a wider part of the street itself, complete with water trough. The privacy of her home was a good trade for the smelliness of others', in her opinion.

The one room was larger than her neighbors', though the ceiling joists were lower — not far above the loft, requiring a slight stoop upstairs. The loft was wide enough for five people to sleep in. With three pallets, one now too large, and a cradle. It had fresh straw on the floor; Jerusha was careful to see to that early each morning before her "real" chores began. She had always kept the house clean, even during her grief when Mordecai died.

A rather fine staircase, not the customary ladder, led to the loft, complete with treads, risers, and handrail, and a large, enclosed cabinet/storage space under it. Mordecai had been a mason's assistant and handyman, and built the stairs when his wife was pregnant with her first child, using his very best, if limited, skills. He had worked at home after his return late in the evenings from Roman labor. Jerusha wondered where he found the lumber in arid northern Judea, but never asked.

Across the room was a fireplace with stone hearth, for warmth, and, frankly, because Jerusha wanted it. Mordecai would deny her nothing that he could build. The children were playing on the hearth now, the baby in his downstairs cradle.

The two women were seated on the lower steps of the staircase, though Leah's bulk occupied most of the space.

"Well, Leah, this is *my* house. No upper rooms in someone

else's building, with a landlord who demands monthly tribute, and is able to throw my family out onto the street whenever he wishes." This was no small consideration, to Jerusha.

"Hmph," Leah snorted. "When you remarry, your new husband will own your home, anyway."

Jerusha was surprised and disgusted. "What makes you think I will ever marry again? I have no father left to pledge me to anyone against my will. Do you think I would entrust my boys to a stranger?"

"You are young. You'll change your mind," Leah said smugly. "You should have a man!"

Jerusha stood and walked into the kitchen part of the large room, hoping work there would take Leah's mind off the subject.

Leah followed, grumbling.

Jerusha was past the actual, though not the official, period of mourning following the sudden death of her husband. Though she had considered him a bit ineffectual, he had been hard-working and attentive. She had liked him. By contrast, Jerusha's adoration of her three sons approached idolatry: her David, three years old and already speaking and thinking coherently; affectionate Jonathan, one and one half years; and Abraham, the baby, at only two months. With them around Jerusha felt richly blessed, whatever Leah thought of her life. The children were the best part that remained from the marriage. Nevertheless, she thought of them as *her* children, not hers and Mordecai's.

But family gave Jerusha another burden: the wearying, if temporary, presence in her home of Leah, the wife of Mordecai's older brother. Their mutual dislike, ordinarily disguised, was not so much adding to or subtracting from her widow's grief, as distracting her from any feelings whatsoever but irritation.

The large kitchen area had an oven with cook-surface and a chimney which sometimes worked. And a small cupboard for food; a large one would have been unnecessary. For kitchen furniture, Jerusha had an all-purpose table taller and wider than normal to facilitate her work; three chairs, one quite rickety.

Leah sat down at the table, avoiding the weak chair out of regard for her weight.

For personal effects, Jerusha had a few pieces of crockery, one spoon—most drinks, soups, and stews were sipped or gulped from the bowl—and one kitchen knife; clay oil lamps, hanging and upright; a box against the wall with her clothes, mostly rags, and his clothes, somewhat better since he had had more occasion to be seen in public and at Jerusalem. Mordecai's clothes would soon have to be remade to fit her and the children. Until then, the children would have only loin rags.

And a little food. Too little.

As she brought items for supper out of the cupboard and put them onto the table, Jerusha noticed the small box made of acacia, with her few remaining coins, all of base metal, and her husband's, now her, phylactery: a small pouch containing a piece of cracked parchment with verses of Scripture. She took the parchment out and looked at it, possibly upside down—she couldn't read. To Jerusha, illiteracy was a symbol of personal independence. Mordecai had tried to teach her, though he would have been despised by his few friends for wasting time imparting a skill which was useless and distracting to a good wife and mother. To Jerusha, his efforts were merely an attempt to insinuate his weak, empty way of life into her purposeful activity: raising strong sons to stand up as free men should. So she stubbornly refused to learn to read. She now regretted her rudeness, though not her determination. Mordecai had died; what good had his reading done him?

On the other hand, what did she have left, but illiteracy and poverty? Her house didn't even have a back door opening to the privy she shared with her neighbors. She faced the daily indignity of walking round the front and down the dark path to the rear, or using the often-full chamber-pot. Oddly enough, the stick-and-wattle wall patch was where the back door should have been. Had there been a feud generations ago, with neighbors using access to the septic hole as the all-important issue?

Then again, what kind of living conditions had Jerusha expected? She had married a manual laborer, and brought no dowry.

The two women began cooking supper, a simple lentil and purslane soup. Lentil and domesticated dandelion would have tasted better, but purslane grew wild and could be found almost anywhere. Jerusha and Leah chopped the onions, minced the garlic, and prepared the olive oil for light frying. Jerusha surreptitiously hid her remaining piece of pomegranate in the rear of the cupboard; the rind was slightly shriveled, but still red with plenty of juicy seeds. Leah was shorter than Jerusha and would not see it. Barley bread, to dip in the oil, would complete the meal, though Jerusha would soon have to change to einkorn wheat, for it grew wild as well, and she could bake it herself. The supper she would serve tonight would be cheap but filling.

After an artificial and protracted pause, Leah asked, "Your husband died weeks ago, Jerusha." She looked appraisingly and enviously at the younger woman's slender body and attractive face. "What *are* your plans for the future?"

"I don't know," Jerusha said with a shrug, certain this would not end the discussion. "Whatever is God's will."

Leah banged the spoon on the table. "Mordecai died constructing a *Roman* building! Don't they have any kind of pension for that?"

Jerusha was expecting the outburst. "I don't think so. Two other men died when the scaffolding fell. One family complained; they disappeared."

"You mean *murdered*?"

"No." Jerusha was tired of explaining things to someone with no understanding of either construction or the Roman and Jewish administrative systems. Mordecai had taught her a little about both. "They probably resettled somewhere else."

"Maybe they were killed because they argued or got angry. There might be a small pension anyway, if you ask nicely." She spoke in a whine.

Jerusha lost her temper at Leah's tone: "And maybe Caesar Augustus will make Mordecai a legate, as a funeral gift." She slowly cooled off. "Honestly, Leah, I don't know what my boys and I will do."

The Romans had paid for Mordecai's burial placing the other two victims in the same plot to save money. They could have saved more money by cremating the remains, in accordance with Roman custom, but this was not a time for unnecessary religious friction with their nominal allies.

"I don't blame the Romans," Jerusha added, "God giveth and God taketh away. But we still have to live." Since Leah had bothered to sound concerned in her last remark, the least Jerusha could do was be more open. "I'm not worried about myself; it's my boys. They can help out when they're old enough, and, praise God, I have no daughter's dowry to save up for; we spent enough shekels for the Redemption of David at the Temple, and the circumcision of all the boys. When I'm too old to work, my fine sons will take care of me. But until then..."

She looked at her children, playing by the open fireplace. She went over and cuddled them. Jerusha was grateful that Mordecai, weak as he was, had not only kept the boys fed, but brought them up in the Law, disciplined them lovingly when it was called for, and had already begun to teach them in the ways of God. *But who would do so now?* She worried.

"Well,... uh...," Leah was plainly searching for the right words to launch into a speech, "The welfare of your family worries me too. You know, Jerusha, I have been your one and only family since your husband and my brother-by-marriage Mordecai was crushed to death, may God give him peace. It was I who provided most of the food we're cooking. But I have four children of my own—three boys, and one girl who eats as much as any of the boys and *will* someday need a dowry." The last remark seemed a bitter response to Jerusha's apparent pride in her lack of such a burden.

Jerusha wondered, not for the first time, why she always thought and spoke of her children with awe and love, while Leah never seemed to mention her own offspring without implied complaint.

"Anyway," continued Leah, "my husband is far away, as usual, in one of his meetings with some gang. Don't ask me what. I am only a woman and not privy to their plots, or strange habits, or whatever else the menfolk do. But," she came to the point of her lecture, "you know I can't stay here with you forever and destroy my own family." She spread her plump hands in a pleading gesture.

"I have never asked you to stay," said Jerusha. She left the boys and went back to the stove so Leah wouldn't mistake her motherly affection for an appeal to charity. If there was anything Jerusha hated it was pity. The occasional pangs of pity she had felt for Mordecai were the main reason she grieved so little for him today.

"Do you have to ask family for help? But even family can do only so much. My children are having to fix their own food from whatever remains fresh, or only stale, or whatever they can beg from neighbors. I live too far away from here to see them more than once in a while. Not that I'm complaining."

Jerusha responded with a hint of renewed irritation. "Didn't you tell me you had a neighbor looking after your children?"

"Uh, yes, but that isn't enough. They need a mother's hand."

"Leah, you have been a sister to me," Jerusha replied. "It's time you took care of your family." Jerusha concentrated on cooking the food so Leah could not see her face.

"Well, she's leaving tomorrow, and has a long way to go. It's past time she went home. Besides, we should start eating earlier. It was different when your father came home nights. He liked to be with you." An early supper also stretched the food further. David stopped eating and his eyes misted over. "I miss Papa. Why can't he come home?"

Jerusha repeated the words she had been brought up with, and tried not to think. I told you all about why he's gone. God gives us life, but we all have to give it back someday. Remember the stories of the Prophets your father taught you?" Maybe it was the peace that flowed over Jerusha while she suckled her child, but she no longer felt cynical or critical. She felt only love for her boys.

David paused to concentrate. "Some were good! Some were bad." He wrinkled his nose. "I don't 'member."

"Well, they were all God's will." Jerusha returned the baby to his cradle, rocked it twice, and came back to her chair. "And so is our life, good and bad."

"I like *good*, better. This food is good. Can we have it...all times?"

Jerusha stifled a small sob, "As often as I can get it, my beloved firstborn."

"Huh?"

"Nothing." She had embarrassed herself. "In a while, I'll get work, then you can have all you can eat."

David grinned, delightedly, "*All* I can eat? Nobody has that much." He then paused, dutifully. "And Jonathan and Abraham, too?"

"Yes, yes, if I can get it."

"But Abraham doesn't *eat* food." Cheering up, "Well, you take care of him, huh, Mama?"

Jerusha ruffled David's hair, and smiled. "Always. I'll always take care of all of you until you're big enough to take care of *me*."

They both laughed. She tickled him until he spilled food, then Jerusha laughed again and wiped it up.

Early the next morning, while she was cleaning the house, Jerusha found her sister-in-law had departed before sun-up with the packages of her belongings Jerusha had carefully readied for her. After cleaning Leah's sleeping-space, Jerusha checked the kitchen cupboard. It was bare of the remaining food Leah had brought, including the salt. That was no surprise.

Jerusha froze when she heard a crash at her front door. Since she never barred the door while housekeeping, but kept it on a light latch, the sound startled her. It was not the over-loud knock of a neighbor or stranger, nor the smashing by a marauding invader meant to instill fear—but the sound of the door rammed back against the wall, as of someone kicking it in only to find little resistance. Jerusha's first instinct was to fix her veil, relaxed or abandoned at home, to cover her hair and most of her face. Two bronze-helmeted Roman soldiers were outlined in the doorway by the bright sun behind them.

Jerusha had seen such men before, usually in orderly ranks on parade or wandering at random through the markets. These two stepped to either side of the doorway, with their spears leveled at her. They seemed determined, though to what end, she could not comprehend. Neither man spoke.

Between them entered another soldier of a type Jerusha had never seen before. He wore a leather breastplate, but only a simple dark-brown helmet with no red horse-hair crest, or red cape, or straps decorated with brass embossings, though he had other strange insignia. He wore the Roman short-sword, but carried no spear or shield.

The man spoke without apparent hostility. "Pardon us, my

Lady. My friends don't speak Aramaic, and your Latin or Greek might be faulty. For that matter, the decurion on my right, a Pannonian, speaks wretched Latin himself, so I'm along to help us Jews who are loyal. An interpreter, let us say.

"So what have we here? A nest for a family of wrens, or a den of stinking vultures?"

"I don't understand," Jerusha replied weakly. By this time David was walking carefully down the steps from the loft, and even Jonathan was working his way down from the top.

"Just don't move, madam." The dark man spoke a few words in Latin, and the evidently lower ranking Roman began to search the house, while the decurion stood in a more menacing pose. The Jewish soldier casually sat at the table. The decurion clearly didn't like the liberties the Jew was assuming, but hadn't decided what he should do about it.

The first place Jerusha saw the junior soldier search was the closet under the stairs. Finding it empty, he moved on.

"You don't know what this is about, do you?" the seated man asked Jerusha. "They never do. Are you or are you not Jerusha, the widow of Mordecai, and the kins-woman of Zachariah, the bloody bandit? Don't bother to deny it. We have already questioned his wife, Leah, though she claims to know nothing of his whereabouts."

"I am Jerusha, and Zachariah is my brother-by-marriage, but I haven't seen him in many months, and I, also, don't know what he's doing."

The Jewish soldier translated into Latin, and clearly urged a more thorough search. Jerusha's veil slid down to her shoulders, revealing her full, glossy hair, and a finely formed, slightly narrow face, with a healthy complexion and without the hollows so often seen in the cheeks and under the eyes of poor matrons, however young.

Jerusha was more angered than frightened by the man's gaze.

"I don't think you'll find Zachariah here. But I might as well offer to pour you some water. I'd offer you something stronger, but we don't have anything, as you can see."

"No, I see that you don't, and I suppose my friends won't find Zachariah here, either. I can say farewell to my popularity with our allies. But I'm glad to meet you," he said with a leer, which Jerusha ignored. "Maybe we'll meet again. I'm one of King Herod's men-at-arms, and high-ranking," he started with evidently unaccustomed bluster, quickly covering it with, "or smarter than most, anyway."

Jerusha could not prevent herself from asking, "Then why are you a lackey of the Romans?"

"Who is whose lackey?" he laughed. "King Herod uses Roman troops for his battles. Romans fought to put down the rebellion against us in Galilee, and many other places. There are only a couple of hundred of us, and thousands of our Roman cats' paws."

The younger Roman audibly muttered a few sentences, while searching.

Herod's man grinned. "He does not love our people or our land. He calls it a 'country of heat, dirt, scorpions, hidden daggers, and holy crackpots.' He does have a point, in a way."

Jerusha noted the Romans looked like veterans, as she had imagined them: Scuffed and cut leather facings, slightly dented helmets, patched tunics, sunburned skin criss-crossed with white scars, and, when they moved, purposeful but careful strides. Beside them, Herod's man would have appeared pampered, but for his sinister countenance.

Jerusha blurted out, "If these Romans are warriors, then why are they hunting down bandits, instead of fighting our wars?"

"Because the bandits are getting organized and they're killing Roman soldiers and officials, not Jews. Or, more importantly, not any of the King's men."

By now, David was avidly watching the red-crested decurion,

and making moves to embrace his legs. Jerusha called David to her, but all she could achieve was a transfer of affection from the Roman to Herod's man. *He's not very choosy,* Jerusha thought.

"Your boy is cute, and will someday make a soldier," said the dark man. "You, on the other hand, would make a good soldier's woman. How old are you, my dove?"

"Twenty-two." Jerusha resented his growing familiarity, and replaced her veils. But because she knew she was without respectable male kin and was too poor to have high connections, the man could say whatever he wished with impunity. *If Mordecai were still alive...,* Jerusha thought, paused, then finished, *he would have done nothing.*

"I have three sons," Jerusha added, hoping to discourage him.

"I prefer experienced women, especially if they're young and pretty," said Herod's man, untangling David as he rose from the table. The decurion, still standing by the door, gestured toward the sleeping-loft, and on receiving an affirmative response from the other Roman he barked a command and the three intruders departed Jerusha's house. She grabbed the rind of last night's pomegranate from the table and threw it at them as they were leaving. Herod's man warded it off with mock horror and a laugh, slamming the door behind him.

Jerusha wished she had thrown a spear instead of a rind. Someday she might.

<hr/>

Jerusha sat crosslegged on the street, with her back against one of the tallest limestone walls inside Jerusalem. She had two of her sons beside her and the baby in her lap. She had chosen this spot for several reasons, the main one being that the taller the wall, the smaller and more pitiful the beggars under it.

Beggary. Jerusha didn't know which she abhorred more:

being forced to pity others, or receiving that pity herself. Before beginning her new enterprise almost a month earlier, Jerusha had reasoned that with all the admonitions and commands in Judaic Law to be charitable to the poor, generous to beggars, bountiful to friends and strangers—give, give, give—it had to be *someone's* moral duty to *receive* all this charity. Maybe she was even helping people, by providing them an outlet for all their righteous piety. Thus far she had detected only a degraded self-righteousness on the part of her benefactors. So she had stopped justifying her new position in life, and returned the perceived though unspoken contempt with genuine unspoken contempt, reserving a generous portion for herself.

Jerusha had, of course, tried previously to work in Bethlehem. But hers was a town of shepherds, peasants, small artisans, and peddlers whose awnings were their only shops. Not many could afford to send their laundry out, or order their food in, or pay for any other services she knew how to provide. There must have been a few richer families, but none near her part of town, and all probably had their own servants. The under-employed were not in short supply in Bethlehem. Beggary was out of the question in such a place, once one had exploited one's immediate neighbors and acquaintances. So here she sat in Jerusalem.

She had to admit her takings almost equaled, and sometimes exceeded, the money Mordecai had brought home, and had given his life to earn. Her boys could eat, though her housekeeping suffered disastrously. What with the five-mile walk to Jerusalem at daybreak, and equally long walk back, over a rutted dirt road littered with pebbles, stones, and boulders, carrying Abraham and often Jonathan too, and stopping every hundred steps to rest herself and the boys, she left home too early and returned too late or too tired to care about the house or to cook more than the most rudimentary and portable food. The Romans were reputed to be the best road-builders in the world: why hadn't they replaced the one between Jerusalem and Bethlehem?

But her feet were getting tougher, and she was learning her profession. Jerusha's and the boys' clothing of rags was well-suited to it. She had learned to arrange her veils so passers-by could see the pitiful expression, which she had rehearsed. Her location in Jerusalem was the best she could find. A large water-fountain in the center of the square, newly built by Herod, where she could refresh herself and where strangers sat to converse and, perhaps, display their generosity to a beggar and her children.

She had her day of rest. Travel was unlawful during the Sabbath, and Sabbath-Eve was cut short to arrive home well before sunset.

Few other beggars were in Jerusha's chosen area. Many preferred the markets, on the theory that buyers had money, and forgetting that only newly arriving shoppers had much, and all had their minds on their own needs and wants. Many beggars preferred locations near the Temple, magnificently rebuilt by Herod, on the reasonable theory that that building, as the locus of piety, would be the center of charitable giving. Jerusha had tried the areas near the Temple Mount, even in the Court of the Gentiles. The endless, repetitive theological disputes among the learned loiterers confused and bored her, and distracted the people from putting money in her bowl. So she had settled on this busy but pleasant intersection, and it had proved a good choice.

Jerusha had considered letting cuts and scrapes on her body, and those of her children, fester awhile unattended, for added dramatic appeal, but was terrified of being mistaken for a family of lepers. So she and her boys simply sat there in their rags with their bowl in front of them. She sometimes cried out for alms, but it was mostly unnecessary. Her only major stage-managing was preventing the boys from getting too rambunctious and appearing too healthy. But, in between throwing pebbles at the wall and studying bugs, they were beginning, unconsciously, to mimic their mother's sorrowful or pleading expressions. The baby's occasional outbursts of crying didn't hurt Jerusha's business either. When David got too restless or talkative, she allowed him to run and play in a nearby, visible street, and sometimes let him escort Jonathan. David's one instruction was that he rejoin Jerusha, running joyfully only when no one was nearby or watching, to which rule he usually adhered.

Today Jerusha and her family had received only two small coins, from poor people, since her family had arrived not long before noon. During the hot, early afternoon hours of rest in Jerusalem, when traffic was usually sparse or non-existent, two better prospects approached the fountain and sat on its limestone edge.

One was a young man, clean-shaven and well-dressed. His clothes were a tasteful blend of Greek and Roman styles; a white tunic with a golden Greek key hem, and a toga-like cloak of fine linen with a silver clasp. Gold-stamped sandals. His hair was cut short in the modern manner. Jerusha recognized him for what she had heard described as a "Hellenized Jew"; almost non-existent in Bethlehem but common in Jerusalem. One who, however patriotic toward Judea in principle or religion, preferred the customs and way of life of more sophisticated lands to the "dirt, scorpions and holy men" of Palestine. *He likely has marble baths at his house, to lounge in daily,* thought Jerusha—*or does he use the new, public Roman baths to idle away his life? Oh, he can't go there; his circumcision would set him apart. Why did I think about that?* As he arrived, the Hellenized Jew had dropped a coin in her bowl, which failed to endear him to her.

The man's companion was clearly a rich Arab merchant, nearing middle age. His darker features, full and artificially curled black beard, colorful silken dress with gold threads, and heavy, gem-encrusted jewelry, all proclaimed this.

businesses, and gardens. Those places might not have been so grandiose, but somebody loved them."

Oh, I see, thought Jerusha, *now this popinjay is interested only in the welfare of the people.*

"...And the supreme act of insanity, installing the Pagan Roman Eagle over the Temple Gate!

[*And devout, too!*]

"Predictably, it was hacked down by two rabbis and several followers. I had to watch while they were all burned alive," he added, with obvious horror.

"That must have been appalling. But come now, you're taking this whole situation too seriously. What was it some Greek philosopher said? 'Only the dead have seen the end of war'... Or intrigue and murder, for that matter. As for the Zealots, the Romans will take care of them... Or *vice-versa*. Meanwhile, you sensible Jews have to keep the present balance, the alliance, if you will, between your King and the Roman Empire. And Herod knows how."

That's the first thing they've said that makes sense, thought Jerusha.

"Herod is old, dying, and mad." The Jew seemed to throw prudence to the wind as his voice rose.

"Wouldn't you be insane," responded the Arab, "if everyone was plotting to overthrow you? He's already had to murder two of his sons, and a third is awaiting execution. Not to mention the earlier killings of two of his wives and one thoroughly guilty mother-in-law. And now this talk of a new-born King to take Herod's throne. Or the throne of whoever is unlucky enough to win the dice-toss to succeed him."

"Well, you can wager Herod has his men looking for this Messiah. Especially since he no longer has to worry about a serious uprising by the nobility, the common Jews, or the Romans. Only the threat posed by one person," said the Jew.

"The child still has to grow up, and Herod will be dead by then. Maybe the Messiah will be another gift of your God like the Flood. In one of my commercial journeys I have heard of fellow learned Easterners—of much higher class than I so they should know—not only speaking of this new King, but actively *searching* for the child, to pay homage." The Arab shrugged. "Not being Jews, I don't know what good the Messiah will do *us*. Your God has never cared much about those of us 'Without the Law'."

"Sometimes it seems He cares little about us who are *within* the Law," said the Jew.

"Well, whatever happens, my friend, you and I won't live to see it, unless, of course, your God chooses to speed the growing process in time to free your people and make your gambling debts good." Then he laughed again. "Meanwhile, let's find a decent wine shop." The two men rose, stretched and smoothed their robes.

So, Jerusha thought, *you rich Jews and Arabs, and the Sanhedrin, and the Romans, and Herod, and the new "Messiah," and the "Zealots," all intrigue against each other over politics, while we, who simply want to survive, are oppressed and slaughtered by all sides. I have three little boys; when they're old enough, I suppose you'll each and all demand they join you, or suffer death?* She spat in the street.

The Arab merchant, not seeing the gesture, dropped a large gold coin in Jerusha's bowl, as he left with his friend.

We can go home early! thought Jerusha, not without gratitude. She arranged her veils more modestly, and started with her family through the back streets of Jerusalem, for the hard journey to Bethlehem.

Jerusha prepared a better supper than usual. This meal cheered the children, making them more lively while eating, and happier when settled in front of the open fireplace. Abraham fell asleep in his cradle almost immediately. Jonathan was studiously sticking his fingers in the cold ashes of last night's fire and applying black soot all over his face. David pushed one of the chairs over so he could sit by the fireplace and kick the cradle in a rhythm he thought was soothing, but which would have awakened a less placid baby and set him to panicked wailing. As it was, Jerusha could leave her children alone for awhile.

She lit her two table oil lamps from the embers in her oven, then, after reflecting, lit the hanging lamps, too, making the room cheerier than it had been since Mordecai's death. The lamps would use up the last of her oil, but the light might last all night.

Of course, the extra light forced Jerusha to notice how dirty and dingy the room had become. This might be her one chance to clean the place up for awhile, she thought, and set to dusting and scrubbing. Her thoughts often returned to the large gold coin she had been given, well hidden in her clothes, and she contemplated taking a day off tomorrow. Jerusha had never seen a gold coin, especially one of that size or design, and wondered how much it was worth. Would a money-changer in her neighborhood have the funds to break it into useable coins? Could she possibly trust him not to cheat her? These worries were less unpleasant than the ones to which she had been accustomed.

On the whole, Jerusha felt more at peace than she had for a long time.

Until the loud knock at her barred door.

CHAPTER 2

◆

A Voice in Rama

On hearing the knock, Jerusha had a moment of panic: Had the Arab merchant tracked her down to demand his coin back, realizing a mistake or regretting his generosity? Had a thief somehow known about the coin and followed them home, to rob her after dark?

The knock came again, louder. Jerusha called out, "Who is there?"

"A friend, with important news," came the answer. "For your sake, and that of your family, open the door." The male voice sounded authoritative, but furtive.

As she unbarred the door and started to open it a crack, the man struck it again with his sword-hilt, knocking it back against her. While Jerusha recovered her balance, the man rushed into the room and quickly shut the door behind him.

Jerusha recognized Herod's officer from his previous visit. "Why should I trust you? I don't even know your name."

"Call me 'Isaac'. You should trust me because you have no choice, my men are camped north of Bethlehem, and we're only a part of the main force. There will be an attack on this town later tonight. I risked all to come here this evening," he said. He did look tired, and uneasy. In a man who had previously appeared so powerful and self-assured, this demeanor frightened Jerusha more than did his words. He continued, mumbling, more to himself than to her, "I *don't* know why I came."

"But why would Herod attack Bethlehem?" she pleaded. The man seated himself at the table, without relaxing.

"There will be blood enough tonight no matter what I do, so I have come to warn you. I like you. I..." he interrupted himself, "and your children." He looked at the scene at the fireplace. The two older boys were looking at him. David seemed to remember him fondly. The man noticed Jonathan's sooty face. "One of them seems to have made himself an Ethiope, at the moment."

"But what..."

"The King has it in his head a little child is trying to kill him. The danger seems to come from Bethlehem, though how a boy under the age of two could wield a dagger, much less a sword or javelin, is beyond my poor comprehension. But we have orders to kill them all."

"Kill *who* all?" Jerusha couldn't stay still in her furious impatience. She sat down, jumped up again, started pacing, and then forced herself to sit again while the soldier spoke.

"All the boy-children in Bethlehem two years old and younger. Lucky we weren't here during the census a while back... there were too many people in town then."

Jerusha's mind balked at the mental image "Isaac's" words conjured. "But King Herod is a *Jew*! He cannot kill the innocent children of his own people!"

"Herod is not a Jew. He and his father were Edomites, Arab Pagans. Antipater had his son circumcised only to secure the Jewish kingdom for him." The officer's frustration at Jerusha's naiveté was beginning to equal her level of impatience. He feigned relaxation, clearly trying to recover the detached cynicism of his previous visit. "And Herod's esteemed allies are Romans. They believe parents can kill any children who displease them until they reach the age of fourteen years. Personally, I think the Roman way works out well. One can see whether the child is turning out right, and then decide whether the child is really wanted. Anyway, our own views don't matter in this.

"You can believe me or not: *We are going to kill the male infants* of Bethlehem later tonight. I had to come alone, in advance, to warn and help you."

"Why? How?" Jerusha's mind was spinning.

"I told you: I like you. My motives are totally selfish. I've been watching you. In the market. And, yes, while you were begging in Jerusalem. And struggling home at night, with your children."

"You never put any money in my bowl, if you were there."

"No. I don't want you to think about me that way. I want... never mind." He looked embarrassed. "So, *how* can I help you? That's a good question. You don't seem to have the presence of mind right at this moment to act on my advice. But advice is all I can give you. Can you listen?"

"I'll try," she said. *And I'll certainly try to understand, and to act.* She couldn't afford not to believe him. Jerusha had no time to think about his more personal reference to her.

Isaac ordered Jerusha to sit down across from him, and then sat straight, leaned forward, and looked into her eyes. Jerusha had never before seen such a cold stare. She willed herself not to avert her eyes.

"First, you must keep your mouth shut," he began. "Any general panic, especially in advance, and we'll have to kill the whole population. Secondly, you must send your three boys out of Bethlehem. Hide them in the mountains and caves south of here within an hour or two, at most, or lose them forever. But you, Jerusha, have to remain behind, or you and your family will *seen all of the town. The boys would be lost within fifty or a hundred steps. They certainly couldn't make it to the valleys and hills beyond without being seen, and they couldn't endure through the night in the wilderness. What am I dreaming about? Neither of the older boys could carry Abraham, or even stay together.* Jerusha could think of no adult who could accompany them and who had no children of his or her own to protect, even if she could risk explaining the reason and urgency of this sudden exodus. She, herself, couldn't take them. The man had meant what he said. She and her children would be hunted down and killed, if it meant mounting an additional military operation.

I will have to hide my sons here. But how will I get replacements... street boys? Herod's man patently knew Jerusalem, but apparently, knew almost nothing about Bethlehem. For the same reason there were almost no beggars in Jerusha's town, there were few street urchins. Those not taken in locally ended up in the city to the north, or, perhaps, starved. *And regardless,* thought Jerusha, *I'd never deliberately lure strange children to their deaths. I'll think about that later.* First, she had to hide her sons.

Jerusha rose and began searching for a hiding-place in the large room. Each place she looked was either too obvious, like the cabinet under the loft stairs and the wooden clothes box, or too small for even Abraham, like niches caused by unevenness in the walls, and the food cabinet. She started to move around her few pieces of furniture before realizing the futility of putting cloths over them. As though soldiers wouldn't look underneath! She gave a thought to the tight chimney, then snorted in disgust. She slowly worked her way around the room, tapping the white-washed walls with her fist and the spoon. None had loose or hollow spaces. Except for the patched place where there had once been a back door. Jerusha began looking for something to pry a board or rubble out of it, and laid makeshift tools out on the table, when the thought occurred that even if she removed enough, she would merely expose the original back door, hardly a useful idea. Not only would it be expected, but any attempt to replace the filler would be immediately visible. And there was no point in using the back door; all alleys and privies would be as thoroughly patrolled as the streets. One glance up at the narrow ceiling joists removed them as a possibility...too low; any irregularity would show, and she could not conceive of a stranger in a hostile house not looking over his head.

Hurry, Jerusha could almost hear 'Isaac'—or whatever his name was—urging, *or you and I will watch your boys die together.*

Jerusha turned her attention to the sleeping-loft, and went up the stairs. The straw pallets were out of the question; the children quickly found each other under them in their seeking-games. The straw on the floor was too thin, and even if she could get enough new straw, it would be highly suspicious. *The fact I'm thinking like this shows it's hopeless.* She stifled a sob and willed her mind to get back to work.

Hurry, or lose them forever.

The walls of her house up to the rafters were very thick. Jerusha fetched a strong chair from downstairs, and moved it around the loft-room climbing on it at intervals. The left wall had joists which supported the rafters, resting atop the entire thickness of the wall, but there was enough space between rafters for small children. Her heart sank when she realized that in the reflected and filtered light from downstairs, the undersides of the cross-boards which held the roof tiles were light in color— *shining in mockery of me*, her disordered mind told her. Anything or anyone placed there would break the pattern and stand out. Jerusha tried the back wall of the loft but found that, having no joists to support, the top was visible its entire length, and gleaming with whitewash and light-gray dust.

When Jerusha examined the top edge of the right wall, she felt a wild relief. The wall supported joists precisely as did the opposing wall, and the rafters were the right distance apart. But over much of the space above the wall, half of the tiles had come loose and fallen off, showing a night sky that was almost black. The cross-boards had rotted to brown-black due to exposure. Rain had not come into the loft because the top of the wall was thick and slanted inward, so the water running off the other tiles had never found its way inside. Jerusha could hide her boys here by covering them with dark rags and blankets. *If* the remaining, rotted boards didn't break, *if* more tiles didn't fall, and *if* the children could stay absolutely silent. Any hope at all was better than none.

[Hurry! Hurry!]

Jerusha went downstairs to bring up the children, carrying Abraham and Jonathan under her arms like sacks of grain, and letting David work his way up. Though she had heard whimpering from them while she was upstairs alone, the older children were now so frightened they were blessedly silent, and placid Abraham was asleep as soon as he was temporarily laid on a pallet.

After collecting dark blankets and examining the spaces on the wall, she climbed the chair with Jonathan, the middle child, and placed him between the two joists left of center, pushing him back as far as he could go without his being pushed off the wall. She stuffed his mouth with a rag, small enough that he could chew on it without choking.

"We're going to play a quiet game. The rag has to be there, but don't make a noise." Jonathan clearly didn't understand her, but he was too scared to protest. Jerusha then covered him with a blanket, insuring he had room to breathe behind the loose part at the top.

Then Jerusha placed the baby, Abraham, in the next space between joists on the right, pushing him more gently, both to keep him asleep as long as possible and to keep his small body supported by the rotted tile-board.

In front of him, on the inside, she placed her oldest. "David, you are the only one who can keep the others quiet, like you did when we were begging. Hold onto Abraham." *Any* sound would be fatal if the soldiers were in the loft, but maybe not if they were downstairs. "You'll hear men tramping about below and up here. Don't make a sound, and don't move until I come up to get you." *God of our fathers, please make him understand me.* After covering David and Abraham with a darker blanket, she carried the chair back downstairs, leaning on the railing.

Halfway down, she said, "Remember, not a sound." *This isn't going to work.* "I love you David, I love you Jonathan, I love you Abraham."

Most of the oil-lamps had burned out downstairs; the better to hide by.

Jerusha sat down at the table. *Now all I have to do is find some non-existent street children and lure them into my house. In a matter of minutes.* She gave in to despair, and sobbed softly. Slowly, outside sounds began to intrude on her consciousness. Distant screams, shouts, and ululations. The sounds of violence and killing and grief. Extreme grief. *Then this whole thing isn't merely a horrible dream.* She was surprised to find she had still held a thread of hope that it was. The street noises were slowly coming closer.

Almost immediately, there was knocking at Jerusha's door. After a short panic, she realized the street sounds were still too far away for the soldiers to be here already, and the knock, though determined, was not powerful enough to be an army bent on mayhem.

She lifted the bar and was again pushed off her balance, this time by her sister-in- law Leah, carrying two of her four children.

Leah leaned her back against the closed but unbarred door and tried to talk, but her wails made her nearly unintelligible. After a few false starts, she blurted, "They said they were looking for *boys*, but they killed my *Esther*! They didn't notice or care she was a *girl*!"

Well, thought Jerusha hysterically, *no more need for that dowry you were so proud and worried about*. Jerusha almost giggled until the enormity of her thoughts struck her. *Is my mind that far gone?* Esther was her niece, after all.

Leah struggled to continue. "After that, we got away. I saw mothers holding up their children's rags, showing female private parts, to prove they weren't boy-children. It didn't help much... blood was everywhere.

"Then they caught up with us again, long enough to kill my Hosea, the image of his father...blood all over the children... Blood all over the soldiers. We got away again...Herod's soldiers... they're coming...They'll get the others!" She was still holding onto her remaining children by a limb apiece, her eyes rolling uncontrollably. Leah had to gasp for breath between outbursts, and was on the brink of hysteria, if not already there.

"Calm down or I can't help you," Jerusha said soothingly, as though she were above all the excitement. She brought a bowl of water from the pitcher. "Now tell me. You live north of town, almost on the way to Jerusalem. Why did you come here? Bethlehem is where the trouble is!"

"I saw the men marching on Bethlehem from the north. I was scared. I didn't know why. I do now. They searched my house but I was keeping ahead of them, carrying and pushing my four. I got lost in the first few streets of town. They caught us *twice*, but the three of us got away." Leah slumped to the floor, and dropped her two remaining sons, Amos, and Samuel the smallest. Both began to cry, with the hoarse sounds of too much practice.

"But why did you come *here*, to *my* house?" Outside, the noise of shouting and screaming, and occasional metallic sounds of resistance with knives or swords, and smashing of wooden furniture, became louder.

Each loud noise punctuated a sentence of Leah's. "Jerusha, you're my only family. I trust you. And you're smarter than I am. I know it. I don't know where Zachariah is. I helped you once, didn't I? Didn't I help you? You can't let them kill my last two. You're young; you can have more, but I...They killed my two oldest in the street. Oh Esther! Oh Hosea! I couldn't fight for them, not with the other two...Leah pauses for breath... Every street I went down had soldiers in the cross-streets! All killing children! Ripping them from their mothers' arms! Soldiers everywhere, covered in blood, they glistened red under their torches, in every street, going in all directions. And the screams from the houses! It's a miracle, God's name be praised, we got here..."

"Such a miracle!" snapped Jerusha. "*I* have children too! Why do you lead *yours* here? Shut up! I have to think, and I'm so tired."

Herod's man had told her, *You're shrewder and harder than you think you are, Jerusha.* Here was the chance to prove it. "Remember, Leah, *you* brought your children here. *I* did not. *You* married Zachariah; I did not. And he is the only man who could have helped us."

"What can we do?" sobbed Leah.

Jerusha almost choked before forcing herself to answer. "There is only one place to hide in the whole house. The cabinet under the stairs. It was cramped enough when you slept there alone. If you keep your children quiet maybe God will be merciful to you." Her voice began to crack. "Your coming here may turn out to be a blessing." *To whom, would be a different matter,* thought Jerusha, shamefully.

Leah looked grateful for a moment, but then shook her head doubtfully. "Maybe we should keep running..."

But Jerusha had proceeded too far. "They're already on our street—listen to them! You can't out-run them once they see you. I give you my word you and your children are completely safe in that cabinet," Jerusha lied. The Romans, and specifically Herod's man, had chosen it as the first place to search.

With Jerusha's help, Leah pushed her children in the small cabinet, and closed the door behind her.

Now I have committed perjury. Jerusha couldn't remember if she had ever lied before. Worse, Jerusha understood the meaning of her greater sin, breaking the Sixth Commandment: "Thou shalt do no murder." That must include participating in murder. She had no other choice, she reasoned; her own children were in danger. Besides, everyone else was killing tonight. At present the street noise was loud enough to cover any few noises from her children in the loft.

Jerusha barred the front door, and sat at the table. There was nothing to do but wait and try to compose her mind. She thought to pray, but was certain her prayers would not be heard. Besides, she had forgotten how. She looked at the table and noticed that of the few items she had placed there earlier for probing walls or removing rubble, one was missing: her kitchen knife. Leah must have snatched it on her way to the cabinet. But there was no time to think. She heard a pounding at the door, which would admit of no other interpretation: soldiers.

Jerusha got up and unbarred the door, knowing it would be broken down anyway; this time, she was able to avoid the swinging door. Three men entered the room—no, four. The fourth, behind the others, outlined the first three from behind with his torch, while Jerusha's remaining oil-lamps showed their fronts.

Three *devils* had burst into her house! *Leah was right,* thought Jerusha, *they were red men!* Breastplates, helmets, arms, tunics, legs, sandals, and their weapons, were all bright with smeared blood. They might all have been painted statues of Satan, as she had always pictured him. Except for one. He wore the dark clothes of the officer who had visited twice earlier. And he, too, had streaks and drops of blood on his breastplate and arms.

Herod's officer shouted in a stentorian voice as in a proclamation, "Bring forth all male children here of the age of two years or younger. This, in the name of King Herod the Great!"

"There are no children here. Leave this house in peace," answered Jerusha.

"What? Woman, I know they are here!" In a much lower tone he said, "Have you lost your senses, Jerusha? Do you want to die along with your children when we catch them? Please tell me I didn't misjudge you!"

"I said," she repeated loudly, "there are no children in this house." Meanwhile, she moved protectively near the cabinet under the stairs, and made exaggerated glances toward it.

The officer grinned, relieved. "Oh, *that's* how you want to play it." He gestured to two of his men who were not carrying the torch. "Search under the stairs and drag them out."

The men forced open the cabinet door and looked in. "There're two children there, along with a woman."

"Kill the children." The soldier re-entered the cabinet. There were shouts, male and female, from under the stairs. Jerusha covered her ears with her hands, but couldn't shut out the sounds.

"The fat bitch stabbed me!" groaned the red-clad soldier, staggering from the cabinet. Fresh blood ran from his side, mixing with the other blood already beginning to darken, before he fell to the floor. The second soldier, backed by the torchman, entered, his sword drawn. Jerusha heard a short scream from Leah, and a longer, but abruptly ended, wail from a child.

"I got them all," said the second red-man, and walked into view, triumphantly raising his sword.

"Have the wounded man carried back to the Citadel," Isaac commanded the executioner. "Get some men from the street, and keep one here with you to take his place," pointing at the wounded man moaning on the floor. The casualty was taken out on a stretcher made from two spears.

Isaac addressed Jerusha, quietly but bitterly, "You have betrayed me. *My* men are *my* sons, as dear to me as yours are to you. You didn't think of that did you? I should have known civilians can't be trusted, but I was blinded by sentimentality.

"Since you supplied the urchins their armed guard, *her* death be on your head as well. All agreements are off."

To the remaining soldiers he snapped, "Search this house from top to bottom. Test all floors and walls; climb the loft and the beams and rafters. Are there not still children here, Jerusha? Let us see, shall we?" Jerusha's last hope fled.

While the replacement soldier laboriously dragged Leah, Amos and Samuel out of the cubicle and into the middle of the room, the other two soldiers, including the torch-bearer, mounted the stairs to the loft. Jerusha noted vaguely that their footprints were red on the steps. At the table, Herod's officer kept an eye on Jerusha, and sometimes a hand or arm, to prevent her from interfering. Soon Jerusha could hear the sound of straw pallets being overturned, and several unidentifiable noises. Suddenly she saw the torchlight upstairs silhouetting a couple of small limbs and a torso. She heard one of her son's screams ending abruptly as she saw the shadow of rapid and final sword strokes plunged across the torchlit walls and rafters.

A soldier's voice shouted down, "Found them! Little bastards were hidden on top of the wall. The biggest one tried to break through the tiles. They're all dead. There were three. I cut their throats to make sure. Let'em stay up there and rot."

Jerusha's own screaming didn't obscure the shouted words, and when she fell on the floor, the mercy of unconsciousness didn't come.

Herod's officer held a strange mixture of admiration and contempt in his voice. "I didn't really think you could do any of it, Jerusha. You might have won, had you not tried to ambush us." He added derisively, "Five dead little traitors and one dead Zealot bandit isn't a bad catch, though they will never make up for my soldier. Think on it, Jerusha. You might have become the wife of an officer of the Royal Guard!

"Nevertheless," Isaac continued, "I keep my word," he said, as he put a large napkin-wrapped bundle on the table. "The food was meant for your boys when they returned, but it ought to go further with only one mouth to feed, thanks to you." He called his men together and they all stamped out without a backward glance.

Jerusha struggled off the floor and went to bar the door, then saw no point in it. She went upstairs slowly, gripping the rail as if to drag herself along. She found her boys, two still on the wall but uncovered, and one on the floor sprawled unnaturally. David. His head had been severed, and lay against the wall. Jerusha wrapped a rag around the head and carried it downstairs, as carefully as she would a newborn baby, placing it beside Leah. She then did the same for David's body, careful to avoid the blood-saturated straw under it, and arranged the complete corpse below. With the other boys upstairs she was able to gather rags from corners sufficient to cover their heads and necks, and carry them downstairs to lay beside David. She took one more trip to collect blankets, which she stretched over each of her sons, and over Leah. Having exhausted her supply of bed-clothes, she went to the clothes-box and brought children's rags to cover Leah's boys.

Jerusha finally fell into a chair and pulled it to the table, laying her head on her arms. She could still hear screaming coming from all quarters of Bethlehem; she would hear it for days, in her mind. After awhile her arm, seemingly of its own volition, reached toward a small loaf that had fallen out of the bundle left by Herod's man. She recoiled, and brought her arm back to cradle her head on the table. The last oil-lamp guttered out.

"Jerusha, wake up! It's me, Zachariah." He shook her shoulder.

Morning had come with Jerusha in the same position, sprawled across the table. The barley loaf still lay near the bundle of food. Jerusha was disoriented for a moment, and then began to scream, as she remembered last night. Her screams rose to a crescendo and then became voiceless, as her body rocked to and fro in inexpressible agony. She had never made such sounds before.

"Hush, Jerusha. This will pass." When, after awhile, he thought she could hear him, Zachariah spoke again, more urgently. "I've looked everywhere near my home, but I can't find Leah and my children. Do you have any idea where they are?" He was pleading. Despite the daylight from the open door behind him, he and Jerusha were on the wrong side of the table to see the dark bundles of horror on the other side. Zachariah appeared as he had for years, except for the worry and suppressed panic on his face and in his voice. His age was showing, with deep hollows in his cheeks. His beard and hair were scragglier than she remembered.

Jerusha pointed over the table to the bundles on the floor.

Zachariah rushed around the table, only to stop short at the six bodies. "No! God of Abraham! It can't be!" He stepped softly to the largest, and pulled the blanket back from Leah's face. He cradled her head, and tenderly cooed, "Leah...Leah..." He sighed deeply. "And which are my little ones?"

Jerusha cleared her throat before snapping at him, "And where were *you* last night?" She then softened her tone, "Esther and Hosea were killed before they got here. Amos and Samuel are on the left. Those are my three on the right." She walked to Jonathan's body to cover his foot where the blanket had fallen off. "They said only two years old and younger. But one of mine and two of yours were older than that. And one of yours was a girl."

Zachariah was uncovering and re-covering the faces of his two boys, moaning softly. What Jerusha said finally got through. "They didn't care. I've seen blood-lust before; there's no controlling it."

Gradually Zachariah and Jerusha began hearing the screams from outside which had died out for awhile during the night. Mothers were awakening to the remembered horror of having lost their children; others had not slept, but, hoarse from screaming, their throats and voices had failed them for a time and had directly renewed.

Zachariah began to mumble prayers, interspersed with Scripture. Jerusha remembered the Zealots were an offshoot of the Pharisees, and deeply devout in their rituals. Zachariah addressed Jerusha, "Can this be worse than the condition of Judea at the time of the Prophet Jeremiah?" He quoted the latter in a low voice, "'In Rama was there a voice heard, lamentation, and weeping, and great mourning, Rachel weeping for her children, and would not be comforted, because they are not.'"

"But *why* did all this happen? Don't simply tell me it was 'foretold'. There has to be a reason; what do you know about it? They didn't tell me *anything* except some babble about an infant king-killer."

"It's more complicated than that." Zachariah sat on the hearth of the open fireplace so he could keep an eye on his dead family. Unconsciously, he reached in for ashes and sprinkled them on his head, the ancient ritual for mourning. "King Herod heard that a new king, a Messiah for the Jewish people, was born recently in Bethlehem, but he didn't know exactly who, or when. Scripture says it would happen in the City of David. But in my readings, not one family in a thousand, in all of Judea, would qualify according to the prophesies. And where were the crowds, the proclamations, the delegations? Have you seen them? So, not having any better idea how to hold on to his crumbling throne, his dynasty, and his worthless, disease-ridden life, Herod decided to kill *all* the male children in this area. He's learned a lot from our Roman masters.

Much good it will do him. Soon, the Romans will end this farce and annex Judea officially."

Jerusha stopped him. "You mean my poor boys were killed because the parents of another child had the ambition to take Herod's throne? I'll wager the rich, who probably include this evil family, were spared."

"No. None. Herod cares nothing about the wealth or position of a few Jews. He cares only about his own life and the last shreds of his power.

"Somewhere there is a mother who, through greed or insanity, made up this story for her man-child. My only consolation is that her offspring must have perished with the others. I hope he died in fear and pain, and his mother is suffering more pain; maybe we can hear her screaming today." Jerusha had never heard such hatred in Zachariah's voice.

"Nothing less will cleanse our land of such greed-inspired blasphemy. I tell you, Jerusha, there's only one way to free our land and God's people. A general uprising against the Romans. That is what we Zealots are working toward."

Zachariah's fulminations died off at the loud cadence of a teamster in the street. With Jerusha's door open, they could hear the creaking wheels of his donkey cart.

The teamster's voice was hoarse from repetition. "Bring us the dead children! We will bury them. We are your neighbors. They will be buried according to the Law."

Zachariah rose and shouted, "In here!"

"No!" Jerusha threw herself down beside her children, with her arm held protectively across them. "I won't give them to anyone!"

"My sister, they must be buried, and there are too many for each family to bury its own."

Jerusha, accepting the inevitable, leaned back on her heels. But when she saw Zachariah kissing the dead foreheads of Leah, Amos, and Samuel, she turned her eyes away, as they filled with tears again.

As the teamster entered, he was surprised by the number of bodies. "What is this, a battlefield?"

"Yes!" exclaimed Zachariah.

"One of them is grown. I don't know if my wagon will carry all these, but it's fresh-emptied, so we can try. Tie a name on each body; we'll mark the graves the best we can, considering the hurry and how close together they'll be crammed."

Jerusha cringed. Zachariah began marking all the dead, since Jerusha could not write. He then helped carry the bodies out, starting with his own family. When the bodies were gone, Jerusha slowly pitched out the stained floor rushes, and poured water on the bloody dirt, scraping at places with the spoon.

The teamster came back in and addressed Zachariah. "Look here, man, we can use your help with all the others. You're strong. With all the digging and hauling, we need anyone we can get. Soon, before disease sets in, and within the one day prescribed by the Law. We'd ask the women to help, but most were mothers, and, well..."

"No," said Zachariah, "I must comfort my sister-in-law."

"As you will." The teamster left.

Zachariah turned to Jerusha. "You asked where I was yesterday. My men and I were five miles north of Jerusalem, ambushing a Roman detachment bringing arms, and a new concubine, to King Herod. We killed them all. The arms would have been used to kill Jews. I don't care where the concubine would have gone; she would have got little pleasure from the King at his age. We wondered why Roman soldiers were doing escort duty; they were far outside of their customary patrols from Jerusalem to the coast. Fair game, at little risk to us. A sound military decision on our part. Now I realize the Romans were there because Herod's men-at-arms had been ordered *here*.

"Our spies in Jerusalem reported to us. Being the only man from Bethlehem, I spent the whole night coming home through rocks and thorn-bushes, with torn sandals and bloody feet only to arrive too late.

"Should I have stayed at home all along? To what end? To be killed as a Zealot weeks ago? To grow fat and happy while my country died and our God was spat upon?

"Had I known this was going to happen, I would have been here, and saved both our families, God willing. I did *not* know, and will allow no civilian to condemn me, while my men are still out there dying."

Again, Jerusha was forcibly reminded of this strange bond among warriors. To her no other affection was significant when compared to the love of a mother for her child. Zachariah tentatively put his arm around Jerusha, who was still seated at the table. "Jerusha, I promise to get you revenge. We're arming ourselves from the supplies of our enemies, and we grow stronger. Our cause is just. The Romans are corrupting the whole country through Herod whom they keep in power, you know. But Herod will be dead soon, and those of his sons whom he has not already killed will be fighting over his puppet throne and the few lands the Romans give them. You *will* get your revenge for Mordecai and for your sons."

Jerusha finally spoke, "My husband was killed by poor workmanship on a scaffold, *not* by the Romans. More likely the work of some sloppy conscript or a foreign slave than a Roman centurion. And my children were killed by Herod's men, not Romans."

Zachariah responded with the tone and emphasis one would use to a child: "It was the great *Roman* Marcus Antonius who installed Herod as King of the Jews...during one of the times when Marcus could tear himself away from his lover, Cleopatra of Egypt. So the blame always comes down to the Romans."

The moment Jerusha dreaded was here. "But *your* family, Leah, Amos, and Samuel." Her tears started afresh. "I must tell you something which you have to know, but won't want to hear."

"What?" he interrupted angrily, "the details of their deaths? That my foolish wife chose to come here, bringing all this death to you? You're right, I don't want to hear it. Leah must have loved and trusted you well, Jerusha.

"Some of the blame goes to the men who sat around waiting for the Messiah, when they should have been fighting. Only you, Jerusha, remain innocent. Finish your grief, then wash the tears off your face."

"But I *do* bear guilt, more than I can ever atone for. Zachariah, I...I..." The time for confession had passed. Jerusha would have to live the rest of her life with the memory of enticing — almost forcing — Leah's family into the cupboard while knowing the consequences.

She continued, on a tangent. "Zachariah, was all this really caused because of the ambition of a false Messiah? I must know, for I, myself, have been tempted into sin. I loved my children more than I loved God Himself. And I have lost all."

"The guilty will atone for us. We'll see to that. Suffer your grief, then fashion it into hate. I must go." On his way to the door Zachariah took some fruit and bread from the bundle on the table.

If Zachariah knew the price Herod's food cost me and his family, he wouldn't touch it, Jerusha was certain. As Zachariah was leaving, she called after him, "I have my own hate, Zachariah, which you can neither increase nor diminish. I do not think this 'Messiah' is dead."

Zachariah pulled the door closed behind him. Jerusha lifted the bar which had failed to keep evil out of her house, and dropped it into its slot with a sound of finality, as though closing her own prison door.

CHAPTER 3

In the Sweat of Thy Face...

Jerusha's movements during the next week consisted primarily of dragging her sleeping-pallet downstairs, where she could doze intermittently, away from the horror in the loft. The only evidence left was the blood of her children, but it was a long time before she could gather rags and a bowl of water, mount the stairs again, and try to clean up the gore, repeatedly. She did a good job of it, even destroying the vast amount of straw which had been blood-soaked, splattered or stepped on by bloody sandals, and hardened, but in her mind she could still see the outline of dark red on the whitewashed walls. She cleaned up the closet under the stairs, too, but that could be closed off, out of sight and almost out of mind. So she lived downstairs, in the kitchen area.

During this time, Jerusha drank some from the large pitcher of water, refilling it from the public trough on the street, and ate the food that remained in the cupboard; but she saved the now-stale bread and cheese the soldier had brought until extreme hunger overcame her loathing. She limited her steps outside the door to her trip for water, and to empty her chamberpot regularly. She said nothing, and tried to think as little as possible. Having no more lamp-oil, she spent her evenings in total darkness. Somewhere in the darkness, lost in the black night of anguish and despair, she changed grief and guilt to hate. The Sabbath came and went without Jerusha's notice, which fact would have been unremarked by her neighbors, occupied as they were with their own grief.

After a week Jerusha fully realized she must survive and, if possible, prosper. She took out the gold coin the Arab had given her, and sought out a moneylender in another part of Bethlehem. She employed her usual caution, if not suspiciousness, in choosing the shop. Those with awnings and portable furniture she dismissed without further thought; she was seeking an interior street-level room, with built-in fixtures, and signs of long occupation: stability and trustworthiness. On the other hand, the place could not face on a busy street; most commercial establishments kept their doors wide open during the day, and Jerusha did not want passersby to observe her financial transactions, or guess she would be leaving a moneychanger with a full purse. She found what she considered the perfect shop situated on a narrow, uncrowded side street, but close enough to high-street crowds to seek help in an emergency. She mentally mapped her route home in advance.

The large number of coins she got in exchange for her gold astonished her, though she had dickered with the moneylender anyway, accusing him of cheating her. He probably had, she thought, if he judged her a thief by her filthy clothing and utter ignorance of the nature of the coin. But now Jerusha had enough useable money to last her for weeks, if she was careful, ate as sparingly as she had until then, and continued to live as a hermit. She would do so.

But even in this later isolation, Jerusha listened carefully to gossip during her few trips to the market, and discovered a surprising economic result of the raid on Bethlehem.

Jerusha had known she could never return to begging for a living. Whatever they meant to *her*, Jerusha's children had served as excellent props to beggary. Long before the night of terror she had noted the fact that childless beggars, however lame or blind, were not as successful as she had been. Nor, she thought, could she again inhabit the streets where she had been happy with her three beloved sons. Besides, as unselfconscious as Jerusha was by nature, even she had noticed that her current bitterness showed in her face, and sometimes frightened passersby.

By patching together remarks overheard at the markets, Jerusha learned that her employment opportunities in Bethlehem had expanded greatly. The generation of boy-children which was annihilated had been too young to add to family income or assist in chores, and yet old enough to add to family expenses, especially in food and services. The result of the murders was that most families would now have more money, whatever their station in life, at least until younger generations of children were born. Simultaneously, a significant number of mothers were, quite literally, prostrate with grief, and unable to accomplish the simplest of household duties. Jerusha considered some of these women weaklings, but knew others were genuinely destroyed mentally or emotionally. Almost all families had previously suffered high childhood mortality –– Jerusha and Mordecai had been exceptions –– and therefore had compensated by increased efforts at fertility, through early and not always voluntary marriage and frequent remarriage. But not until now had such devastation visited the whole town. And this was in addition to the continued, natural deaths of older children and infant daughters. Many mothers lacked sufficient emotional resilience to adjust. Jerusha was stronger than most and intended to survive at all costs. Increasingly she was coming to believe she had a mission, though she was not yet sure what it might be.

Jerusha knew if she wanted employment, she had to appear respectable and clean –– but not prosperous. Mordecai's old clothing was easily redesigned, with a few items, including modest veils, underclothing, notions, and feminine details bought cheaply at the markets. Unlike many female job-seekers, she owned a house which prospective employers could visit to verify her respectability. Most importantly, she practiced courteous, or subservient in her opinion, expressions, even an occasional smile. With a few more days of practice Jerusha appeared young, eager, and sympathetic, at least superficially.

What to do for a living? Laundry? She found two old barrels which she scrubbed out, and bought cheap chemicals, dyes, and sweet-smelling herbs. Perhaps food? She had always been an excellent cook, and bought enough staples to last her through her first few meals; the customers would have to pay for the meats and more expensive herbs and vegetables. Delivery would be no problem; she could run fast enough to serve hot food or cook it at the houses of patrons.

House cleaning only required her presence and energy, on an hourly, daily, or weekly basis.

Jerusha soon acquired these employments and more: sewing; watching after children who had survived the Raid; nursing; paid companion to the elderly and lonely; caring for the occasional domestic animal; even some little carpentry and repair work, the skills for which she had learned from Mordecai.

But within a year she discovered her services had come in to such demand she could reject certain types of employment. She began by refusing any work which involved caring for children. Each child reminded her of her own sorrows and guilt, without assuaging them. Then she gave up laundry and house cleaning, as too strenuous for too little return. Finally she could no longer abide companionship to the weak or elderly; it had forced her back into feigned pity.

By the second year the only employments she accepted were cooking and sewing, at which she was becoming quite accomplished. Jerusha's dinners, personally delivered, were improved not only by her own innovations, but by rare fruits, vegetables, and seeds, herbs, and spices, as well as game common to the area near Bethlehem and permissible under Jewish dietary laws. Seldom did she cook a meat without plums, apricots, dates and nuts combined in such a way as to provide new tastes without revealing the ingredients. She discovered the shops and stands where she could buy the finest quality of fresh and ripe produce at the most reasonable prices: pomegranates, eggplant, saffron which she also used for dyes, figs, grapes, olives, hibiscus for tea, and hyssop for both tea and medicinal poultices.

Similarly, as a seamstress she found materials no one else did. Not only silks, satins, and velvets, but strange-colored dyes from far-off lands, gold threads that did not break after the second or third wearing, and beads, which though not true gems, were colorful and of a gleam to shame some of the more expensive stones. Jerusha invented ways of stitching that took less of her time and yet resisted wear and unravelling as no common stitches did. She developed a curiosity about new and interesting clothing styles, sometimes walking to Jerusalem to study sophisticated travelers from all parts of the world. Despite her developing taste, she kept her own clothes simple and cheap. She knew her place.

Jerusha was shocked to learn how many husbands managed to survive their grief over the death of their sons and the incapacitations of their wives to attempt to satisfy their sexual desires with her. But she successfully resisted them without the loss of a customer. Moreover, she left them all ashamed of their advances. Her secret objections were not moral, but visceral. Some of the men were quite attractive and personable. But all were men: Like Mordecai, like "Isaac," like the Helenized Jew and the Arab, like Herod, like the Roman soldiers. Like her sons might have become had they been allowed to grow to maturity. But her sons had not been allowed to grow up, because of older males, like the ones who wanted her now. Men who did nothing to save the children of Bethlehem, either their own or hers. Or, of course, Leah's.

Jerusha, still young and quite attractive, was also properly approached by single men of her own approximate age; bachelors and young widowers, honorably courting. Female death in childbirth was frequent enough that widowers were common. Some were encumbered with a child or two, a situation Jerusha could not tolerate while jealously husbanding her own unhappy memories. Because the Raid had caused such family chaos in Bethlehem, the old class system of arranged marriages, complete with dowries, was temporarily suspended in the vicinity. Jerusha wondered whether the loss of a generation of children caused a mass impulse to mate and produce replacements. It certainly had not in her own case.

But she could neither deny her vague attraction to some of them nor her own occasional sexual desires, however diminished and suppressed. Once or twice, Jerusha considered indulging in discreet though illicit coupling with one or another of her more persistent suitors. She knew a possible conception from such a union could be terminated, in Jerusalem, if not in Bethlehem. But the thought always eventually brought her to the revelation that such a procedure was too excruciatingly similar to what had happened in what she now habitually thought of as the Night of Horror. The concept of probing into her most secret of places to slice up another baby was, ultimately, unthinkable.

By her third year of independence the competition among Bethlehem residents who wanted Jerusha's services had driven away many of her original customers, who were, anyway, giving birth to more children, thus limiting their ability to pay for luxuries. This was no disappointment to Jerusha, who considered their joy after each new birth to be a betrayal of the memory of their own children, and hers—and Leah's, who were killed during the Night of Horror.

As the normal, though less-than-prosperous, economy of Bethlehem slowly returned, the comparatively well-off increasingly employed Jerusha's services, at much higher pay, requiring fewer hours of toil on her part. A few of the local trade associations attempted to discourage Jerusha, but somehow they were quieted by anonymous customers of hers. Jerusha's sewing skills now far surpassed those of her wealthier customers' household servants, though she knew some of her clients could have patronized expensive and fashionable tailors in Jerusalem. She was tempted to conclude they were motivated by a desire to support the bereaved of Bethlehem in general, or by a loathsome pity for Jerusha herself. But her long-term success, along with the glaring lack of express gratitude on her part, indicated otherwise.

Jerusha continued to live frugally, and over the years her money accumulated in hiding places. Money was easier to secrete than three boy-children. The only improvements to her own house were a larger and well-stocked cupboard, the thorough repair of her roof, fresh whitewashing, and new bedclothes and linens. She could now sleep in the loft again, with only occasional nightmares of her sons' dying screams. Jerusha finally removed the patchwork masonry blocking her back door, so she could more easily use the communal privy. The prohibition against this must have dated before the memory of any of Jerusha's neighbors.

Jerusha's new access to the space behind her house allowed her to transform it into a small garden by bringing richer soil, bundle by bundle, and buckets of water from the street trough. She produced the finest peas, beans, garlic, leeks, endive, onions and mint, which could also be used for prolonging the freshness of milk. The cucumbers could be eaten or used as poultices for bruises, and her vetch, when boiled with garlic, made an effective cough medicine. She grew these for her customers as well as herself, while leaving her patrons ignorant of her sources and therefore dependent on her.

In order to maintain good relations, Jerusha avoided offending Judaic pieties, especially since many of her acquaintances were Pharisees, so she remained secluded at home during Sabbath, Passover, and other holy times.

Jerusha's religion, never strong, had undergone an extreme transformation since the Night of Horror. She had always thought of Judaism as more a matter of actions than inner beliefs. In her youth, she had felt mild contempt for the few acquaintances who turned against God because of some disappointment or harm that befell them in their lives. God supposedly reigned over the nation of Israel; He was not a personal friend and protector. To expect Him to answer one's every need or whim was not only selfish but unrealistic. People were injured, died, and were victims of disasters. To demand otherwise, through prayer, was silly. But after That Night, there *could* be no God, unless He cared nothing for an entire generation of Bethlehem's children. Jerusha spent several nights trying to reconcile herself to an almighty God, but she found herself unable to do so. Being illiterate she knew no Scripture, other than the scraps she had heard in synagogue when she had bothered to listen. Her father had taught her less at Sabbath dinner, when he spoke at all. Since no one knew whether she attended Synagogue or the Great Temple, she could safely avoid both. The high and holy days were perfect for concentrated work on her little vegetable garden, highly secluded from pious eyes by her house and the back wall of the common privy, on two sides, and the ramshackle, twig walls between them.

In general, once Jerusha had lost interest in God, she questioned all of the habits which she had always considered to be "moral". She was astute enough to know she had to be considered honest and virtuous by her neighbors and customers, but she soon concluded being regarded as such, and actually being so, were distinctly different matters. The more her clients trusted her as a seamstress, the more they would assume all the gold beads they deposited with her for their finest gowns would actually be sewn into them. They would never notice she secreted away a few. Had she been caught, she would have explained that too much gold on one garment was gaudy, and the extras were being saved for that customer's very finest gown. But this eventuality never occurred. Indeed, some customers asked her to buy the expensive ornaments, took Jerusha's word for their cost, and never counted them.

This system worked equally well for costly material; Jerusha now always bought more of the expensive cloth than she needed, sometimes double the amount, and saved the remainder. Even small pieces of silk made beautiful veils. Jerusha would always remember the very first complete gown she made, and sold for a very high price, which had cost absolutely nothing in material and little in labor.

She began to apply the same rule to her cooking, and found she could claim considerably more as her expenses. Interestingly, the more she increased the fees for her labor, the more her work was sought out.

All this was only right, Jerusha reasoned, since she could not remember anyone ever going out of their way to be fair or kind to her. Jerusha reminded herself that she never caused harm for its own sake; her clients, being rich, had merely been lucky, and luck was not virtue; her petty embezzlement was, indeed, their own fault for being too lazy or careless to notice; and she herself was not greedy. In fact, one look at the way she lived would prove luxury was not her goal. Besides, considering what had happened to her beloved and unavenged boys, in a town full of cowards, no one had the right to criticize.

Perhaps, Jerusha mused one day, the old-wives-tale that one vice led to another, was true. She didn't allow herself to dwell on that idea. Those who had taught her such adages always worshiped a useless God in whom she had no interest.

Jerusha had made a few small local investments which she risked only after thorough investigation. Being illiterate, she was forced to rely on local scribes for contracts, but her innate shrewdness caused her to employ writers far removed from each other to read and prepare the same documents. She consistently made a small profit, which supplemented the earnings from her work.

After enough time, she was willing to risk more money for larger holdings. Jerusha could not engage in lending for interest, as usury was against both Judaic and civil law. However, as a partner, even a minor one, she was free to invest in any lawful concern. She questioned the scriveners whom she had learned to trust, and they informed her that truly large sums of money were to be had in major ventures, using "factors." But factors varied widely in trustworthiness and other aspects of character.

While appearing to be motivated only by curiosity, Jerusha memorized the names of the more unsavory factors. The scriveners gave her a few names, always with the injunction to keep their names secret, which she had every intention of doing. Naturally, Jerusha asked whether their untrustworthiness related to their investors, or to the victims whom they cheated in favor of their employers. Though many of her informants immediately answered, "Both," she soon learned through a little more questioning the grudging admission that these factors could not have remained in business long had their benefactors regularly also been their victims. "Dogs are loyal to their masters," as one scrivener put it.

"Nevertheless," warned another when she repeated the phrase, "Dogs have been known to turn."

You would say that, anyway, having an honest man's contempt for the more subtle mind, Jerusha thought, but she was careful to provide a bonus for those scriveners who supplied her information.

She then looked up those factors who were reputed to have brought in the most profits to their investors, whatever their principles. For investment opportunities she eliminated from consideration such widespread operations as shipbuilding on the coast, large agricultural ventures, the slave trade, and the most profitable of all: Financing far-roving merchant caravans for contingency profits. Those were all too far from home and beyond her ken.

Jerusha decided to attempt to establish monopolies in the produce and meat markets, as well as weavers and tanners, and, at a greater, but calculated, risk, local produce farmers and shepherds to supply them all, about which businesses she was somewhat knowledgeable.

On a trip to Jerusalem she took the trouble to buy an ancient signet, unidentifiable because its original owner was long dead. It was affixed on a black marble obelisk, and was meant to sign clay tablets or wax seals. Her reason at first was to disguise that she was both illiterate and a woman, but, after realizing she would have to meet each of the factors in person, the signet was still useful to establish or protect her identity in case one of her tablets or scrolls was intercepted, misdirected, or substituted.

The factors she carefully selected did not report to her at regular intervals, or in much detail, but Jerusha noticed her profits growing substantially, even though she trusted them with very little money at first, increasing the amounts gradually. Only then did she begin to observe that several of the stall and shopkeepers at the marketplaces, people she had patronized for years, closed up their shops and left Bethlehem quickly, without explanation. Their locations invariably re-opened soon afterwards, with the same quality goods but at higher prices. Jerusha discovered that she herself was now making healthy profits from both the wholesale and the retail parts of each of these businesses. The factors were taking large fees, but Jerusha was more than compensated by her increasing wealth, most of which she reinvested.

In a few months she was contacted by one of her factors, Shema ben Izar, with a problem. Jerusha knew Shema as one of her less scrupulous agents, and had the physical characteristics commonly assigned to his type: fat, greasy, and shifty-eyed. He had never, however, betrayed her. He informed her that one of the strongest trade organizations in the region was putting great pressure on him about his operations within the field which she had assigned him: the weavers and tanners. On his own, he had expanded the enterprise to include a marginal tailor and sandal-maker—though never cutting Jerusha out of her profits. But, naturally, this came to the attention of the association.

Jerusha pondered the problem, and then asked, "Why can't we take over the association?"

Despite his worldliness, Shema was taken aback. "But there are many members; it would be impossible."

"Why? Take over another not very popular retailer or two. That should grow our operation enough to earn entry. After this, subtle bribes and threats should get us majority control of the association. We can then change the rules to favor us slightly, always keeping enough independents to give the appearance of fairness. I will send you enough money to accomplish this. Send me your best estimate." Unknown to Shema ben Izar, Jerusha already owned the major supplier of raw wool and hides, on whom the artisans depended, enabling Shema to accomplish the task with minimum opposition.

As shrewd as his reputation was, the entire plan had clearly never occurred to Shema. Jerusha could not tell whether his expressions showed timidity, shame at not having thought of it himself, or admiration. Perhaps all three.

After a moment Shema replied, "It shall be done, my lady." She doubted *this* dog would turn on her.

Jerusha left his office, which looked as disreputable as he did, wondering whether the ruthlessness of factors had not been overrated. But from that date her wealth, and her fame among a chosen few, grew proportionately.

Someday, Jerusha knew, her ventures in Bethlehem would expand enough to earn her too many enemies, invite official inquiries, or even have a harmful effect on the local economy. But by then she could move her operations to Jerusalem. Assuming she would still be interested in such matters.

Despite Jerusha's prosperity, and now fully established independence from God and man, she was increasingly restless. She was free of a weak-willed husband, society's contempt or pity, poverty and overwork. She had no material ambition. She had no desire for greater respectability, especially if it involved the bother of a husband, the cost of religious or social involvement, or the repetition of anything she had previously known. She even lost interest in improving any of her not inconsiderable skills.

By now, Jerusha was of a class as high as the town of Bethlehem had. She was no longer an "artisan," but an "honored tradesman", beneath only the inherited priestly class and nobility, which stayed in Jerusalem anyway. Jerusha's status gave her certain privileges, without corresponding public responsibilities. She did not pride herself, as most of these rights were as useless to her as the one that declared that during the entrance of the King or Governor in the streets of Bethlehem, in formal procession, she had the right to stand or sit, even in a reserved seat, if she wished it. Jerusha never attended such processions, partially because of her contempt for crowds and partially because she was unsure whether female as well as male craftsmen were due such honors.

Jerusha also knew certain crafts were despised, and suspected their low status could be traced back to "women's work." These included weaver, flax-comber, tanner, pigeon-trainer, peddler, barber, physician, and launderer. Other occupations, she presumed were disapproved of due to an out-dated prejudice of their "unclean" nature, including ass-driver, camel-driver, usurer, herdsman, tax-collector, butcher, and bath attendant. Other lowly careers such as tinker and sailor were despised for reasons Jerusha could not understand and didn't care. Of course, Jerusha now employed men for many of the despised tasks. But since she personally engaged in none of them outside of her home, the subject was as uninteresting to her as her new-found status.

Jerusha had let only a few of her old clients know of her advancement for fear that her prominence or prestige would interfere with her search for the possibly poor family whose energy, desperation, or greed had led them to try to wear the royal red through their young son, thereby causing the other children of Bethlehem to don blood-red.

Jerusha had no idea how to seek out that family. She finally knew her mission involved vengeance for her own children, and expiation of her guilt for the loss of Leah's children. Jerusha had learned years earlier, through market gossip and the chattering of her customers, as well as by personal observation of increasingly arrogant Roman soldiers, that King Herod had died. She had spat when she heard that, mildly shocking one of her customers. She also knew Herod's remaining kin were squabbling over his throne. The Romans had, of course, taken advantage of the situation and had formally annexed Judea as a province of the Roman Empire, setting up a governor. The Jewish kings now ruled little outside of their own palaces, if that. Such intrigues had meant little to Jerusha, but there was less talk in Bethlehem of the false "Messiah," whose reported birth had brought so much misery to the town, and in whom Jerusha retained her morbid interest, increasingly unsatisfied.

Jerusha's home and business life had reached a predictable and comfortable plateau; but comfort was not what she sought. Jerusha continued to cook and design clothes for a few of the rich, to stave off boredom, to give herself a visible means of support, and also defray her own costs for the ingredients and materials, though she was now paying mostly herself for the goods.

❖

Another year passed before a new major change occurred in Jerusha's life, for good or ill, and it appeared, as always before, with a knock at her door. Jerusha no longer panicked at knocks. Indeed what more could anyone do to her than that to which she had already been inured? She unbarred the door and opened it fully, without regard to security.

"Jerusha...?"

"Have I changed so much?" she snapped. She had immediately recognized her brother-by-marriage, Zachariah. He was older now, his hair and beard white and thinning, his face sunburned with deep furrows. But his features, always prominent, were more so now, making him almost a caricature of his old self. There was still about him the never quite reconciled air of commitment and courage almost to the point of foolhardiness, coupled with an amused casualness of manner. She had always known his moods to be complex, changing rapidly from manly resolution, to the sweet selfishness of a child, to the most devout piety. After all these years fighting for the Zealots, which would dominate today?

"No, you haven't changed that much," he said.

"You're not a good liar," she replied, inviting him to the table, where she had laid out sewing beads for a lady's robe. Zachariah pulled out the same tall wooden chair he had used years before, and lounged in it as though at home.

"Pour yourself some wine, and have something to eat out of the cupboard." From the way he readily complied, showing no hesitation or surprise as he arose and surveyed the well-stocked pantry, Jerusha knew the man had been well informed of her current prosperity.

When he had seated himself again with a bowl full of plums and figs, Zachariah chided her gently. "You used to pour for the menfolk."

"And it was always water. Now it's wine, and I don't fetch." She chose not to add,...*and now there's only one man, and he's a starving fugitive.* "To what do I owe the honor of your very rare company?" she asked, aping the speech of her more high-bred customers. She sat at her usual chair.

While eating a fig, Zachariah glanced appreciatively around the room. "I see you've re-built your back door."

"Already planning your escape?" She flashed one of her rare smiles, though it felt more cynical than she had intended. Jerusha then changed chairs, and turned from sewing to chopping onions.

"My dear sister, the smell of your onions does not improve the taste of your figs." When Jerusha did not desist, but began grating garlic as well, Zachariah made a dismissive motion with his arm and came to the point.

"Let us be serious for a moment, Jerusha." He sat up straight in his chair. "You are a widow, with no grown sons..."

"Or any young ones, as you will remember."

"...No grown sons, nor any other close male relatives, other than me..."

"Or female ones, as you will also remember."

"Jerusha!" His indignation overcame him. "Are you mocking my poor wife, my Leah?"

"No," she said, genuinely ashamed. Jerusha alone knew, and knew too well, why her sister-in-law had been dead these many years. "I'm truly sorry."

Zachariah was mollified, but wary. "There is, as I was saying, no one to protect you and look after you. Especially now that you are known to be a woman of substance."

"I wondered when you'd get to that. Is this a proposal of marriage?"

Zachariah seemed startled, but Jerusha took it as at least partially feigned. He must have considered such an arrangement. "No," he said. "Scripture and Scribal tradition of the Oral Law are ambiguous on that point," the perfect Pharisee again. "Try as I might, I cannot make out whether it is my duty, or forbidden to me, to marry you. And, as you might guess, my access to the scribes and rabbis is limited. Nevertheless, my duty to look after you as your nearest male kin is absolutely clear."

"*Your* duty! *Your* prohibition! Do *I* look like *I* need or want a husband or guardian of any kind?" She hurled her words derisively now. "I have lived alone for years, and you have never noticed nor cared. Now that I am established with my own house and a not-inconsiderable business, you come sniffing back to see if you can live off me. Even if I permitted it how long do you think it would be before the authorities discovered I had a bloody Zealot outlaw living in my home?"

"A long time, if ever," Zachariah replied easily. "When the Romans annexed Judea and at those times when there was a change in Roman governors officials and troops were also replaced, and I have been operating in higher but less visible positions. I doubt any of the remaining officials know my true name, and none of them know my family. My worst danger always came from King Herod's spies who worked for the Romans, but now our brave Jewish soldiers have been barricaded in the Antonia for some time, as resentful of Rome as they are afraid of her. My past would never endanger you." Having spoken with seeming confidence, Zachariah's voice took on the tone of a jealous child. "You don't *have* a patron, do you?"

"No. And I don't need or want one," she said emphatically, chopping onions furiously, and wishing they were Zachariah's fingers.

Resuming his rabbinical voice, "I am the head of the family. Our Law and our customs require that you accept your male next of kin as such. I can enforce my right to control both your property and you, if necessary."

Jerusha injected as sweet a tone in her voice as she could manage, not having tried for so long: "And I will have well-selected customers reacquaint the Roman and Jewish authorities with your past.

"Every woman in Judea is well aware our country, unlike some others we have heard of, is a patriarchy, and most women like the idea of it. We don't know how any other customs work. I'll be happy to build a shrine in my house honoring you and all other men, lit day and night with the most expensive candles. I will address you as 'My Lord,' even at home. I will follow you on hands and knees in public. But if you or any of your gang members try to get your filthy paws on any of my business, or take control of any of my life that's important to me, I will kill you one by one, starting with you, an outlaw, remember. Is this entering your thick head? Because if not, I will begin right now." She pointed the knife delicately at his throat.

Zachariah's surrender was as rapid and good-natured as if his earlier threats and cajoling were simply meant in jest. For all Jerusha knew, they might have been. He must have been very good at his high position with the Zealots. Zachariah smiled, relaxed again in his chair, and ate a plum. Jerusha now knew, for the first time in her life, she would never again have anything to fear from a man.

"May I please spend the night here, my lady?" he asked softly.

Jerusha gentled herself. "Yes. And I will prepare you the same supper I am preparing for my few remaining customers. I can promise you it will be worthy. A meal like you have seldom, if ever, tasted." Jerusha's heart fell for a moment when she realized that Zachariah would be sleeping under the stairs, in the closet where his wife and children had died through her actions. But she maintained her self-control.

"When you left here last, Zachariah, you promised to avenge our boys. Have you done so?" She stared at the table.

"Many a Roman widow would swear I did."

"As I told you before, my children weren't killed by Romans."

"Many of Herod's men, as well as other Jews, helped the Romans and in other ways got in our way and paid for it. But King Herod is long dead, as are most of his sons, and our only remaining real enemies are the Romans."

"Haven't you forgotten one?"

"Who?" he asked, genuinely puzzled.

"The false Messiah whose family's ambition caused the slaughter."

Zachariah thought a moment, and then said, "I've never heard of him since. He must have died that day, along with the others. Of course, my more timid friends among the Pharisees are still praying for the one, promised Messiah. I favor preparing his way with the blood of his enemies."

Jerusha had long considered conquering armies and tyrannical kings to be matters beyond her ken or control—as acts of nature, like a plague or famine. But a single family so ambitious as to set their child up in rebellion and secretly hide him behind innocent children, *their neighbors*, to be murdered in *his* stead, was beneath contempt. No it wasn't—it was worthy of the highest and purest hatred and revenge against the pretender. *Didn't I do something like that to save my own children?* No, it was the ambition of that unholy family that had turned the town into a killing-field. It was left for her to be the instrument of retribution.

There was no point in berating Zachariah anymore. She would let him change the subject.

Having sat through Jerusha's stony silence, Zachariah suddenly laughed softly. "Anyway, if I can't retire and live off you, I'll have to go back to killing Romans. I'm in charge of all operations in the countryside outside the city of Jerusalem. My men can't get foodstuffs as easily as town-dwellers can. Now that you own all the produce in the world, will you share with us?" He resumed a serious expression. "Whether you understand it or not, we're fighting for you and your countrymen."

Though at that moment Jerusha cared little about the liberation of her countrymen or anyone else, she recognized Zachariah's sincerity, and she had always admired courage. "I'll pack you a bundle—no, many bundles—and leave them by your door under the stairs."

After a pause, Jerusha asked, "What is it like? Killing, I mean?"

Zachariah shrugged. "I haven't personally killed anyone in years. That's not my work anymore. I can only try to remember... The first one I killed only in self-defense. We had tracked down a small patrol of them. They turned to face us. I confess to an unmanly fear, but I knew, being unarmored, were I to try to run away my back would be a fine target for their spears; and their swords if they could run as fast as I. So I killed a Roman strictly to save my own life. I was too relieved afterward to look at his corpse. Later, I killed for the fellows beside me. There was satisfaction in that, even in the gore, for my friends who had fallen. We always fought as a close-knit group, however small, and we felt a love for each other outsiders cannot know. Are you sure you want to listen to all this, Jerusha?"

"Yes. Here, have a slice of cheese to go with your fruit." She not only served and sliced the cheese, but poured more wine. "Go on."

"After time and understanding it became as it was supposed to be. The reason I was a Zealot in the first place. Someone had to fight and kill and if need be, die, for the Jewish nation. The Roman blasphemers who invaded our land had to be removed. I was good at fighting and was proud of it. Don't ever let timid stay-at-homes tell you there's no glory in a righteous war, Jerusha. Honor and glory are a soldier's, and a partisan's, only real pay. Without it there would be only indiscriminate, perpetual slaughter, plunder, rape, and anarchy, with Satan laughing at it all. Blame Father Adam if you want. Glory and honor are discipline. For unit and self. God blessed my arms, and I thanked Him for it.

"But all things pass; toward the end of my more active life, I suppose I turned into something of a butcher, with a detached view concerned only with efficient killing techniques: the best cuts, the most effective chopping and stabbing, together with all the blood and sweat that accompany a good butcher's profession. Then I knew it was time to accept the higher and safer stations I was offered. I was getting older. There are many ways to serve the Lord, and fighting Roman soldiers in open skirmishes and ambushes is very little of what we do.

"Odd," he grew reflective. "I don't remember the faces of those I killed. Do you think me heartless, Jerusha?"

"No," she said, "but I would want to remember their faces."

Zachariah spent the afternoon watching his sister-in-law cook. The earlier talk of violence did not affect her art. Zachariah ate a supper of lamb which he declared better than he had imagined possible, then helped Jerusha with deliveries to her customers. He went to bed early.

Zachariah awoke in the late morning. When he emerged from his cubicle, Jerusha greeted him, "I let you sleep. You needed it. Besides, I had a lot to do."

Then he noticed a mountain of bundles by his door, and that Jerusha was dressed in what could only be traveling clothes.

"I'm going with you," she stated matter-of-factly.

"You can't!" Zachariah spluttered.

Jerusha led him to the table where his breakfast was ready, and gently pushed him into a chair. "We don't have time to argue.

I've been working since last night and before dawn. The food and other provisions will be carried in a donkey-cart I bought—be quiet, I'm talking. I've arranged for my neighbor to look after my house. It will be well-protected. I have left word with each customer that I have been called away on a family emergency. My other...interests, will be looked after by other people. I can return and check on things from time to time. My little garden will die of neglect, but..."

"My men don't have the time or inclination to care after curious onlookers."

"I'm coming to participate, not watch."

"Jerusha, you must be well into your thirties by now. You could be a grandmother..."

"No, I couldn't," she said.

"Sorry; I didn't mean to bring up bad memories. But our fields of operations are called the 'wilderness' for a reason. Even my rear-base of operations is nearly unapproachable, and I allow no women there, much less one to whom I have a special duty."

"I have no interest in your base. I'm going to support your fighting men wherever they are. I want to learn about what killing really feels like, and maybe take a small part in it myself." Before Zachariah could protest, she added, "I can cook, nurse, mend, wash, carry water and weapons, and other things, and I can keep the men supplied with food. I am strong, more so than many of the men, I'll warrant. I can travel as often as they do, and as quickly," she said, hoping it was true. "And if worse comes to worse, and they prevail over us, any little time the enemy spend killing me will give one of your better fighters a chance to get away."

One thing Jerusha had concluded over the years: The family, and the boy child, whom she had been hunting, could not still be in Bethlehem. Either he had been smuggled out of the town before the slaughter of the children, or he had been well-hidden.

The last thing that ambitious family would have done was stay in Bethlehem among those they had so cruelly betrayed, and made Jerusha a betrayer. The boy should be a young man now, and visibly of an age not common in Bethlehem. Was he hiding in the wilderness, planning another attempt at snatching a crown? Or in Jerusalem, where all the power was concentrated, even under the Romans? Anywhere but Bethlehem, and Jerusha would seek him and his family out. If it cost her her life.

Zachariah brought her thoughts back to practicality. "Are you aware that you haven't mentioned one of the services which fighting men—even some of those who fight for God—sometimes expect from a woman?"

"That's why I bought a dagger this morning...quite concealable."

"I fail to see the advantage of losing a man to your knife rather than a Roman spear."

"I have dealt with many different men; I'm sure it won't come to violence," she replied, dismissively.

Jerusha made it apparent that to stop her, at least at this stage, Zachariah would have to kill her himself, rather than leaving it to the Romans or the wilderness. His inevitable surrender to her plan was as graceful and rapid as before. Zachariah even smiled. He displayed a grudging admiration for this remarkable woman.

Jerusha was surprised he never demanded her full motive. Maybe he knew, or suspected, as much of it as she knew, which was very little and somewhat confused.

"Well", Zachariah said, after drawing out breakfast as long as possible perhaps in the forlorn hope Jerusha would reconsider, "let's get on with achieving the crucifixion of my last remaining relative."

CHAPTER 4

◆

A Righteous War

The first three days of the journey were the hardest. Jerusha thought her feet and calf-muscles were strong, but she learned better in the rock-strewn hills and gullies of the countryside.

"It's worse walking through the deserts to the west," Zachariah observed, though Jerusha hadn't complained.

The alternating boulders, loose pebbles, dust, and thorny vegetation were all Jerusha thought she could bear. After much questioning, Zachariah admitted they were heading toward the northeast of Jerusalem. Jerusha's hope they could rest in the villages on the way was quickly squelched by his casual mention that they were avoiding all habitations of man. They took no roads, or even paths made by livestock. The donkey-cart held together, despite occasionally needing pushes and leverage out of holes. Jerusha was satisfied she brought enough water for the donkey as well as herself; Zachariah was festooned with water bottles and leather bags. They ate from Jerusha's stores.

On the fourth day it rained. Jerusha could not remember such a storm. Maybe city life and a tile roof were not so boring as she had thought. It was impossible to proceed through such blinding sheets of water, so they camped on the side of a gully, which continually threatened to fill and drown them. Jerusha had brought oiled canvas to protect her as well as the goods in the cart. Zachariah had his own. Jerusha sat high on the wall of the gully, ensuring that her canvas was over, as well as under, her. It did little good. The rainwater seemed to prefer descending and eroding the dirt under only one of her buttocks, knocking her off-balance and into another little stream. After sliding into the water several times, Jerusha found a flat rock to sit on, and bundled herself up from head to toe.

Most of her face had to remain exposed under her improvised hood in order to permit breathing. The coarse veils with which she had replaced her silken ones, for traveling, would stifle her if permitted to cross her face. That was her first full exposure to Judean mosquitoes. They swarmed under her hood. After she made a few half-hearted attempts to shoo them off, her face was numb enough to ignore the mosquitoes and get about two hours sleep during the night. The next morning her entire face was so swollen she could hardly open her eyes. *What am I doing here?*

Zachariah seemed to understand, and though he had no healing potions—she tried several of hers; but they were for wounds, not insects. His assurance that he would guide her by hand until late morning, when Jerusha could see again, was somewhat comforting. The rain stopped.

Then she discovered mud. Not the inch or two often covering the streets of Bethlehem, but seas of it. Walking through soaked flatlands was a bad dream. Her walking-stick was useless; she had to rescue it more often than she did her feet. But climbing was worse. Every step had to be completed at least twice, and countless times Jerusha slid all the way down a hill or gully and had to start over, wishing for a rock for a foothold, only to find the stones and boulders, which had bruised her feet before, seemed to disappear after a rain. Jerusha was glad she brought extra sandals; she lost one in the mud. She wasted much time looking for it, and only when Zachariah pointed out that its mate was in tatters, anyway, did she give up.

Upon Zachariah's suggestion, Jerusha cut criss-crosses on the soles of her remaining sandals to improve her traction, though it would help only with shallow mud or wet rocks.

Finally, they arrived in the camp which Zachariah identified as being in the mountains several miles northeast of Jerusalem. Zachariah had shown her no map, and Jerusha had little sense of direction. At the beginning of their journey she had had no idea what to expect, but she couldn't have expected what she found: Less than a dozen hungry, ragged men, filthy and surrounded by their own refuse, ranging in age from young boys to old men. All stared at her.

"Men, this is Jerusha. She has brought many things for you," was Zachariah's introduction.

"What good is she to us?"

"First, she answers only to me." He directed this comment especially to one of the older men. "She can cook for you, but serves none of you, and has my full trust. Meanwhile, I have other patrols to check." He turned to Jerusha and said, "God go with you," and left. Jerusha considered following him, but knew he would rebuff her, and she could not survive out here alone.

For what seemed like minutes, Jerusha stood where she was. One of the boys came up and kissed her hand. Some of the men leered at her. Two turned their backs on her and walked away. The rest tried to pry the canvass off the donkey-cart to see what Jerusha had brought, until she chased them off with her walking-stick. After that, no one spoke.

Jerusha gathered her pride.

"I'm not a servant, and I will be treated with full respect. I'm here to help you as long as I feel like it. So far, it looks like the sun won't set on my presence...or that of my supplies."

Her mention of supplies reminded her that she herself was hungry, so she decided to attempt to win their trust by setting up a camp kitchen. Her experience in cooking for housefuls of guests differed little from serving a gang of partisans. As she fetched each ingredient from the cart she had to threaten one or two impatient men. But after most of an hour she had a meal sufficient for more than their number, and, once the men saw and smelled what she was doing, they stopped interrupting her, or allowing others to do so. She served the men in bowls she had brought, though some had their own.

Jerusha even managed to set up a food-line, though none of the men had ever seen one before. After the first men had tasted, they kept order on their comrades through their growls and commands, and she had no more trouble.

The men had been careful to thank the Lord, though no one had bothered to thank Jerusha. After their bellies were full, Pharisees that they were, the men went through animated prayer-services, completely unintelligible to Jerusha. This concerned her—she might soon be discovered as an interloper. Then she recovered distant memories of her childhood: Women, including her mother, were not required to show the outward piety of men; they could even avoid synagogue and the Temple, most of the time. Had Jerusha remembered this earlier, she could have devoted more time to her garden and other pursuits with less caution. After their prayers, no one spoke to her again but went directly to sleep. *I suppose that means they trust me. But, do I trust them?*

For safety's sake, Jerusha had found ways, throughout the afternoon and evening, to remark to each of the men that she was armed, usually as part of a discussion of possible enemy surprise. That would have to do.

Jerusha found a place on a precipice, soft because of the loose soil, and hoped it would not rain again, or she would surely be washed a mile away. From her perch she could see, in the far distance, the edge of Jerusalem, slightly south of the disappearing sun. All was lush green or green-black at this time, due to the olive groves and scattered shrubs and trees. Jerusha had never seen such greenery. She wondered how long before over-cultivation would turn such an Eden into the arid plains she had known while growing up. All was beautiful, and impossibly far away from her spot in the wilderness. Jerusha had long known olive-oil was almost the only export of Jerusalem, and now she knew why. Beyond the city she could see the western sand, where there were true deserts, complete with treacherous dunes. Beyond that was the ribbon of sea.

After feeding the men next morning, Jerusha initiated conversations with them, always individually, to discover the function of the unit, as well as discover differences between the men should the information prove useful. As for the former, she was highly disappointed. None admitted to any action against the enemy for the past week—their procedure was just to await orders, then track down the Roman patrol if it was small enough, have a fight, move to a new campsite, send a runner to inform Zachariah where it was, then wait for orders again. They did nothing on their own initiative. The last "patrol" they had fought was one Roman officer and his slave out hunting lions. They killed the two men through the back with javelins, from behind boulders, then robbed the corpses and left them to the vultures. The partisans did not eat the horse and donkey, as they were unclean under Judaic law, and the men were very hungry when Jerusha arrived.

Learning the differences between the men occupied more than a week of Jerusha's time, which was otherwise spent cooking, mending, nursing, and most importantly, teaching the men basic sanitation. Apparently, these men had never heard the ancient military/political axiom, "[Excrement] rolls downhill." In Jerusha's talks with the partisans, she avoided the two youngest boys as much as possible; they were approximately the ages her sons would have been by now. Worse, they quickly formed an attachment to her, and the last thing Jerusha wanted to be was a surrogate mother. The old men were garrulous, which made them useful for information, if boring at times. The men of middle years, two of whom had turned their backs on first meeting her, seemed to be torn between desiring Jerusha physically, and their religious principles, making their attitudes totally unpredictable. Jerusha almost wished they would try to seduce or rape her—such emotions and passions she understood. During the next few weeks, Jerusha might have even welcomed such overtures, if only for a change of pace.

Most frustrating for Jerusha was trying to discover who the leader, or captain, or chieftain, or strongman, of this bunch was. She had never lived in an unstructured society, and it made her nervous. But each of these "men" seemed more ineffectual than the others, and decisions were not decreed, or discussed and voted on, so much as enacted by default. No one cared to oppose the one person who might, for any reason, express an opinion. She found herself making most of the daily decisions. Patriarchalism seemed to have broken down here, and Jerusha was not comfortable without it. Jews had no female rabbis, and she was not willing to become the first.

Since the men observed the Sabbath strictly, Jerusha cooked most of the food in advance, and tried to look as inactive as she could during the Holy Day, though she performed other chores when no one was looking. She suspected one or two of them were on to her tricks, but none ever said anything.

After a month, Jerusha finally conceded she had nothing further to learn from these men, and decided to return to Bethlehem. Her supplies were running low, anyway. Soon after she began packing at twilight so as to avoid drawing attention to her movements, a rider came into the camp. She would have welcomed Zachariah, if for no other reason than to berate him for leaving her alone with these louts, however devout. The horseman was not Zachariah, but presumably a messenger from the Zealots, evidently unarmed. Most of the men didn't bother to take notice, so it was up to Jerusha to greet him. The horseman slid off his saddle onto a medium-sized boulder. He asked Jerusha for the headman, and when told there wasn't one, looked disgusted but not surprised. He announced himself as Jesse, and when he heard her name he reported to her.

Jesse announced that a small patrol of ten Romans was searching the mountains to avenge the lion-hunter and other Roman losses. They were, however, led by a centurion, one who usually commanded a hundred or more men, and could be expected to be experienced in such warfare. The centurion would be wary of traps, a deceptively retreating enemy, and overhangs of rocks or cliffs. There were two passes the Romans could be expected to use, each of which were described to Jerusha, using a map hand-drawn on parchment. Jerusha didn't know if she could read a map, but there must be someone in camp who could.

When Jerusha pointed out that the men she stayed with were about equal in number to the Romans, and without armor, the messenger was unimpressed. Either because he had an inflated opinion of her group's fighting ability, or because he had little interest in the outcome, Jerusha could not discern. The rider remounted and disappeared, without so much as asking for water or feed for his horse. This engaged her suspicious nature, but she suppressed it as well as she had her notice of the rider's slight accent in his use of Aramaic. She had met Samaritans and Galileans with much worse speech, and how could she know where this rider came from? Israel was a large country. The expensive parchment added to her unease. She put those thoughts out of her mind for the time.

Jerusha talked to the men the next morning, but heard no

useful ideas. Most were accustomed to obeying orders, whatever their source. A few of the older men were nervous about confronting equal, or near-equal odds, especially without armor or sophisticated weapons, and without the element of total surprise. None seemed happy at facing battle, but none appeared to be cowards.

It wasn't clear just when Jerusha took command, nor did anyone mention the fact. In the beginning, the men would glance at an older man as though to get ratification of something Jerusha said, but he regularly nodded, and soon they stopped checking.

Clearly, at least in this camp, Jewish attitudes about women had changed completely. Jerusha asked the men for their maps if they had any, and someone who was taught to read them. Only two maps were forthcoming, and one of them was useless—it was scratched on a large potsherd, as most temporary or field maps were, etched more or less elaborately, depending upon the map's usage. This one, however, marked only streams, water-holes, comfortable resting-places, and whatever other things were of a selfish value to this map-maker. It had no indications of either hills or paths. The other map proved more useful; it was carefully drawn on papyrus, and outlined both the paths Jesse, the rider, had supplied. The new map was in surprising detail by comparison with the rider's and potsherd maps, but it also showed a third path between the other two. She searched the messenger's map, but not only did it not sketch that path or gap, it showed, by a series of small angles denoting hills, a ridge, rather than depression, where the low-lying path should be. Jerusha found that understanding maps, once she learned to orient them, was far easier than she had expected. *Perhaps I should have learned to read writing, when my mind was younger and more agile?* But maps were just pictures, after all, and what few symbols were necessary were simple to decipher with a little help. Jerusha had always had imagination, and the ability to reason from the abstract to the concrete, and *vice versa*. There was no avoiding the conclusion that the third, middle path should have been on the map given her by the horseman and had been deliberately and hastily omitted. No effort had been made to put other natural features in, or conform the non-existent ridge to the surrounding topography, or add small gullies or dips within or leading from the "ridge." Now Jerusha's suspicions were confirmed in her mind.

The horseman was a Roman.

The rider would not have been sent if his Romans were closer than the better part of a day's march away. Simpler by far to catch her Zealots where they were that night, and slaughter them while they were asleep. But then why warn them at all? Except to find and fix them where they were *wanted* by the enemy before he approached? Therefore, there was time, if the partisans acted quickly, to examine the two paths offered by the rider, and the phantom one he omitted. Jerusha skipped any morning meal for the men, causing grumbling, but no worse, and had them use both maps to take her the almost two miles in a circuitous route over rough terrain, to bring them to the two paths delineated on both maps. As Jerusha had suspected, both approaches were straight, well-worn, and without boulders or twists to permit or disguise ambushes. The third, middle path, omitted from the rider's map, was, of course, real, though the opening was difficult to find between boulders, cliffs, and undergrowth. Jerusha examined it herself. This hidden path not only had large rocks along its length, but, better yet, had two sharp-edged niches in it, opposing each other, each just big enough to hide an ambush that was at all competently designed. The walkway was narrow enough to constrict the enemy at the right places. For a moment, Jerusha had a panicky fear the Romans had planned on her selection of the middle path, so they could use one of the other, smoother paths, at greater speed, and attack from the ear. Then she realized no Romans would know of her, nor would they expect tactical skills among a small gang that concentrated on lone lion-hunters. Nor did the enemy have the time or inclination to draw a map of such elaborate double-deception. One trick should be enough to fool these disorganized bandits.

Jerusha permitted the men to return to their camp, only to disappoint them. The comforts and supplies that were there would have to wait. She wanted to test the men on their weapons of choice. Throughout her stay, Jerusha had observed the men continued their weapons practice—which was one of the few regular habits they had. But their practice-field was away from camp, and Jerusha had had other chores, so she never watched. Besides, she had never dreamed she would be a field-commander of soldiers. Now she was suddenly, and keenly, interested in whether these men knew how to fight.

There were two bowmen, the youngest men, who were quite proficient, if not expert. Each carried ten iron-tipped arrows. Next were the four javelin and spear throwers, each with four of the former and two of the latter weapons. Since these were older men, they had the upper muscular strength necessary. The elderly men were surprisingly good at slings. Although lacking the upper-body strength of their juniors, their arms were tough and wiry, and their wrists well developed and remarkably supple considering their ages. The elders were proficient with both cloth and leather slings, and the jointed wood rods which enhanced short-range accuracy. They also had bagsful of the new iron and lead shot, with and without spikes, so preferable to random, unweighed stones. One man even had elongated shot, which could be propelled in a spiral for greater distance as well as accuracy. Jerusha had always pictured David, in his battle against Goliath, as swinging his sling repeatedly above and around his head, only to now learn slings were used in one, skillful vertical arc. Jerusha was disappointed to learn there was no swordsman among the men; two of them wore swords in camp because the weapons were dull and pitted Roman refuse, and they used them only to clear brush, had there been any, or to impress women, had there been any of them to impress. There was no time to train men in the use of swords, even if Jerusha had the knowledge.

Only after she was satisfied the men were as competent as she could hope, did she remember that she herself was unarmed except for a six-inch dagger, useless for combat. *Well, I'm a woman, not a soldier.* Nevertheless, she took the long, sharp iron spit she used to roast a side of mutton, if only to employ as a pointer to show the men where to stand and wait. Then they all returned to the upper opening of the supposedly non-existent middle path up the mountainside.

Would there be enough time?

Jerusha walked down the slope to the two places she had earlier considered for her ambush. The two sites had to be *within* the gully made by the path. She thought marching infantry, especially if massed, might make a better target from in front than would individual helmeted heads from above. Since the two sites opposed each other, each had extreme advantages and disadvantages, depending on the direction of enemy approach. If her concern was that the Romans knew of her discovery of this path and therefore would use one of the two more-traveled paths to get behind the partisans, then placing her ambush on the right looking downhill would be suicide. Behind the natural wall was, due to the twist in the path, an excellent place to hide a dozen men, with plenty of room to use their weapons, even slings and javelins, between the rock above and around the gully-wall. But all the men would be totally exposed if the Romans descended from the partisans' rear.

Using the large niche on the *left* of the path presented some of the identical advantages, if the enemy were to come *down* the path, and the same disaster if they came *up*. Would it boil down to how smart the Romans thought this band of outlaws was? Did anything Jerusha said to the horseman the night before make him reject a direct approach up the path? She would *have* to choose, and she chose Roman arrogance as the deciding factor: Why would they travel twice as far to play two deceptions on a stupid bunch of undisciplined bandits? Jerusha would place her ambush in the *right* niche. The enemy would come directly up the path. She hoped.

But Jerusha would hedge her bets and station each of her best two runners and climbers, at each end of the path, to hide and wait. Whichever saw the enemy approach would run behind the short ridge and draw the other men to the right ambush site depending on the approach. If he was too late to place himself at the start of the ambush, he could still shoot arrows at Romans from their rear, using rocks as cover. As soon as Jerusha knew for certain the enemy's line of march, she could still change locations for her ambush—they were only fifty feet apart, and the twist in the path and gulley would cover the maneuver. If the men were very quiet. *If* the Romans weren't very cautious. If, if, if. Jerusha vaguely remembered such desperate "ifs" from years ago, but put the thought out of her mind.

Jerusha then explained her plan to the men, and it astonished her that they all seemed to understand it — they, who had never discovered the construction, or even the purpose, of a latrine.

The two young bowmen took their opposite positions quickly, quietly, and invisibly. The other men were placed in their right-side ambush, with each man in the position in which he could best use his weapon. Jerusha had dreaded this part, but was pleased the men knew their exact places better than she ever could have. Then the one thing Jerusha least expected occurred: The men started praying. Not quietly, not standing at the ready, but noisily, animatedly, complete with prostrations, dust-showers, and what she considered weeping, wailing, and groaning. She could understand almost none of it, for the caterwauling was mixed Aramaic and Hebrew, and idiomatic in neither. Zealous Pharisees; what should she have expected? Her panic rose, until she looked as far as she could in both directions, and saw no sign of the approach of the Romans. The bowmen at each end of the pass remained silent, and, she hoped, watchful. The others finally returned to their positions and complete silence.

It would be a long time before Jerusha would learn this temporary distraction saved her from the infinitely more stressful wait between when an ambush is prepared and when the enemy might, or might not, walk into it.

It was fortunate that the twists in the gully and the ambush positions prevented the gap from becoming an echo-chamber, for a few minutes after the prayers stopped Jerusha heard what at first seemed to be a desert insect crawling or burrowing over her head, but was, in fact, her archer from below the path hurrying along the rocks to report sighting the enemy approaching. He estimated it as a "decade" which Jerusha now knew was about ten men, but she was impressed the bowman knew this. Jerusha sent an equally swift youth to bring back the uphill archer to join the ambush. She had chosen the right site for it, after all.

The time now seemed endless to her, but the men were quietly readying their weapons. Since Romans never marched in step, not even on parade, the only sound she could hear from them was a strange shuffle and a few clinks of metal, gradually increasing. Jerusha could not resist finding a chink between two rocks from which she could see the advancing Roman column; it was just rounding the lower niche which she had rejected. To her, the scene was breathtaking, despite the film of dust on the uniforms and shields. The officer was in the lead, mounted on his richly caparisoned horse, all silver, gold, and red. Jerusha now knew this was the rider she had spoken with the night before. The massed men behind him were only slightly less colorful, all in shiny bronze and silvery metal, flashes of crimson and red-brown breastplates.

They carried their tall lightning-emblazoned shields at their sides to help them climb, rather than in front, which would have offered some protection had they suspected anything. And they were all marching directly toward Jerusha, as if to pay homage.

At the precise moment the last part of the Roman column reached the place where the walls of the gully restricted the soldiers the most, not far in front of the ambush, all the partisans let fly with whatever projectiles they had. Half the enemy was on the ground in less than a minute. Many of these were not gravely wounded, but in shock they had been attacked and hurt at all. It made no difference to the Zealots; they darted from their positions, slit the throats of those who were down, and scurried back. Through the dust Jerusha could see at least five arrows in Roman bodies, though she only had two bowmen. They must have concentrated on the rear of the enemy to hinder escape. Javelins and spears were harder to see from in front, and shots from slings were impossible, but all of Jerusha's men were in a frenzy of activity, and enemy soldiers kept falling to the ground. The mounted commander was in front. He wheeled toward the rear of his men immediately, but when he saw all was lost, he turned about again, right next to Jerusha, which was his misfortune. During the confusion she had crossed the path and was therefore on the near-side of the commander's horse, which made it almost impossible for him to use his short-sword, also on the near-side, against her. His one spear must have been thrown at the first sign of danger, but as it turned out later, to no effect.

Jerusha swung her arms back and down with the handle of her sheep-skewer, and on the up-swing aimed just below the mounted Roman's thick leather breastplate. Afterwards, she could not remember whether she had really been aiming at his private parts, which, as she later learned, would have been well-protected by the pommel of his saddle. As it happened, she sideswiped the pommel, went up and under the breastplate and its felt padding, and through his entire body cavity diagonally. The force of her thrust drove the spit almost to its bent turning handle. To Jerusha's disgust, the officer fell off his horse toward her rather than away, onto the dusty pathway. She was too stunned to do other than stand there, when the officer spoke, almost in a whisper:

"But...but...you're a woman! A...c...*cook*?" That was when she drew her dagger from her sleeve and cut his throat. She wiped the dagger on his tunic.

She paused to study the dead officer's face, carefully.

When Jerusha was able to stand again and look around, her first thought was that it was her duty to count her dead and wounded. She barely considered the fact that she now thought of them as her *own* casualties, rather then those of a band of Zealots with whom she happened to be sharing the same countryside. She was saved from demanding a count by one of the older men who reported to her in a voice that not only commanded respect, it showed respect. For the first time it bothered her she didn't know his or many of the others' names.

"I've checked everyone, my lady. None of ours are dead, and only one is wounded — in his arm, nothing to worry about."

"'My lady?' Since when have I been addressed that way? Am I that delicate?"

He looked at his feet. "I thought it sounded more polite than 'Captain.'"

Jerusha tried to ignore the implications of these words. "What about the enemy?"

"All dead. All ten soldiers and one high-ranking officer. We managed to kill the horse, too."

Jerusha looked and walked around the gully, having to cover nearly its length. There was little blood on the Roman bodies, though plenty at and in the ground behind their necks, and on their faces where some slingshots struck home. She supposed the bloodlessness relative to what she expected was the result of using small or narrow projectiles, instead of hand-to-hand sword fighting. Or what had happened at Bethlehem. At first she regretted the death of the horse, thinking it would have been a useful pack-animal in the long march they must now make. Then she realized that had the horse escaped, it might have arrived in Jerusalem and raised an alarm before they had gone a great distance from this place of death.

Since no one else spoke, Jerusha ordered the men to recover all the weapons they could, their own and those of their enemies, rob the dead, and collect all the armor.

"But, my lady, we're supposed to be Judean peasants and shepherds. We can't wear armor."

"You can hide your weapons until they're needed, can't you? Why not armor? I don't want to see people killed through open-weave wool. But don't take that officer's armor. It's fancy-worked and silver-gilded as well as gold-encrusted. Someone is bound to keep it as a trophy, or give it to a lover, or sell it. An innocent person will be crucified. Also, remove all metal markings from the other armor. I don't know what it means or how recognizable it is, and neither do you. Make the leather as nondescript as possible. And did I forget to say? Do all this instantly. We have ten miles to go before we can rest."

"We can't carry all this!"

Jerusha replied as sweetly as she could, "With all my food you've eaten, my water you've drunk, my wine you've filched, my crockery you've broken, and everything else you've wasted, my donkey-cart back at camp is almost empty. But be careful, if it's overloaded and the donkey dies, you'll be pulling the cart yourself.

"Until we get back to camp, divide the spoils equally among the men."

"Yes, my lady."

"Have you back-tracked the Romans with a couple of armed

men, for a supply wagon? If so, bring it to the camp." There was none.

Jerusha almost forgot one thing. She returned to the dead officer, and twisted the mutton spit buried in his body, in several directions so that distinguishing between that wound and one caused by a javelin or spear would be difficult. Then she removed the rod and wiped it on another Roman's tunic. She had no idea what the authorities would deduce from the use of a kitchen implement as a weapon, and had no desire to find out. Besides, she would need it again to cook with, after a very, very good scrubbing. She detailed a man to run to camp for an oilcloth. Knowing horsemeat was forbidden to Jews, as soon as he and the others were out of sight again, she cut off the most edible parts of the officer's horse, wrapped the meat, and rejoined the rest at camp as soon as possible.

Jerusha had considered the possibility there would be no camp to which to return; that the Roman officer, who had known exactly where it was, would have sent a detachment to destroy whatever supplies they had. But Roman over-confidence had exceeded even her expectations. The camp was undisturbed. Jerusha supervised the loading of the donkey-cart, while caring for the beast during breaks. She needed to insure all spoils of the victory had been camouflaged, and especially that the blankets were stacked on top. They had been needed only on the coldest nights, but now winter was approaching, and they would be needed every night, and even at times during the day, at least until the men were out of the mountains.

Jerusha considered destroying all evidence of the campsite, but that would take too much time, especially with her improvements to it, and since they were leaving, what difference did it make how many men had lived there? Their number would probably be wildly exaggerated by its Roman discoverers, anyway, out of wounded pride.

Her men first hinted, then pleaded, for food; they had not eaten all day. Jerusha handed out what cold food was left, then promised a complete cooked meal that night. Jerusha had already concluded that a ten-mile march over this terrain would take two days. Though her sense of direction was still bad, she knew they had to go to the foothills far north of Jerusalem and a few discreet questions let her know roughly where that would be.

Jerusha's last act in the camp was to treat and dress her young archer's wounded arm. The cut was on the outer bicep, caused by a dying Roman's sword slash while the partisan was probably cutting this soldier's or another's throat, though the boy still had enough scruples to avoid mention of it. Jerusha's work allowed her to try to find out their names without admitting her previous ignorance. She learned that the boy's name was Nehemiah and the other young archer was his brother, Joab. After binding Nehemiah's arm, Jerusha gave the unguents to his brother and ordered him to change the bandages every two hours, and to let her know immediately if any green color or pus appeared. Both boys thanked her effusively, and she praised their outstanding work both as sentinels and fighters. They beamed like flattered children, filling her with conflicting emotions, of which the greatest was the urge to escape their growing attachment.

"Pray for us!" they both shouted as she left them, which superstitious act she had no intention of doing.

The ten miles were more like twenty, considering the climbing and descending the Zealot band had to suffer. Before the first sunset, the men fell into fervent prayers thanking the Lord for victory. At least these weren't as loud or physical as those that had panicked Jerusha before the ambush, but she still thought it prudent to search for the nearest stream and wash the blood off her clothes and body, and scrub the skewer, returning only after the religious observances were over. The next day gave

Jerusha more time to learn her men's names, though she still didn't know why she felt she had to know them. She doubted she could keep the Aarons, Ezekiahs, Menans, multiple Davids, Josiahs, Melchizedeks, Arams and Jedidiahs distinguished. She began to remember and identify the men themselves, however. She also began to learn their individual virtues and vices. She even perceived signs in herself of the much heralded love of brotherhood-in-arms, though she did not know it came from shared danger and respect, and would have denied it had its cause been pointed out.

Jerusha prepared an outstanding supper the first night, though the spicy stew consisted mostly of horsemeat which she had to disguise as mutton; any toughness would be ascribed to the age of the meat, and none of them had ever eaten horse meat. She kept the men well-fed and happy, until the second evening, when she announced they would have to split up the next morning. They were reaching the foothills north of Jerusalem, and a band of men coming from the mountains would be exceedingly obvious to the authorities, especially after a fight such as they had won. They would have to separate by miles and hours.

Jerusha asked each man if he had a place to go for the leave time he would have coming, and a place or person to return to. Most had families to visit, either their own or their children's, except for a few who were looking forward to staying together in Jerusalem to see the sights, though they quickly advised her they would visit the Temple first. She assumed their money came from the dead Romans, since none of her men had been paid. Jerusha announced that she herself would drop behind with the donkey-cart. A simple woman, with a fixed residence in Bethlehem, would be less suspect. Each of the younger boys offered to escort her, but she rebuffed them sharply.

Jerusha, of course, had no idea where to go. Jerusalem?

Bethlehem? With what explanation for her absence, or profit to show from it? A cartful of weapons and Roman armor? And then go back to cooking and sewing for the rich?

Only an hour or so after the last man had left did she spot a rider heading toward her, whom she immediately recognized as Zachariah. He looked worse than ever, but she now knew this as a disguise. Though how it corresponded with his fine horse, she had no idea. He would undoubtedly be executed as a horse thief, rather than a Zealot chief.

Once in speaking distance, Zachariah greeted Jerusha with, "*Shalom.* So how's our heroine today?"

"Heroine?" she spat.

"Oh, I think wiping out a Roman patrol without the loss of a man earns some credit."

"Then why did you have such contempt for me that you abandoned me with the rabble in the wilderness?"

"Actually, I'm very glad I did, as things turned out. I admit to leaving you at the fringes of the fighting. I didn't want you killed the first day. But did you find the men to be rabble?"

"Yes!" she stated emphatically. Then, after consideration, "No."

"They're good fighters, aren't they?"

"I suppose so."

"They're among my best, though I'll admit they're not very fastidious. They were sent out there to rest. And they needed a good cook."

"I thank you," Jerusha said sarcastically. "How did you learn about the enemy patrol we ambushed?"

"Well, first we heard about it from the Romans in Jerusalem. They sent another rider soon after hearing the patrol had left. I also questioned each of your men as they entered Jerusalem. Extensively. We control the Ephraim Gate. It's in the north wall and quite small. We obviously can't enter through the nearest— Herod's—Gate, near the Antonia, and the next one is the main gate to Damascus, large and well-traveled, and as well guarded. So we have a distance to go.

"By the way, your men love you, you know," added Zachariah.

Jerusha was shocked. *"Love* me! They barely spoke to me for a month or so."

"That's their way," replied Zachariah. "Besides, they didn't know until the end that you were a born tactical genius. You know, I've heard of such people, but I've never met one. I certainly never suspected that my younger brother married one. Nor did the men, until the planning for the fight. Then the officer and sergeant among them kept quiet, and obeyed you."

"But...but..."

"Oh, shut up. What more glory do you want, than the destruction of a patrol and killing a tribune?"

"A tribune? He said the patrol would be led by a centurion."

"So you spoke to him?" asked Zachariah, seating himself on a rock.

"He first came dressed as one of your messengers."

"Pretty good, wasn't he? He spoke four languages natively, and his Aramaic was good enough to fool most of my men. His only weakness was a pride that equaled his talents."

"How do you know so much about him?" asked Jerusha.

"Oh, he's been around here much of his life, Marcus Gaius Pollonia. Or was. He was just about the only officer not transferred after King Herod died and Rome stole the country.

"As I said, vanity was his only vice; hence the silver and gold armor I heard about. That was his ceremonial uniform; he should never have worn it in battle. I'm glad you had the sense to leave it there. Though from my point of view a purchaser or recipient from your men wouldn't have been so innocent, possessing such a trophy without the courage to earn it the honorable way. Do you know what Marcus' position was?"

"I told you; at first I thought he was your messenger, then a centurion."

"He was a tribune, specially assigned to the Roman Governor. From one of the most patrician families in Rome, and one of the richest. His principal duties were those of Intelligence Officer for Judea. He knew almost as much about us as we did. Your skirmish saved dozens of men from crucifixion. Did you really kill him with a sheep-spit?"

"Yes."

"Pity. A Roman boar-sticker might have been more appropriate, though he wouldn't have appreciated the difference."

"Why was he out there in the wilderness?" she asked.

"Pride again," Zachariah shrugged, rose from his rock, and began tying his horse to Jerusha's cart. "Our tribune was a repulsive man once you got to know him. I have a theory that worldly success doesn't come from money. Any person or group with power can get it away from you. Nor does success come from power. Anyone with the right personality can get enough devoted patrons or followers who will take that away from you, too. No. What no money, official power, position, or talent can get you is an appropriate personality, and *that* will get you everything else you could want on this earth. I consider this a tragedy, for an attractive or commanding personality does not constitute virtue— as many of our virtuous but less ingratiating prophets discovered. Unfortunately, Marcus was born, as I said, with a remarkably irritating manner, and, whatever his talents and successes, he was falling out of favor with the authorities. Even his family in Rome didn't want him back; he must have spoiled many a patrician banquet. Promotions came slowly, and he was unlikely to get any more. Despite having survived annexation of Judea as well as a change of emperors—you do know Augustus died and his kinsman, Tiberius, succeeded, don't you? That's right; you were in the wilderness. The various successions haven't made any difference to us. Marcus also made it through four governors, including the current one, Valerius Gratus. Your Marcus was exceedingly valuable to Rome where he was, and nowhere above that. So, being Marcus, he had to show off (in the wilderness against a few bandits). He wanted a field success, however small; we hadn't been giving him much business lately.

"You know, you liberated me, personally. I've spent several years avoiding and hiding from him, and even tried an unsuccessful murder. Marcus was the only Roman who knew or suspected who I was. My only hope was that he might have thought I was dead by now. I'm finally a free man. I might even bathe and get some decent clothes." Zachariah took Jerusha's arm and urged her forward.

"Where are we going?" she demanded.

"The sun will set soon and we have to get in the walls."

"Then what?"

"Then you'll go to our headquarters. It's a slum neighborhood just inside the wall, where most of the tenants either don't know who we are, or don't care, or are passive allies."

"I've had enough of rough living; maybe I should go home," she said without much conviction.

"Of course, the most wanted outlaw in Judea, with a cartful of captured Roman gear. Don't worry; your quarters are large and I've assigned men, and women, to make them comfortable. They've been working full-time for two days. There's a tile bath, and I must admit that you smell a little ripe, too."

"And in return I can cook and clean for you?"

"No. You'll have your own servant. Don't you realize how valuable you are to us?"

"No," she replied emphatically, "and I've been used before."

"We're all used; isn't that what being of value to our fellow man means? But wait until you've seen your rooms. You can leave whenever you want, and even send messengers to Bethlehem. The

Romans don't know your name or where you live or, as yet, even that you're a woman. Their loss of Marcus's services is already crippling them."

This quieted her long enough that she allowed herself to be led into Jerusalem proper.

CHAPTER 5

Headquarters

Jerusha found that the city wall was as thick as it was at the Southern gate, which she had passed daily many years before, but this arch was much lower and narrower. She noted that the guards gave no sign of recognition as Zachariah passed, and Zachariah and she were not barred entrance or searched. Once she was within the wall, the stench of the slums assaulted Jerusha's nostrils. She remembered the smells of Bethlehem, but they were not this foul. Many weeks in the mountains had accustomed her to fresh, clean air, except when she was passing by the refuse and excrement of her men. She would not stay in this place.

Soon they entered a gated courtyard lined with colonnades, where the air was noticeably better. "My men live on both sides," explained Zachariah. The courtyard had obviously once been an atrium but the elaborate fountain had been remodeled or broken into a horse trough. Finally they approached the entrance to the tall, central part of the compound. The door was of simple oak, cross-braced and studded with iron, and flanked by a Mezzuzah.

Once inside, Jerusha could breathe pleasurably again. The upstairs window lattices stood open. She saw flowers arranged in vases, and incense matching or complementing rather than clashing with the flower scents, an offense she had noticed in the homes of some of her richest clients in Bethlehem. Most important was the absence of certain smells, indicating the existence of good indoor plumbing.

"See," said Zachariah, "we learned something from the Romans."

They stood in a small ante-room with an oil-lamp ceiling fixture high above. The room led to a carved staircase, which Jerusha ascended after Zachariah's motion. At the top of the stairs was a larger, white-washed hall, ending at the two windows with adjustable pierced-wood shutters. This hall had a few pieces of carved furniture bearing more flowers, and a brass Menorah.

"On the left," Zachariah announced like any thoughtful host, "is your bedroom. On the right is the bathing-room at the far end, and the privy at this end. Food and wine will be served in your bedroom."

"Who has admission to it?" she asked, suspiciously.

"Anyone you admit, or ask your servant downstairs to do so. You and she have the only keys, and there's an iron bolt on the door."

Jerusha entered the bedroom. It was almost larger than her entire house, with a platform for her bed, a large fireplace outlined in figured tile, carved corbels holding up the ceiling joists, latticed windows on two sides, a few fine pieces of furniture, a wardrobe, and, most surprising of all, frescoes on the walls. And, of course, the ubiquitous hanging oil-lamps, all burning. Her first reaction was to reject the place as a bordello, until she realized that all the pictures were of baskets of fruits and flowers, except for a pastoral scene on the longest wall. Surely, a whore-house would have more suggestive pictures? Then Jerusha vaguely remembered that Judaic Law forbade images of "all things in heaven or on earth, or in the seas," and inquired about this.

"Our Scribal Tradition determined long ago that that Law only applied to images that are used as objects of worship. Do you worship pictures of apricots?" he asked innocently.

She ignored him.

Jerusha crossed the hall and entered the bathing-room. The light-green tile bath was about three feet deep. It was a large oblong with two steps down into one end, a ramp to recline against at the other end, and enough room in the center for her to splash around in full length, if she cared to. On a table were large bottles of bath-oils and beside it two very large urns for hot and cold water. There was also a large brazier, with a shallow metal bowl beside it, for heating the water as well as the room. The fire had been set. The only other object, other than a hook for clothes, and the ever-present oil-lamps, was a full-length mirror made of recently polished metal.

Standing in the doorway, Zachariah explained, "This house was built before the Romans introduced hot and cold running water here, so we have to prepare our water. It wouldn't be a good idea to have Roman or Roman-trained plumbers rebuilding the place."

The last room was similar to the communal privy in Bethlehem, except that the floor was polished tile and a marble lip extended above the hole, high enough for comfort, and a wooden lid clearly meant to cover it. Also a large urn, full of water, to rinse the hole.

Back in the formal hall, Jerusha asked, "Do all of you Zealots live like this?"

Zachariah thought. "None that I know."

"Then how did you get it?"

"Some long-dead Hellenized Jew must have owned it, before the neighborhood became a slum, and the original mansion divided up. We keep it for special guests, when we get one, of which you are the first that I know of."

"Where is my donkey-cart?" Jerusha remembered.

"The military items are being distributed where they are most needed. Your personal things are being packed for you. We're taking the cart and donkey because you won't need them anymore, and someone has to take care of the poor beast, and you'll be living in luxury."

"Hah!" was the most elegant response to come to her.

"Would you like to meet your servant?"

Zachariah clapped his hands and shouted, "Ruth!" *She must have been spying*, thought Jerusha. The girl who entered was young and very homely, but had large hands and feet that looked accustomed to hard work.

"Take off your mistress's clothes and burn them," said Zachariah. "Lay out new ones, for day and night, on her bed. Light up the fireplace. But first heat the water and prepare her bath. I don't care how many trips it takes outside," he commanded.

Jerusha felt she had to object, "Are you the master here, or am I?"

"You will be, when you adjust to normal life."

"And until then, I'm a prisoner?"

Zachariah shrugged. "You can leave tonight, if you wish, and miss out on the best night's sleep you've ever had, and a delicious supper, not to mention the bath."

"I'll die of boredom."

"I doubt it. We also hold our highest meetings here. You should be entertained, even if your stubborn ignorance forbids you to listen." He added, "And some of our leaders are very good-looking." He ducked as Jerusha threw a sponge at him. "Just see how it goes." Then he invoked the blessing of God upon her and left for the night.

Jerusha entered her bedroom as soon as Ruth put bath-water on to heat. While she was there, another servant laid clothes out on the bed. Jerusha examined them slowly and carefully.

Some were no better than those Jerusha had made for herself, but some, especially those that were to go closest to her skin, were of the finest silk. Some she thought immodest, even though other clothes would cover them. The fireplace had been lit and banked efficiently. Jerusha dawdled as long as she could to let the bath-water heat. She would not take off her filthy rags until the servant was out of the room. That left her crossing the hall naked, but she peeked first to see that Ruth was out of the bathing-room and not to be seen.

As soon as Jerusha stepped into the warm bath, she almost jumped out again. The warmth was strange enough, but the liquid did not feel like water. It smelled wonderful, but it also felt both oily and astringent to her skin, and had colors shimmering in it. Then she remembered the table full of oils that must have been added. This was quite different from the cold water baths in her tin barrel-bath at home. Surely, this was the luxury Zachariah had spoken of.

First, Jerusha used the sponge which she had recovered from near the door to scrub the dirt and dried sweat off her skin. On a tile shelf she found scrapers, even those small enough for finger and toe nails, as well as brushes, hard and soft. When at last she felt clean, she just relaxed, occasionally swishing about in the bath. She found there was room enough not only to splash, but to reverse her position, head to toe. She even swam underwater a bit, as much as one could do in two feet of water. Then she relaxed longer, this time facing the opposite direction. Occasionally she caught a glimpse of her head and shoulders in the full-length mirror, but she grew used to this and ceased being startled or embarrassed.

Although Jerusha had always cleaned herself thoroughly, even in her most private places, she found it more pleasant this time. It must have been the oils. The more she gently rubbed herself there, the more pleasant the feeling became. Before long, it was not just pleasant; it was exciting, more than she would dare continue. She slowed her breathing and stretched in the warm, sultry water. Only then did it occur to her, in an instant, that she should have been experiencing her menses—the woman's curse— at about this time, and she had not. Nor had she for two or more months. Jerusha knew she could now follow whatever urges she had, without fear of pregnancy and children to compete with the memory of her own David, Jonathan and Abraham.

Just then there was a knock on her door.

"Who is it?" she shouted, almost screaming.

"Ruth, my lady, to give you your rubdown."

"No!" She saw the full-length towel hanging on the hook. "I'll dry myself. You may go home."

"But your supper is hot and waiting in your bedroom."

"Then I'll eat it there." Jerusha thought a moment. "Get the dishes late in the morning with breakfast. Snuff the lamps everywhere but the bedroom and here before leaving." Not being used to the phrase, she added, "And thank you very much, Ruth."

Jerusha climbed out of the bath, reached for the large towel hanging against the wall, dried off, and wrapped herself in it. She had considered avoiding the long mirror out of her habitual modesty, but after her excessive enjoyment of the bath, it seemed hypocritical. Besides, the light-green tiles of the bath had given her skin an almost deathly pallor and she wanted to assure herself that it was only an illusion. She stood up straight in front of the mirror and let the towel drop to her feet. It was the first time in her life that Jerusha had seen her entire body, and totally naked at that. Before, she had seen only those parts visible by looking down, and even then they were either clothed or barely visible in a dark metal bucket of cold water. Even back when she and Mordecai had made love, they were both dressed in night clothing of some sort, if not entirely covered by a blanket. Until tonight, in the bath and before the mirror.

Jerusha first examined her face. A few short months ago she had known a dozen or more women about her age in Bethlehem, mostly her customers, and she had come to expect networks of deep wrinkles on all women approaching forty. She was startled, almost embarrassed, to find her skin so smooth. A hint of crow's feet beside her eyes; no creases down her face or cheeks, but, irony of ironies, slight laugh lines near her mouth, on a woman who almost never smiled, much less laughed. The greenish pallor had not only been an illusion, but her face was slightly tanned from the mountainous wilderness for she had covered herself as much as practical while there. When the tan went away, so would some of the few facial wrinkles she had. Her hair was still a glossy nut-brown, with only a thin streak of gray. Jerusha now knew that her face was highly attractive, with her large, and wide-set eyes, almost black, her straight and slender nose, and wide, full lips. Maybe the latter would have been more noticeable had she smiled more often. She practiced once or twice in front of the mirror.

It could only be put off so long, so Jerusha stepped back a bit and looked down, and was again surprised. Her waist was narrow. She had to assume it was larger than when she was a bride, especially after bearing three children, but she couldn't tell — as a bride her modesty had never permitted her to dwell on her body. The stretch-marks from childbearing were still there, but not that noticeable. Jerusha's hips were firm, and her upper thighs were very slender, round and firm, as she had noticed in the bath. It must have been all the climbing and walking in the wilderness, and, before that, running all over Bethlehem making her deliveries. Her calves, of course, were correspondingly heavy and muscular. Jerusha was glad that the towel covered her callused feet. Her arms, as well, were distinctly muscular, yet feminine in contour.

Finally, of course, Jerusha had to consider her breasts. She was more familiar with them, having to handle them whenever bathing, dressing, and often binding them for freedom of movement while working. But she had never given thought to their sexual attractiveness, if any. As a bride she once briefly feared they were too small—not flat; indeed, quite round—just small. It never had mattered much; Mordecai had not been overly interested in that part of her anatomy, and there was always enough milk for her children. Now, Jerusha discovered, their size had helped defy gravity somewhat, and the slight sag inevitable for her age was nowhere near repellent, unless men were fanatically choosy, which she had never found them to be.

Yes, Jerusha told herself without vanity, she was extremely attractive for her age. She could have passed for a woman well under thirty.

I've wasted enough time on trivialities, she scolded herself, and wrapped the large towel around her, though not without a shameful suspicion that some other day she might try to catch a glimpse of her backside, and a closer examination of some other angles and places.

She hurried back across the hall to her bedroom, which had been fully warmed by the large fireplace.

The food smelled so good that it extinguished the aroma of the incense. It was laid on a small folding table set in front of a straight wooden chair. From her experience as a cook Jerusha knew immediately that her supper consisted of finely-slivered young lamb, garnished with some sort of fruit and fresh vegetables, braised not boiled. Soft barley bread, and a few delicacies and spices with which Jerusha was unacquainted, completed the essence of the meal. She tried to compare the food with the special dishes she had prepared in the past, but could not. It was done too differently, though, she concluded, at least equally tasty. The wine was better than she remembered in Bethlehem. She ate greedily, rested awhile to let it settle, ate some more, savoring slowly, then carried the table and tray into the hall outside her door. She suddenly found that she was extremely tired and sleepy. She snuffed the lamps in the bathing room, and then in her bedroom.

Jerusha put on the silk night-wear which Ruth had laid out, and climbed into bed, only to be immediately pleased again. She had never lain in a bed that was not stuffed with straw. Beating down protruding stalks, or even pulling a few out of her skin, had been a nightly ritual. Jerusha had no idea what this bed was stuffed with, but it was definitely not straw. It had to be a cloud, her drowsy mind told her. Her last thought was of the fresh mountain air coming through the lattices in her upstairs windows, far above the smells of the city. She only wished her sons could have once experienced such comforts, a thought she instantly suppressed.

⬩

"Please wake up, my lady," Ruth said, while gently shaking Jerusha. "Your breakfast will get cold."

"But I just ate," muttered Jerusha, when her brain cleared sufficiently to speak.

"You've been asleep since not long after sunset last night, and it's the noon hour now."

Jerusha forced herself out of bed and opened a latticed window. The sunrise should have been peaking over the distant mountains, according to her lifetime of habits and observations. It was instead directly overhead; at least she couldn't see the sun, and the city was blindingly bright. She slammed the lattice shut.

Breakfast consisted of warm bread and a soft goat-cheese which spread easily over heated bread, a mound of red pomegranate seeds with a tiny spoon, and several figs. She found she could eat it all with pleasure. Ruth left the room discreetly. When she was ready, Jerusha changed into street-clothes, a modified Roman stola made of wool, and adjusted the new sandals she found, also in the wardrobe. At just that moment, Ruth re-entered. *Could she have been spying?* Removing the dishes, Ruth said, "My lord Zachariah will be visiting in a while, if my lady has no objection?"

"No, let him in." Ruth quietly closed the door behind her. *So run report to your master,* Jerusha thought meanly.

It was almost an hour before Zachariah came and knocked on her bedroom door. During that time, Jerusha remembered the sensuality of the night before, and seriously considered whether Zachariah would be useful to satisfy it, and her other emotional needs. No, she concluded finally, and, she knew, forever. They had much in common, even personalities. He had a sense of humor, obvious to everyone. Jerusha thought she had one, despite all she had lived through, but if so, it was so dry that she doubted anyone, even he, knew of its existence. Maybe Jerusha's unloved sarcasm wasn't the same thing as Zachariah's attractive humor. But above all things Zachariah was truly a Pharisee and a Zealot, and she was—she didn't know what—but not that. Also, it would resemble incest, in her mind, and at every moment. Jerusha didn't care what Scripture or God said, one way or the other. It would be incest, and ultimately, if not immediately, disgusting. However much she liked Zachariah as a friend and relative, he could never be her lover.

The final, and fatal, consideration that guaranteed there would never be anything romantic or sexual between them was that Jerusha had virtually murdered Zachariah's wife and children, and even if he could ever forgive it, she could never forgive herself.

"Are you up and dressed yet?" he asked through the door.

"You know I am. Your spy told you."

"When will you outlive your peasant suspiciousness? *Of course* your servant has to know what you're doing, to help you, and will inform visitors as far as discretion allows."

"Hah!"

He entered. "You could also improve your vocabulary."

"And you, Zachariah, look almost human when cleaned and trimmed and decently clothed."

"So do you. Almost."

Jerusha admonished, "You never told me, or even let me guess, that you had access to such luxury accommodations, servants, clothing, and foodstuffs. I feel a fool for my occasional sympathy for you, ragged and starving in the desert."

"Do you think I would risk the mission and my men's lives just to satisfy my sister-in-law's curiosity? I tell no one any more than I have to. Besides, this isn't mine; it belongs to all of us," Zachariah concluded in his formal tone.

"But I was hoping you were coming to tell me what's going on," she said.

"Militarily? Let's both sit down." He made himself comfortable on the edge of the bed, since Jerusha was sitting in the only chair. "As you should know, our main operations are toward the West, between Jerusalem and the coast, mostly Caesarea. We intercept supply wagons when lightly guarded. Also shipments of Jewish slaves. The freedmen make good recruits. From their viewpoint, the Romans are justified in still calling us 'bandits,' not even rebels. Though we are currently attacking only soldiers. We can step up our actions a little now that we have your armor and weapons. Of course, we won't don the armor until just before a fight. If you were hoping for a big, bloody battle, you're out of luck. We don't have the men or the discipline."

"I noticed," she interrupted.

"We do have spies on all the roads and paths, and plenty of knowledge when Romans are on the move, or make a mistake."

"How can I help in all this?" Jerusha asked.

"I don't know yet. I was hoping you could help strategically, not tactically."

"What?"

"In the overall, national plan for liberation, not just in a skirmish, patrol, or ambush."

"I don't know about any big plans."

"Obviously," he said. "That's why you're here, instead of sitting on some anthill, waiting."

"I'm still waiting."

"You'll learn here," he said with conviction. "Meanwhile, you can write to Bethlehem. After the Sabbath I'll provide my most trusted scrivener and messenger. You can keep up with your business dealings. You can even go to Bethlehem when you want to."

"I suppose I should thank you for that!"

"I'll hold some meetings here, as much to keep you entertained as well as inform you."

"Are you then the chief of the Zealots?" Jerusha asked, almost in awe, which tone she quickly controlled before the question was complete.

"No. We have dozens of 'chiefs,' if you want to call them that. And our men are volunteer militia, not an army. They can come and go as they please, more's the pity. Even in the middle of a fight.

"But when a few of us rise to our level then we receive, and must deserve, greater trust."

Jerusha knew that Zachariah was coming to the important part of his visit.

"I've known you since you were a child, Jerusha. Even then I knew you were different from the rest of us. You know, for a long time, I was in love with you."

"Then why didn't you do something about it?" she demanded.

"You know perfectly well that marriages are arranged, and I

was chosen to marry Leah. But that's beside the point. I knew at the time that you were not a Pharisee. For that matter, I now doubt you're even a true Jew."

"You knew my mother!"

"So you were born a Jew. A child of Abraham. But since that night...that night in Bethlehem...I've had my doubts about your religion. Are you aware that as you entered this house with me you didn't even show respect for the mezzuzah beside the door? But that was just the last of dozens of signs."

"So what?"

"So everything. If God loses interest in our cause, nothing else matters. We are Pharisees. More than that, we're not willing to pray loudly and sit still, piously waiting for the Messiah to come. We're working, fighting, and dying to prepare his path."

"*Do you know who this Messiah is? Or where he is?*" Jerusha interrupted, vehemently.

"No, but he is coming, Scripture makes that clear. We must prepare the way for him, with righteousness as well as arms. When I questioned your men, they admitted they never saw you at prayer or services of any sort. They naturally assumed that you performed your obligations to God while they were away at their weapons practice, or when you were wandering in the wilderness, or rehearsing combat tactics, which, to some of them, is the same. Frankly, I don't know what you were, or are, doing," he concluded.

"Neither do I."

"Then what *are* you, just a blood-thirsty bitch?" Zachariah was no longer willing to mince words. His face was hard, harder than Jerusha had seen it since long ago in Bethlehem. "I know you don't care about the Roman occupation, one way or another. What are you after?"

"I don't know," said Jerusha. "Someway, someday, somehow, I will avenge my children. And yours." Though full revenge for the latter, she omitted to say, would require suicide.

"The Romans didn't kill our children as you keep pointing out, and King Herod is long dead. What now? You can't hate all your life."

"Can't I? But as I said, I don't know what I'm after. I beg you to never mention the 'Messiah' to me again."

"He's whom we're fighting for!" exclaimed Zachariah. "You know we will always talk of him."

"*You're* fighting for him."

"And you?"

"Maybe I'm practicing," she said, after a moment's consideration.

"Practicing? For what?"

"I don't know! I don't know! How often do you have to hear it?"

"How can we trust you?"

"By my actions. I kill Romans. I don't harm Jews. Don't you have *any* non-Pharisees in your band?"

"Yes," Zachariah replied. "We have a few adventurers, escaped slaves, fugitives from justice, and simple troublemakers. We even have a Gentile."

"Then consider me one of those."

"Not in my headquarters, with one exception. And I wouldn't want to think of you that way, anyway." Zachariah rose and stalked out. A moment later, he stuck his head back in. "Look, can you at least keep quiet about your religious opinions, if any, and go through proper obligations and the motions of piety while in public?"

"Certainly, if it pleases you. Teach me any extra rituals you want." She gave him a wave of dismissal and Zachariah went away. "Maybe we can fool God," she added, after the door closed. Jerusha passed the Sabbath in her room.

On the first day of the week, true to his word, Zachariah sent a scrivener and a messenger to Jerusha. Ruth announced them at midmorning. In keeping with her nature, Jerusha questioned them extensively about the length of time they'd been with the Zealots, how well they knew Zachariah and his family, about their families, Bethlehem, its economic life, any possible conflicts of interest they had there, and if they had family staying with the Zealots who could serve as hostages to insure their return or silence. She then sent the messenger to wait in the ante-room downstairs, with Ruth to watch him for any attempts to approach her room, and sat the scrivener at a small table and chair that Ruth had brought. Fortunately, he had brought a sufficiency of papyrus, ink, and pens. Jerusha dictated nine lengthy letters inquiring about the status of her business affairs and house. Many letters had identical passages, because Jerusha had left no one matter with only one factor. She believed strongly in duplication, so she could compare responses. She would not give names or locations to the scrivener; those were for the messenger only, to be written on covering sheets, sealed with her signet, which she always kept on her person. She therefore had to make hatchmarks on the letters, so she could remember which went to whom. She demanded equal caution among the recipients of the letters, and made no mention of where she was staying. Her signet would identify her letters, and she had previously described to the recipients unobtrusive and apparently accidental smears or marks by which their letters could be absolutely identified. Early on in this paranoid ritual, the scrivener would have thrown the work in Jerusha's face and left, were it not for his loyalty to Zachariah and the fact that he was well-paid.

Jerusha then took nine sheets of papyrus for the covers, and sent the writer away, watching to see that he passed the messenger without speaking. When the outside door was bolted, she called the messenger upstairs, and dictated names and locations for the covers according to the hatchmarks she had made, supervised his actions in every detail, and sent him to Bethlehem, although it was by then late afternoon. He explained that he would not return until the next day at the earliest, given the number of deliveries and delays for responses by the recipients, but had been given money to stay at an inn. The messenger also informed Jerusha that Zachariah would be sending a well-armed man to follow him to the inn at Bethlehem to insure that he would not be followed or intercepted on the way to or from the town. *Maybe Zachariah does have some sense, after all,* thought Jerusha. Then all she could do was wait. She found that the delights of luxury and leisure were beginning to wear thin.

Jerusha's messenger returned the next evening, carrying nine return letters and two small leather purses of gold. She kept him standing, while she had Ruth summon the scrivener. She had those parts of the two letters read to her wherein the recipients described what they had sent at her request, and she then counted the money. Still she was not satisfied, and had the scrivener point out to her the mentions in the letters of the amounts, to try to determine herself if the figures had been scraped out or altered by the messenger. All the identifiable marks of her factors were in the right places, so none of the letters were forgeries. Afterwards, she let the messenger go with Ruth, but bade the scrivener to stay.

He was permitted to sit. He read all the letters to Jerusha, slowly, most of them several times. Any slight contradictions between them had clearly been differences of emphasis, outlook, or personality, which she had already known about each of the factors. One of her correspondents was clearly a pessimist, over-cautious in his calculations and risk-taking, and Jerusha considered replacing him, but he nevertheless reported respectable profits, and perhaps a balance was needed among her factors, most of whom appeared almost jubilant. Another factor was sloppy in his itemizations, and showed little profit. Compared to the volume of business he conducted, it was clear that he was cheating Jerusha. She determined to dismiss him as soon as possible; until then, she would simply send him no further instructions or, of course, money. Each correspondent recorded the fee he had extracted from her funds for himself, amounts she considered excessive, but comparable to those admitted by the others, and she had little else with which to contrast them.

In short, Jerusha's business ventures were making her quite a wealthy woman, though no single factor of hers was aware of the totality of her ventures. She had been earning more money while she was away than she had while in Bethlehem. Further, her house was being excellently maintained. She sent the scrivener home in the late evening, with one of her last silver coins for his extra pains and time, as well as his honesty, now finally clear to her. She sent Ruth to deliver a coin to the messenger, as well. When all had left, she burned the letters in the fireplace.

Ruth's absence allowed Jerusha to prepare for and go to bed without concern that anyone would notice her omission of devotions or religious observances. The Sabbath would arrive again in four days, and she did not know how to continue to avoid it. But for tonight, she slept as contentedly as she ever had since that terrible night.

During the next few days, the absolute monotony of her life at the headquarters began to become oppressive. She slept comfortably, bathed often, ate excellently, except for the fasts which the Zealots enforced on her tiny household at what seemed to her unpredictable and ridiculous intervals. She was waited on assiduously or left strictly alone, at her whim, and had no duties or work to perform. It occurred to Jerusha that many a woman would envy her life now. But she was restless. She thought of a walk into a better part of Jerusalem, and perhaps a stop at a wine-shop, but hesitated due to her ignorance of how such an excursion might endanger the Zealot headquarters or herself. Further, she was unsure of local customs concerning women in the streets alone, and the awkwardness of making small purchases with her gold coins. She would wait until she could question Zachariah.

Worse, Jerusha's occasional nightmares were almost unbearable, despite her comfortable bed. Mostly, Jerusha relived that awful moment when she saw the shadows of her boys; limbs being chopped off to their shrieks followed by their silence of death. But increasingly her dreams included what she could not have seen—only heard: the bloody murder of Leah and her children, in the cupboard under Jerusha's staircase. Nevertheless, in her mind's eyes she could observe everything that happened in that enclosed space. Not one detail of horror was omitted or softened over time.

Two days later, Ruth said that her lord Zachariah had asked her to announce that he would be pleased to share the coming Sabbath meal with Jerusha, at her quarters, together with the family of one of his officers, and escort her to the Temple for worship the following morning. Jerusha was tempted to shout "No!" But it occurred to her that this might be a test, which, if she passed, would allow her participation in the councils of the Zealots, greater information, and greater freedom.

"Tell him I would be honored to share this holy time with him and whomever he wishes."

She spent the next day and a half questioning Ruth about religious rituals and ceremonies. She spoke casually, and, when she had to be direct, disguised her interest as that of a provincial unaware of possible differences in a big city. Much of what she heard refreshed vague memories from her childhood and her time as Mordecai's wife, but Jerusha was always unsure whether she was allaying suspicions or creating them.

CHAPTER 6

The Council

On the Sabbath, well before sunset, workmen brought a long but low trestle table into Jerusha's upstairs hall, along with four upholstered lounging couches suitable for dining in the Roman and Oriental style, and a clean, white tablecloth. They placed two standing oil-lamps in the center of the table, along with several small silver dishes which must have been intended for some ritual use later. Jerusha thought it best to stay back until summoned, while a few food-stuffs were brought up. Just before sunset, Zachariah arrived with a man in early middle age, and his rather plain wife. Zachariah stood before his couch at the head of the table as the patriarch, and when the couple stood before adjoining couches on one side, Jerusha felt it safe to enter and stand at the remaining couch opposite them. The men wore yarmulkes, while the unknown woman wore a scarf, similar to the one Jerusha had donned. Jerusha and the couple were introduced, and the lamps lit. So far, so good.

Zachariah immediately commenced a long chant in Hebrew, of which Jerusha could not distinguish much. The names *Elochim* (God) and *Adonai* (Lord) were mentioned what she considered an excessive number of times, as was the Messiah, though she must expect this from Pharisees and Zealots. When there was a general movement to be seated, she did the same. Each served himself, as the servants were at their own Sabbath meals. The food was not as savory as usual, though whether this was another religious custom, she didn't know or remember.

The next forty minutes were a blur to her; no normal conversation occurred, but instead numerous Hebrew phrases, and short rituals, which she hoped never to repeat if she could avoid it. When the guests left, Zachariah said, "You did well." This would have to do. And tomorrow was the temple. Fortunately, she could remember how to behave in the Women's Court even without Zachariah near her. She went to bed slightly depressed. Despite all the religiosity, Jerusha had never felt farther from God in her life. In the morning, the dishes would still be there, and she would have to eat cold food or leftovers all day, as no work was permitted on the Sabbath.

Temple was just as she had remembered it years ago; the Women's Court with a few scattered men, including Zachariah, and the boredom, tempered by the slight comfort of nostalgia, and some appreciation for the physical improvements to the hall, until Jerusha remembered that it was King Herod who built them. Afterwards, Zachariah took her back to her quarters, with barely a word between them.

After three dull, totally predictable days, Ruth informed Jerusha that Lord Zachariah wished permission to hold his war council in my lady's upstairs hall that evening, and Jerusha's presence and contributions would be deeply appreciated. This time Jerusha did not hesitate to agree.

The trestle table, now with seven plain, wooden chairs, was set up in Jerusha's hall again, and at the appointed time council members were escorted in by Ruth, with Zachariah in the lead. He took the head of the table, and Jerusha placed herself at the last seat on the left, when the others sat. While fruits and nuts were set out and the wine was poured, each of the men, in his own manner—shocked, annoyed, or merely interested— took obvious note that for the first time, there was a woman in attendance at the council. Evidently they had not been warned. No patronymics were used, but the five unknown men were introduced by their given names: Joel, Hezekiah, Moses, Asa, and Eleazar. As Jerusha was introduced to them, she noticed a somewhat different reaction to her from each, ranging from deep respect, to curiosity, to at least once, enmity. Zachariah must have told them earlier of Jerusha's success in the ambush, without mentioning her sex.

The meeting was a disappointment to her. It began with the usual invocation to God, led by Zachariah, but rarely got more interesting. These men were supposed to be discussing over all war plans, but none talked about anything but small operations; an attack against five guards traveling, or a tiny unit here, the armed theft of a supply wagon there, the liberation of a few slaves there, who were just as likely to be re-enslaved by these men. And, petty details of what supplies and equipment each officer would need to accomplish his mission. Zachariah said nothing, except to encourage each to speak and ensure he be listened to. After the last man spoke, Zachariah asked Jerusha if she had any thoughts.

"Well," she said, "Each of these leaders has more experience than I," she made herself smile at each in turn, "but can't we do something on a grander scale? I mean, for each Roman we kill, the governor can send for ten more from Rome. They must be crucifying our people at a faster rate than we're killing them, and they don't stop at combatants."

"True," Zachariah admitted. "But we don't have the men or support for a large scale battle." Almost the same words he had used to her before.

"Are you suggesting that we are already defeated?" she asked.

"Of course not. When the Messiah arrives, he'll be at the head of a host, with all the power and glory of Heaven."

Jerusha stifled a sarcastic or even blasphemous reply, with effort. "And what until then? Enlist the Sanhedrin, our priests who are scared to death of the Romans and continue to exist only at Rome's pleasure? The other Pharisees, who prefer prayer and ritual to action? The Hellenized, who are profiting comfortably? The Essenes, who pray and fast in the wilderness? Our shepherds with their staffs and crooks? Herod's descendants, who hate us more than the Romans, and are too busy surviving their ambitious kinsmen to bother?"

"No," he answered. "Have you any other ideas?"

"None," she had to admit. "Except that perhaps we should give some attention to the political and military *leaders* of the Romans. They might care about their safety and comfort. Of course," she added, "I'm only a woman."

"Thank you, Jerusha," Zachariah replied. "We'll give your suggestions careful consideration. Meanwhile", he addressed the others, "I'll arrange to get your men what they need, so far as is possible." Zachariah exchanged blessings with the men, and all said a few words in Hebrew.

As the men filed out, Jerusha wondered whether Zachariah had used her at the meeting for his own, secret purposes. She barely noticed that one man had lingered behind. She remembered his name as Asa, and recalled that the other men, having left in clumps, wouldn't have noticed his absence.

For once, Jerusha decided to say nothing while he stood in front of her in her upstairs hall. Asa was just sophisticated enough not to shift his weight awkwardly from one foot to the other. He had clearly prepared a speech in case he was challenged by Jerusha. He was not.

"Well, I...uh, that is to say...uh...," he stuttered.

"Yes?" asked Jerusha, affecting the manner of a great lady.

"Well, I liked what you said."

"Thank you. Which part?"

"Uh..."

"Would you like to step into my bedroom? There's an upholstered chair there, and a fire."

Asa blushed. Jerusha ignored it and let him in the room. All the time she was appraising him as a man. About her age. Embarrassed around strange women, and certainly not a smooth-talker, but above-average height, broad shoulders, muscular, no excess fat visible, pleasant face, and his comments at the council had been cogent, if not very original. Brave, and a good leader of men, as well as discreet, or he would not be here. Asa would do for her purposes.

Jerusha had heard from the giggling girls in her childhood that men were seduced by women's beauty while women were seduced by men's speech. It was evidently the reverse in her case.

"You're not, uh, married, or pledged to anyone, or...anything?" Asa asked after he was seated.

"Not that it's any of your concern," said Jerusha, purely for the sake of form, "but I'm a widow, have been for many years, have no prospects nor intend to have any. What about you?"

"I was widowed as a very young man, at the birth of my only child, and then he too died shortly thereafter."

This news made Asa a mixed bag. He could not be an accomplished lover, given his short experience and his religious proclivities.

On the other hand, Jerusha wasn't ready for someone who expected too much of her.

It was clear she had to take the initiative. "It's chilly tonight. Let's lie on the bed, and cover ourselves with blankets. I'm tired of standing, and the position of your chair doesn't allow for much conversation." He complied. A good sign: neither of them had mentioned the obvious fact that a slight push would have put his chair in perfect alignment.

Both remained fully dressed, but pulled the bed covers over them.

"You must understand," Asa said, "I'm a very observant Jew, a Pharisee, and, I hope, a righteous man."

"I'm sure you are," Jerusha replied, "That's why we have a Day of Atonement—just in case you ever had anything to atone for."

"Oh, no one is perfect!"

"That's the problem," sighed Jerusha. "I have many things to atone for. Lately, they have mostly been a matter of impure thoughts of the flesh." Enough excuses. She began to undress him under the covers, and he reciprocated. Jerusha found that with the heavy cloth and all the entanglements, the proceedings were not only complicated, but amusing enough to have to stifle a laugh. Especially as outlined by the firelight, the spectacle resembled a fight to the death between two very large and clumsy animals. But stifle laughter she did, out of respect for Asa's sensitivities. Even after they were undressed, both remembered they had not removed their sandals, and quickly did so. Jerusha was disappointed that Asa did not explore her body with his hands, but she used her imagination. Then Asa mounted her.

It was much as Jerusha remembered Mordecai doing so many years before, but there were several significant differences. Asa was stronger and larger in all parts of his body. Both Jerusha and Asa were physiologically ready for mating; Mordecai had often caught her unready, with awkward and sometimes painful results. Asa didn't talk about trivialities during the act, so Jerusha was free to think her own thoughts, which now centered on her tile bath and her attempt to experience that level of excitement. Jerusha enjoyed the proceedings—but building to what, she didn't know. The two men with whom she had done this had two things in common: it was over too soon, and there was no attempt to fondle Jerusha's body before or after the act. She wasn't sure why she resented that. After her breathing returned to normal, Jerusha had a vague thought that the absence of love or affection or commitment on both their parts was a detraction. She briefly felt like a prostitute; except that she herself had been the aggressor. She now felt little more than a slight boredom with Asa.

Then Asa committed the unpardonable sin: he apologized for his act of fornication. First to Jerusha, and then to God. Jerusha promptly ordered him to dress and leave. He was puzzled, but complied. *Never again with a Pharisee*, Jerusha decided. Maybe she could *teach* Asa or another, but it might not be worth the trouble, and it might undermine his respect for women or his religious faith and thus the cohesion of the movement. No. Maybe her bathing-room would be a better release.

Jerusha called down to Ruth to let Asa out and bolt the door behind him, with the excuse that they had been discussing tactics on his next, most difficult, assignment. Ruth appeared to believe her.

Several days, including at least two Sabbaths, of luxury and boredom ensued. *Maybe she should go home; looking at ledgers, whether or not she understood them, must be better than this.*

She settled for communicating with her factors in Bethlehem using the same elaborate and over-cautious procedures as before, and demanding the same scrivener and messenger. *Zachariah must be getting exasperated at such time-consuming methods*, she surmised. The replies Jerusha received were, after thorough examination, much more satisfactory than before, and the bags of gold, meant for non-existent expenses, held considerably more than before. Jerusha was now, without a doubt, a rich woman.

Then, one evening several weeks later, it was announced that another council meeting would be convened in her hall. *What if Asa is in attendance? What can we say to each other?* Jerusha need not have worried; Asa was convalescing in a private home after receiving a serious wound. She didn't even ask what caused it. In his place was a tall stranger, who, she was told, had been absent before due to being on personal leave. The man didn't look right at all. Alone among the Pharisees, he was clean-shaven. He was too tall, had a short, pudgy nose, and freckles, which she had never seen on anyone but small children, and a larger jaw than Jerusha had ever seen. The rest of his body was in excellent proportion to his height. He was introduced as Khimrik, a strange name, perhaps even unique. But he must have been trusted by the Zealot command. Jerusha thought she had better concentrate on the meeting, if she would ever learn anything.

But before she could listen to any of the litany of insignificant skirmishes, past and future, Khimrik lifted back the hood attached to his heavy winter robe. He had worn the hood lower over his brow than was common, and had had a small silver clasp fasten it at his throat. When he pushed the hood back, she was startled to see what the bulky cloth had hidden. Khimrik's hair was bright yellow, very fine, and worn long, and his eyes were pale blue. The eyes looked innocent beyond belief, but was there a hint of amusement there? Jerusha had heard that not a few Romans had yellow hair, cut short. She had never seen it, as almost every Roman she had ever observed was wearing an all-covering helmet, but she had seen several Romans with blue or gray eyes. *Perhaps*, she thought, *all men with light eyes had yellow hair?* But if this man was a Roman, what was he doing *here?* Her curiosity would have to wait until the reports and deliberations of the council were over. She found it difficult to catch up with the discussions.

"So," Zachariah was speaking, "Marcus' death is still helping us. I wonder with whom they will replace him? The Romans have unmasked none of us lately. Without intelligence, they have to garrison their troops thinly along the roads to the coastal ports leaving us to pick and choose our targets, at times most convenient to us. Your reports show increases from one to three or so supply wagons. Our ambushes kill a few more Romans. Fewer of their officers confiscate estates with an eye to comfortable retirement. They have stopped their small, efficient patrols. We collect a few more spoils.

"But my sources report another Roman legion on the way. They are all veterans from fighting the barbarians to their north. Meanwhile, the roadside forest of the crucified grows."

Khimrik spoke, smiling, "You Jews play at war. You avoid torture, killing women and children, destroying crops and villages."

Jerusha noticed that Khimrik's accent wasn't Galilean, Samaritan, Roman, or any other she knew.

The man called Joel turned angry and barked, "I refuse to argue religion with you again, Khimrik, but we are commanded by the God of Mercy, so drop this fruitless point."

Khimrik laughed, "I heard that the ancient armies of Israel did everything I said, and worse."

Joel spoke again. "That was when God was in *direct* command, and spoke with us almost daily. None of us claims such authorization now, except to abide by the laws of a just war."

"Do the Romans?" rejoined Khimrik.

"They are not under Judaic Law. If we cannot win justly, we are not ready for the Messiah."

"Oh, quit your hypocrisy," snarled Khimrik. "You know that you don't kill Roman women and children because there are almost none here. You don't destroy crops and villages because they're all Jewish, and you've never learned that if they're not fighting on your side then they're against you. Or totally useless, which is much the same thing. Neither do you destroy the governor's residence or the arena or even the 'Pagan' temples because you have not the strength...you are weak." He laughed.

"See?" exclaimed Joel, "Khimrik the Blasphemer is a traitor.

He thinks our cause is contemptible." Joel then muttered almost to himself, "Gentiles and women; what next?"

"No," said Zachariah. "Khimrik's no traitor. I've seen him fight. And he always wins." He spoke the latter pointedly, but at whom, Jerusha was unsure. "However, Khimrik has reminded me of a point that was brought up at our last meeting, by Jerusha, over there. The Romans are too comfortable. Think on it: The common soldiers and lower administrators have no choice, they're ordered here. More and more of them come from Rome's far-flung provinces and border areas like Spain, Gaul, allied Frankish tribes, Pannonia, Sicily, Greece, Anatolia, Armenia. Anywhere but that great city on the Tiber, whose residents pay, use relatives, or hide or run away to avoid coming here, whenever they can. Their leaders, from the governor on down, however, are almost all from Rome itself, and are all volunteers, however reluctant. They might not like it here, but service in such a troublesome province helps their promotions and careers, and avoidance of Judean service for Caesar harms the same, while outright refusal of it could be fatal.

"If Rome's best and most competent leaders begin refusing, or learn the avoidance techniques of their co-citizens, and they have relatives influential enough to succeed more often, what will happen?"

"The Romans here will be leaderless and go home!" exclaimed Hezekiah, who rarely spoke.

Jerusha now knew why he was usually silent; he was not very intelligent, whatever his other virtues. Hezekiah had been trying to conceal his limitations, relying on a saying, as worthless as all other common sayings. It was from Proverbs, she thought, that "even a fool is thought wise if he keeps silent, and discerning if he holds his tongue." Jerusha knew this rarely worked for long; better to speak, and perhaps sometimes say something which appeared very subtle, or even uncommonly brilliant, if accidental. But this was not Hezekiah's day for seeming bright.

"No, my friend," Zachariah responded kindly. "Tiberius Caesar will not give us up until the Messiah forces him to. But you all saw what happened to the new aqueduct when its original chief engineer returned to Rome and his work was taken over by an inferior, awaiting a suitable replacement. It took several years to repair the damage.

"What will the opposition to the Messiah be like when the governor is an incompetent distant relative of the emperor who couldn't figure out a way to avoid such a posting? When the logistics officer, improperly trained, sends all the food to one of our regions and all the weapons to another, or blocks everything at Caesarea awaiting the right form of documents out of fear of making a mistake or acting on his own? When, to bring this closer to home, the new intelligence officer finds it more comfortable and far less dangerous to stay in his quarters and invent his estimates until his time here is up? In short, when Rome can send only its second or fourth-rate leaders, because her best won't come, or *can't* because they're dead? I believe that long after the Messiah has liberated Judea the Roman Empire itself will fall, not because of its lack of soldiers or will, but because of incompetence at the top levels. Though why this will happen I don't know; but we can help it along here. For the foreseeable future, Judea will still get a few Romans who are intelligent, brave, and dedicated, but those three qualities rarely go together."

Nevertheless, Jerusha was certain that Zachariah believed that all three qualities coexisted in him. Maybe he was right.

"Roman leaders dead?" Hezekiah queried again. "Will we invade Rome then?"

Definitely not his day, thought Jerusha.

"No," sighed Zachariah. "The skilled Romans would be killed here."

"But they don't fight, often."

"I know, my friend. But they walk about in Jerusalem. Sometimes heavily guarded, sometimes lightly guarded, and often unguarded at all."

"Is this lawful?" asked Joel, perceptive, but legalistic as usual.

"I know of no prohibition against it, and several of our groups practice it often. The Romans call such killers the *Sicarii*. We call them dagger men," said Zachariah.

"Do you, Jerusha, know of any proscription against such warfare?"

"No," she replied quickly before Joel could challenge her credentials in the Law.

Once again, Hezekiah ventured, beyond his depth. "But how does this square with the commandment, 'Thou shalt not kill?'"

Zachariah was beginning to lose his patience. "What do you think we've been doing all these years? The commandment reads, 'Thou shalt do no *murder.*' We're contemplating no killing prohibited by our Judaic law, or the laws and customs of war—as uncodified and ambiguous as they are. Just now you thought, Hezekiah, that you were quoting the Scriptures. I wish as many people *listened* to the Scriptures, or read them, as quoted them. There must be at least fifty places where killing of people is not only *not* discouraged, but actually commanded by God. Justification for the killing is always described in those passages. And these killings are only sometimes left to men in authority. Often, everyone around is commanded to participate. Frankly, offhand, I can think of not more than a dozen places where killing is specifically forbidden in the Scriptures. Fortunately, almost all the things that would *lead* to unjustified killing are strictly forbidden to us, if not the Romans. Therefore, let us hear no more of the wrongfulness of Zealot orders to kill. We are not Romans; we do not invade other lands; we do not force people to convert to our belief. Most of our punishments for crimes consist of money fines. It is *respect* for life that causes us, under special circumstances, to execute, but never to murder."

Except for innocent children in Bethlehem! Jerusha's mind intruded.

Joel doggedly responded to Zachariah, "There is a difference between killing armed men in a fight, and sneaking up behind someone in the street with a dagger. I think rabbinical scholars would agree with me."

"In all good sense," Ezekiel concluded the discussion, firmly, "How could it be more lawful to kill soldiers and men who have no choice, who are under orders, than to kill those above them who devise and enforce those orders?"

There was general approbation around the table.

"But who will be our dagger man and do that kind of killing?" asked Joel.

"Of murder," interjected Hezekiah as his last word.

"Leave it to me. I'll find one," said Zachariah, and added, "If there are no further questions, we are adjourned." He rose, as did the others.

Once they all stood Jerusha asked, almost shyly, "Has anyone here ever heard, or heard of others hearing, of a family leaving the town of Bethlehem, almost twenty years ago, perhaps in disgrace?"

Their blank looks told her all she needed to know.

"Then let me ask one more question. Has anyone here heard of a young man, not of royal birth, claiming the throne of Judea..."

"Who would want it, now?" said someone and at least one other laughed.

Jerusha continued as if uninterrupted, "...or claiming to be the Promised Messiah?"

Several people exclaimed, almost simultaneously, "Blasphemy!"

"Just asking; I didn't say he *was* the Messiah. Indeed, I know he is not."

Zachariah calmed the hubbub by declaring that if they found him, they would kill him. He gave the closing prayer in Hebrew, which prayer struck Jerusha as longer than the previous one.

As the Council broke up, Jerusha noticed that Zachariah was more active than usual, scurrying to say a few words to each departing member, then drawing them together into small groups and changing subjects, then shuffling groups, and raising other subjects. He followed this pattern from the large hall all the way out the front door. Jerusha found herself swept along in the dance. It wasn't until she was in the courtyard that she understood the purpose for this apparent confusion. She was suddenly alone with Zachariah, with no one the wiser, and bundled in a hooded cloak he had previously stored near the door. It was chilly outside.

While Zachariah guided her along the corridor to the left, she complained, "Why was this silly ceremony necessary? You can speak with me privately anytime you want."

"I need to talk to you in my quarters, a few doors further along down here, and we need absolute secrecy, even that we met."

Jerusha admitted to her curiosity concerning how Zachariah lived, so she let herself be led. She was ultimately disappointed; a simple barracks-room, no fancier than her main room in Bethlehem—but with a martial flavor she did not expect in the hiding-hole of a partisan. This was due, she discovered, to a few carefully displayed Roman trophies Zachariah had captured over the years, including what appeared to be a solid gold laurel wreath of a very high ranking officer, mounted on a carved head. There was also a carved and gilded standard with four markings, though Jerusha could neither read it nor be certain that the markings were letters. The standard was surmounted by its Roman Eagle and embossed underneath with the numerals—or letters, for all she knew—of the legion it came from, with battle and campaign medallions and streamers attached. Zachariah noticed her examining it and added, with glowing pride, "The

Romans worship these standards and their idolatrous eagles, and will fight to the last man rather then let one be captured. They did, but we concentrated our forces at that one spot, and carried it away. They still have units searching for it."

There were two mounted Roman short swords, with hilts of different designs, giving Jerusha no idea as to whether they were of different units or were captured many years apart. There may have been other trophies, but Jerusha didn't recognize them. The room was as clean and tidy as a soldier's room should be.

"These can get you killed," she said off-handedly of the trophies.

"So can almost anything at headquarters. Besides, I might need a bit of a disguise someday." She gave him a hard look. "All right, I'm human, I still have pride in my accomplishments," he laughed.

"What I need to talk to you about, Jerusha, is..."

"You want me to be the murderer the council talked about."

"Well, uh, yes..." said Zachariah hesitantly.

"Fine. When do I start and whom do you want killed?"

Zachariah pulled out two camp stools for them, facing each other. "Let me explain a few things. Our unit has always fought as one, with conventional tactics. So we have no one with experience in...this. And there aren't any books on the subject to study."

"I don't read, anyway."

"I forgot. Well, there are no rules except that there *are* no rules. Some common sense: the *sicarii* (dagger men) must plan well in advance, and should take every advantage they get. Also, their faces should be completely unknown to the Romans. Certainly a woman would be unexpected. And you were the one who explained the reasons for this tactic in the first place."

"You're wasting time telling me the obvious," snapped Jerusha. "And stop saying '*sicarii*'. Murderers is more honest, as Hezekiah said, and I prefer. Still, wouldn't a man be better?" she asked.

"No." he answered. "You've forgotten that we soldiers are brothers'? Glory? Honor? These are masculine traits, more suited to fighting in a group. And you. You're different. You don't seem to have any real affection for your comrades or respect for your superiors."

"Then men aren't as committed to the cause, or whatever it is, individually? They have to have a gang to urge them on?"

Zachariah was becoming visibly uncomfortable. He said, "Don't credit excessive virtue to your sex. *You* don't seem to like women any better. Of course, where poor women's only work is to care for their families, homes, and the menfolk, they don't tend to congregate. You didn't have friends in Bethlehem, and the whole time you've been here you've never cultivated the other men's wives. As far as I can tell, whatever isolation brings you, you prefer it to humanity."

These remarks made Jerusha increasingly agitated; she got up from her chair and started pacing. Then she considered Zachariah's words seriously, and responded with deliberation, "When other people aren't actually vicious they're cowards or utter fools."

"Well, that answers *that* question!" Zachariah replied with a slap on his knee. "But you may not like certain other changes that must be made in your life. You can't live at headquarters anymore. I've found you a fourth-floor room near, but not too near, the governor's residence and his major administrative offices.

"I will send you a messenger designating your new target every once in a while with whatever information we have about him. Tell the messenger what you need in return."

"Your last 'messenger' was a Roman tribune," she reminded him, while in the middle of the room.

"From now on," he replied, "any messenger of mine will have a Roman denarius which he will show you, displaying the outline of Caesar Augustus' face, before the messenger speaks."

"How would I know one fat Roman face from another?"

"Oh quit your quibbling! *Any* face on a silver coin is a strange way to introduce oneself, except to a whore. So don't dress or lurk as one!" Zachariah calmed himself. "Memorize the first coin. And don't come back to headquarters unless I summon you for a council."

"Don't worry; I've grown thoroughly tired of this silken palace for pampered cats in which you imprison me."

Zachariah was wounded. "Haven't we done everything here to make you content?"

"I'm bored. I'm bored out of my mind."

"Well, we have a number of books, no, you can't read them. You understand we can't have live entertainers. And letting you wander around Jerusalem always to return here would be dangerous."

"As an independent killer I will be free to come and go as I want, without endangering anyone, won't I?"

"Yes, within the neighborhood chosen for you. And before you strike."

"Then, to repeat myself, when do I start?"

"In a few days," said Zachariah. "I can't have you move out the morning after the council has discussed the plan. *No one* but you and I can know what you're doing. I do have one surprise for you, though you seem to know everything. It was meant to help persuade you if you balked. Your first victim was chosen purely for your own appreciation."

"Who? I don't know any Roman." She was less than interested, and slumped into her chair. His next few words made her jump to her feet again.

"A man named Isaiah. An old, retired leader of Herod's Men-At-Arms. You knew him many years ago as 'Isaac'."

CHAPTER 7

The Dagger Man

The shock made Jerusha almost physically ill, as she suddenly relived that night in Bethlehem and Isaac/Isaiah's murder of her family.

"It won't do our movement any good, but it ought to offer a little satisfaction to you for the sake of your David, Jonathan and Abraham."

"How do you know who he is?" she finally asked.

"We have had people in the Antonia, from time to time. And once Isaiah was retired, the other guards gossiped about him in detail with both admiration and hate, and in your case, envy. His companions saw you, and he described you to others."

"His death will also serve your purposes, Zachariah. Revenge for your poor Leah, and your little ones Amos and Samuel. He killed them, as well as mine; did you know that?" Jerusha sat in the camp stool again, glad to share her anger with him.

"Yes. I considered that, and envy you your assignment."

"By the way, if you know who Isaiah is, and probably where he lives, then you should know at least something about the False Messiah!"

"How can I investigate someone who was killed in infancy? The real Messiah is coming. The false one is dead."

"He's *not* dead. But this Isaiah soon will be." Suddenly, Jerusha knocked over her camp stool, threw back the bar on Zachariah's door, and returned to her quarters alone. Ruth let her in after a quick look through the grille. On the way up the stairs, Jerusha was already planning her killings, at least the first one, but on entering her bedroom her plans left her head. There was Khimrik standing straight, facing her door, and wearing nothing but his loinclout.

Jerusha's first thought was how he was the finest specimen of a man she had ever seen, even in his middle age, but it was quickly followed by her resentment. "How did you get in here?"

"That skittering around which you and Zachariah performed on leaving."

She threw a blanket over him and commanded him to sit. This time, there was a second chair opposite him, arranged by her so she would never be faced with the same awkwardness as she had been presented in the case of Asa. She sat in the second chair, and looked hard at Khimrik.

Jerusha said, "I don't even know your patronymic."

"In my native land we don't use patronymics, only descriptive terms. But I'm Khimrik, the only surviving son of Khunan, King of a tribe that lives between what the Romans call the land of the Corintani and the Cornovie."

"King? Then why are you here?"

"My father was murdered by a neighboring king, Brant, who also took the kingdom, what there was left of it. Not even the name has survived."

"Then why aren't you back there exacting revenge and recovering your birthright?" she demanded. Jerusha felt personally affronted.

"Oh, I suppose because my father murdered Brant's father to

start with, in the hope of taking *his* kingdom," he laughed, "and my 'subjects' never having been used to stability, are probably perfectly satisfied with Brant as their king. We don't take these dynastic changes as seriously as you. Though I must admit both Rome and Judea tend to have a few such squabbles, but they usually keep them in the family. The Caesars and earlier consuls have always been Roman, or at least Italian, and almost all from one or two family lines."

Jerusha could not understand any fighter who was not motivated by conquest, vengeance, or guilt. Khimrik obviously was uninterested in revenge. And as for guilt, he appeared to feel none in any sense that Jerusha could understand, or he could express.

Although Jerusha would normally have no interest in such matters, the strangeness of the situation, and of Khimrik himself, intrigued her. "Were there religious differences between the two kingdoms?"

"I wouldn't know. There might have been, but our practice has always been that the conquered people accept the new king's religion, habits and customs. We're not as stiff-necked as you Jews are. We're more interested in the truly important things, like land and gold."

"Where is, or was your kingdom?"

"On a very large island in a distant sea. The Romans call it Britannia."

"Is that as far from here as Rome?"

"More than twice as far, though in roughly the same direction."

"No wonder you look so different from us. I didn't know the world was so large!"

Khimrik laughed again. "It's a lot bigger than that."

"What did you do, with neither father, nor king, nor country?"

"The same thing most of us disinherited princes do; looked for another tribe who would ally with me. But I was only fifteen years old, having been trained by my father to be a soldier at only thirteen, not giving me much time to learn inter-tribal intrigues. I was the only one of importance to escape alive. Had I been more experienced I might have had more sense than to approach a small Roman raiding party. I didn't know they were only scouting, and had little interest in more conquest at that time, much less getting involved in local squabbles. So they just made me into a slave." Khimrik obviously enjoyed talking about himself, and Jerusha was inclined to indulge him. She gave the expected sympathetic responses. Did his handsomeness make her more patient with him?

"It wasn't so bad," Khimrik chuckled. His humor was beginning to irritate her. *Didn't Khimrik take anything seriously?* "*We* were quick enough to enslave *our* enemies, or even travelers." He apparently sensed her interest. "It's getting uncomfortable sitting here so stiffly. May I relax or move around a little?"

"Not until I have all the answers I want. You looked comfortable enough when I walked in." Jerusha herself took the liberty to stand, sit, or move around while interrogating him.

"Ask whatever you like." At least he didn't laugh this time.

"How did you get here, and become one of the leaders of a Jewish Zealot band, at that?"

"It's a long story, but one I enjoy retelling. Though it would go better with wine, even the sweetened vinegar you call wine down here."

"No."

"Very well. My master was a good one. Certainly better than we would have been to one of his kind. And took me to see the world, or at least those parts his Legion traveled through. Marcellus let me fight alongside him many times in Gaul. Then we crossed the river Rhine, a gross mistake, but we were under the idiot Varus. He set us up in a fortress, and stayed there long enough for all the Barbarian tribes under Hermann, or Germanicus, to be united and surround us. I rather liked the Barbarians; we had more in common than I had with the Romans. I found I could even speak some of their language. But then Varus marched us out in a column into the Teutoburg forest, and the enemy attacked us on all sides. We were...what is the Aramaic word?"

"I hope 'completely destroyed,'" Jerusha said sweetly.

"Yes, but I prefer the word 'annihilated.' Only a few got away. I took Marcellus out of the fight, changed his garb, and went south with him, while the other refugees went north. And I was still a very young man.

"The Barbarians captured three standards with eagles on them: The 16th, 17th, and 18th legions. I got one of the standards away from them, and never let Marcellus see it, though he probably knew anyway; he was in a different legion and furious at Varus. I kept it hidden under our goods in a cart, wherever we went. It's in Zachariah's quarters now."

"I've seen it," she said, smiling. "But his story of how it got there is a little different than yours."

"I know. As if any Zealots could have destroyed a legion and captured a standard! But whatever he likes. Though later it did take me two days to go back to the Roman post north of Jerusalem, find where I hid it, and bring it back here. Many lies are told about the Roman wars with the Barbarian tribes. Usually after each glorious victory, the Roman commander is given a 'triumph'. A parade in Rome led by his captives and attended by Caesar and most of the population, with the commander all dressed in gold, in a golden chariot. It has been said that the Germanic tribes were more often 'triumphed' in Rome than defeated in Germania."

"I wonder who lies the most: Zealots or Brittanic?"

"Don't interrupt my lies.

"Before we came here, I lived in Rome for years. The women there are something to behold, and have few inhibitions. I think my master took great pleasure that his slave was one of the most desired lovers by women of all classes. I even enjoyed the long trip to Judea—the first thousand miles or so are green and lush. But after being here for over a year the monotony finally oppressed me. So one night I covered my hair and beard in black grease and walked out of my tent. There were few patrols to avoid, and I found native robes. I learn languages quickly."

"Did you kill your master before leaving?"

"Now, why would I want to do that? But I knew I had to stay away from the Romans; a number of them knew me. However, the only trades I knew were fighting and slavery, and the latter didn't appeal to me any longer."

He stifled laughter. "So I had to look for a fighting group and your people were the nearest I could find. I could cover my hair and keep my eyes in shadow, but my beard kept growing out red. So I shave it. There are enough Jews who follow the Greek and Roman custom of shaving, so with care I can wander around Jerusalem, so long as I avoid passing Romans. Your band thinks it's a brilliant disguise, and since I'm a Gentile, they don't consider me bound by your customs. I have the best of all possible worlds."

"How can the Zealots trust you? You're a freak in both body and conscience." She beat the bedpost for emphasis.

Khimrik looked as offended as she thought he was capable, which wasn't very. "My people don't have much of a god, if any. Certainly not a rule-maker like yours whose every wish you are supposed to obey in every aspect of life, just so you can feel righteous. Instead, we Britons can do pretty much whatever we can get away with. But this doesn't mean we're what you'd call 'evil.' I'll admit, our few virtues and vices are probably just an odd assortment of old customs. I got the impression you, Jerusha, were free of the tyranny of gods, too, but you don't seem happy about your freedom." He looked puzzled.

Jerusha ignored his comment.

Khimrik continued. "I myself have only two iron-clad laws,

but which I, not any god, made up. The first of these is courage, without which I'd rather be dead. The second one is loyalty. I can't even imagine myself betraying any person or people to whom I owe it."

"You were disloyal to your slave master."

"No, I wasn't; I never pledged him my loyalty, nor did he ask me to. The capacity to pledge loyalty is what makes one a free man, and I was a slave. I *have* pledged loyalty to the Zealots, and have proven it, and will prove it, any way they want."

"Have you no other morals?" asked Jerusha.

"Well," he considered, "a little one. I like most people, and I never go out of my way to hurt anybody, but that's my nature. My father was the opposite, I remember."

"But you spoke at the council in favor of total, merciless war!"

"Only if you want to win. If the outcome doesn't matter, any strategy will work. But I thought the Zealots *did* want to win. If not, there'll always be another war I can fight somewhere or another. I'll follow whatever rules I'm given."

"What do your men think about your religious or moral values? For that matter what does Zachariah think of them?"

Khimrik shrugged. "I'm a good play-actor, as any good leader has to be. And also any good subordinate. Not about anything I consider important. But Jerusha, you are being cruelly immoral to me. I've said I was uncomfortable. And I do have another virtue you are thwarting: I'm very good in bed, which brought me to this room in the first place. Is the examination over? Can I get up and stretch? Do you have any wine? Can we get into bed?"

"Yes, to all of those," Jerusha was startled to hear herself answering. She was now to be a dagger man; what were other offenses compared to that?

She poured the wine, and Khimrik took a long swallow. They almost lept into bed, but only after Jerusha remembered to shut the door bolt, remove her sandals, and drop her clothes to the floor, all of which took only a moment. Jerusha's first surprise came when she saw Khimrik's uncircumcised penis. She didn't know whether she was frightened or curious to the point of fascination. Her next experience was clearly, and intensely, pleasurable. Jerusha had also never hoped for a man who would spend half-an-hour exploring all of her body with his hands and fingers. By the time he was ready to enter her, she was almost at the stage of demanding it. He complied. There was no comparison with Mordecai and Asa. Throughout the mating Khimrik never ceased fondling her. Her excitement grew to an almost unbearable level until something within her gave way and then she felt the greatest moment of satisfaction in her life. But that was not all. After a few moments' rest, Khimrik repeated the same act from various different angles and directions, and moved her body with gentle force so as to accommodate different positions, none of which she had ever thought possible before. After a long pause, when Jerusha was almost ready to fall asleep, he roused her, and started over again.

When they were both through, this time for the night, Khimrik lay back and remarked, lazily, "You don't have many visitors in your bedroom. Why not?"

Jerusha was slightly offended. "What kind of woman do you think I am? If I choose a man it's because I want him. Alone."

"You Jews talk a lot about morals, but if you *won't* stay chaste, there are few things more unethical than discriminating among men. Some men are better lovers than they look, I hear. But anyway, choosing favorites is selfish and cruelly insulting to all the unlucky ones. And in a fighting group, it destroys morale."

Before Jerusha could think of a cutting reply, she could hear Khimrik's soft snore. Anyway, he was probably right. She dropped off to sleep shortly thereafter. Jerusha awoke, late the next morning, and Khimrik was still there, now sleeping quietly.

She used the time to consider the night before and what it meant to her. Jerusha clearly had enjoyed the proceedings more than anything else she thought possible—deliberately excluding, as so often, the time she spent with her children. But it was over, not likely to recur, and, realistic as she was, she resigned herself to that fact completely. Besides, she felt a twinge of an uncustomary emotion. *Could it be shame? Surely not.* Later that week, she would begin her new life as a solitary murderess. Khimrik was merely an interruption, however welcome at the time. Only when she had settled her mind, was she willing to wake him, gently.

Some conversation seemed appropriate, and she was still curious about Khimrik's life, so as soon as the man had wiped the sleep from his eyes she asked about his future.

"You know you can't keep fighting for us forever, since you don't believe the Messiah is ever coming. As fine as your body is, it will grow older. And no Gentile will rise much higher in the movement. What will you do?"

"First, I'd like to know if you enjoyed yourself last night," Khimrik asked, receiving only a curt nod in reply. His clear disappointment left him with nothing to say except to answer her question. "Oh, I haven't thought it out entirely. I'm thinking of entering the slave trade. Far south of here, maybe in Africa. You're sure you don't want us to do it again?" Khimrik's question seemed more like a courtesy to her.

"I'm sure. How can you think of the slave trade, having been a slave yourself?"

"What is the next step for a slave but to become a master? Though I'll probably just be the middleman; there's more money in that. I'll sell them to Arabs, or Edomites, or Egyptians, or Romans who won't know me so far from their homes. Don't go self-righteous on me; you Jews own slaves. Worse, you enslave your own tribe."

"We have strict laws on who can be enslaved, how they must be treated, and when they must be freed."

"You don't treat them as well as the Romans and the Greeks

do. I speak from personal observation. Besides, I'll probably buy or capture only black Nubians. I understand they are more docile, muscular, and altogether better suited to enforced servitude. Your Jewish Scriptures call them 'hewers of wood and drawers of water,' simply because they're descended from somebody named Ham. I'll teach them a few more tricks than that. Some of them make good gladiators; I've seen them in Rome."

Jerusha didn't know whether she was mildly shocked, or merely interested. Khimrik was already dressing to leave.

He paused to add, perhaps thinking out loud, "Most Roman slaves are captured enemy warriors, and they knew the risks. Slavery is better than death. They have equal intelligence, are allowed to use it, and are reconciled to their lot, as I was for years. Nowadays, the slaves owned by the few Greeks who can still afford them are usually bought, and know no other life. There are a few forest tribes in northern Gaul and the Frankish holdings who become useless slaves and often end up beaten or killed. Bad business. I hear that the Nubian and Ethiopian blacks aren't very intelligent, so they won't cheat you, fight you, or run away. Most of them were captured in inter-tribal warfare amongst themselves, and our treatment will never be as bad as what they are used to."

"That sounds...awful," Jerusha stammered, though she didn't know a word or argument she could use against Khimrik's reasoning. But she really didn't care about foreigners, anymore than her own people. And who was *she* to judge him?

Khimrik finished dressing and left the room, with a final, gentle kiss to Jerusha's foot.

◆

A few days later, after Jerusha had erased all evidence of Khimrik, she heard a knock on her door. It was Zachariah, wearing his old, threadbare clothing and carrying an empty bundle-bag.

"What now?" Jerusha snapped.

"Time for you to move to your new quarters," he replied softly. "Your new mission."

"But why the costume?"

"I'm your poor country brother by marriage, finding rooms for his widowed sister, who is also poor, but has been left enough to survive on. Therefore, pack only your simplest clothes. No silk or satin. I've already picked the rooms."

"Did I remember to thank you?" she said sarcastically. Then, "Will I ever return here?"

Despite the question, Jerusha was indifferent to the reply.

"Of course. You're still on the council, and we must have meetings. To *live* here, regrettably no. We can't have you traced back." He continued, with a twinkle in his eye, "Also, your, shall we say, nightly activities have become known."

"I'm surrounded by spies!" Jerusha hissed.

"No, you're just a bit careless. Better watch that in your new career as a dagger man."

She gave him an evil look, but after packing she followed him out into the noisome streets with never a look back.

Jerusha's knowledge of the city was slight, but even she could discern Zachariah was leading her in circles, sometimes doubling back on their path. She supposed that made sense, to protect their headquarters. Finally they stepped out of a dark alley and were standing in front of Herod's principal palace in the Upper City.

"What are we doing here?" Jerusha demanded. "Will I be living under their noses?"

"No. Your rooms are in an alleyway off the plaza. We need you midway between Herod Antipas' home and the Roman governor's house, when he's not at his palace in Caesarea. That way you can disappear in the alleys between, as needed after you've carried out your orders."

"How will I get those orders?"

"I told you how to recognize my messengers. They'll also bring money. If you've brought any of your own, give it to me now; they'll bring enough for a poor widow to live on."

Jerusha, having grown used to being supplied whatever goods she desired, for how many months? Could it have been years?, had forgotten to bring her hoard of coins. She told Zachariah about them and asked him to conceal them. She knew by now she could trust him.

Zachariah then led the way down another alley, in which there were numerous recessed doorways to upper floors, but no shops on the ground floor, just more rooms. The fourth doorway was hers. They ascended four flights of a narrow stairway, smelling slightly of urine, to Jerusha's new quarters.

The "rooms" turned out to be one room, with a partial divider; not as large as either her previous bedroom to which Jerusha had become accustomed, nor her own large room in Bethlehem. But with an oven with holes for a stove, and a well-stocked pantry for which Zachariah claimed credit. She would have to buy perishables and delicacies in the market. There was one shuttered window, facing the street. There were a few sticks of furniture, and a bed which she could already see was stuffed with straw. The room was freshly cleaned and white-washed, for which Zachariah again claimed credit.

Jerusha's first words were, "Where does Isaac or Isaiah the first victim you promised me, live?"

"In a moment. You must draw your water from the stall down the street to your right. The bathing tub is near the bed. There's a common privy downstairs behind the door."

"Isaiah?"

Zachariah paused. "The years have aged him, and he is now

lame. He wears a blue sash with a decoration of some sort on it, over his shoulder. He never misses a parade, whether Roman or one of the rarer Jewish ones. There's a Roman parade tomorrow. Somebody's birthday, probably some Roman god or tyrant. Isaiah always stands in the front row, if he can. And since they are sparsely attended, he usually can. All parades pass in front of the palace, to your left, or the governor's mansion, at the end of the alley to your right."

"Where does Isaiah live?" Jerusha demanded.

"Three doors to your right, across the alley. He lives by himself. Here's a small bag of coins to supplement your kitchen." He handed it over.

"How can I reach you?"

"You can't. But I'll keep in touch through my messengers."

"Then get out," she commanded. "I know what to do. I've dreamed of little else for years. I still have my dagger, and know how to use it."

"Be careful, and very cautious; I don't want this to be your only mission. Also, don't steal anything. They search the neighborhood for thieves, though not so much for perpetrators in blood feuds or political killings." Zachariah lectured as he left the room, and then the house.

At last Jerusha was totally alone, as she had not been since Bethlehem. But now she had a clear goal. One which left her more restless and impatient than she had ever been before. She had planned to spend the entire late afternoon and evening thinking about her sons. Everything each had ever said or done; but prudence demanded she first become familiar with the entire neighborhood as well as she could. She hoped she would not encounter Isaiah during her reconnaissance.

Jerusha dressed with care. She chose mismatched clothing that befitted an old woman, and practiced sloped shoulders, since she had difficulty maintaining a crook to her entire back. Taking soot from the oven, she darkened her face; if it would not increase her wrinkles sufficiently, at least it would make her look dirty enough for people to avoid. Her veils would not mask a direct view, but old women often became sloppy about facial modesty. She wished she had a walking-stick; she would have to get one soon. She scuffed her sandals against the stove to make them look cheap and worn. At the last minute Jerusha thought of fashioning her tote-bag into a sort of backpack, to give her the appearance of a traveler, or even a vagabond, but feared it might hinder her mission. When she was satisfied, she descended the steps and went out to the alley.

First, she traveled to the king's palace, the way she had come. The plaza in front of it was empty. There was a major thoroughfare through it, where she assumed they held their parades. But Jerusha could not consider herself ever using such a wide road during an escape. On the other side from her were narrow alleys, identical to the one from which she had emerged. She didn't think she would use these, unless she were discovered, cut off from her own alley, and had nowhere else to run. The others on her side of the plaza had shops, even wine-shops, which, in the afternoons or evenings might be full of patrons, as they seemed to be now. Although Jerusha had no intention of hiding there and being trapped in one of the shops, they might distract pursuers long enough for her to reach her dwelling. Also, they would provide street traffic to mingle with, as they did even now.

So much for the area of the palace. She went back down her alley, affecting a hobble and studiously avoiding the doorway she had been told was Isaiah's, across from the water trough. At the end of the alley was a cross-street of which she had not been informed. She looked both ways and could see nothing she considered dangerous to her. Finally she saw her own alley continue on the other side of the street, so she followed it to find no other cross-street, and the alley ended at a much larger plaza, obviously that of the Roman governor's residence. Jerusha looked to her left at the structure, so alien to Jewish architecture, with its bright colors, grooved columns, and idolatrous images.

Jerusha briefly wondered how many Jews had their homes stolen to be flattened for this monstrosity and the plaza in front of it. She also idly wondered whether it was the scaffolding on this building which had collapsed to kill her husband, Mordecai. None of this scene seemed truly interesting; just the two highways which crossed the plaza, either of which could be used for parades. She further noted that the other side of the plaza was crowded with new Roman-built mansions instead of alleys and narrow streets. There was nowhere to go when pursued but back to her dwelling as quickly but circuitously as she could. Jerusha would have to plan for all this. At least all the alley row houses she had seen in the neighborhood were essentially indistinguishable, being stuccoed and freshly whitewashed, most likely by the Romans as was their style, even over smooth-cut, solid stone. There were no clear street signs, either. Jerusha returned to what, she supposed, she must now consider "home."

Jerusha lay in bed, after pounding down stray fibers of straw. She thought of her son David, he of the continual questions, who was always first for food, and who always asked for more; but Isaiah, in exchange for sexual favors, offered to save David, if Jerusha could only do the impossible and get David south of Bethlehem. She thought of Jonathan, who never took food for himself without offering some to little Abraham, though he was still breastfeeding; but Isaiah had joked about Jonathan and offered to save and feed him, too. She thought of little Abraham, who had suckled on the breasts which Khimrik later profaned, and who never knew what was going on that terrible night; but that had not spared him. Isaiah had ordered them all killed, with limbs lopped off and throats cut. Jerusha had watched.

Then she thought of Leah and her children, Jerusha's nephews, what were their names? At least the ones killed at her home? Maybe Jerusha had honestly offered them possible shelter? No, she had known that Herod's men, especially Isaiah, had already searched under the stairs, and she had all but urged him to search there again. To save her own children. But surely Jerusha wasn't responsible for Leah's attack on Herod's man. Then again, what would she herself have done had she been armed and cornered with her boys?

No, Isaiah was personally responsible for the murder of all the children and no one else was. Except herself.

But there was someone else. The false little king, whose family's greed had brought all this misery, and he was alive! He would be in his mid twenties by now, but where could he be found? And how could he be recognized? At least she would be more likely to learn of him in Jerusalem, as part of a large movement with many spies, and located at the center of all Judean power, than she would have been in Bethlehem. Though she had learned nothing so far. Perhaps, Jerusha thought, if she could read Scripture, she could learn the prophecies of the Messiah that might lead to the discovery of this impostor. But she would never entrust this task to a scrivener, and how could she know that the false Messiah's family had read such Scripture, or even bothered to mimic the prophecies?

Meanwhile, Isaiah would have to suffer Jerusha's wrath. She swore to herself her revenge against him would be as complete as possible. Perhaps even satisfying. The next question was how? That question could wait until early morning, before any parades, when Jerusha's internal alarm would awaken her.

Jerusha woke as early as usual, after a fitful sleep, but feeling ready for her work. She had forgotten supper the night before, and there were no perishables in the pantry, or time to cook what food there was. There were many shops in the next alley, and she could buy something to eat on her way to the Roman plaza and Isaiah. With her stomach growling, she made her other preparations.

A place to hide her bloody dagger after the deed? Somewhere in her clothes. She planned to kill Isaiah in his own rooms after following him home, and then she would only have a few yards to go to her door up the alley. But blood would take time and effort to clean off completely, and even a few drops might leak through her clothes. There was no way of knowing if Isaiah kept an oilcloth of any sort. Jerusha examined whether her bundle-bag could fit around her waist, under her long shawl. It could, with a few quick stitches; luckily she had packed a kit for mending clothes. After preparing it, she carefully lined the interior of the bag with sheep-lard from her pantry. Which would not only hinder leakage, but its odor might disguise the distinctive smell of blood, repel others who were too close, and enhance her attempt to appear much older and repugnant. Before the act, of course, her dagger would remain in her sleeve, along with a small whetstone in the loose leather sheath, which she used to keep the edges almost translucently sharp and almost painless. Jerusha had no idea how long the bag would last, if needed for other missions, but she could always discard it far away. Human and butchered animal's blood were the same. For that matter, the lard would help it burn in her oven, though creating a stench for a while, despite the one window. If she needed to replace the bag for other missions, just one of her heavier robes could make several more. Surely some of her targets would have to be killed in the open, without time or place to hide the dagger, except in her bag.

Jerusha dressed exactly as she had the night before, remembering to apply the soot and practice the slope of her shoulders. When she was ready, she descended the stairs and stepped out into the early morning, first to search the next alley for a pastry or fruit store.

It didn't take Jerusha long to find more than she had hoped for:

a small shop selling sliced lamb-filled pastries. She bought two by placing the money down, receiving a look from the shopkeeper that she was really not welcome, and hobbling outside with her food as quickly as she could. When she got to the center of the alley she wolfed the pastries, which tasted surprisingly good to her. From a neighboring shop she bought a walking stick, leaving even more quickly, with its supposed aid.

Jerusha wondered for a moment how she could accomplish such mundane tasks, considering the bloody plans she had devised for later in the day. She concluded it must have been whatever it was that kept her sanity, indeed her calmness and efficiency, when she had faced ten well-armed Romans in the wilderness. Or the murder of her children. She returned to her own alley, so there would be no chance of becoming disoriented on her way to the Roman parade. She knew her sense of direction was still less than secure.

By her reckoning, based on the few Roman parades she had seen, this day's parade would not begin long before noon, which gave her time to sit at the water trough and keep an eye on Isaiah's house. She obscured her face with her veils, carefully. The house was shorter than the others, only two storyes. Through the unshuttered window on the ground floor she could hear the sounds of an older child and his mother. Evidently Isaiah lived in the upper rooms, if Zachariah was right and he lived alone. By this time Isaiah should be near or at the parade site. Jerusha could only hope that later the family downstairs would be out shopping at the market when she followed Isaiah from the parade. Prices at the stalls were cheaper as the day wore on. The walls of the tenements were thick enough to block out sound, but Jerusha did not know if the floors and joists, and ceilings, if any, were. And she expected to cause noise.

After a few minutes Jerusha proceeded down the alley, across the intersecting street, and into the plaza in front of the governor's house. Although she was still early, a few people were criss-crossing the plaza to get good views of the parade. Isaiah was apparently still not there, so Jerusha leaned against the walls of a dark alley. She should be able to see his blue sash among the white togas and occasional uniforms, and the stolas of the Roman women. There were Jews in their traditional robes, and a few Arabs, but not many of either.

Jerusha approached the front row but one and suddenly saw Isaiah nearby.

CHAPTER 8

Blood

Despite the years, Jerusha could not mistake Isaiah's hawk nose and arrogant expression—whether he reserved the latter for Roman and Jewish parades and Herod's massacres, or whether it had become a permanent feature of his face, she didn't know. But it was the same face she had watched three times previously; twice on the day when her children were killed. Age could not obscure his appearance. It was only after these observations she noticed the simple crutch supporting his left leg, and the light-blue satin sash hanging off his right shoulder down to his left hip.

Jerusha watched almost nothing of the parade, not even when the Roman soldiers were led by loud, colorful drummers, trumpeters, and soldiers in lion skins and heads, so interested was she in Isaiah. She did hear one item of interest, when some well-dressed Jewish woman referred, dismissively, to an especially elaborate changing of the guard that was to occur tomorrow, before Herod Antipas' palace. *I must remember that, if I fail today.*

Jerusha waited until the parade ended, and Isaiah made signs of moving, before she shook off her forced paralysis. She hobbled twenty paces behind Isaiah, as he limped toward his dwelling.

Even after they both turned the corner into their mutual alley, he never looked back. Whether this was stupidity or a sort of unconscious community among the lame, she couldn't tell. But she was glad she used her walking stick and exaggerated her non-existent weakness. She kept pace with him, but only at a distance. No darting in and out of doorways.

When Isaiah finally entered his doorway, Jerusha sat at the water trough across the street, and still heard the sounds from the family dwelling below him, a family who might listen.

Jerusha could not hazard any risks unless absolutely necessary; therefore this would not be the afternoon for her revenge. She might as well go to the market; she couldn't eat out every meal, not on the little money Zachariah had given her. After her shopping, Jerusha returned to her room, filled with growing impatience. The woman and her son downstairs from Isaiah would have to leave their house eventually. But she wanted it to be tomorrow, during or soon after the changing of the guard at the palace. Now that Jerusha could easily identify Isaiah and knew his home she had no cause to worry about parades coinciding with the absence of Isaiah's neighbors—she could approach his door any time of the day he had the building alone, knock, and stab him when he opened the door. But that would be too short and clean, allowing Isaiah little time for fear, much less suffering torture. Also, she felt something was appropriate in tracking him home from the kind of elaborate royal or Roman ceremony that Isaiah seemed so attracted to.

Once she was home, Jerusha cooked her supper in her room. That night was not filled with thoughts of her children, but of Isaiah in torture. These thoughts did not leave her tired as her thoughts the previous night had; if anything, she felt more energy.

In the morning Jerusha dressed as she had the previous two days. The colors of her clothes were so drab she doubted anyone could possibly have remembered them. Not bathing would only add to the image she wished to project. She did not forget the soot, walking-stick, or sloped shoulders. On the street she checked the nearest sundial carefully; timing was important to catch Isaiah at the plaza. She was on schedule.

Jerusha hobbled down the alley to her left this time, toward the king's palace. Her plans were slightly different today; the plaza afforded plenty of alleyways to hide in, and it was not long before she spotted Isaiah, in the front row as before, with his sash tied in the same manner. When she studied his face, she was not surprised to see that his sneer *was* now a permanent part of it. Now sure of his habits, she did not stand too near him. The changing of the guard was usually a paltry matter, but clearly the Jewish authorities had attempted to make this one rival the Roman parade of the day before, if not in uniforms then at least in pomp and duration.

Jerusha had seen enough parades to know when the end was near, and left in sufficient time for her intentions. She proceeded to the water trough in front of Isaiah's house, and sat on the rim. This morning, to her great relief, there was no sound from the rooms below his. Though, the tenants could be napping in the unseasonably warm weather this early spring, with their shutters closed. Therefore, she went to their door and pounded on it with her stick in an authoritative manner, then scurried to the middle of the alley, without forgetting to first look both ways. The only people in the alley were two men walking away with their backs to her. When she reached the middle of the street Jerusha instantly resumed her persona as a shuffling old lady with no particular destination, or hurry to get there, but her eyes never left the downstairs door of Isaiah's building for long. No one appeared at the door. The rooms must be empty, so today she would get at least partial revenge for the death of her children.

She shuffled to a darkened doorway near the trough and waited. Not long after, Isaiah limped down her alley, satin sash gleaming, and started up the stairs of his house. Pausing a moment, Jerusha slipped into his doorway behind him and quickly removed her sandals. Fortunately the steps were of stone, and would make no noise. She was never more or less than six steps behind him as he climbed laboriously. Briefly Jerusha wondered how Isaiah managed his limp, not being a combat soldier except against defenseless children. She was still close enough that she had to wait for him to unlock his room on the upper floor. If through bad fortune Isaiah should turn around at his door or before it, Jerusha would have immediately assumed a more stooped appearance and mumbled something about a "Rebekkah" who had lived there, and scuttered out at any question or challenge she received. But such didn't happen. Jerusha hurried the rest of the way to catch him before he fully entered his room.

Jerusha's attack came after Isaiah had pushed the door open and stepped into the door frame, stabbing at his leg. She kept her arm partly extended to protect her clothes from blood, though there turned out to be very little of it, and none was spurting. Human flesh was either softer than that of the animals she had butchered, or her blade was honed sharper than any other she had ever used. *Good: no blood on the landing.* It might take days or longer for the body to be found. She had aimed at the center of his good, right thigh muscle not far below his buttocks. He was tall, and this was not very difficult; his robe was either tight or smoothed by his movements to expose the target area. From her experience with animals she knew a main artery was close to the groin, so she had deliberately missed it to ensure Isaiah would not quickly bleed to death. Isaiah slid forward but fell backward, Jerusha herself stepping back just in time. Isaiah now lay sprawled across the room on his back. Beyond her most optimistic expectations, his head had hit the floor inside, but toward the door which she quickly closed and bolted. His crutch went skittering across the floor. His outcry was brief.

Now Jerusha walked around Isaiah's body to where she could watch his face and the door at the same time.

She settled in what was an unexpectedly comfortable chair, conveniently situated at Isaiah's feet.

"What is this?" Isaiah stammered; no sneer now. "I don't have much money!"

"I don't want your money, 'Isaac.' Don't you remember who I am?"

"No!"

"Do you remember killing children in Bethlehem one night? Slashing, hacking, and dismembering their defenseless little bodies?"

A pause. "That was years ago..." The sentence was broken and stuttered; the pain must be settling in. "I don't remember you."

"These clothes are a disguise. Do you remember Jerusha?"

"Maybe...it was long ago." Isaiah began to moan. At least he didn't scream.

"That's a very pretty decoration on your sash. Did you earn it by killing babies?"

"No," he gasped.

"I'll wager you remember *everything* about when you earned the medal, no matter how long ago it was. You said it was a long time since you slaughtered my children. Strange... it's like yesterday to me," Jerusha sighed. Thoughts of that night flashed through her mind.

"I was only carrying out orders!" While he spoke, Jerusha began to bind his hands in front with a leather thong. She must watch and be careful; she did not know how much training Herod's men had had with knots.

"'Obeying orders'? I thought you couldn't remember anything," she said. When she felt secure, she settled herself back into the chair.

She then asked, "Despite the orders, couldn't you have

resigned, or deserted? Or at least had the decency to kill yourself?"

"That's not for me to decide. Oh, help me; I think you've broken my thigh bone."

"I doubt it. My knife isn't even chipped." She looked around and found a washcloth, in case it might be needed as a gag. "Do you remember any of my children whom you killed?"

"I was only doing my duty! And I think I remember giving you a chance? I don't remember much. But my good leg will be useless, now!"

"Good. Oh, I forgot about the lame leg." Jerusha rose from the chair, stood over Isaiah's lame left leg which was still crooked part way up, and smashed her bare foot down as hard as she could on his upper thigh, until she heard a gratifying snap.

Before Isaiah had filled his lungs for a scream, she stuffed his mouth with the washcloth. Carefully, so as not to choke him. She sat down again. Jerusha waited for his stifled scream to die out and his eyes to reopen.

"You can't remember my boys, or even Leah's?" She knew he couldn't answer, but she couldn't restrain herself from asking. She tried to focus her thoughts. Her mind continued to skip around between her children, what they were like, what she had witnessed that awful night, and what she still had to do. "Do you remember the false king or Messiah who brought you to Bethlehem in the first place? I'll remove the cloth so you can speak. But only about the pretender. One lie, and you will die. Horribly. Are you over your screaming? I didn't scream much when you tore my heart out that night."

Isaiah nodded his head as well as he could.

When she removed the rag, he moaned for a while, and then whispered, "We never knew whether we had found him. How could we?" Jerusha quickly replaced the washcloth tightly.

"Proving you killed him might have saved your life. But I doubt it," she spat.

This time Jerusha did something as unexpected to her as it was to him. She walked, spraddling, up the outside of his legs to his hip, avoiding the blood, and hiked his robes up to his waist. She then ripped off his loinclout. At the last moment he realized what she was going to do, but little sound escaped his gag. Isaiah made a feeble attempt to clamp his legs together; his lameness and wounds prohibited. Jerusha had never seen such terror in anyone's face; his eyes were more open than she would have believed possible; his noises were, of course, gibberish.

"Don't worry, I won't damage your glorious decoration, or even the satin sash if I can help it." She raised her own robes above her hips to keep them clean of blood, and tied them there, never letting hold of her dagger or taking her eyes for more than a moment from his immobilized hands. She used her dagger to unman him quickly, throwing the offensive parts into the corner of his room. Avoiding the spreading blood Jerusha moved onto his left side toward his throat, and cut it to the spinal column. *What a spindly neck; all skin and arteries.* She jumped back to avoid the spurting arterial blood. His pretty blue sash was ruined after all. Pity.

Jerusha washed her hands and the dagger in the washstand bowl, and placed her knife in her lard-lined bundle-bag. She carefully took the rag from Isaiah's lifeless lips and wiped what blood there was off her legs and her feet. As the water in the bowl turned pink, she poured it in the far corner and refreshed it from Isaiah's large, almost full ewer. After carefully inspecting and rearranging her clothes, she was satisfied there was no blood on them or on her. Jerusha stepped carefully around the body and the spreading pool of blood. She opened, passed, and then closed Isaiah's door behind her as she left, shutting out that part of her life. She went down the stairs and reattached her sandals on the dark stoop, a normal enough act if she were spotted, unless the downstairs family returned too soon. They would remember her later. But Jerusha was lucky again. She looked both ways into the alley from the doorway, and was relieved to see once again the little street traffic there was was walking away from her. She returned to her room, unseen.

Jerusha felt no desire for supper, but lay in bed thinking and dozing. For the first time in years she felt no immediate needs, nor did she feel any regret for what she had done. Her long-term goal had been dulled for the moment, and the murder of Isaiah dwindled in significance during the evening. She knew her ultimate mission in life had not yet been achieved, but at least one step was taken. She still had to find the false Messiah, whose sole accomplishment was the murder of innocent—utterly innocent— children. Revenge for her own children, and expiation for Leah's, demanded it.

The next day Jerusha spent in bed, except to satisfy her hunger, and use the common privy. For two or three days she feared a knock on her door before she was convinced that her bloody actions had gone undetected.

◆

Jerusha hoped she would not receive her next mission from Zachariah too soon; she wasn't ready. In this, she had her way. She spent several weeks awaiting a messenger.

Despite Jerusha's earlier belief, true to some degree, that Isaiah's death would close a chapter in her life; it had to fit in with the rest of her existence and her new occupation. So she spent many hours, evenings and nights, thinking about such matters. Her first killing, of the tribune, had been almost as mechanical as Zachariah had described his last killings—a job to be done without emotion—fear, passion, revenge, or even a cause worthy of it. Whereas killing Isaiah was clearly out of revenge. Jerusha knew that from now on, "dagger man" that she was, she would be assigned Romans or others whom she had never met, but always without the camaraderie of "family" or gang. Each killing would be one-on-one. Zachariah had hinted to her of this, and challenged her that unit combat was a masculine satisfaction. Indeed, she would feel freer acting alone than part of a team. Now came her first test as an individual, anonymous killer. She was still not so sure of herself.

Jerusha answered a knock one evening to see a non-descript Jew at her door, covered with an oilcloth dripping from the unseasonable rains she had not even noticed. He held his hand out with a silver coin displaying the face of some caesar or another — she still couldn't distinguish between them. She let the man in and listened as he recited his carefully memorized speech. Her occasional interruptions caused him to have to start again at the beginning. The essence of the instructions were that she was to kill a high-ranking Roman, the replacement for Marcus whom she had killed in the wilderness. The only name she was given was "Gaius." More anonymity.

She was told that an intelligence officer for the governor, Gaius, was learning too quickly and too much, though he was not yet as dangerous as his predecessor had been. This Roman regularly wore his white toga instead of a uniform, which could be distinguished from others by the red stripe around the hem signifying he was of the senatorial, or highest, class. In her years of studying styles for her sewing, Jerusha had noted that a corner of the toga was regularly worn over the left arm, presumably to show that Roman citizens did not have to engage in manual labor. Jerusha knew there was no guarantee, whatever Zachariah's messenger said, that Gaius would even be wearing his toga. Many Romans in Jerusalem wore only their underlying tunics during the hottest months of the year. It was now well into spring, but not warm enough that Roman pride of citizenship should permit the abandonment of the toga.

According to the messenger, Gaius was almost completely bald, about forty years old, and quite short for a Roman. He often walked with one or two companions to the governor's residence in the late afternoon, whether or not the governor was in Jerusalem.

Gaius lived in an apartment, though reputedly a lavish one, in the first Roman mansion at the beginning of the plaza fronting the residence. For such a distance, Gaius never took a horse or hired a litter, which were rare enough in Jerusalem anyway, but always walked. Jerusha would need only keep her eyes on one stretch of territory. *And discover how to murder a man accompanied by friends in broad daylight, and then manage to escape freely to the safety of her alley hideaway.*

The messenger brought a small bag of coins which were welcome, in as much as Jerusha was running low on money. All of her attempts to learn more from the messenger were a waste of time. He obviously didn't know any more. Nevertheless, Jerusha did have a message for him:

"Tell Zachariah I'm bored enough to want to come back to one of his council meetings after this mission. Also, I want a scrivener sent to me early one morning, the scrivener I used before." Just before the messenger left, Jerusha seriously frightened him by unsheathing her dagger and cutting off a two foot square of his oilcloth.

"Don't worry, Zachariah will buy you a new one. He knows where to get the money, and I don't know where around here to buy oilcloth, even if he gave me enough coins, which he didn't."

"But...but..."

Jerusha abruptly dismissed him, and he hastily withdrew into the shadows.

After the messenger left Jerusha got out her sewing kit and fashioned a small lining out of the slick cloth by folding it and leaving enough room for a flap on one side. She both double-folded and double-stitched the sides so that no needle holes unnecessarily aligned with others. It was large enough to drop her dagger in quickly, but without any unneeded space. Using the lining of her heaviest robe as a template, Jerusha cut and sewed a pouch, much easier to hide than her bundle-bag, with a strap long enough to go over her shoulder and yet be concealed under her robes and shawl. She used a spare sandal-thong to attach the pouch tightly around her waist so it would not bounce should she have to run. Now she could finally rid herself of her bulky, smelly lard-bag. Though it was still raining outside, with any luck it would be dry tomorrow—with perhaps even a breeze coming into her small window. People wouldn't smell the lard burning, or chimney smoke, from the alley four flights below. Even if they did, they would simply mistake her for an incompetent cook. Of course, the authorities would be thorough, searching for the murderer of a high official.

It was also time to change her disguise. She wanted to be mistaken for a poor widow, not as a local deranged woman of the streets identifiable by every visible item of her clothing and every odor. Notoriety was not part of her plan. After honing her dagger again, she picked out her clothing for the morrow; equally mismatched, and almost as drab, but not as eccentric as she had previously worn. Jerusha now knew how to apply the soot only to accentuate her wrinkles, not dirty her entire face. Her sloped shoulders were becoming second nature.

Awakening at sunrise, Jerusha saw it would be a clear day with the requisite breeze, so she could burn the lard and cloth that formerly held her dagger. She then indulged in the first bath she had permitted herself for so long she barely even remembered the tile tub at Zachariah's headquarters. Jerusha had all morning and much of the afternoon during which to plan how she might encounter Gaius.

In the midafternoon she casually worked her way down to the oblong plaza, never glancing at Isaiah's house. It no longer existed for her. When Jerusha first emerged into the Roman plaza, the sun dazzled her, coming, as it did, after a cleansing rain. Unlike its Judean counterparts, this Roman plaza had a number of marble benches placed around it, and she was able to rest at one of these while adjusting her eyes. There were also trees or rather, saplings, circling the park, a novelty to Jerusha, as the Jews in Bethlehem and Jerusalem rarely wasted effort on such adornments. The house she wanted was the first on her right, and she was early. She spent time looking at the black obelisk centered at the opposite, front end of the plaza, almost an exact copy of the marble one holding her signet. There was writing all around the big one which would mean nothing to her no matter how closely she looked. There were, however, large blank spaces under it, for Roman proclamations, judging by the tattered remnants of the previous ones.

Now she could only wait, perhaps for days, until a bald Roman with a red-hemmed toga walked the length of the plaza, with enough friends but not too many, in a crowd of passersby that was neither too thin nor too thick. Jerusha had learned through all her years of being alone how to, if not entertain herself, at least keep her mind occupied. If not forever, at least indefinitely. This was no worse than her six to eight hour days as an almost immobile beggar, albeit she no longer had her children upon whom to lavish her occasional attentions and loving corrections.

Jerusha's patience was tested that day. Many people passed by, but very few in togas, and none with a red striped hem. If she was hoping for crowds, she was disappointed again, in that most people were walking in groups of two or three, large spaces between them, like pigeons without a feeding source. She could never lose herself in such a scattering. By early evening she gave up, returned to her dwelling, and prepared the kind of bland supper she had lately accustomed herself to. Delicacies, expensive spices, good wines, and the freshest fruits, vegetables and meats would not suit the character she was portraying, on her trips to the marketplaces.

She sat at the plaza through the next two late mornings and afternoons observing no difference in the passing scene, except for that caused by her occasional change of benches, and therefore her angle of view. She began to suspect that devoting many more hours to her vigil would probably accomplish nothing but draw unwanted attention to herself.

Jerusha finally appreciated the loud, pious animations in which her men in the wilderness indulged before the Roman column approached her ambush. It did no harm to her plans, and the anxiety it caused was nothing compared to the two days she had waited for one Roman to wander into her ambush on the plaza. She had learned that fear was always preferable compressed than dragged out over days with no inkling as to the outcome or the length of wait.

Jerusha wondered again what she was doing here. She had no hatred for her Roman prey, nor anything to gain by his death. But Zachariah had given her part of what she had wanted, and though she had little concern for the sanctity of anything else, Jerusha still respected the importance of promises. And she still believed, if anybody could, the Zealots would help her track down her eternal blood enemy. Eternal? Her hatred for the false king grew stronger every day, and would do so until she, or he, died. If some Roman official here or there must die first, it was none of her business. She was only following orders. *Had she heard that somewhere recently?*

Through both of those days of waiting in the plaza, Jerusha's early mornings were spent at home handling her growing financial empire in Bethlehem. Her scrivener had finally arrived, but without her previous messenger; it would have looked like an official delegation. As much as her nature would allow, Jerusha had finally come to trust Zachariah's functionaries, so the time spent for her correspondence was considerably shorter. In accordance with Zachariah's instructions, she asked for no bags of gold. The responses, which came shortly, were more than satisfactory. Because she harbored doubts about her factors, Jerusha didn't neglect her duplications, comparisons between replies, and reading between the lines. The time required for this still allowed her to concentrate on her primary mission at the plaza in the later mornings and afternoons.

The fourth day was Sabbath-Eve, but her plans for Gaius, if successful, would be completed before sunset, and shortly afterward she would be at home, away from pious eyes. At about the noon hour, Jerusha finally saw her quarry. The description she was given was sufficient for positive identification: from baldness, to height, to red hemmed toga. As expected, he emerged from the first Roman-built house on the right. Her hopes rose, only to sink when she observed Gaius was quickly joined by four acquaintances, and that there were no others in the plaza to offer her concealment. Another wasted day. The next day, Saturday, would be equally useless, as she must spend the daylight hours indoors in accordance with Jewish law.

Lacking anything else to do for the rest of the day, Jerusha studied the marble pavement of the plaza. It formed a colorful mosaic design, mostly browns, pinks, and gold-streaked whites. She had seen mosaics on some of Jerusalem's buildings in Roman-occupied neighborhoods, but never as smooth paving stones. Unused to large artworks, it took her a while to try to piece together in her mind what this one was supposed to depict. The main figure was that of a large beast, lion or wolf, but with exaggeratedly large and full teats. Under it were two human male figures, not merely immodest, but without any clothes whatsoever. Jerusha had certainly seen enough naked children on the streets of Bethlehem, not to mention her own three boys at home, that she was not shocked, except *these* figures were apparently gods or heroes to the Romans, though they were engaged in the horribly unnatural act of caressing or kissing the teats of the beast. The Romans must worship such disgusting behavior. If Judea's conquerors had as little regard for children as they were reputed to have, and as Isaiah had indicated by the Roman parental right to kill them before the age of fourteen, then these two heroes must be grown men, despite the proportions the artist had mistakenly given them. From all this confusion Jerusha could only conclude that Romans were sexual perverts, as were their gods and heroes. And she had thought *Jewish* theology stupid. But nothing she could remember from it would equal the bestiality glorified by the Romans on their main plaza. The only excuse which Jerusha could make for these foreigners was that, in crossing the plaza at random, they stepped on their gods' faces, private parts, and even the mammary glands of the beast.

It was at this point Jerusha noticed an ancient Jewish woman who had been sitting at the other end of her bench, watching her, and sliding closer. This did not surprise Jerusha, as she had often been approached by lonely widows in the hope of a little gossip, which she seldom had any to give. But now Jerusha had decided that simple courtesy to them would make her appear less eccentric. Rude rejection, over-familiarity, or any uncommon behavior would cause her to be remembered forever in an old lady's life. Such people had very little to occupy their minds, and Jerusha had no intention of giving this one more. Jerusha did not look at her companion until addressed.

"Aahh; the sun is nice out here, don't you think?"

Jerusha thought the sun was about the same anywhere, but replied with a smile, "*Shalom*. But nowhere is as nice as my native Bethlehem," she shrugged, as though resigned to homesickness. "God's Will." Mentioning her hometown was a calculated risk;

many in Jerusalem came from Bethlehem, and for all she knew her accent might have given her away if she attempted to dissemble. And a good whine added to her age.

"I've never been there, but I'm sure it's a nice place," responded the crone.

This conversation was going nowhere; Jerusha might as well try to learn something. "Are those paving stones supposed to show off some Roman gods?"

"No, the boys are supposed to be the original founders of Rome: Romulus and Remus, or so I've been told."

Jerusha ventured, "Then that might be why the Romans don't show much respect for those images?"

"They don't show respect for any of their images," the old lady seemed happy to talk. "You must not know Jerusalem well. They have images of all their gods and goddesses everywhere they can put them without zealous Jews smashing them. But the Romans never actually show them any respect. They just use their gods' names as oaths. The only thing they honor is that big golden eagle, because it stands for the almighty Roman Empire. Though *I* wouldn't want to be caught insulting the image of one of their gods."

Jerusha grew suspicious. "How do you know all this?"

"I used to...well, I used to be around Roman soldiers a lot..." Then it was the old woman's turn to look suspicious, as well as embarrassed. "No! Not in that way! I...I used to sell things to them. How dare you accuse me of anything else!"

The woman moved away quickly down an alley. Jerusha realized she had nothing to fear from her erstwhile companion, but the encounter got her to thinking. *So the Romans no longer revered or feared their gods. Their religion was dying; observed only for political or social reasons, if at all.*

Being a non-believing Jew herself, Jerusha would naturally not be shocked or offended by impiety concerning any religion of any country. Other Jews would be, or be pleased the Romans showed the superiority and truth of Judaism. She also understood the social need for religion in general, however indifferent she felt toward society. Without a common code of ethics, handed down from a supernatural but unimpeachable source, no one could be trusted. Sin and crime—were they truly the same thing? Judaism implied so—would run rampant; and society, commerce, and the State would fall apart. Even the family would be useless, with brother against brother. People would revert to savages. As Khimirk's people had proven. Savagery. Jerusha's Night of Horror, but worldwide.

Yet neglected religion could still serve its purpose so long as individuals were hypocritical enough to give it lip service, as Jerusha herself did. And, she suspected, as did many of the Pharisees, with all their outward show. And so long, of course, as *most* people practiced their beliefs in sincerity and devotion. Or at least showed it; hence the Pharisees? No, she knew too many who *were* true believers. This line of thought was going in circles, and Jerusha was getting confused. She was satisfied the sloppy Roman practice of religion made Judaism look better.

Why was she rethinking all this now? She had rejected the last of it years ago; when her distant God couldn't save her boys, or Leah's, or any of the boys in Bethlehem... *Some* of the families there must have been pious and prayerful and righteous. But only *one* was saved; the one whose family was the most evil in all of Judea.

The sun was setting, the Sabbath had begun, and Jerusha went home to boredom.

On her sixth day in the plaza, the first day of the week, a major change occurred almost without her noticing it. Small groups of people began congregating around the base of the black obelisk near the Roman residence, as though waiting for something, and chatting with each other to pass the time. She only glanced at the growing crowd for a moment. Jerusha never looked in any one direction or at any one thing too long. So she turned her head just in time to see her target exit from the house at the opposite end. He was accompanied by only one friend, and their interest appeared fixed on the black obelisk and its crowd, which they approached.

Jerusha moved slowly to a closer bench, not only slope-shouldered but limping, holding on to her stick as though it was all that protected her from a broken hip or worse. She repeatedly looked downwards around her feet, as though she had dropped a coin, a piece of clothing or even a bit of rag which would mean nothing except to a poor old woman.

After sitting at the new bench a few minutes, Jerusha arose and approached the crowd carefully, giving herself opportunities to scan it for signs of danger. She noticed that the proportion of Romans to Jews and others, and the mixture of social classes, were the same as at most random gatherings. Since she intended her attack on Gaius to come from behind and to his right side, she placed herself to his left rear, separated from him by two elderly Jewish men. When she glanced down, she found she was standing on Romulus', or was it Remus'?, face. Gaius' friend was standing in front of him, so he should present no problem. Now all she had to do was discover what this gathering was all about. She could take no chance that its purpose might interfere with hers. Within a matter of minutes she knew.

Two well-dressed men, a Roman and a Hellenized Jew, marched from the main gate of the governor's palace to the base of the obelisk. People stepped aside to let them pass; they stopped, flanking a green stone step. A lesser functionary, judging from the way he had to thread his way through the crowd, pasted a large sign on the base of the obelisk facing the people. Though Jerusha couldn't read any of it, the shapes of the letters showed it was written in several different languages. The Roman official mounted the block first, pulled out a scroll from his toga, and started reading loudly. When he had finished, there was no sign of approval or disapproval from the people. He then pulled out a second scroll and read from it. Since the speaker was Roman, it stood to reason that the first scroll was in Latin, the second in Greek. Jerusha would have to wait until the Jew had read his own scrolls before she could know what the announcement was about; a matter which could conceivably be of great importance to her. *But would Gaius and his friend wait around that long?* They had heard the Latin version. Many other people softly resumed their chatting as soon as they had listened to the speech in a language they could understand, but a few wandered away. *Would Gaius leave, ruining the best opportunity Jerusha might have for a long time?*

Though his friend appeared bored, Gaius stood still, looking surreptitiously at various people in the group.

When she finally heard the speech in Aramaic, it turned out to be of no importance to her whatever. It was decreed that due to the number of Hellenized Jews who were adopting Roman clothing customs and wearing rings somewhat similar to the official gold ring of Roman citizenship, for security reasons, persons entering important Roman governmental buildings must be more easily identifiable by nationality or loyalty. Therefore, small shrines to Roman deities were being installed at the entrances to such buildings, along with a bowl of incense, hot coals, and a spoon. Those who chose not to burn a bit of incense at the shrine would be considered Jews and would be required to state their destination and purpose within the building. In the most important structures, or at times of heightened security, such persons would be escorted by a guard while in the buildings.

There could not have been very many listeners to whom this decree would cause much interest or inconvenience. Yet Gaius stayed in place and continued to look around the remaining crowd, almost all of which was in front of him, though facing in different directions. Jerusha concluded that as the governor's intelligence officer, Gaius was either trying to determine which languages appeared improbably known to certain people, or was examining the faces of suspicious persons so they could be identified if they later wore a different guise or came to Gaius' attention in some other way. It occurred to Jerusha, rather late, that due to his political position, Gaius probably prepared the decree himself for the approval of the new procurator, Pontius Pilate, and wished to see public reaction to it.

Very shrewd of him. *Too* shrewd. *Were those on his staff equally intelligent?* Would someone notice that two murders would shortly have occurred only a few streets apart? Her serious concern began to fade. What would the torture-killing of a long-retired Jewish soldier, clearly an act of passion or revenge, have in common with the well-planned, political murder of a highly placed Roman official? At least Jerusha hoped the second killing would appear well-planned. If it didn't, it would only be because she had been immediately caught.

None of these thoughts interrupted her slow progress behind Gaius to his immediate right rear. She glanced down idly again to find she was now standing on Remus', or was it Romulus'?, face. Jerusha suddenly had two additional strokes of good luck: Gaius' short stature forced him to rise to the balls of his feet to see as many faces as possible, and as Jerusha arrived in place, Gaius had just turned his head and upper torso so as to observe the far left of the crowd, the opposite direction from Jerusha. His slightly precarious balance would make any sudden move on his part, such as a fall and shout, appear accidental, for a brief fraction of time. This might be all she would need. Even without such good fortune, this was the moment to act. The speech was at its end, the crowd would quickly disperse, and with it would go Gaius.

Jerusha didn't have to think about her actions now. She had practiced, made corrections, and practiced again before she appeared at the plaza the first time, and had continued to do so every evening since. As to the aim of her dagger thrust, her years of studying clothing of all manners and how they were assembled and sewn had always involved enough curiosity that she knew everything there was to know about the Roman togas she had seen. Despite what appeared to be a voluminous amount of heavy cloth held up as if by magic, she knew that the toga, when properly folded, was only a relatively narrow garment worn over a thin linen tunic. Also, most of the heavy material was worn on the sides of the body, mostly the right, in folds beginning a couple of feet beneath the armpit, though there were some shallower folds diagonally across the chest leading from the left shoulder, and at the back. That knowledge made it quite clear that the most vulnerable place on a well-dressed Roman, especially when approached from the rear, would be under his right arm near the lower ribs. Therefore Jerusha could expect to meet only the resistance of Gaius' thin tunic if she aimed her dagger at his liver. She could well hope the toga would ride high enough to disguise the wound while Gaius was falling. Her experience with animals was insufficient to identify the exact location of a man's liver, so she would have to move the dagger quickly up and down inside his body, particularly since she knew the liver could take some damage without death necessarily resulting. The only alternative would be a frontal attack, for which she was certain she would not be afforded an opportunity. Her exaggerated stoop would make her shorter than Gaius, despite his lack of stature—another consideration for the plan she had adopted. Jerusha would hold her walking stick in her left hand and use her right hand for removing her dagger from her left sleeve, a quick thrust and wiggle, then withdrawal of the bloody dagger into the bag fitted for it and now hanging on her left side, slightly forward. She had checked the bag a moment before to insure the flap and mouth were open, under her shawl. Her left arm with her stick would hold the shawl out to avoid blood-stains. Jerusha had honed the dagger almost excessively every night before each trip to the plaza. The only improvement which Jerusha would have liked would have been a slightly thicker application of soot on her face to disguise it more during her escape, but she could not have known in advance which day Gaius would appear, and a filthy face every day would have been out of the question.

The knife thrust went in quicker and easier than Jerusha could have hoped. She used all the strength in her arm and the dagger movements inside the victim's body offered her no problems or slowed her down. The dagger was in its pouch before Gaius' shout could be heard and before he was on the ground. Gaius' friend turned around and knelt beside him with soothing words thinking he had fallen down accidentally; since the victim had landed on his side, precious seconds would pass before any blood could be seen through the now bunched toga. Even the red hem helped disguise the act.

By that time Jerusha had taken a step or two to her left and pushed gently forward into the crowd. Since most of the people in it were by now blaming their neighbors animatedly for bumping into them, which Jerusha helped with a few clumsy movements, her progress went unnoticed. She must have made herself the shortest in the crowd, for she saw no faces, and, of course, no one looked into hers. A few in the group had seen something serious about Gaius' condition, or just didn't want to be where there was any commotion or trouble, so they ran or walked as quickly away from the scene as they could, forward or sideways, well covering Jerusha's slower walk to the nearest dark alley. Once there she looked back quickly; a dangerous move if so many others weren't doing it, and saw she had been right in escaping forward rather than retreating. Those who thought they had any authority or were willing to be involved were staring behind where Gaius had stood and fallen. Presumably, they were searching for some evil-looking man running away.

Jerusha knew help—guards or physicians—would take many minutes to arrive. Although she had secured her escape, those minutes would ensure Gaius would die from his wound, if he wasn't dead already. *Poor stepped-on Romulus and Remus hadn't been of much value to their descendant.*

At the first cross-street Jerusha turned left toward her own alley, just before the small shops. They would offer some groups of people, for cover, but these people would soon be rounded up and questioned. She was much better off hobbling alone in her own alley, with her doorway only a few yards away. Once in the safety of her room she trembled slightly, a reaction uncommon to her, then washed the dagger and the inside of her pouch in her bowl. She added sticks of dry wood on the coals she had left burning, and then slowly poured the pinkish water on the fire, careful never to spill enough to quench it.

After a light supper, Jerusha slept moderately well. The next day all she could do was wait inside. She knew the more often she ventured out the more chance, however slight, of being recognized as having been at the plaza. The safest place for her would be Zachariah's headquarters, but the twisted route taken to this house, combined with her wretched sense of direction would have made it impossible to find.

So she waited. And waited. By the third day her food supplies were getting low and stale, so she risked a trip to the nearest and cheapest market. It was heartening her shopping went unnoticed. At least no incidents occurred. But she limited herself to only four stalls. She had also left her stick behind and dressed as the younger woman she was, though still poor, which she wasn't.

The next day a messenger from Zachariah finally arrived. He showed her his coin, face up, at the door, but declined to come in. From the way he kept checking his clothes she deduced that he was the same messenger Zachariah had sent before, and that he had not forgotten her mutilation of his oil-cloth on his previous visit. He made a motion for her to follow him. Knowing that the man would be as unconversational as before, Jerusha concluded that she was leaving this place forever. She made a quick inventory of her possessions and retrieved only the bag for her dagger, her money, and her signet before joining him on the street.

CHAPTER 9

Simon

The return trip to headquarters began on a circuitous route, and Jerusha's escort explained that, due to the murder of a high-ranking Roman on the plaza some days ago, one had to be careful in that neighborhood. *Then she had been successful!* Interestingly, the messenger's rote recital of his earlier instruction to Jerusha had apparently so deafened him to its meaning he didn't realize he was the one who had given the explicit orders to kill Gaius.

When they arrived at headquarters, Jerusha found she could already recognize it from a short distance despite having seen it only twice, the night she arrived and the day she left. Unfortunately, she could also smell the fetid stench of the neighborhood in which it was situated. Nevertheless, after the squalid rooms she had recently occupied, alternately tormented by fears of approaching arrest and numbed by crushing boredom, this felt like a homecoming to her.

Her guide escorted Jerusha up the stairs to her old waiting-hall, where he introduced her to a seated stranger, with an almost brusque "My Lord Simon, this is my Lady Jerusha," and withdrew, leaving the two alone.

"Shalom," said the man, who rose perfunctorily.

"Where's Zachariah?" Jerusha demanded sharply, the first words she had spoken for over forty-five minutes.

"He won't be back until late tonight. He has asked me to look after your needs."

"Are you his servant, then?" Jerusha noted his northern accent. A Galilean?

"I'm his equal. As much as anyone can be another's equal, God's viewpoint to the contrary. I understand you have fulfilled your orders in an exemplary manner." Simon's tone was respectful, but tinged with a strange note of sadness. That tone vanished shortly, to be replaced with a conversational voice. "Please be seated at the table. It has been brought up for the council meeting we will hold after Zachariah returns."

As she accepted his invitation, Jerusha noted the stranger had seated himself in an imposing high-backed chair at the head of the table. She studied his figure, which initially appeared commanding. Simon was tall and slender, but not slight. His black beard was clipped close and dotted with gray; his brown hair was curly and equally short. The only truly remarkable feature was his eyes: Overly large and liquid in appearance. He seemed to be a couple of years younger than Jerusha, though his solemnity might make him look older to a less astute observer.

"I haven't seen you at any meetings before," Jerusha said.

"I was at the last two while you were busy in another part of Jerusalem. And my work has changed in the last few months. I was a field commander, if leadership of a group as small as mine merits such a grand title. Now I just plan strategy."

"Do you know if any of the others of Zachariah's council have changed assignments?" Jerusha asked this merely as polite conversation while she further assessed the figure before her.

"Zachariah keeps people's assignments private, between him and them, though it can't always be done. Khimrik, our one

Gentile, is dead. Killed in what he would have thought of as a glorious attack on a much larger force of Romans."

Poor Khimrik, Jerusha thought; now he would never know if the black Nubians were as docile and unintelligent as he had believed. Of course, his death would have absolutely no effect on the slave trade. Jerusha suddenly remembered the last letter from her most diligent factor informed her that she was now heavily invested in the slave trade herself, as well as merchant caravans and foreign shipping and other ventures about which she knew little. Now Jerusha had nothing with which to fault Khimrik. She wished she had been less critical of him while he was alive, though she doubted he took her comments to heart, any more than he did anything else. And he had *smiled*, as no one else in his army seemed to do, except perhaps Zachariah. She would miss Khimrik; light-hearted self-confidence had always attracted her.

Servants now brought in wine to refill the mostly empty urn already there. Cheese, fruit, olives, nuts, and bread were spread on the table. Jerusha dipped her bread into a curved dish of olive oil, but found it had too many spices mixed in to suit her palate, though there were plenty of other refreshments. After she and Simon had partaken for a while, Simon asked, simply, "Why?"

"Why what?" Jerusha was puzzled.

"Why are you in the Zealot movement?" Simon appeared as though he really wanted to know. He paused again, and then spoke openly, without any air of mysterious omniscience which a lesser man might have affected. "Zachariah is my closest friend. He has told me about you, at least superficially. What happened long ago in Bethlehem... your heroic service with us Zealots, and even...shall we say...your less than total devotion to our faith, or the coming Messiah. You could live a much better life with all your money."

"You talk too much," Jerusha said.

Simon laughed heartily. "Actually, your kinsman, Zachariah,

almost equals me in talk. But he's dropping behind. Must be getting old. My reasons for being a talker are simple, but many. First, I want to know everything about everyone I meet, and people don't open up to the silent. Second, I have no secrets about myself and am happy to tell you anything you wish to know. Third, I don't care what personal affect my actual words have on you. I don't want to impress you, frighten you, bore you, excite you, and I don't care if what I say has any of those results. Also, I sometimes speak to straighten out my own thoughts; you just happen to be here at the time. Does this bother you? I've found that self-centered or secretive men tend to be silent. Or men who are afraid of showing their ignorance. I'm not worried about that. Oh yes, and there are those who have such contempt for other humans they consider their own thoughts too valuable to share and the thoughts of others too worthless to hear. I pray I'll never fall into that category

"But this time I've wandered *too* far off the subject. *Why* are you among the Zealots?"

Jerusha began to wonder if Simon was merely a chatterer. But that character did not go with his eyes. Or his serious manner. "Were you a teacher?" asked Jerusha.

"No. Never knew the subject well enough. The one I would want to teach. But I might try some day."

Jerusha might as well see where the talk would lead. She continued, "Back on your subject, I know you were going to list off for me all the good things I could be doing with my riches," Jerusha said with a large hint of irony. "Give to the poor, so they will always remain so and dependent on others? Donate to the Temple to further enrich the priests in their flowing golden robes and surrounded by the rich tapestries Herod the Great gave them? I'm afraid even my wealth can't compete with his. Scatter my money among the needy so within days or weeks everything would be just as before except for the fools hoping for more such generosity? Oh, of course, there are the Zealots; were you going to build up to that? A modest legacy or ten might help your cause."

Simon replied, "Actually, I hadn't thought about the last, though I suppose a few coins might hold us over until the Messiah comes. But God will provide our wants, or, more importantly, what we should have."

Uh oh, Jerusha thought, *here comes the heavy theology.* But Simon didn't follow up on the subject. He glanced around the hall. "We're not at council yet. Can't we be more comfortable? We might have several hours to wait."

Jerusha felt a wave of disappointment. "You mean my bedroom?"

"Of course not. I meant better furniture than straight-back chairs. I'll send for two dining couches, under the windows for fresh air."

"Oh," she shrugged. For some reason she could not explain to herself, Jerusha suddenly felt defensive. She looked herself over. "You know, I don't usually look like this; I just came back from a mission where I had to pass myself off as an ugly old crone." Without giving her actions any conscious thought, Jerusha licked an inside corner of her robe and cleaned her face as well as she could, smoothed out wrinkles, brushed off any loose dirt from her clothing and shifted position to a more attractive posture. Only then did she lower her veils in a manner which made it appear they slid down of their own volition.

Simon asked, "Why should your outer appearance matter to me?" Since his question was clearly rhetorical, Jerusha let it go without reply. Simon ordered well-upholstered couches and they were placed with their raised portions at opposite ends. The servants left as quickly as they could; whether this was a sign of respect, dislike, or fear, Jerusha could not discern.

When the two had settled themselves, Simon on the left and Jerusha on the right, a long moment of silence passed.

Simon finally spoke on the previous subject. "You are rich. Why don't you get out of this, live well, and do as much good with your money as you can?"

"While you wait for your Messiah. Do you really think he will come?"

"I know he will. And soon...though..."

"Though what?"

"I'm not a theologian, but I have studied Holy Scripture. And have thought long. I suspect the Messiah won't come as a king or a warrior. I have to admit, however, that I have no idea how he *will* come, if not as such." He reached to the table for more fruit. Jerusha had moved the delicacies closer to their couches as he spoke.

She now turned his question on him: "If you're not absolutely sure of your cause, why don't *you* leave this movement?"

"I am still a Pharisee and a Zealot, despite details. You are neither...in your heart. But maybe we're both fools."

"If you know Zachariah as well as you say you do, you should know I have a mission which is far more important to me than anything you people are fighting for."

"No, I don't know. Perhaps Zachariah didn't choose to tell me. But it seems", he added, "that each of us has his own motivation. Though mine wouldn't make any sense at all to you. I suppose I should still be a blacksmith in Galilee, where I was born and raised."

"You were a blacksmith? You don't have the body for it."

"What do you know about bodies? Don't answer that," he smiled.

So, Jerusha thought, he has at least heard rumors about me, and has a sense of humor. The latter is sometimes an indication of intelligence, however hidden. Simon's tone suddenly became wistful, and he looked away from her. Jerusha sensed he was going into another soliloquy, perhaps a long one, but she could always interrupt him or take a short nap if it was boring enough. Any first impressions of Simon which might have raised his stature initially had dwindled due to his talkativeness. Intelligence aside. Now he would have to earn any awe or high respect from her the hard way.

Simon began, "When I was young, I had family connections and a very successful carpentry shop I had inherited from my father and elder brother. But I found that kind of work to be tedious. Besides, there are only so many pieces of furniture possible, especially in a land with limited lumber, however much profit I could charge.

"I had been married, but my beloved wife died in childbirth. My son was a fine young boy when he became determined to go to the Temple, to rise or not, as God willed. Not dedicated officially, and too old to be so, but he would have accepted any work in connection with the center of our faith. After a while I stopped hearing from him. It was time for a change in my life.

"Iron was easy to obtain, and linked itself to artistry. After a short time I found that my body was really not built for heavy iron work, as you noticed, but my artistic skill was, for light work, at least. If you don't use your muscles daily over a hot forge, they diminish. It doesn't take as much physical strength to create beauty (or kill Romans, as I later found out). An artist, if you don't know, works ten times as long as an artisan, but gets paid half as much. Not that I cared."

"If you were a skilled blacksmith," Jerusha was beginning to be impressed again, "then you must have been an honored member of a guild, second only to the Sanhedrin in prestige. Certainly above us mere merchants. Why would you give that up to degrade yourself as a simple artist?" Jerusha was incredulous.

"Artists of 'wise hearts' were chosen by God, Himself, to build the Ark of the Covenant. We still know their names. An artist works because he has to for his own soul, not for money. Though money does come in useful."

Jerusha considered aloud, "I was of the lowest caste, slave excepted, but I, also, do what I want regardless of the class or pay, though I venture I earn more than you. Becoming a skilled worker even for a time was my path to riches."

"But can you turn out four iron chairs with sixty grape leaves, over two hundred grapes, with holders for a cup of wine in each arm, which won't rust, and which you have to hide to keep the Romans from using or stealing?" he laughed.

"No."

"...And in which the grapes don't touch each other and yet still look bunched?"

Jerusha laughed. "Think of how many weapons you could produce for the Zealots."

He smiled. "I have made them weapons. But they're so pretty they're rarely used." He turned serious again. "Actually, since Galilee has been the center of most unrest and rebellions, I was often called on as an armorer by one side or the other, at high wages. In Jerusalem, I only pray I'm on God's side."

"You quit being a unit commander with the Zealots. In close combat, I presume. You are now a strategist, or tactician, I forget the difference. Did you get tired of killing? You're not too old for it."

"Not in that way." Simon paused a moment, turned his head to the left and looked piercingly into Jerusha's eyes. "Nor did I become cowardly or squeamish. Squeamishness is a serious vice. God may have given it to us as a warning sign to make us think about what we are doing or about to do, but if our action is righteous, squeamishness should be suppressed as ruthlessly as any other weakness.

"At the very beginning, some of my men might have considered me weak, because I demanded after a fight when we were in command of the field, or the sand dune, that we bury the slain enemy, complete with services and prayers. One man reminded me that the Romans had different death customs and religious views. I informed him I was not responsible for their ignorance, just my knowledge. Piety never interfered with my fighting. I prepared myself spiritually before the fight and prayed afterward. But I can't think of anything more useless than a doubt-filled soldier. I tolerated only happy warriors *(Zachariah's words!* Jerusha remembered) in my unit, and I set the example. I am no longer a happy warrior. Since I've been at council, I have always advocated mercy when at all appropriate. Never on legalistic grounds. Nor because I thought Romans deserved it, nor out of prudence. I'm not sure why, except that we're all sinners in the eyes of God."

"You still talk too much," Jerusha said. *Didn't he know knowledge, however trivial, was power, to be hoarded like gold?*

"I guess I'm a didact."

"What's that?"

"A teacher. Who doesn't get paid. And usually is unwanted. Or an intellectual. I over-explain everything. And though the Scriptures are harsh on idle chatter, I ensure my chatter isn't idle, but works very hard." He smiled again. "You should be grateful; most men don't consider women fit vessels for their talk. I have been regularly criticized for talking and even arguing with women."

Jerusha remembered Mordecai's attempts to teach her to read, and that his efforts at conversation weren't successful. Her husband had tried, but never said anything worth remembering. She didn't know what to make of his extreme opposite, sitting across from her, dipping his bread in the oil, and talking. Succeeding where Mordecai had failed.

Simon swallowed the wine that remained in his goblet and poured himself more. "On our earlier subject, don't misunderstand me and think I consider myself less responsible for battlefield deaths now that I am on the council than I was when I was in the field. If anything, I am more responsible; before, I could kill only a handful of Romans, and now I can kill dozens. And I don't feel very good about it." She could see the sorrow in his eyes. "But I want to know more about what we're doing than I knew out there.

"Do you hear any sign of Zachariah coming back?" he asked.

"No."

"All right. Then I'll keep talking about what interests me. You might understand something. Or you might not. More importantly, it might help straighten out my own mind. You and I, or at least I, know we Jews are God's chosen people. And that God means for us Israelites to be free of Roman rule. How this is to come about, I don't know. And if *I* don't know, then none of my acquaintances knows, either, though some of them think they do.

"Does that sound arrogant? I do not claim knowledge or intelligence as a virtue. Indeed, I tend to think of intelligence as a curse. At any rate, it's an accident of birth and a double-edged sword. I fight hard against this, my only vanity, and force myself to accept true wisdom—love of God, patience, and admiration for those without intelligence, as far as my nature permits. Which isn't enough." Simon smiled. "It takes much to impress me with your mind, as you do."

"I haven't said anything important," she replied.

"Your questions and reactions have; perhaps more than you know. Also, of course, there's all that Zachariah's told me about you."

Jerusha began to notice that the wine, unwatered, was slightly affecting her, especially since she had eaten little of the food. She wondered now if it might have acted similarly on Simon, who had obviously begun drinking before she got there.

"What did your men think about what you admit is your intellectual arrogance? That doesn't strike me as a quality that would endear you to them."

"Every good leader must learn to be a good player, as well."

Where had she heard almost those exact words before? Ah, yes, Khimrik—though he had been talking about hiding his lack of religious belief. Which characteristic would require the most dissembling? Which was the most unforgiving by underlings? Had she heard the idea even before Khimrik? Hadn't Zachariah referred to the unpopularity of a brilliant, though vain, Roman intelligence officer? Jerusha asked Simon about one of the few things she, somewhat resentfully, considered to be a sign of a good mind. "Do you speak Latin or Greek?"

He laughed. "Greek, of course; my Latin isn't very good. But then again, almost all Romans, like many Jews, speak Greek, or the *Koine* version. Some Roman soldiers and officers recruited in the provinces don't speak any Latin at all. Why do you ask?"

"I speak only Aramaic," said Jerusha. Strange, almost everyone in Judea spoke and read languages of which she knew nothing. Was she in over her head? No, she knew what she *wanted*, which was more than Simon knew. After a pause, Jerusha said, "You never answered my question. What are *you* seeking here?"

"God," Simon answered quietly but with an intensity that startled her.

Jerusha ventured, "Is there any human whose judgment you trust beyond doubt?"

Simon hesitated. "Oddly, there is. My younger brother. The one who works the family carpentry business. He's my half-brother. He was born after me, to my father's second wife. He's very wise. No, he's not here, nor do I think he would want me here."

"Then he would expect you to take full advantage of the Day of Atonement for your actions or doubts?"

Simon looked at the table. "I'm not sure that's enough. We Jews have always tended to think of ourselves as a People, and have sometimes forgotten to think of our individual souls. Maybe that's partly why I left fieldwork. My own soul." He mused. "The Day of Atonement...no, that is not enough. I do, of course, believe our sins must be atoned for, I believe in our resurrection and I do seek paradise and fear hell, and know everything we do leads to one or the other. But we can't pick and choose which sins or virtues we think more important than others. We can't compare ourselves with other people; our virtues and sins with theirs. All of God's law must be obeyed. Which, in itself, is nearly impossible for individuals. But I can't be carried in on the shoulders of my nation."

Jerusha assumed a look of contempt. "Just like a man! Your *own* personal righteousness is all that matters, and forget about your People." She made the comment just to throw Simon's speech off course. *She*, naturally, cared nothing for the spiritual status of herself *or* her "people." She punctuated her remark by throwing a fruit rind on the table, and vaguely noticed that throwing things without intention of hurting anyone or anything was becoming a habit with her. Was this "just like a woman?"

"Thank you," Simon said sarcastically. "Now I've got selfishness to worry about, too."

Usually, Jerusha felt no respect for weak men, but somehow she sensed strength in Simon if he only could get past his present confusion.

Jerusha casually shifted as though uncomfortable on her couch. "Would we be more at ease talking in my bedroom?" she suggested, shocking herself. *Her bedroom?* Jerusha remembered that just a while ago the thought had disgusted her. Was mere talking seductive? Well, at least *Jerusha* had made the suggestion this time, not the man. Simon seemed sincerely touched— *Touched*—but turned her down, and for a reason she did not understand at all.

"I am betrothed. It is impossible."

"I'll never tell her," she responded sharply, though she sensed that was not his concern. "Do you love her?" she asked, despite her dislike for that useless emotion, other than for her children.

"I've barely met her; she has a sweet face. My mother-by-marriage knows my betrothed, and vouches for her. And for all the right reasons. I would trust her judgment with my life."

"Are you that enslaved to your mother? And not even your real mother?"

"If you knew her, you would have the same feelings. But now it's you who are wandering. At the risk of sounding like the most fanatic Pharisee you have ever met, there is my future family, too. I wish to approach it in purity. Sex isn't its own end. Or have you found it to be so?"

"No, but it can be a nice diversion."

"So is a fig dipped in honey, but I wouldn't risk my family for it. Look at it this way: Had it had not been for my well-known chastity, I would not have been chosen to accompany you this afternoon and evening. And I'm glad I was chosen." He smiled, brightening his entire face again.

For some reason, Jerusha sensed a profound difference between Simon's refusal of her favors and Asa's long ago acceptance and subsequent repentance.

"Do you have difficulty remaining chaste?" she asked, again shocked at the direction their conversation was taking. And at her own whim!

Simon answered, thinking out his words, while still staring at the middle of the table:

"Temptation isn't a vice if controlled. I have wanted money, but I never turned to robbery. In the field I often went hungry, but I never embezzled my men's food. Why should wants, however strong, be the master of my actions? Besides," he brightened, laughing and looking up, "before long I will have a wife, and lust will be irrelevant. But *you* never answered *my* original question fully, and it's related, I think, to my problem. Why are you involved, and so deeply, and bloodily, with the Zealots?"

Jerusha never thought she'd tell anyone but Zachariah, though it seemed to come easily after Simon's honesty with her. "The same reason you're in the council: I want to learn something. I am searching for the then infant false king and Messiah whose ambitious family caused Herod the Great to kill the children of Bethlehem, including my three boys," she replied, her voice husky... "and some others close to me."

"This impostor was an infant?"

"Yes, but his family wasn't, and he has not renounced their ambition in all the years since, as far as I know."

Simon paused. "I never heard much of that atrocity in Bethlehem, since I lived in Nazareth, but I'm not surprised, knowing the character of Herod. Such information would have made him insanely jealous. You want revenge, and Herod is dead. That leaves the family of whom? Do you know?"

"Didn't I say I was still searching?"

"Are you certain there is or ever was such a false Messiah?"

"Yes. And I will find him."

"Is that your proper job? Or anyone's? Why not leave him to God? God will not be mocked by an impostor, or a mass killer."

"Do I strike you as someone who will leave anything to God? Especially when my sons' deaths are involved?"

"Strange, I've found guilt is a stronger motivator than hate, but perhaps not with you."

Did this man, Simon, know about Jerusha's blame for the deaths of her nephews? Simon could only have learned of it through Zachariah. Did *Zachariah* know? It wasn't possible. *That* she knew as a fact.

Before Jerusha could explode with indignation that she should bear any guilt for that night, Simon stood up and paced around the table, showing no awareness of the effect of his earlier words,

"I am as horrified as you by the thought of a false Messiah. It makes a mockery not only of God, but of the death of every Zealot and every Roman in this war. The True Messiah will make himself known, and we, among others, will surely recognize him." As he became more animated, Simon's face began to redden. "Let me beg something of you. Do not come to the council meeting. Zachariah cannot openly give you honor for what you have done, and everyone else will wonder why you are there. Meet with Zachariah in advance, and receive your orders, if you really wish to carry them out. Do not come back here again. This is said by a friend...more your friend than you may ever know."

"Actually," said Jerusha, "those were my thoughts exactly about the council. But you sound as though you are trying to dissuade me from obeying orders."

"Tonight," said Simon, "The council will change our strategy, despite all my efforts to prevent that change. We are one of the few bands that have limited ourselves to killing Romans. Now we will also begin killing collaborators. And you, Jerusha, will be one of our most dangerous weapons."

"I'm flattered," she said. "And I'll avoid the meeting as a favor to you. But I don't see that Jewish traitors should be harder to kill than Romans."

"For the sake of your soul, please leave this place...return to your home. Those are my final words to you, and my prayer." Simon paused, fixing her with a piercing glance, then abruptly turned and strode out of the room.

Jerusha had, just at this one meeting in what used to be her upstairs hall, thought extensively about two men: Khimrik the confident; Simon the searching. Khimrik the shallow unbeliever; Simon the deeply devout, and in such a way that she had tolerated hearing about subjects she would not have given a thought to previously. Khimrik, who would never ask for or accept advice; Simon who actually listened to her and respected her mind, as no man ever had before. Khimrik the lover; Simon the thinker. A strong body versus a strong brain, in two brave men.

But there had been other men in her life, and she felt some guilt she had not given them a thought. Most obvious was her husband, Mordecai; but however hard she concentrated she could not come up with a mental picture except that of a good, though boring, man. Asa, of course, but he wasn't worth thinking about. Isaac she *would* not think about. Zachariah; he talked even more than Simon, but it was spread over many years and many visits— and how could she take a man seriously who didn't even take himself very seriously except in matters of work? The rest of the time he was precisely the "idle chatterer" she had wrongly thought Simon to be. But then what was Simon's work? She was becoming as confused as Simon.

Simon was, above all other things, a *teacher.* Jerusha had never had a real teacher, but she recognized one when she met one. Whatever his confusion over certain matters; whatever authority he lacked; however much she had thought him at times an idle chatterer; she now knew he was a teacher, and his failings only proved his real gifts. It would have been interesting to have been his student.

As Jerusha pondered these thoughts, and the dusk was setting in behind the window lattices, she heard the front door open and knew Zachariah had finally arrived. She would turn to what and whom she knew and understood.

She stopped Zachariah as he was about to mount the stairs, turned him around and propelled him out into the courtyard, toward his quarters.

Jerusha remembered that Zachariah's room was on the right side of the yard, so her lack of a sense of direction didn't matter, especially since Zachariah went straight to his door when it became apparent she wanted only a private audience with him.

She slammed the door shut behind them and bolted it as soon as they were inside.

"Is there some reason," he asked sweetly, "why you want us to stand in the dark, or would you like me to light some lamps?"

"Yes, yes, of course, get on with it!"

"Thank you, my lady."

Jerusha could hear him move to the stove and see his outline as he bent a taper down into the coals, which must have been kept hot for him during his long absence by a (communal?) servant. Zachariah took his time lighting the two oil ceiling fixtures and then several table lamps which had been strategically placed under or near what must have been his favorite trophies. Before he finished, Jerusha could restrain herself no longer.

"Who gave you liberty to tell that stranger upstairs my life history?"

"What stranger?" Zachariah lit the last lamp. "Oh, you mean Simon?"

"Of course."

"Now look here, Jerusha," his voice had a sharp edge to it. "I told you when we last met in Bethlehem that we are a family. I don't know how to explain this politely, but Simon ben Joseph is the best among us. I have fought beside him for years. I would trust, and, indeed, have trusted, my life to him, and my affection for him far exceeds any I have for you, despite our kinship and despite my obligations to you." He towered over her grimly by the end of this speech.

Jerusha was taken aback. "How many others did you tell?"

"None. You have seen how carefully I run my councils and watch what I say." Zachariah relaxed enough to sit in the chair he had used during her last visit. "I told him nothing of your personal mission here. Its inherent silliness might have lost you his respect. Or did you blurt it all out to him?"

Jerusha was abashed. "Yes, I did. I suppose it was foolish of me."

"Possibly not. Knowing Simon as I do, he told you his doubts as well. When he trusts someone, he holds nothing back about himself. And I had a feeling you two would get along well," Zachariah laughed. "Think of it: friendship between the most pious and devout member of our group, and a woman who can only be described as the least so. But your secrets are safer with him than you seem to have thought they were with me. Would you like some wine?"

"No, I had enough in the hall upstairs." Jerusha took the remaining chair and momentarily lapsed into silent thought. Finally, "Simon told me that you are changing tactics or strategy? That our targets are now Jewish traitors."

"Good. Now I won't have to explain it to you in council. We are the last Zealot group to fully realize the necessity of inspiring fear and respect among our own countrymen. But it's not just traitors, as such, that we're after, but collaborators. That includes all that any Romans consider as friends, whether or not these Jews have actually harmed us or helped the enemy. Does this bother you, Jerusha?"

"No...no." *Apparently some of Khimrik's opinions had effect even after his death.*

"Then I see no reason for your attending the council at all. I'll discuss your next mission. You'll find it different in many ways."

CHAPTER 10

Lady Jerusha

"Your next target is named Habakkuk ben Abishai. Do you know him?" asked Zachariah while they were in his quarters.

"Not by such a name."

"We know little about his familial line, but that's irrelevant." He took a sip from the goblet he had poured for himself.

"If his house is even in question, I assume it's prominent and rich?"

"Yes; otherwise he would never have fallen in with such bad company."

"How will I know him?" Jerusha asked.

"He should be easy to recognize. He's fully Hellenized and wears a large clasp of a pagan idol; a green dragon, I think, made of emeralds and set in elaborately worked gold. Probably stolen from Persia or somewhere, and given to him or sold by a Roman officer."

Zachariah took another sip. "He's past middle-age, white haired, clean-shaven. He has taken to wearing a toga, or at least as close to the style of a toga as his seamstress could copy without violating Roman law, which limits real togas to citizens of Rome.

Since he uses the jeweled clasp to hold his cloak together, it is always on the left side of his chest, which should make it relatively easy to deduce the position of his heart."

"Actually," Jerusha admitted, "I've never had more than a vague idea where a man's heart is."

"Interesting thing for a woman to say," Zachariah smiled. "It's just to the victim's left in his lower chest. Most recruits, I've noticed, think it's somewhere in the left shoulder, leaving wounded Romans for us to have to kill afterwards. A dagger should pass under his breast bone then go slightly upward, and to the killer's right, which avoids both the armor-like sternum and the ribs while hitting other useful places on the way and ending, with luck, in or through his heart." Zachariah indicated the places on his own chest. "You're shorter so that should help.

"He goes almost every day to the most expensive market in Jerusalem, and wastes hours choosing delicacies. He must not trust his cook to meet the standards of his sensitive palate. The crowds may be larger there, which could either work for you or against you."

"Wouldn't I stand out atrociously in such a crowd?" Jerusha asked.

"I've selected nice rooms for you near the market. Your dress and manners we will discuss later. Actually, your speech has come a long way, considering your origin."

"Has this Habakkuk ever acted against Judean independence?"

"Not that I've heard. Probably not, or he'd have been made a citizen of Rome as many of our people have. Joel hates him worst of all, and all he can come up with is a personal snub. Joel has always been very poor, and resents the rich, despite loud profession of devotion to nothing but God's Law. But we have to start somewhere, with someone on friendly or business terms with the Romans. Why do you ask, does it matter?"

"Not really," Jerusha said. She remembered Joel as the member at council who took the most legalistic side of every argument, and went out of his way, in gestures and dress, to appear almost painfully pharisaical and self-sacrificing. But she didn't think Joel's motivation was very important, considering that her *own* motivation had much less to do with the Zealot cause. "You do know your good friend Simon ben Joseph tried to discourage me from taking such assignments?"

"He's getting married soon. The manly virtues decline at such times. He'll be back to his own self once the novelty wears off and he resumes his proper place in the patriarchal system," said Zachariah, rising from his chair as if in dismissal.

"And what is *my* 'proper place'?"

Zachariah ignored the question. "By the way, have I ever gotten around to thanking you for the excellent job you did with Gaius?"

"No, as a matter of fact, you have not."

"I'll reward you tomorrow."

The next day Jerusha found herself reclining on a couch across from Zachariah's at the inside corner of the best of one of the few fine dining establishments in Jerusalem.

Zachariah had explained to her that although the poor cooked for themselves at home, this was not the universal custom, even discounting the outdoor pastry shops Jerusha had used on rare occasions. Most rich Jews had their own cooks, who lived with them, or delivered to their home, full or part-time, as Jerusha had done in Bethlehem. So many Jewish religious practices involved food, such a rich family would only seldom eat at any sort of dining establishment in Jerusalem. Gentiles, on the other hand, had courting customs that called for dining out, and lacked the Jewish disapproval of women unescorted by their husbands and families disporting themselves in public, so dining establishments flourished in some foreign lands.

Also, the Romans, even in Jerusalem, maintained their custom of the *orgy*: A few to a dozen or more families who were friends ate at each others' homes, alternating hosts. Because these dinners lasted hours sometimes, often with a musician, poet, or other entertainment, Jews assumed the worst and attributed lustful and other immoral activities to Roman orgies, which were usually just rotating dinners. Zachariah thought the Roman custom superior because it allowed foodstuffs to be purchased in bulk, and permitted the cooks a week or two off before having to cook for anyone but themselves and perhaps other servants, excepting occasional cold cuts. But the orgy, like the Jewish customs, led to a dearth of first-class dining establishments among the Romans as well as the Jews in Jerusalem. So he was lucky to find a place such as this.

Jerusha had rarely before seen such luxury as she saw here. For that matter, she had never been inside any place that served food to seated customers only. She had used outside benches, arranged so as to feed the hoped-for moving crowds in trough-like manner. Some she ate at did not even have awnings for protection from sun or rain. And the food was best forgotten as soon as possible, if its quality was not so low as to reassert itself periodically. She had usually found herself hurried along in such establishments. Indeed, when she was in her costume of an old hag she had not been allowed a place at the bench, but given her food on a piece of used papyrus or a large leaf so she would not even use up floor space for long. Once or twice Jerusha had found herself waiting in line, and when she finally paid for her food the innkeeper had spilled the food on the filthy street and made no effort to replace it. She had begun to think her experiences were those of all unfortunates without their own private cooks or kitchens. Or perhaps the way lone women were always treated.

But here, the walls were freshly whitewashed except where they were frescoed with artistic renditions of hanging meats, game, and fruit. Below the decorations the walls were all wainscoted red, in the Roman manner. Jerusha reckoned the rich Jews couldn't keep their hands or chairs from dirtying the walls either. There were tuns of wines and beers along one wall. All the edges of the vats were bronzed or gilded with grapes and grape leaves or sheaves of grain, though with none of the disgusting gods of drunkenness favored by the Romans. None of the openings leading to the service areas had doors, but bronze-beaded curtains, presumably so the customers' needs could be seen to unobtrusively. The floors were tiled in interesting colors, and there were enough servants that each diner had his own. A large, over-weight and shaven-headed man, with a short scimitar at his waist sash, had greeted them at the door. Jerusha would have thought of him as a eunuch in harems she had heard of through stories told to her as a child, if she did not know eunuchs were illegal among Jews. The tables and red upholstered dining benches were lower than she was accustomed to at home or at the Zealot headquarters but she was surprisingly comfortable. In one corner a young man sang to the notes of a lyre. Jerusha knew nothing of music, but the sounds pleased her.

"I hired the singer to give us more privacy from eavesdroppers," said Zachariah.

"Why are we here?"

"Oh, several reasons. To thank you for that matter with the Roman. Secondly, to offer you one of the finest meals in Jerusalem. Kosher, of course. The third reason will make you angry, and I can't have you making a loud scene here; so control yourself."

"All right," she snapped, but softly. "What is it?"

"To finish your education as a lady."

"Oh, if that's all, do you think I've ever had pretensions that I *was* one? Or ever cared?"

"No," replied Zachariah, "but on your mission against Habakkuk it might be a matter of life or death for you to appear to be a lady. Your speech is almost perfect, or what mistakes you make can be attributed to the region you come from. I give your surroundings at headquarters, and your proximity to me, of course, credit for that. Also, your natural gift for mimicry. But there's more to being a lady than sounding like one."

"Then continue my education."

"You have to help by conversing, and letting me judge," said Zachariah.

"I thought we came here to eat."

"I reserved the place for the entire afternoon. Besides, you can talk and eat at the same time, though I told them not to bring the food until later."

"What should I talk about?" Jerusha asked.

"Anything interesting to you."

Jerusha had an idea about how to use this opportunity. Her feeling of isolation was caused by not knowing her way around Jerusalem; being trapped at headquarters, under other people's command, or lacking knowledge of their surroundings. The only exception was her killing missions, on which she was taken to her new quarters by a circuitous route so her knowledge would be limited to the small space between her new rooms and her target. A few streets at most, chosen for her. Jerusha did not actually resent this, because she knew the security reasons for it. Nevertheless, she intended to have some freedom in Jerusalem, secretly.

Jerusha would learn her way to her new target by memorizing it to overcome her weak sense of direction. She would talk here about the buildings in Jerusalem so she could later observe every physical object along the puzzle path on which she would be taken; streets, houses, parks, designs of any sort, until at least the area from headquarters to her next assignment in a higher and better part of the city would be familiar to her.

"Well, talk about something!" whispered Zachariah.

"I was just trying to think of a subject. I am limited in my learning at headquarters. To start, this place doesn't look like anywhere I've ever been."

"Because it was designed as a cross between Judean and Roman architecture. And decoration. A whim of the owner, since Romans don't eat here."

"I've noticed a few differences between the two styles but I can't describe them well. Roman buildings seem built in exact shapes, with fancy decorations, often at the tops of columns. But always evenly spaced, I suppose to draw attention to the overall shape. When the buildings aren't white all over, each color is limited to one architectural—is that the right word?—detail or chosen to go well together to show off the balance of the complete design. Judean buildings don't seem to follow much of a set pattern or shape. We use stones of clashing kinds and colors on the same building. Are our structures built only for function, or don't we Jews care about beauty, other than baubles? I'm sorry, I don't mean to insult my own country, but I spent years studying the styles of fine clothing and copying them, so I've developed an eye for design."

Zachariah was clearly appreciative. "You're quite right on the architecture, but don't blame your countrymen too much. The Jewish buildings grew over many centuries, and the use of space was of greatest importance. Also, each generation who built on had its own ideas. The Romans built almost everything here during a short period of time, and with only a few architects to compete, all longing for the Rome they knew. They also had machines to build with we couldn't imagine. Notice anything else? Take your time; we can stay here all day."

"Well," Jerusha paused. "I've only been in a few rich Jewish houses. But, both inside and outside, our builders stick their decorations on without plans. Columns don't match; they might be smooth, striped, spiral, all on or in the same building. Colorful badges stuck at random places. Judean streets are cobblestoned, while Romans' are more smoothly paved. Uh...cloths, tapestries, and silks in clashing colors. I'm talking only about the wealthy, of course; the poor have only sticks and stones. The *others* have too much decoration. If the owner can afford it, beads, gems, tiles, bronze fixtures, clutter..."

"Whereas," Zachariah interrupted, "all the Romans need are their huge, gilded, idolatrous eagles? Put in the most central and elevated place?"

"You're making fun of me." Jerusha made an almost girlish pout.

"No. I am very impressed with your perceptiveness. Though until your vocabulary expands enough, stick to subjects you really know about. Like clothing."

That was all the help she'd get this time, but certain guesses were confirmed, Jerusha thought.

Jerusha looked down at her luxurious clothes, a glance Zachariah could not have missed.

"You can't be looking at your clothes all the time. What did you expect? Hemp?"

She would have responded with a scowl or worse, but she was already learning her role.

Jerusha thought back over that morning. Zachariah had sent what she supposed must be a lady's maid, to dress her and arrange her hair. Jerusha had always been fastidious in her cleanliness, except when portraying a poor crone. The maid took liberties to correct minor points of her mode of speech, which offended Jerusha somewhat, for the girl had not hid her surprise at how well the older woman spoke at the time. Jerusha's manner of walking needed no correction for her natural pride had always kept her posture, back and head straight, costume allowing. When she saw the clothes laid out for her on the bed, her admiration prevented any outburst. Everything was of Sidon and Damascene silk, in complementary colors. When she put them on, the careful folds made her almost afraid to sit down. There was jewelry of all sorts and especially an ostentatious tiara for her hair, obviously made of solid gold. Her sandals were chased in gold-leaf. There were several items of clothing which she had never seen before, and had to be taught how to wear. The maid even applied a bit of face powder, though not nearly the face painting associated in Jerusalem with loose women. When she finally was in a position to see her entire head in the polished mirrors, she found her hair arrangement was more elaborate than she thought possible. She would have to memorize how it was done.

There had been no effort to color the gray streaks; ringlets were formed down both sides of her face, although the tiara held in place the double veils of silk that would both hide and show the rest of her hair; the veil fringes crossed over her shoulders. When the work was finished, Jerusha did not recognize herself in the long mirror of her bathing room. She had thought the clothes which Zachariah had lent her while she was at headquarters were of the best quality. But compared to this finery the others looked dowdy.

The greatest shock was when Jerusha stepped outside the building and found a litter supported by four slaves, with heavy curtains, gold fringes, and a step to let her mount, although the legs of the litter, when it was put down, were short enough she could have entered it without a step. The contrast between such elegant transportation and the stenches of the neighborhood in which the Zealot headquarters was situated made Jerusha want to laugh out loud, if such displays were in her. She hoped there was some sort of censer in the litter, or at least it had been doused with perfume. Jerusha moved one curtain just enough to see inside, and found Zachariah, smiling, and dressed as expensively as she. During the trip to the dining establishment he warned her to keep her curtains closed.

"I had to go to a lot of trouble for this contraption. I told the agent we were going to a wedding reception, so he wouldn't be so suspicious about sending his best litter into a slum. Even poor people do their best for weddings. Though I wish you hadn't put that gold thing on your head until you were in the litter. Of course, I told the slaves nothing and I hope they are experienced enough that nothing surprises them. When you leave the litter, say nothing to them nor even look at them. I told you long ago that being a commander requires mimicry. So does being a 'lady', however hypocritical it may seem in practice."

Now here she was seated in a luxurious establishment, across from her friend and kinsman, and plotting mayhem.

Zachariah interrupted her reverie. "Let me see your hands."

She showed them to him with the backs up.

"I wanted to see your palms and fingers," he said ironically. "Right now I can only see that you keep your nails in good shape," he added.

She turned her hands over with a twinge of fear. She had never studied them. After careful examination, Zachariah said, "For a woman who spent much of her life doing manual labor, it's surprising that whatever calluses you had are now gone, and your hands are almost as smooth and soft as any lady's in Jerusalem. Do you oil them regularly?"

"No more so than in the oily water of the bath at your headquarters."

"Try to speak with more of a lilt. Perhaps you can mimic a little baby talk?—No, that would over-do it."

Jerusha looked around. "Why is there only one woman here with this gaudy jewelry I'm wearing on my head?"

"Because it is known as the Crown of Jerusalem and it can

only be worn by the Jewish nobility. On the Sabbath it's the only piece of decoration a lady can wear at all. Wear it the day of your mission, for no one would suspect anything or admit if they did. It also explains why you have the temerity to be out on your own without other ladies or a male escort. There will probably be a few other women with one at that market."

The first course was finally served, and after eating daintily with her fingers, Jerusha looked around for a rag to wipe her hands on. In an instant the servant was there with a finger bowl, which she used. The food was delicious; though the only identifiable ingredients were yogurt and grape leaves, in which any manner of other food stuffs might be wrapped, except, of course, meat, which was forbidden in contact with yogurt under Jewish Law. Jerusha also had to admit to herself that even this early in the dinner she could tell the food here was better than at headquarters, and even than in her own home, at the times when she could afford the finest ingredients, and she had always considered herself the best cook imaginable.

She had to assume her eating methods were perfect, as Zachariah had watched her intently, throughout, without comment.

The second course consisted of slivers of fish with fruits and spices mixed in a crunchy coating. She could not help but wonder how the fish was brought from the nearest large body of water without the slightest staleness.

The next course was slivered lamb. It seemed impossible, but each course tasted better than the one preceding it. It was as though the food was arranged not to show off its own wonders so much as to form, all together, a steadily improving sequence heading to some culinary climax she could not even imagine. Leave one item out and the dinner would be diminished by more than that loss.

Jerusha also, however, discovered that each course required

different utensils and little ceremonies. Although she learned quickly, they appeared sillier to her each time. "I give up!" she said softly. "I knew rules existed. For that matter we practice many of them at headquarters. But I thought the whole reason for manners was to make people comfortable and feel at home. These rules do the opposite."

"They're supposed to. At home you act 'at home.' The reason for rules and ceremonies is to distinguish between classes. With enough practice, they do cause comfort because they teach you who is worth your time, and the topics of conversation. They eliminate the awkwardness of mixture, and the embarrassment or insult caused by misapprehension and immediate retreat. Learn them," he commanded.

His face showed nothing but polite flirtatiousness.

"I will. But only to prove something to myself."

To make her point she copied, perfectly, Zachariah's slightly flirtatious facial mannerisms, adding to them a slight artificial surprise, as would be expected from a lady in such a situation.

Jerusha was quickly learning new flavors. The wine was without a doubt the best she had ever tasted. Once again the servant miraculously appeared with a fresh finger bowl. If they were to continue this conversation, they would need more privacy. She turned to the waiter and asked with a sweetness she did not know she had in her, and yet with the slightest hint of firmness, that he return only when she or the gentleman signaled to him. She whispered to Zachariah, "I think I did rather well. What else do I need to know?"

"Well, you should have left it to me. But this evening has been a very good start. I can't possibly teach you everything. Since the action will take place in a high-class market, I can make a few other suggestions. Don't haggle with the tradesmen; if the price is too high, pretend to lose interest and look at other goods for sale. Also, do not try to reply to tradesmen who speak

Greek—*Koine*; ignore them and move on. Finally, and most importantly, remember that they are there to serve you; not you to serve them. Do you think you can develop the command voice? If not, learn to speak indifferently, as though bored. Never over-pay anyone; it's a sign of desperation."

Jerusha asked, "Why do so many Judeans speak Greek? I've never met or heard of a Greek in my life."

"Do you remember many years ago, when I told you the great Roman general Marcus Antonius established his old ally Antipater and therefore Antipater's son Herod, now known as 'The Great', as King of Judea? It was to help him in his rivalry with Julius Caesar of Rome. They had both been in love with Cleopatra, queen of Egypt, though at different times. Marcus sought two goals, a political advantage over Caesar, and the admiration of Cleopatra."

"What does that have to do with..."

"Don't interrupt. The important fact is that Cleopatra was *not* Egyptian; she was Greek, as had been all the kings and queens of Egypt for hundreds of years. Long before the Roman Empire existed, the Greek Empire ruled the world and the Great Sea, and traded goods with everyone. Fortunately, trade was about all they wanted with us Jews, and we were happy to oblige. The Greek Empire wasn't interested in bothering our religion. Some of the more pleasing details of Judean architecture we happily adopted from the Greeks. So we, and the world, learned Greek to make trade easier. In Judea, all but the lower classes learned the language. Much later the Roman Empire so admired the culture of the Greek nation they had conquered, that now almost all prefer the Greek language and use it except officially and when in Rome. Greek, not Latin, is the universal language. That's why we use *Koine* Greek as a vague class distinction. But if you should ever want to remain a lady, it's not Greek you should learn, as much as history. I've done all I can, there.

"The rest of being a lady you will have to learn for yourself, but never forget your courtesy and bearing."

"And what if I get really angry?"

"Don't. Emotions are for the secrets of home."

"But I have no real home."

"Then have no emotions," he concluded, to Jerusha's dismay.

After a pause, Zachariah voiced what he had obviously been delaying, "You, Jerusha, have one major obstacle to ever becoming a true lady. Your insane obsession with revenge for your children."

Jerusha was on the brink of an explosion when her new found self-control forced her voice down in volume and tone. "Isn't mother love one of the greatest virtues people have?" she asked gently.

"Hard to believe, you actually sounded like a lady at the very moment when I thought today would be proven a total waste. But this calls for a little philosophical thought. Every virtue, when carried to an extreme, becomes a vice, and sometimes a very serious sin. One of the most common, and the easiest example, is love between a man and a woman. One of the first gifts God gave us. The dark shadow which stalks it is lust, which causes fornication, violations of women, adultery, neglected and sometimes murdered children, and any number of perversions. This is not why God gave us romantic love. Another virtue is courage; it defends an innocent person or an entire people from barbarians and tyrants and foreign conquerors. But it can also lead to unrighteous wars and unnecessary violence between people just to test or show bravery. Another is love of humanity, which sometimes leads to neglect of one's own family. Also willingness to work to provide security; its shadow is sometimes greed, even enough avarice to rob, or kill the innocent to hold on to a throne."

Jerusha's attention picked up at this.

Zachariah continued. I can cite countless virtues countered by sins: eating, gluttony...drinking, drunkenness...wise-stewardship, miserliness—excluding only those virtues which concern our duties to God, under His terms.

"But I have come to believe that one of the most dangerous virtues is filial love, what you would call parental or family love. Without it our ancestors would have killed off the entire next generation as noisy and useless infants. Yet Scripture is full of warnings against its excess. Whenever it begins to interfere with other virtues, love for and obedience to God, the proper raising of Godly children or leading a righteous life in any area, it instead becomes a great vice.

"In *your* case mother love is clearly ruining your life. Worse yet, periodically it makes you a head splitting bore around *me*. If I thought it would do any good I would command you never again to mention the murder of your children, or your compulsion for revenge, around me, on pain of death."

Zachariah laughed. "But then I would have to kill my best dagger man. I await, with trepidation, your screeching response."

There was a pause before Jerusha smiled, sweetly. "Why, what on earth have you been prattling on about? I've been working on separating a piece of flesh from this bone without getting a splinter in my finger. I thought the kitchen here was more careful. But please go on." She raised her eyebrows with polite anticipation, while thinking that if Zachariah ever knew what she had done to *his* family, he really would kill her.

They were brought several other courses, few of which Jerusha could recognize, but ate with ladylike gusto until Zachariah told her to slow down, and stop before the end of the meal. Zachariah and Jerusha spoke for a while further, then he paid the bill and they left, with at least three servants bidding them *Shalom*.

As they entered their waiting litter, Jerusha asked ironically, "Did I do all right?"

"Well enough, considering the time we had." He mumbled under his breath but loudly enough for her to hear, "I suppose there are enough eccentric rich ladies that mistakes would be put down as individual quirks." They returned to headquarters without further incident. Jerusha was certain what little instruction she had was enough to piece together the behavior of a lady.

"One more thing," she demanded, "Now that we're alone. *Do* you know any more about the false king and Messiah?" She asked this while he was exiting the litter.

"No! We're wasting time." He wanted to slam the curtains but they just swished.

The next afternoon Jerusha's escort to her new dwelling wasn't the man she had become accustomed to, but a better-dressed one. She was able to distinguish landmarks and count streets, making her glad for the customary silence of her escort, so she could memorize the passage as well as possible. When they entered the major thoroughfares with which Jerusha would be familiar, sometimes from as far back as her time as a beggar, she could stop counting and scrutinizing. Until then, she examined every turn, building, fountain, odd intersection, and paving style. When they did reach familiar territory, she was relatively confident she could find her way back to headquarters despite her weak sense of direction. Continuing to go over her inventory mentally wouldn't hurt. They arrived at twilight.

The destination turned out to be a wide residential street, well-lit with torches, less than four streets from the Temple Mount. Jerusha realized she had often traversed this years before, on the way to her favorite intersection for begging; with its large limestone fountain. She knew, before her escort announced it, that the most expensive market in all Jerusalem was only three streets farther. Other beggars, less successful than she, had set up for business there. All the houses on this street were expensive; only the priestly classes and the richest merchants could afford to own houses here. Although built in the Jewish style, their homes had large portals, often surrounded with stone carvings, or small courtyards protected by high walls inset with elaborate wrought-iron gates. An occasional house had been divided into large, expensive apartments, and one of these was where the messenger handed her a taper which he had lit from the torch beside the entrance. He then took her to a second-storey door and left her, bidding her "*Shalom,*" a common-place farewell which nevertheless struck Jerusha as ironical considering her current mission.

By this time in her life Jerusha was not easily impressed, and the rooms of her new quarters were no novelty to her. She used the taper to light the ceiling and table oil lamps as she went from place to place. The bathroom had a large iron tub. No tile or marble, but hot and cold running water. The bed was raised, but her rooms contained little furniture, though most pieces were of good design, and there was a large wardrobe. The lattice windows had doorways behind them, with balconies overlooking the street below. She sat on the bed, and found it to be as comfortable as her old one at the Zealot headquarters. This time she had no qualms about digging a small hole at the bottom of the mattress with her dagger and discovering what she should have known all along: The "clouds" she had slept on were feathers. Her kitchen was in a nook, but had a large pantry, and the largest, most elaborately designed combination oven-stove she had ever seen, with large stacks of both firewood and coals beside it. The lamps supplied more light than she would ever need. There was no public room to speak of, but she did not intend to entertain. The common privy would likely be downstairs again, behind the door she had passed on the way up. After putting out the lamps, Jerusha undressed quickly, flopped on her bed naked, pulled up the blankets, and fell asleep almost immediately, despite the remaining twilight outside.

She awoke early the next morning to a knock on her door. She threw on the clothes she had, and opened the door finding the same messenger as the night before, now leading a donkey laden with traveling bags containing the clothing needed for her new persona. A sizable sack of coins was also included. Zachariah had thought of all this before she had a chance to. So, after the man left, she might as well bathe, and select appropriate rich matronly clothes, to explore the market.

While bathing and then examining herself in the polished metal mirror, Jerusha discovered that despite her handsome and enhanced appearance under Zachariah's tutelage, she had aged somewhat since she had taken stock of herself early in her stay at headquarters. That had been not long before her sexual exploit with Asa, but had the aging process proceeded further before Khimrik? If so, had his interest been merely charity, or had he been indiscriminate in his lusts? Worse, had her aging been what really caused Simon to refuse her favors? No, his religious scruples were sincere. Now, she thought, her looks would no longer allow her to be discriminating with men. She would have to obey Khimrik's moral maxim of fairness: to offer her favors to any and all who wanted them. If she ever offered them again at all, which she knew she would not. The stoop in her shoulders which she had feigned on missions was not yet permanent. The new, but shallow, wrinkles on her face were plentiful enough she would never have to use soot to accentuate them again. And her breasts—well, despite her usual lack of vanity, she preferred not to dwell on that part of her anatomy now. At least she had not grown fat nor too thin. She had remembered while bathing to clean her fingernails thoroughly and file them with the iron file on a table near the tub. She remembered that Zachariah had especially noticed them. All of this mattered to Jerusha mostly as an aid to selecting her clothing for her work at the market.

Jerusha knew that unlike her, most women, especially wealthy ones, tried to conceal their age, and dressed in such a way as to exaggerate their remaining charms and diminish the rest. She strove instead to look matronly and dignified, without a foolish snatch at a bogus youth. A careful balance, especially in the choice of jewelry, not forgetting the Crown of Jerusalem. Since most women who shopped at this expensive market were wives of Hellenized Jews, they were likely to have large and varied wardrobes, and dressed carefully whatever their age. Unlike the Pharisee women, however rich, who made a virtue of modest, and usually homely, body coverings.

Few Romans or their wives came to this market, for though it sold food imported from all over the Mediterranean World, it followed Jewish dietary laws and therefore deprived foreigners of some of their favorite delicacies, including all shellfish and some fowl and other meats. Jerusha must blend in with the most typical customers—the Hellenized. She could expect to be addressed some times in the Greek language, but would always find something to distract her attention. At the worst, her accent while speaking Aramaic would mark her as coming from Bethlehem or farther south, and it might be expected that a southern provincial who had married into a rich Hellenized family would still have difficulty with Greek, so no vendor would persist in that language.

Once again, though, her years as a seamstress with an eye for fashion would serve her well.

Jerusha had selected, for her first day, a peach-colored Roman stola, with pleats at the top and cinched with a gold rope, and those under-dresses of which large parts would show, in a lighter shade, almost ivory. Her sandals were, of course, gold-stamped. An ivory-colored, silk head covering held up by the Crown of Jerusalem. From a long, narrow box Zachariah had included, Jerusha chose one strand of pearls, and a large ring of sardonyx, for contrast, along with a wedding ring.

The total effect was what she wanted: a rich, Hellenized Jewish wife or grandmother, of advanced middle years. Just before descending the stairs, Jerusha remembered that she had forgotten her dagger, and regretted that stolas were virtually sleeveless in spring, at least in Jerusalem. She would buy a shopping bag, and keep her dagger and case in it, as well as her purchases, hoping that at the moment of attack she would not pull out a fruit. Until she could get the bag, her case and knife would have to be hidden under the lower folds of her dress.

Jerusha originally planned to have breakfast at a pastry shop on her way to her destination, just as she had on the first day of her mission against Isaiah, but these memories brought back to her how different this setting would be from the streets and plazas of her earlier job. The crowds would be large, and the majority of women in them would look and act like her. The market had always been a peaceful place. The only person who could guess her intent would be her victim, and that only a second or so before he was dead. Spending all day at the market and returning every evening would not be suspicious. It was all there was for wealthy women to do during the long hours before large dinners, parties or receptions. Most importantly, there were a number of small but expensive food shops, with outdoor tables and chairs, where she could eat in a leisurely manner, and from which she could examine the market and the people in it. When she tired of eating she could always move to a wine shop with the same outdoor accommodations and continue her observation while sipping slowly at a glass of mixed water and wine. Her previous victims had relatively set times when they might be expected; Habakkuk ben Abishai might decide to go shopping at any time and on any day that the fancy struck him. Fortunately, her costumes and the crowds would permit Jerusha to while away the hours for a number of days without drawing attention to herself.

CHAPTER 11

Habakkuk

After descending to the street and walking several blocks to the market, Jerusha chose a small shop, situated at the long side of the market near its center, and seated herself at one of its five tables, facing the morning crowds. She ordered fruit and a lamb pastry, keeping in mind that she should eat sparingly if she were to spread out her time as a diner as long as possible. Jerusha was gratified to notice the shopkeeper served her with the same mixture of deference and feigned boredom which he could be expected to feel toward all wealthy women. The high prices disappointed Jerusha, but she was ready for that. Zachariah's money-bag contained an abundance of coins from the lowest to the highest denominations. She placed more than sufficient money on her table and noticed that none was taken by the shopkeeper. Apparently the habit when dealing with customers of her new class was to collect only after all dining and drinking was finished. She would have to remember that. She sat back and began her vigil.

A preliminary survey of the market from end to end revealed that among the patrons were rich, Hellenized women, a light scattering of ostentatiously pious Pharisees, and a few private household cooks, distinguishable by their clothing. As yet, only a few men. After a long while she spotted a vendor with a cart of dry goods. She motioned him to her table, and bought a sturdy shopping bag with two sets of well-sewn handles, for hand or shoulder. She transferred her pouch, with its dagger, to the shopping bag. Her motions could not have been observed. She even continued eating with one hand during the operation. She placed the bag on her table, insuring that it was folded and closed to all eyes.

It was time to consider what might turn out to be the most difficult part of her task. Zachariah had carefully explained that Habakkuk could be easily recognized because he would be dressed in the Roman style. He would wear a toga, presumably. Indeed Zachariah had implied so, mentioning that Habakkuk held it up with a large brooch. But it would not be a Roman toga. Would he be distinguishable by a shorter cut to the garment? Hanging from the wrong shoulder? Different material? More simply or voluminously cut? A certain hem, unremarkable to her but a clear signal to every Roman that something was wrong? The possibilities seemed endless. Would the excess material hang over the wrong forearm? Too many pleats, too few, none at all, sewn into the wrong places? Would the difference be in the tunic beneath? Sleeves too long or too short? The entire tunic cut differently? The brooch with an idol would be of little help; most Romans wore such, though they would be unlikely to be in this market. Jerusha's years of observing togas with the eye of a seamstress might similarly be useless. Her only hope was that she would get an opportunity to identify the brooch, to see if it was made of emeralds worked with gold. Of course, the only way to study it would be to stand directly in front of Habakkuk for many seconds, before her attack, without causing him to be suspicious. He would have to be a moron for her to accomplish that.

She would think about it later.

While surveying the sea of faces and costumes in the marketplace, Jerusha also studied wares in the stalls, push-carts, and loose baskets, visible from her seat. Jerusha had always known she had a discriminating eye, but she was unprepared to discover that the foodstuffs here were not much better than those she had selected in Bethlehem's markets in the past. There *was* far more variety here. The three most obvious items of produce were plums, chickpeas, and cucumbers, often stacked in different partitions on the same plank tables. Could they all have come from the same farmers? No, surely there must be distributors; then why were they so fresh?

Not far from her table a cheese maker displayed his fine-smelling goods. Jerusha considered. She must have been here well over an hour. It had been quite a while since she ate her meat pastry and the clay bowls had been cleared away. She slowly sipped the water she had ordered. Surely she was now free to order cheese without violating the Jewish prohibition against combining animal flesh with its own mother's milk, or a derivation thereof, like cheese? Of all the practices of Judaism, especially its dietary laws, the only one Jerusha sincerely admired was this one about the proximity of meat and milk. If anything was sacred, in its spiritual sense, to her, it was the concept of mother and offspring. Of any species. She could butcher a mother ewe or nanny goat, but she found it cruel in the extreme to use the milk of the dam to cook or garnish the dam's own offspring, however mature. It was repugnant and against the law of the God she had worshiped as a child. But more important, Jerusha had also been a nursing mother once.

Jerusha thought it prudent to practice and test her new role as shopper. Now, before the appearance of her victim, was the best time. There was only one other diner at her shop, a younger woman dressed as expensively as she was. The lady was at a table close enough to hers to overhear. A good test. She summoned the cheese maker over, first checking for a sufficient interval between his customers.

He walked quickly to her table. "Would my lady be interested in my cheeses?"

"I was wondering if you made any of them, and are the others local or imported?"

The cheese maker was well into a long reply in what Jerusha assumed was *Koine* Greek, when she interrupted him:

"There is another cheese vendor on the other side of the market..." She looked uncertain as to whom she should patronize.

The man learned his lesson quickly. "What I meant to say, my lady," he spoke in Aramaic this time, "And please forgive my pretentiousness, was that the rounds and wedges on the left are my own, from my goats. The large tray in the center has cheeses from other parts of Judea and Samaria, mostly from milch cows. The cheese in the tray on the right is imported from all over the Mediterranean, but the most prized are at the front of the tray, the finest Greek and Anatolian feta cheeses, goat, of course, and some combined with the best herbs. See the green and blue specks? In the back I have a tray of very soft cheeses from the north of the Empire, but they must remain fully covered to prevent any melting. May I bring over a tray?"

"I would like to see your own cheeses, if I may." Jerusha made no effort to rise.

The cheese maker quickly moved to fetch the tray, the weight of it slowing his return trip almost to a stagger.

The young lady at the other table, clearly hearing the exchange, gave no sign of having observed anything she had not heard and seen numerous times before.

Jerusha saw that the cheese tray contained large rounds, smaller ones, half-rounds of each size, wedges, and tiny taster slices. After a taste she chose a wedge of the same cheese to eat here, and one of the smaller half-rounds. It would keep all day in her shopping bag and she would have some for supper.

The cheese maker, after being paid, said, "Thank you, my lady. *Shalom*. Have a pleasant day," and scuttled back to his table under the weight of his tray to where another customer stood waiting.

As she savored her wedge of cheese, Jerusha observed that the only other vendor in her field of view had a large metal barrel of fish, alive and swimming as much as they could in a closed space. She like fresh fish, but knowing when she would return to her apartment she would not risk spoilage.

As soon as Jerusha finished her water, the shopkeeper collected her mug and his money, leaving the change; more of the tables were occupied. She examined the milling crowd once more, then took part of the money off the table, and resumed her walk down the cobblestone sidewalk length of the oblong market.

She paused to buy three excellent looking figs from a basket and two rare oranges at a built-in stall facing the market. At the far end she found what she had hoped for: an open-air wine shop. Wonder of wonders, the chairs were hollowed out at the seat for comfort, which her aging shanks appreciated. Here she could sit and survey the area for hours, if there weren't too many customers.

Off to her left, Jerusha saw a family of beggars squatting on the ground at the end of the market. The wine shop and other vendors would shoo them away, but they would always return. *Fools*, Jerusha thought, *even amateur that I was I knew that market patrons were either preoccupied by their own acquisitiveness, or, on leaving, mindful only about how much they had overspent and how they would never waste money again!*

The needs of beggars were antithetical to those thoughts. Nevertheless, Jerusha walked over and dropped a few coins in their bowl, suspecting she earned the same contempt from them as she had so freely felt for her patrons many years before. Afterwards, when she returned to the wine shop Jerusha sat front and center and ordered a glazed, earthenware urn of expensive imported wine—the local product was always cloyingly sweet—a similar pitcher of water, and a mug; the last item came with a stem, again the first glass of that sort Jerusha had ever seen. She mixed her wine and water in equal proportions, and was overwhelmed by the delicacy of the taste.

But it did not distract her enough to lessen the shock she felt when her target suddenly emerged from a near side street and entered the marketplace.

She knew immediately that he was Habakkuk ben Abishai. His toga was identical to those of any of the multitude of Romans' she had seen, except for one blatant detail: It was blue-gray in color. *That* must be the sign; all Roman citizens would be required to wear *white* togas ; they were all she had ever seen Romans wear.

That's odd, Jerusha thought, *with his wealth he should have been able to finagle for himself Roman citizenship like many of our rich countrymen. Perhaps he did identify with the Jews, after all.* Habakkuk's toga was an impressive shade, the color of a storm cloud receding at the approach of the sun. That image was reinforced by the garment's hem which had a large, perfectly embroidered gold Greek key design. The parts of his tunic which showed were pale blue, with a narrower hem, also gold embroidered. Entirely gilt sandals. With all the gold, the sun appeared to be pushing away not only clouds but evil itself with them. Even Jerusha's spirits were lifted, enough to put her mission out of her mind for a short time. The Romans could keep their tiresome white togas.

Although Zachariah had given her only a sketchy description of the man himself, she confirmed her recognition of Habakkuk immediately. He was older than she, clean-shaven and his smooth waves of hair, carefully coiffed, were silvery white. Many Hellenized Jews straightened their hair if they had inherited a not-uncommon tendency to excessive curliness, but most who did so went to insufficiently skilled dressers who failed to reinstate *any* waves. Habakkuk clearly found the best. His waves looked casual, but were designed to enhance the shape of his attractive face. Ironically, the Romans prized tightly curled hair however artificially created. As Habakkuk stood on the walkway looking the length of the market, Jerusha saw his large brooch of emeralds and wrought gold. She could not discover what, if anything, the brooch depicted, but she had no remaining doubt this was her man. Moreover, Jerusha tried, but could not shake, her conviction that she had seen this man before, when she was younger. Strange that men changed with age more slowly than women. His face was darkened by the sun, probably by sports, his body still muscular. The lines on his face only enhanced his appearance.

Jerusha watched him walk among the tables, booths, indoor shops and those under awnings without having to leave her chair. He was methodical, and examined every item which caught his attention, carefully, with impeccable courtesy to the vendor when he turned the latter down, either for quality or price, usually finding something among his goods to flatter. Jerusha could overhear most of his conversations, and noticed that when he was addressed in Greek, or even in what sounded like Latin, he would reply in the same language for a few words then change to Aramaic. Was this national sentiment, despite his Hellenization? Habakkuk selected a few items, whether produce or more substantial goods, slowly, with effusive thanks, putting them in the bag he carried almost hidden in the folds of his toga. He was, in short, the first true gentleman she had ever seen. Jerusha still remembered the loud haggling and screeched insults among the stalls of Bethlehem.

She had decided she would not kill Habakkuk today, however propitious the crowds. Tomorrow would be Sabbath-Eve. If he still practiced Judaism he would shop tomorrow for his ritualistic meal with enough leftovers for Sabbath Day; if not, he would entertain Roman friends that evening and need even more provisions and delicacies. Plenty of time and opportunity, and she could choose the size of crowd she wanted, depending on how near sundown she chose to strike. Jerusha vaguely wondered whether, if the stabbing occurred at sundown, would anyone break Jewish Law to doctor her victim?

There was no rush. She watched Habakkuk cover the market with a practiced eye.

After a few more selections, probably for a solitary dinner to be followed by a larger one tomorrow evening, Habakkuk left, having spent something more than an hour. Jerusha remained to enjoy her wine.

But when and where had she seen him before?

The next day Jerusha wore a light-blue stola, with the same minimal jewelry, so as to display some variety and still be recognized by the owner or employees at the wine shop, should she need an alibi. She might have to spend the entire day there, and she had been generous the day before. Simultaneously, Jerusha would appear to have a large, expensive wardrobe, as any lady in her assumed position would have. She also chose a less transparent scarf, so that while actually committing the crime, she could pull the veil forward and disguise her face for the time it would take to act and escape. She would do this as far down the market, and away from the wine shop, as Habakkuk's buying habits would permit.

Jerusha stopped by the short counter of the shop where she had eaten the day before, and purchased one meat and one sweet pastry and a small bowl of wine. The sweet would serve as breakfast and the meat as lunch, supplemented by anything she liked from nearby carts, stalls, or tables. She had never had wine with breakfast before, but she knew many did...and beer, which she hated, was commonly the first meal of the day in places other than Bethlehem. Regardless, she needed an excuse to sit at the wine shop from early morning until as late as necessary.

It seemed it would not be very late. Jerusha mixed her wine and water to taste, drank some of it, and swallowed the last of her honeyed pastry, when her quarry appeared at the same intersection as before, and as suddenly. But what irony! Yesterday Jerusha had worn peach with ivory, while he had worn shades of blue. Today she was wearing light-blue and *his* toga was of peach, tunic of ivory, both with heavy gold-embroidered hems, though the embroidery was of leaves and grapes, not his previous Greek key design. The other points of his appearance were identical. Jerusha checked her shopping-bag to insure the watertight knife-pouch was open and the dagger in easy reach. She hung the bag from her shoulder, and paid her bill, so she could leave the moment she chose.

The market's customers were increasing, almost to a crowd. It seemed everyone knew that not only the freshest, but the finest, goods were sold early. Jerusha watched her quarry choose some hard-skinned fruit at a vendor across the narrow end of the market from her. While pausing, he did not forget coins for the beggar family. He then chose some cheeses at a nearby stall. His shopping-bag was considerably larger than yesterday's. Soon, he moved diagonally to a vending table and bought several different selections of bread. She discerned his method to be one she had employed when she was a gourmet cook in Bethlehem. Start at one side of the market with the less perishable foods, then methodically work one's way down that side and up the far one, taking occasional cross trips to the center aisles only when especially attracted, since the center was reserved for late-coming vendors, often with inferior goods. In this way, by the time one came to the highly-perishable, true delicacies one was near the end of the expedition, and ready for rest or refreshment, or to go home. Jerusha now left her table, abandoning her remaining pastry, and any extra money the waiter would accept as change, and retraced her steps to the other end of the market where the eggs and squawking chickens, and those no longer squawking, were displayed. She crossed the path and plotted a slow course back to intersect the direction of her quarry. Whose passage, considering his elaborate courtesy and pleasantries, would be slow indeed. More to her interest, it might impede the crowd's flow of traffic.

How much easier it was to murder children in Bethlehem than adults in Jerusalem.

By this time Habakkuk was at the green grocers' tables, selecting cucumbers and a leafy vegetable Jerusha did not recognize. He happened to be followed by two groups of women, four in each group, chatting with one another and pointing out and commenting on wares. Why was it that groups of women shopping chatted continually and loudly, never listening to each other? In front of Habakkuk were two more groups of women, of three each, with the same habits. All these women might keep pace with her target, or push ahead. Jerusha would have to be prepared for either. Meanwhile, she blended in with the many unattached female shoppers going in her direction, taking care to appear to be accompanying different ones, in turn but not enough to arouse their curiosity or suspicion.

As Jerusha approached Habakkuk he was walking straight ahead, not looking at the wares on either side. The women, behind and in front of him, were, on the contrary, preoccupied on both sides of the cobbled walkway, as were the women on either side of Jerusha. There could be no better moment. When she was directly in front of him, Jerusha pulled her scarf forward, seized her dagger from its bag, and thrust underhand, somewhat upwards, just under where his breastbone should be, toward his heart. The edge was sideways to allow for the possibility of passing between ribs. Although Jerusha put her entire bodyweight into the stab, her extended right arm and upward angle would have made her move appear almost graceful and natural to anyone not carefully examining the scene. Jerusha saw Habbakkuk's eyes as her knife entered its full measure. He made no sound, at least none that could be heard above the usual market babble.

The instant Habakkuk began to fall, Jerusha snatched his brooch, ripping it from his toga with her left hand, while quietly removing the knife with her right.

Habbakkuk fell toward one group of the women behind him, and they pushed back without looking, seemingly to avoid any rude interruption of their search for the perfect squash.

Jerusha immediately resumed her walk forward, concealing the dagger simultaneously, only slowly increasing her pace. The small crowd of women beside and behind her never stopped exclaiming over or decrying the wares on each side of them until Jerusha was well out of the tableau. She was at the other end of the market before she looked back. Utter chaos...but no one who seemed to have any idea what to do.

Jerusha was tempted to return to the wine shop she was now near again; the dagger was back in its pouch, which was closed and next to the brooch in her shopping-bag, and there was no blood on her hand or arm, or her garments. But luck could only last so long; she must leave. She did not want to sit and think... definitely not to think. In the past, Jerusha had returned to her rooms, but her new quarters were in an expensive part of town, where neighbors either knew each other or carefully observed strangers. Also, such an escape would require her to reverse direction and pass within a street or two of her crime, and it was too early for this. Fortunately, continuing straight in her present direction would bring her to the Great Temple, and at noon on Sabbath-Eve the crowds there would begin to grow. Near sundown the throng could be followed in all directions for a mile or more without suspicion. Remembering Zachariah's words, she removed all jewelry, especially the Crown of Jerusalem, and hid the latter alongside Habbakkuk's brooch.

Several hours of feigned piety on Temple Hill and in the Women's Court would help to settle Jerusha's whirling mind. She walked the incline toward the Temple, barely noticing that the cobblestones gradually grew from the size of melons, common through-out Jerusalem, to a cubit-square, hand smoothed, presumably to show the increased grandeur as one approached the Temple. By the time sundown approached she knew what she had to do. She had brought the money Zachariah had given her. She need only return to the market to get her bearings and find her way to the Zealot headquarters.

Jerusha had no difficulty following the thoroughfares back to the general area she sought. Remembering and finding the landmarks she had memorized on her way from headquarters— troughs, fountains, architectural designs on corner houses, intersections, number of streets before a turn—were more difficult, but not impossible. It seemed one with an excellent memory did not need a good sense of direction.

When Jerusha entered the courtyard of the headquarters it was fully dark. She headed straight for Zachariah's quarters; good Pharisee that he was he would be at home to celebrate the Sabbath supper. Without considering whether he might have guests, Jerusha thrust his door open so hard that if it had been bolted she could have seriously injured her wrist.

Zachariah pulled a long dagger from somewhere near him. "What's the meaning of this?" he shouted forcefully, if not very originally. "And who or what are you?" In keeping with tradition, he had only his candles lit, but Jerusha could see he had no guests.

"How much did you know about Habakkuk ben Abishai?" Jerusha demanded.

"Oh, it's you, Jerusha." Zachariah put back the dagger. "What are you doing back here? Have you done your job? I suppose so or you wouldn't have used the past tense. I would have sent a messenger in a few days, if you had waited."

"I asked you a question," she said coldly, closing and bolting the door behind her.

"Nothing except what I told you before. Other than that, only what Joel said. Yes, I know, he had his own motives."

"And he's a liar."

"At times," Zachariah admitted. "But that isn't important. We're setting an example for collaborators."

Jerusha's voice became softer. "My memory of Habakkuk came back while I was at the Temple. I had watched and listened to Habakkuk when I was a young beggar in Jerusalem, before the Night of Horror. While he was sitting and chatting with a friend at a fountain nearby. He struck me only as a rich young lounger. I resented him, because he had the leisure to discuss politics; because he put a coin in my bowl, which I considered patronizing at the time. Now I am rich, maybe more so than he was, and I've learned from Joel how envy can rot a man's soul. It's probably what motivated that evil family in Bethlehem. I now know Habakkuk identified fully with us Jews in his heart, whatever his idle interjections to his companion. He was very young then and perhaps a bit callow. Maybe I also resented his beauty. He has grown old gracefully and after two days of watching him I have observed nothing but kindness."

Zachariah broke into her reveries. "Do I detect a note of love?"

"I am not in the habit of killing my lovers."

"You forgot one detail: the brooch honoring a Pagan idol which Habakkuk wore daily. Since I know you are not a thief, I know you didn't steal it. What, exactly, was it?"

Jerusha looked at Zachariah with contempt, and reached into her bag. She dropped the emerald-studded brooch in his earthenware plate. "You mean this? I had a chance to study it at Temple afterwards. The stones form intertwined circles, no idol, probably given to him by a lover or wife. And you might as well have the Crown of Jerusalem back." It bounced off his wine goblet.

Zachariah initially looked surprised, which was the first time Jerusha had seen him so. Then his face turned red, even in the candlelight. "You idiot! Do you know what you've done by taking this brooch? Whatever Joel's prejudices, *our* only motive was to perform a clearly political slaying, something to frighten the uncommitted. Now you've made it look like a random, common robbery! The killing is totally useless to us!" Zachariah was now standing.

"I'm beginning to think all your killings have been. Regardless, tell Joel I will no longer be his slave to do what he doesn't have the manhood to do himself. Nor will I be yours." Jerusha pulled out a chair and sat stiffly in it.

Zachariah calmed a bit and sat down. "Let's not be hasty. We lost Khimrik. We lost Simon ben Joseph to marry his betrothed. And *I* made it possible for you to improve your language and habits from those of a peasant to those of at least a provincial lady. Your work has been inestimably helpful for our cause in the past, and I have always shown my gratitude."

"And just what help have you been to *my* cause? I thank you for Isaiah, but that killing served your personal revenge as well. You are merely stalling my demands regarding the false king. Remember, you helped make me a skilled dagger man. There's a certain challenge to it. I might just come up, when bored in Bethlehem, and kill Joel. After that, who knows who might become my mark? Especially if anyone tries to force me back into your enterprise..."

"Your private mission is too important to you to waste such time in pointless violence."

"You took time from *your* cause to order the death of an innocent Jew, to no advantage, just because he was a Jew who wasn't a Zealot. For that matter, because he wasn't even a Pharisee. Well, most Jews aren't. You have a lot of work to do. But first, I want you to sit still and listen to my demands."

"I'll certainly consider them," he said, lounging back in his chair. "At least, after the Sabbath, which you have desecrated enough already."

"You'll do them now, and without this Sabbath nonsense. If necessary hire Gentiles or Arabs."

Zachariah declared, somewhat stiffly, "The Lord commanded that the Sabbath be kept holy not only by us but 'by the stranger in your gates.'"

"You didn't work very hard to make me keep it while I was a guest here. Nonetheless, you'll do as I say or you'll get some nasty surprises. Can you kill a sister-by-marriage on the Sabbath, with your dagger there? Well, I can kill a brother-by-marriage, with mine.

"Now, first, I demand that you collect up all my money. What I came with when I first arrived, what my factors sent me on three occasions, that which I hid and revealed to you, that which you took from me to protect, and so on. You can throw in a few denarii for my expenses. I know the few coins you gave me for that purpose came from my own hoard. Don't try to cheat me. I spent many hours with nothing to do but count my money, and I have an excellent memory."

"What about *my* expenses, least of all was a new oilcloth for my messenger?" he asked.

"That was for *your* missions. Next, I require a small room here for the night, not in the main house, as far from it as possible in this compound. And anyone who tries to visit me later during the night will die. Are you writing all this down? Get some papyrus and ink or a clay tablet." To her amazement, he did...unpredictable as always.

"Next, a donkey loaded with a few provisions, only enough to get me to Bethlehem and a few days more, and a few non-perishables. Also, neatly packaged on the donkey will be good clothing, top to bottom. Not as fine as some I wore here or on my last mission for you; just enough to make me look decently successful or well-married in a small town. No jewelry; I'll leave you what I have on here. No, or very little, silk. You must have what I need here somewhere, or you could not have provided whatever was needed, whenever it was needed.

"That's it. I will leave at sunup. The Romans keep the city gates open despite your Sabbath. Oh, and one more thing, one set of proper clothing for a Roman serving-woman, so I won't draw too much attention from you fanatics when I travel tomorrow on the Sabbath. Send it all with a servant, to my room, which you'll show me when we leave here. I'll say goodbye now."

"What do you expect me to do with this brooch?" he asked docilely.

"Hide it for a long time, then sell it to feed yourself when you're starving again, as you will be someday, after you've given up your ridiculous cause."

"And when you've given up yours?"

"When I have quit trying to avenge *your* children as well as my own, and lost interest in the false king, then you'll know I'm dead. But I know he's not in Jerusalem. At least not now."

Jerusha suddenly remembered she was very hungry, so she snatched as much of Zachariah's Sabbath meal as she could stuff in her sleeves and the folds of her gown, regardless of grease-stains, and left the room without another word, but held the door open for him to follow and then direct her to the new room for her last night living and killing in Jerusalem.

❖

On the road to Bethlehem, her thoughts were repetitious: *Fool! Idiot! Donkey! Stone-head! Moron! Sounding gourd! Mush for brains!* Jerusha continued abasing herself: *Nightsoil fills your skull! Dolt!* What had happened to her brain since she had left Bethlehem? Had she ever had a brain? All that time spent in Judea and without seeing what even Zachariah, with his blinders for everything that did not serve his cause, must have known all along. She almost felt as though she had caused the death of her boys and Leah's all over again, through lack of concentration.

Obviously, to anyone but a fool, it would be clear the would-be king would not have been allowed to grow up in Bethlehem, where he would be the only male of his age, or one of very few, nor would he be in Jerusalem where his new enemies would be seeking him.

These unusual musings prevented her, during her seemingly endless retreat to Bethlehem, from taking notice of the stones over which she stumbled and bruised her feet continually, or the thorns through which she had to force herself and her donkey. The toughness Jerusha had built up over many years had been pampered by the smoothly paved streets and wooden and tile floors of Jerusalem, and the feel of soft cloth and polished and upholstered furniture. Her mind was occupied only with regret over the time she had wasted looking for the false king.

Jerusha had thought that in the great capital city of Jerusalem, center of her universe, she would certainly meet or hear word of the false king. Everyone went to Jerusalem sooner or later, and who more than a man who thought himself the rightful owner of the city? But in all that time neither she, nor Zachariah, nor emanations of gossip, had given her any knowledge of the evil boy. She had thought it out at the Temple for a long time and had reached only one logical conclusion, other, of course, than the death of the ambitious family or their child, which she would never accept as true.

Clearly, Jerusha had exaggerated the significance of the massacre of the children of Bethlehem and its importance to

Judea as a whole. By the time she had arrived within the most distant sight of the hovels of Bethlehem, glistening or sweating in the sun, she finally absorbed that when seen from anywhere else, her hometown was a small and insignificant village. All news of interest radiated from Jerusalem, where Herod "the Great" had murdered most of his own family and was surrounded by insurrections, intrigues, mass executions, and burnings alive; and his sons provided for more excitement and gossip. These would have been of immensely greater importance to that huge city of gossip-mongers than the killing of a comparatively few backward children in a backward town. These excitements would have erased everything else, even an ineffectual Zealot uprising, as they seem to have erased Zachariah's memory of his family, and Jerusha's witness to the loss of his children.

The world had shrugged aside all memory of the slaughter at Bethlehem. Maybe it was knowledge of this mass amnesia which was driving her mad. Jerusha was all that was left of her family which mattered, and of the horror that befell it. Not a rock, nor a weed, nor a goat, nor a child, nor a human being, remembered or cared. It existed only between her ears, and when she died, it would never have happened.

Upon returning to Bethlehem, she found it had not changed. Her adventures had led her to expect *something*, but it wasn't there. She returned long before sunset and stayed in her house for several days, which she discovered to be in good condition, except for dusting. Any attempt to restore her garden would be hopeless.

Jerusha contacted her factors over several weeks so none would have any idea with whom she would be visiting next. All of her factors, indeed, all business people with whom she had had any dealings in the past, had assumed that during her time away from Bethlehem Jerusha had been engaging in highly profitable ventures. The gossip in that small town had amplified such speculations beyond any reasonable likelihood. Money was worth gossip but dead children were not. As the tradesmen's respect for Jerusha had grown, so had their fear of her, until she found that even the least honest among them seemed willing to absorb a loss rather than cross her. She dismissed two of them anyway, based on discrepancies she had noted in their previous communications. At least she thought this was the reason; it might have been that she was merely feeling out-of-sorts due to her disappointment over the failure of her mission. She wasted no time pondering her motives, for they would make no difference in the long-run. Jerusha hired an eager young broker just getting started in Bethlehem to replace the two she had fired, being careful to pass the word to others that he was under *her* protection while omitting any mention of what he did for her.

She knew such a state of affairs could not continue long, but was willing to take advantage of it while it lasted. If necessary, Jerusha could reinforce fear by other means.

It was almost comical to her to discover how easily she could accomplish all this. She made a show of checking over the books and scrolls; the factors had either forgotten Jerusha could not read, or assumed she had learned to do so during her long absence. Fortunately for her, Hebraic letters, and therefore Aramaic ones, were of a design that was excessively bottom-heavy, as she had noticed on signs and other casual lettering. Jerusha would thus not be found out by holding a sheet of papyrus, a scroll, or a book upside down. She had always known reading was done from right to left.

After what Jerusha considered a decent interval—enough time for her enhanced reputation to make the rounds—she examined all of her bank accounts, open and hidden, and with but one day's advance notice. She had shrewdly deduced this would cause her dishonest bankers to panic and supplement any shortfalls with their own money, at which time Jerusha would withdraw all of her money, only to invest it elsewhere, leaving the culprits destitute and keeping firm control over what was hers. Of course, Jerusha did not know for sure whether any of the factors or tradesmen were actually dishonest or had in any way mistreated her, but her policies still seemed prudent to her.

She confirmed that she was by now heavily invested in long-distance merchant caravans, as well as in the Nubian slave trade. This did not dismay her, as she had never forbidden such investments, though the latter enterprise now struck her as ironic, considering her long-ago argument with Khimrik in Jerusalem.

Only after seeing to her most serious business interests did Jerusha begin to relax at her home as much as possible, despite its occasional ghosts.

A routine of designing two or three gowns per month for rich clients, and maintaining her house, and trips to the market stalls, especially since she now owned most of them in Bethlehem, with neither the surprise of new produce or merchandise, nor the secretly thrilling irritation of haggling, still left long stretches of boredom. She began, and soon became a master at, designing fine jewelry. Was this new occupation somehow connected to Habakkuk's brooch? She didn't know or want to think about it. Jerusha took to long walks around the entire town, and skirting the edges of the countryside. Jerusha did not know whether these walks were for her health, or to escape the smells of the village, or on the miraculous chance she might still catch sight or hear of her ultimate quarry. However, these walks also forced her to notice for the first time that her joints were getting old, at times, and her bones were getting weaker. She had always kept her muscles in a condition good enough to disguise these other advancing signs of old age even from herself.

At least she had no more males to bother her. She was still slender, but her figure had become shapeless; her hair was now totally white, stringy and thinning; her face was wrinkling, and she had developed a genuine, though slight, stoop. Although in her mid-fifties, she looked older. Not frail, though only an opponent with the nerve to test her muscles would have known it. Whom her appearance did not discourage, her outbursts of bitterness did.

During the nights, her evil dreams came at more frequent intervals. Although she had no faith in the interpretation of any kind of omens or dreams, Jerusha began to suspect that Zachariah would come back, however rude she had been to him in the past. He always had. And he was almost all there was to her life, for whatever reason, and for what little it was worth.

CHAPTER 12

First Sight

When Zachariah finally did return, he found Jerusha scrubbing her tabletop. This time, her brother-by-marriage did not even bother to knock, but entered and sat at his old chair. Jerusha was slightly surprised at his presumption, but somewhat more at his appearance. Zachariah looked the bandit once again, or rather a caricature of one—but immensely, unbelievably, older. For a moment Zachariah struck her as a cadaver, a ghost, or some other dead, but still walking, thing.

So I was right, Jerusha thought, *you did end up a pauper—or costumed better than I thought.*

Jerusha barely looked up but said, tiredly, "So, Zachariah, you return for your periodic visit. I have nothing to offer you or your men—or that I *will* offer."

"This is not what I visit for, nor has it been for many years. 'My men,' you call them. My men are almost all dead. Killed in forgotten skirmishes. Starved or frozen in the mountains. Crucified along the highways in neat rows. The Zealots as a movement are stronger than ever, and I expect to hear much from them in the future, if I live that long. But I don't know these young men. I can just barely remember thinking like them. I still do them small favors at times. Deliver a message, pass gossip on to them. Gossip. That's what I'm reduced to." A speech of this length seemed to exhaust his lungs.

"Here, have some bread, and oil to dip it in." Jerusha served it with a goblet of wine. "So, do you have any gossip for *me?*"

"I could talk for hours, if I had the strength, but you wouldn't listen, and I'd probably get mixed up."

"No, I wouldn't listen," she lied. "And why should I? Who helped my family when we so needed it?"

"Are you still on that? I tried, but I came too late..."

She relented. "I'm not angry at you any more, my brother. There are other causes, my fault, that have estranged us. So, if you would gossip for Zealots, why not for me? What goes on in the world?"

Zachariah attempted to speak off-handedly, but failed. It became clear to Jerusha what he had to say now was important, and it was the reason he had come.

"Nothing much new," he hedged. "That make-believe king of the Jews who caused the Night of Horror," Jerusha dropped her rag and came to his chair to catch every word, "well, he was born about the time of the census, and he was spirited out of Bethlehem shortly after his presentation at the Temple."

"How would you know all this?" asked Jerusha incredulously.

"All I've had to do since I ended my active service was to talk and listen. With all kinds of people. You might have noticed when you were in Jerusalem that I could mingle with all classes, knew their clothing and customs, and even the idioms of their speech. And I have been looking for that family as long as you have, Jerusha, though I would never have told you. It would have distracted from, and perhaps even destroyed, your concentration on your more important missions." Zachariah ignored Jerusha's angry glance, and continued his narrative; he now had her rapt attention. "I never learned his or his family's name. Their vanity was apparently not as strong as their sense of self-preservation. The killing being over and King Herod dead, the family eventually returned to their home in the north. Nazareth, I understand."

Jerusha could barely restrain her anger, which Zachariah ignored. *So, I don't even have the satisfaction of imagining the family skulking around town all those years; they probably never gave Bethlehem another thought! Or worse, they gloried in their escape.* When Jerusha felt the tension too great, she burst out with, "How could a family, especially an ambitious one, reestablish itself so far away in less than a generation and not have had to become beggars or some such?"

"I told you the boy was probably born at the time of the census. It was the only census Rome ever required of us. But every family had to return to the home of its ancestors. My family has always lived in Bethlehem as long as anyone knows, so we wouldn't have had anywhere to go, and such things as the census wouldn't have bothered us. But the boy's family residence for several, maybe many, generations was a town far away. Like Nazareth.

"You probably didn't even notice the crowds who came for the census. Most of the outsiders would have stayed with friends or relatives, even if they had to cover the floor with new pallets. A few would have stayed at the small inn. Many might have slept in the barns, liveries, or in whatever out-buildings were about, or even in the streets. But none would have come this far up into the slums just to sleep in the gutters."

Zachariah paused to soak a piece of bread in oil, and chewed it with his remaining teeth. "My own recent search quit when I found even the inn no longer had any idea who had stayed there. With such crowds, at that time, no local people would have kept track. A few now mutter his birth here fulfills one or another of the prophecies." He took a sip of wine. Perhaps it helped his throat, for Zachariah's voice was growing stronger.

Jerusha cursed herself again for the youth she had destroyed trying to find signs of this flit-around family in one region.

Despite the many years, she could remember as if it were yesterday, moments of that night, testing her walls for hiding holes...climbing the stairs with each bewildered child...stuffing them under the rafters...seeing the red men going up to the loft...shadows of her children's limbs...carrying David's head downstairs...and, yes, betraying Leah and her boys. While "God" looked on, untouched.

Zachariah hazarded to resume his monologue. "Now the man's in this area again, while preaching all over the country. Calls himself a rabbi, and more, I hear."

Jerusha almost shouted, "Is he near Jerusalem?"

"How should I know? He was headed south, last I heard. He and the simpletons who follow him. The man travels around Judea performing tricks. He is a carpenter's son and trained as such. He owned his own shop in Nazareth, and was foolhardy enough to give it up."

Several of these comments rang a bell in Jerusha's mind, but she had no time to think. She stamped her foot. "A carpenter? A skilled craftsman? I should have known! The richest class but for some merchants and the priests! None of humble birth could have caused such suffering as he and his family did. And why hate a real king? It is the middle and rich, the ambitious, the glory-seekers, the would-be tyrants who have created the Herods, the Romans, the intrigues and insurrections and all those who rule, or would rule, in order to kill us and favor their friends."

Zachariah interjected, "Aren't *you* rich, also, Jerusha?" with a parchment smile.

She paused for a moment. "So skilled craftsman wasn't enough for this boy's family—food, comfort, his own workshop, being addressed with an honorific, status, a front row seat at all processions, without even the obligation to stand as the highest and mightiest passed—these still weren't enough? They had to make him king?"

Zachariah interrupted sardonically, "The boy couldn't very well aim for the priesthood, since that position is inherited, as are most at the Temple itself. Where else could their ambition lead?"

The return of Jerusha's anger, intensified, forced Zachariah to try reason, "When this man was a baby, was it his fault his parents were ambitious?"

"Was it our fault that our children were murdered because of his family?" she snapped. "He has had over thirty years, half of them as an adult, to change or modify his plans, whatever his parents would have liked. Yet now you tell me he is traveling over all of Judea, collecting followers. I wasted my time in Jerusalem because I thought that city was the center of power. This impostor was smarter: he knew Jerusalem was only a bunch of Jews under Romans and without real leaders, walking on eggshells, while the population which have always been behind successful revolts and usurpations, was scattered over the countryside and in small towns and villages.

"And now he's near here. His family no longer interests me; only the former infant, now grown man, with a probable army ready to support him."

Zachariah added, without much conviction, "Some even say this rabbi is the Son of God."

Jerusha smashed a clay pot on the table. "Son of God! Messiah! King of the Jews! What next? Emperor of Rome? God Himself? A magician whose greatest trick has been to make countless babies disappear? Your four children. My three."

Zachariah was still trying to calm her. "Some say he heals the sick, and makes the blind to see. Many believe in him. But who knows? By the way, among your list of complaints was an implied charge of blasphemy. When did you regain your piety?"

After it was clear to Zachariah that neither his remaining sarcastic humor nor his hope for gratitude nor occasional attempts to placate her, were having any affect on Jerusha, he stated, "You're in no mood for visitors. Fare you well." After a short bow to her, he departed with one last remark, "Take care, Jerusha. Whether this man's mob rises and wins an insurrection, or loses one, you might be in danger."

Jerusha dropped the door bar behind Zachariah. She knew she would never see her kinsman again. Would her memory of him be of a beloved brother? Beloved? Yes. A ragged gossip who outlived his value to anyone? A brave leader of fighting men? A devout Pharisee? A charming host? A thinker, talker, philosopher? Only a jokester with a sarcastic turn of phrase?

Or the first and greatest victim of her treachery, so many years before...

Jerusha added to herself, *Fare you well forever, Zachariah, my husband's brother, whom I have wronged more deeply than you will ever know. I go to avenge us both.* Jerusha then spent much of the night sharpening, cleaning, and polishing her dagger which had become rusty and dull.

◆

Her same old knife should do. Clothes should be poor; tradeswoman. There was not much point in cleaning the house for her voyage, but knowing her habits, she knew she would do it anyway. Jerusha wouldn't ask anyone to keep an eye on the house while she was gone. It would not be for long, and might endanger an innocent person. Though why she cared about anyone else now was beyond her imagination. Jerusha thought of boarding up the house, but there was nothing noticeable in it worth breaking in for; she would eat the remaining food before departing. Afterwards, Jerusha would either be dead, or return to her old life here a fully satisfied woman. There was no doubt Jerusha would carry out her plans to their end. *I've always heard they crucify women, too; I wonder what that would be like?* What bothered her most was that the victims of crucifixion were completely naked, and she had always been extremely modest. Not even curiosity had driven Jerusha to the areas just north of Jerusalem where the rows of unclothed criminals were planted. She wasn't a coward, nor squeamish; just uninterested at the time.

Putting such thoughts out of her mind, what else should she do or plan, now? So many things, material and non-material, had been of at least some importance to her before, but there had always been immediate reasons for that. There seemed few now, except necessities for her journey.

She would need money; plenty of money. From large gold coins to the meanest tokens. Need she have other dealings with her factors or tradesmen, other than bankers? No; they had always known to expect her only when they actually saw her or received a communication from her. If Jerusha disappeared, they would most likely find profitable ways to cut their ties.

For the first time in her life, she need not bother herself about anything in the distant, or even not-so-distant, future. This would be her most exciting adventure, and her last one, whatever happened.

Jerusha spread what little shopping would be required for her journey over several days, to lessen suspicion; there would be little or no connection between items she bought. First a strong basket, tightly woven, meant to be carried on one's back and shoulders, and reinforced throughout, especially at the shoulder straps. Like those meant for tradesmen. A much smaller basket designed to fit just inside the larger one, for storing smoked fish, cheese, and less perishable items to feed her during her trip, or perchance to sell. How long would the trip take? The gossip Jerusha had listened for informed her this rabbi, this false king, and his followers and listeners were last seen not far away, to the southwest of Jerusalem, not far from Bethlehem. This was her opportunity.

She used a young tradesman with whom she was slightly acquainted to buy her a donkey; Jerusha knew it would be strange to do so herself, considering the current class structure. The ass was loaded with large skins of water and a few items she could not carry. All the loading was accomplished in the remains of the garden behind her house.

The basket she herself carried would be filled with, other than the items she had already chosen, small loaves of barley bread for sale. Jerusha would be a food peddler, one of the few occupations she had never tried. There would be, of course, a few skins of olive oil so the new king's subjects could dip their bread. Hard cheese and smoked fish. Jerusha also obtained wine for those who could afford it, though gullible as they must be, they would probably not know bad from good.

It was time to begin her search. She started on the main road northwards. Fortunately, this was the first day of the week, and Jerusha would not have to worry about superstitious Sabbath rituals. It seemed that the rabbi and his followers were heading toward the main southern gate of the Capital City. When she was most of the way to Jerusalem, and a few rises away from him, she spotted a number of people who could only be the pretender's would-be subjects. Jerusha stopped to keep her distance. A cluster of people suddenly came out of the main gate of the City, obviously chasing the false king with small stones in their hands. The two groups clashed; the king answered them at length, but made no effort to defend his followers. After a while, the angry mass returned to the gate from whence they had come. It was two days before the rabbi and his followers continued on their original path eastward. During much of this, Jerusha hid with her donkey among brush and saplings which were growing in a ravine out of the immediate sight of either side of the scuffle.

When Jerusha's target and his group began moving again, it changed direction slightly, now moving parallel to what could be seen as the longest wall of Jerusalem, and contained the main gate Jerusha had always used on her daily trips to the City while a beggar. They must have received some news, for surely a small number of hecklers would not have deflected such an ambitious rabbi, nor deprived him of the adoring crowds a would-be king obviously sought. *For that matter, why was he dawdling so long to claim his kingship?* It would not be long before someone younger would appear with better credentials and certainly more followers.

Indeed, the small group stopped where there was a rather large rocky hill, and his gang made preparations to stay on it.

Gradually larger numbers of people began to approach the hill from Jerusalem; first single men, then couples, then families, and finally small crowds. All seated themselves on rocks or in depressions in a circle around the hill with the rabbi still standing on top talking with one or two of what were apparently his closest friends.

It was only when the hill was spread with those who had come to hear the rabbi, that Jerusha decided this would be her best opportunity to begin the last stages of what she had always known was her only purpose for continuing to breathe for the last thirty or so years.

By slowly circling the crowd, and therefore the hill, starting on her left, she would appear to be just another peddler who specialized in the poor. Jerusha was surprised to see on closer inspection the audience consisted of all classes, judging from their clothing and accents, so there would be customers for all her goods. The more customers, the longer she could remain unnoticed.

She started with the outer ring so she could be lost in the crowd if there was a rush back to the city due to any disturbance. Most of the people were now sitting on shallow hills or leaning against rocks so they could see the top of the elevation, however distant. Some faced their friends but could turn slightly to see the rabbi. All appeared to be talking among themselves, indicating Jerusha had missed nothing and would have sufficient time to study this "king."

Jerusha learned to divide her time between her feigned interest in her customers and her genuine interest in the figure at the top of the hill whenever he or someone in his group appeared to say or do something that might affect her plan. In the beginning, she caught herself ignoring buyers, and had to correct for that, though she kept her voice low. Only after circling the entire first row of the uneven hill did she feel safe to move another row upwards circling in the opposite direction, working her way slowly.

Many bought from her: bread, olive oil, fish, and wine of the cheapest kind though a few had better taste in libations. She tossed the money carelessly in the nearest basket she had to hand. Fortunately for Jerusha, no one was studying her movements after paying, and she had not had to search for change. None offered her a coin of high value, and Jerusha kept her prices as cheap as they would have been in Bethlehem, so no haggling would be necessary. These folk were careful enough of where they placed their feet or sat that Jerusha could make her way with ease.

She couldn't help feeling contempt for the crowd, but what she showed on her face thus far was no more than the average peddler felt for all customers; sellers were expected to show only a very minimum of courtesy to those whom they inwardly felt they were favoring. On her return trip around the circle, Jerusha felt secure enough to find a temporary niche for herself, and most of her donkey. She did not want hungry people beleaguering her just then. Her niche was between two families who had brought their own food and therefore had no interest in peddlers, so Jerusha could relax for a short while.

That gave her time to examine the rabbi, still some distance away. He was in his early thirties, which would make him the right age for her target. He was of average height and slightly ascetic, though nowhere near as much so as the Essene cult who made a virtue of starvation. The rabbi's clothing was plain, but not ragged. His green cloak was particularly fine for one which was clearly homemade. His face was entirely Semitic, but she supposed attractive to another young Semite, though she had formed an opinion over many years that most easterners preferred western features, though they would never admit it. This rabbi's hair and beard were well-groomed. Not one to stand out in a large enough crowd, usually, but in a way, he did. Perhaps it was the respect and occasional courtesy which he received from almost all sides. Her personal hatred did not make her blind to the reactions of others around him. All this she could see easily for it was still mid-afternoon.

For the first time it struck her that she was not only in literal view of her quarry but in what would probably be the last stage— Minutes? Hours? A day or two?—of her life. She could not afford the slightest error, miscalculation or so much as a vaguely inappropriate facial feature on her part. Every word, step, and deed must be executed to perfection, no matter how trivial it would normally be. A lifetime of habit, attitude and mannerism must be erased if inappropriate to her role. Casual cynicism, or, at the other extreme, commonplace courtesy, must be instantly examined for its effect on her mission. Jerusha could not remember ever having had to be so much in control of herself. Her past murders as a dagger man now seemed to her like a random walk through the streets in which accident or luck determined most outcomes. Here there could be no surprises.

One of the strangers from the next small bunch within the audience neared Jerusha. Since they had a basket of provisions, Jerusha guessed she would not have to bother with business, so she opened the conversation.

"That man at the top; who is he? What is he doing?"

Perhaps the stranger had conversed with the company she already had, and still sought to chat about her expectations until some sort of speech or address came from the summit. "I'm not sure, but he might be the Messiah we have all been promised for so long. I heard him speak to us all earlier, or at least those of us who were near the Temple in Jerusalem. Were you there?"

Jerusha's lack of response had no effect.

The stranger sat down on a tuft. "Whoever he is, he seems like a good man. He spoke of love. The love of God for each of us. And of the dignity of life in this world, even for the poor. I'm not poor, but I'm not rich, either. This man asked for no donations, and none were taken. But there was more the man talked of; or what seemed to me to be much more. The rabbi spoke for quite a while about the next world, which he calls his Father's Kingdom. Where there will be no rich or poor, no injustice or hate."

After a short pause, Jerusha asked, "And you believe him?"

"He seemed to have nothing to gain from me or anyone else, so I believe he was sincere."

"So is a madman. But if he can gather a crowd this size to listen to him, he must be making a large amount of money some way or another. Yet I see no bodyguards protecting him."

"Why should a man who asked for no money need guards?"

Jerusha spat in a way that, within the class she was assuming, would be considered discreet. "In these days, almost any well-known man needs guards. Where is he from?"

"They say Nazareth."

Nazareth. The last few clues were coming together, as if they were needed.

As the woman made signs to leave, Jerusha offered her a small loaf of bread to show she meant no harm.

"We bought some—and a little wine—from you earlier. We can wait until the rabbi has finished speaking again, when we will go home."

Jerusha managed a thin smile. "Here are two loaves and a small skin of wine for you and your family and friends. Or you can eat them later."

The strange woman looked confused. "We do thank you. We thank you in the name of...our Master. I can use that word for he seems to be bringing out the kindness in others in addition to his teachings." As the woman worked her way to her previous location, Jerusha leaned to hear her whisper to her companion, whom she had not seen on the other side of the donkey, "Did he not say God would provide? I told the peddler we were not poor, but she must have known the truth."

Jerusha suddenly felt revulsion on hearing this, for in her courtesy she had merely caused the most evil man which she could imagine, the man who provoked the death of her boys, to rise in esteem. And even allowed some of it to rub off on herself, Jerusha, who knew her own guilt in killing Leah and her nephews.

Jerusha remembered years ago, when Zachariah was leading her into Jerusalem after her ambush in the wilderness. He spoke of his "theory" that neither wealth nor power brought success, for both could be taken away by a man or group who could attract enough devoted followers. Is that what this rabbi was? And Jerusha's recent customers, and the others on this hill, devoted followers? Jerusha must be careful.

Her disgust almost caused her to continue her circling approach in its original direction but she realized in time the need to reverse paths regularly so as to be less noticeable. It made no difference, for when she was halfway up the hill, having sold few loaves and little wine lately, she found her way blocked by a man with crossed arms and spread legs that implied he intended to stop her. His eyes looked straight into hers, and there was no way of avoiding him without causing unwanted attention. Jerusha was high enough up the hill to have reached what might become her closest proximity to the rabbi or "master." She quickly pushed the dagger farther up her sleeve.

To the intruder she adopted a whining tone. "Who are you and why are you blocking me? Do I need permission to sell bread?"

"My name is Simon, and I am doing all I can to avoid embracing you as an old comrade. Do you not remember me among the Zealots?"

Jerusha stifled her shock on recognizing the iron-artist with whom she had talked at Zealot headquarters. She put on her sternest expression. "So now you serve a different master. Or is this another Zealot band? I once heard one of *Herod's* men ask almost the same thing I am asking: 'Is this a nest for a family of wrens or a den of stinking vultures?' What would happen if I denounced you as 'Simon the Zealot'?"

"Nothing," he laughed, "I'm often addressed and introduced that way now. Of course, few know in which sense the word 'zealot' is meant. My zealotry for our Master is well known."

Jerusha ignored this. "Anyway, as I said, I don't need a permit to sell anything here."

"I don't think you came to sell bread, or fish, or wine." Simon smiled.

"So I came to hear your master at the same time. What difference does it make?"

Simon seemed to relax, but remained visibly alert. He said nothing for a while, but made no sign to move.

As the time stretched out Jerusha became slightly nervous, a feeling to which she was unaccustomed.

"If you expect me to pretend to be a convert, or reconvert, to your cult or your political cause, you will be disappointed. Has all this crowd taken an oath of some kind to your master? If so, I would fear for it. But even more would I fear for all Judea."

Simon paused. "No, most have come only to listen. Some will later follow my master. Some will not. But among them there might be one or more who wish harm to him. Are you such a one?"

"I am a woman and old. Why should *he* fear *me*?"

Simon clearly dismissed the thought. "*He* does not. He has told us the time of his death, and resurrection, have already been decided. But I have not his faith, and therefore *I* fear you."

Jerusha stepped aside for a moment, irritated, only to find herself pressed between two boulders, almost out of sight of the crowd. She had forgotten Simon had been a trained Zealot warrior. He was almost as old as she was, but bore his age well, with visible strength and agility. He quickly stilled her mouth with his hand, and then whispered, "You may speak, but only softly."

Jerusha nodded her head and as soon as she had the chance she spat out her words, quietly but viciously. "*His* faith, you say! *Your* faith! Guesswork! There was a time when I shared such fantasies. Now I understand only those things which are *real*, or derived from them by thinking."

"As is faith," Simon interrupted. When he saw her anger rising, he reminded her, "Be careful not to raise a scene." He continued in the teaching mode she remembered from before, "You learned the word 'faith' from believers. Faith is merely reason sustained when the path is lost or hard to find. The flesh is weak, and wants to quit. One retains only the memory of what reason taught one before. This is my view of 'faith.'"

"You still talk too much, Simon."

By this time the rabbi had finished addressing the group.

Jerusha had listened at times, but dismissed what she heard as pious dribble. The rabbi had returned to conversations with two or three close followers.

Simon let Jerusha up from the corner formed by the two boulders. Much of the crowd left, but a number built cook fires and wrapped themselves in blankets.

"If you doubt my motives, why do you let me up?" Jerusha asked.

"Oh, I think I have an idea of your motives, but I know my abilities better, as I do those of my Master. Stay here for the night, if you wish. I will be on watch, and I will alert others to watch for you also." He started to turn, and then changed his mind.

"I think I'll take your dagger, for now."

Jerusha spat at him, but that only made him smile. She complied with his order.

"You have changed, Simon."

"You have not. Do you have any other weapons?"

"No," said Jerusha. "But why should you believe me?"

"Because you've proven yourself a killer, as was I, but not yet a liar, at least to me."

Simon pointed to a comfortable looking grass indentation slightly farther from his master than they were. "Sit or lie down over there. You might even listen, if the master speaks again. Do not approach him for any reason."

"I have patience. Having maintained it for thirty years I can wait a bit more. I stay, of course, out of curiosity," Jerusha said and prepared to settle in where Simon had indicated.

"Thirty years? Oh, yes, you mentioned something about that when we had a long talk at headquarters."

"I spoke of nothing concerning you."

"No? Anyway I'll be right up there near our Master. My bluestriped robe will be easy to recognize. I'll be this side of him." Simon walked away.

For the first hour a few spectators came to Jerusha for bread or cheap wine; her donkey marked Jerusha's location. Once in a while she listened to the rabbi when he spoke to some small group who would approach him. He was seated on a flat rock as darkness fell, yet some people still came. Jerusha listened during any such talk. But she heard only more of love, repentance, righteousness, or the afterlife. The last subject bothered her the most because the only reference it had to her was the death of her sons.

Jerusha decided she would not listen to him any more. She blocked out the teacher's words with the old children's trick of drowning out her adversary, by repeating to herself the names of her boys continuously, and monotonously, in the same sing-song order. She began to include her nephews, but forgot names occasionally and returned to the list of her own children. She was suddenly aghast at the thought of digressing from thinking to mumbling names, and had even been on the verge of putting her hands over her ears as children do for the same reason. She rapidly looked around in panic only to see the remains of the crowd setting up tents, rolling themselves in blankets, and building small fires to ward off the cold or cook what foodstuffs they had brought with them. They had heard nothing from her, but Jerusha knew she had come close to endangering her entire enterprise through momentary compulsiveness.

Just before total silence settled over the hill, one more couple approached her to buy.

"Would you have some bread?"

The customer replied, "Yes, please, three loaves if your price is honest."

"My loaves grow cheaper as the buyers go home, and as the bread gets less fresh. Would you like some wine or cheese or dried fish?" The customers declined.

"I would have brought more," said Jerusha, "but I didn't know the preaching would last so long. Why do you stay? Will your master speak here again tomorrow?"

"I don't know. If so, we want to hear him. If not, we might even follow him."

"Why?" Stifling her frustration, "Have you no lives of your own?"

The man answered, "I begin to wonder. The master speaks of eternal life with God, if we follow him. An unending love."

"Or at least unending puzzles," said Jerusha turning back to her donkey and her goods.

❖

Jerusha awoke at the slightest hint of sunrise and quickly concluded she was the first in the camp to do so. Her eyes sought out the rabbi, only to see that he had been watching her. For how long, she did not know. She made no move, out of curiosity as to what would happen next.

During the night the thought had entered her head to carry out her mission with the false king at once, but the hill was moonlit and so silent that her chance of success was slim. Indeed, she had never heard such silence as when she was weighing the possibilities. So she did nothing during the night. Only later did she remember that she was without her dagger, anyway.

Simon, the second person she saw this morning, approached what she had begun to think of as her nest.

"*Shalom*. You can have your knife back," he said tossing it lightly beside her.

"Why? Have I passed your test?"

"No. As a matter of fact you failed it. I, however, have passed it."

Jerusha was exasperated. "If you're going to be such a talker, you might at least leave out the riddles, especially before breaking fast. Why did you give me my knife back?"

"You might need it to cut your food with. Your bread is a bit stale by now, and you must have been smart enough to bring salt fish or other meats. Have some water. Without it you can't eat," Simon added.

"Can't eat? Has my food been poisoned?"

"Now *you* are afraid of *us*?" asked Simon.

"I'm never afraid, just cautious. Especially around riddlers. There must be something which you can discuss in a straightforward manner. I noted last night you have changed since headquarters. More confident, somehow; a good characteristic. Make a clearing in the dust here and settle down beside me. I'll share some of my food with you."

While making himself comfortable, Simon commented, "From a woman as rich as you, I would normally be looking forward to a sumptuous feast. But since you are playing the poor peddler I assume your food won't be any better than ours, but I'll throw in a few twigs for a fire and leave the preparation to you."

Simon continued talking as Jerusha worked her usual magic on the ingredients she had brought with her. "What change in me you might have noticed," Simon turned serious, "was brought about by two major experiences in my life, and one led to the other. You will remember when we last talked, learning that I was betrothed. I'm married now and have been for some time."

"Where is your wife? I don't think I've seen her near the summit of this hill. Have you tired of her already?" She had a hint of a sneer.

"No; she's in Nazareth taking care of our boy and still suckling our youngest. Her brother works the blacksmith shop. My absence from her is the only thing preventing this from being the happiest time of my life. I do not say that as a dutiful husband; I think you are astute enough to have gathered at our first acquaintance, that I am always sincere, and open."

"That's not the way you described the attitude you displayed around your men during combat," Jerusha interjected.

"I was describing the qualities of leadership, which requires some aloofness. You don't consider me your military leader, do you?"

"Certainly not. But go on with your endless talk."

"The man who stood with me at my wedding was my youngest brother. Do you remember my mentioning him?" Jerusha shrugged. "Well, he's the one to whom I left the family carpentry business when I decided to become an iron-worker. I also told you he was the only person whom I would trust in everything. His judgment was proven at the time when he did not wish for me to join the Zealots, and I decided to do so anyway. However useful I might have been to that cause, I always sensed I was wrong to be there. I think I hinted at that to you. So, I left them some time ago. Then everything began to change. I'll tell you about it after we have eaten."

CHAPTER 13

Circling The Quarry

Soon the food was prepared and served on skewers, or wrapped in grape leaves, or laid on large, dried leaves to hold loose bits of meat and fish with a sauce, which Jerusha assured Simon was made with no manner of milk, cream, or cheese, since she always observed the Jewish dietary laws. *Or at least*, she thought to herself, *the one forbidding meat to come into contact with dairy*; Jerusha had not forgotten the horsemeat when she was a Zealot recruit, and a few other lapses when they were convenient and there was no possibility of being found out. Jerusha served watered wine in small crockery mugs.

As the meal was finished, Simon started to help Jerusha clean up, but she preferred to control all her property, its remains, and even its evidence.

Simon arose to take his leave. "Fare-thee-well, Jerusha. Thank you for the best food I can remember for a long time." He dusted and prepared his colorful robes to walk away.

"What?" she asked before he took two steps, "Simon, the talker, is preparing to depart?"

"What would you have me speak of?" asked Simon, with a blank look on his face.

"I don't know. Why did you leave the Zealots?"

Simon sat down again. "I found what I was seeking. Didn't we both say that was the reason we joined?"

"But you never found it at headquarters? You joined another cult? This one?"

"It didn't happen then," Simon answered. "As I said, I gave up the Zealots. I went home to marry a wonderful woman. Then something happened there, actually in Cana, nearby. I saw a miracle." He looked almost embarrassed.

"You mean magic? I would have thought you would be the last to believe a trickster. Was he hired to entertain the wedding guests?"

Simon laughed. "Far from it. He was my younger half-brother, who stood for me at my wedding. It was his own mother—my father's second wife, after my mother died—who asked him to perform it, though he had never done anything supernatural before that I know of. He objected, but he adored his mother and would never disobey. I am certain he would not have performed his first miracle for anyone but her, and she would never have asked him to were it not my, her husband's son's, wedding. The miracle was also for me..." Simon was drifting.

He gathered his thoughts. "The reception was very well attended; too well. The wine ran out much too soon. No one in our part of the country would fail in hospitality, so the hostess, his mother, asked my brother to remedy the situation. He solved it by addressing an amphora of purest water and—well—turning it into wine."

Now Jerusha had the urge to laugh. "That's it? Water into wine? Perhaps the first order of wine hadn't run out soon enough for your sobriety, or that of your guests. No heavenly portents, raising the dead? People flying about? Or the much more common 'miracle' of a pregnant bride without the carnal touch of a man?"

Simon smiled at the last example, as though he were holding something back. But Jerusha had known him as the most open of men. "No. The miraculous wine was very, very good. The guests commented on it. All miracles are through God, and He is as interested in our minor needs and wants as our greatest ones."

"If one is going to perform an impossible act, this one seems rather trivial."

Simon was beginning to show slight irritation. "'Impossible'? How do you know it was impossible? Have you ever seen a lion stalk its prey? A lunar eclipse?"

"I don't even know what that one is," she interjected.

"Have you seen an elephant? Or a heavy ship get built, and float on water much lighter than it is?"

"I've seen the last, or at least a small boat, but I admit I don't know why it floats; I hear that they do." Jerusha wasn't as bored as she expected to be.

"So 'possibility' depends entirely on whether you have seen something, or heard about it often enough, and it fits in with what you've already stored up in your vast vault of learning. Would that we all had your scholarship!" He sounded angry. "You're more gullible than I thought, Jerusha.

"Well," Simon concluded in a more conciliatory vein, "I'll admit this wasn't one of my brother's more impressive miracles. But I'll always be grateful that, if nothing else, my brother got me out of a very difficult position. You see, it was my duty to provide all the refreshments. But I severely underestimated the amount of wine required for my own wedding. Worse, in comparison to my half-brother's wine, mine was distinctly inferior. No one failed to notice it. Of course, my wine was not miraculously produced.

"Must a miracle always be earth-shaking? Must it reverse all evils since Father Adam and Mother Eve? Can't it sometimes be powerful enough for those who have eyes to see, ears to hear, and lack a mulish prejudice against God's miracles? It opened my eyes because it supplied the one detail which I had not seen in my brother. I would soon have powerful proof."

"Of what?"

"Later."

"Peace," Jerusha concluded light-heartedly. "I'm sure your half-brother must be a very good magician. Or Vintner."

"Is 'magic' all you can call it?" Simon appeared sincerely curious. "Did you listen at all yesterday afternoon and evening?"

"Yes," Jerusha made a brushing motion with her hand. "But too much of it was about love, which I don't trust, or about his 'father's kingdom,' and I have little interest in a carpenter's shop, however richly decorated."

"Either I overestimated your intelligence or underestimated your stubbornness. Do you lie awake at night practicing it?" Strange that however light Simon's tone, his eyes remained large and damp. "After most of a lifetime of listening to my brother's wisdom and feeling and witnessing his love, I finally felt the call to follow Jesus to help in his mission, and I still am doing so. Though I go home regularly. Jesus has no home his real work will let him accept."

"Then your master's name is 'Jesus'?" Jerusha asked, feigning indifference.

"He's known by various names; Jesus ben Joseph, Jesus of Nazareth, of the House of David, Master, Rabbi. He calls himself 'The Son of Man'. And he's not really my half-brother. My own mother is certainly long dead. Once, I thought we shared the same father in Joseph of Nazareth. Since then I have great reason to believe Jesus' real father was more miraculous than you are ready to believe. That would make Jesus, literally, my foster-brother. But few know of this, yet. So half-brother will do. Or brother. Our families are so tightly-knit in the North we, and others in our position, are commonly called brothers, as are even our cousins. I understand your families are not that close—because of King Herod. Why so much interest?" Simon sat back comfortably.

"Oh. Oh, I don't know." Her mind was racing on several levels including her relationship with Leah, whose strings she had helped cut. But also about what she suspected would be Simon's next question because he had never dwelt on it before.

"Wait a minute," he said. "You clearly have a mission with us, and Jesus. Don't I remember you and Zachariah talking of a grudge stretching back many, many years—one that motivates you over all other things? Yes, yes, but Herod the Great is dead, as is anyone else that could be a party to this grudge. Or is he or they? I demand to know, does it concern Jesus?"

"If it did, would I tell you?"

"No," said Simon, coldly. "I think I'll have your dagger back." Jerusha handed him her dagger.

"Jesus has no interest in protecting his own life, as I told you before. But I do. You do know I carry a sword?"

"No. Is that why your robes are colorful and striped? To cover the sword? I thought your master preached peace?"

"So do I," said Simon. "But how long would we survive around Judea, with our small treasury, totally unarmed? We're not usually surrounded by a devoted crowd. People have thrown stones at us. It seems to me it wouldn't take much to destroy our mission forever, though our Master has implied this is impossible."

Jerusha wondered what that mission was. Not wealth. Power? Unlikely, at least as far as his poor followers are concerned; but what is the false king's intent? Jerusha had devoted her life to the belief that Jesus' ambition for power destroyed her own family. It *must* be true. "So you quit the cult of the Zealots in order to join the cult of Jesus of Nazareth. Any others in mind for the future?"

"Not really." Simon rose again. Jerusha listened for the distinctive metallic clinks or squeaking leather that might indicate a sword hanging behind Simon's loose outer robe, but heard none of which she could be certain, nor did she see the outline of such a weapon on her side of his clothing. Which meant absolutely nothing.

"I don't think I wish your company for awhile," said Simon without any visible emotion. Someone called to him from across the campsite. "I must be going. I truly hope you someday find what you're looking for. *Shalom*."

After he left, Jerusha felt the need to make some serious plans. On her midnight walk to the makeshift women's communal latrine she had looked around the moonlit hill and estimated a third or less of the crowd lay sleeping, and she considered it safe to assume that at least half of the remainder would leave at daybreak or perhaps after a short sermon by Jesus, before he and his closest followers continued their journey. Jerusha searched around her and was relieved to see the rabbi Jesus still among them, now wearing a white robe, not far from where he had been the night before.

Why would Joseph and his wife pick the *youngest* son to be king or Messiah? Why not the oldest son? Or Simon; he was intelligent enough to pass, and could make himself popular with the right people. Also, why waste all that time away up in Nazareth? Maybe it had something to do with Scriptural prophecy, about which Jerusha knew nothing. Perhaps someday she would ask Simon, if she were still alive, and if all panic hadn't broken loose and if... and if...and if. She remembered thinking in such pointless mazes several times before.

Now Simon knew or suspected her bloody goal, and would have no reason to keep it secret from his targeted brother. Or dozens of others, for that matter. How many people had, or would soon have, the assignment of watching everything she did? Or just killing her and putting an end to it? If so, there was nothing she could do about it, so she might as well continue following the crowd and looking for the best opportunity she could, without the element of surprise, or knowledge of her surroundings, without a weapon, or anything, but luck. Well, she never thought she would live long. Jerusha would follow her original plan. Doubts were unwelcome, and were a weakness.

At daybreak about two dozen people were packing their scant goods and heading back to Jerusalem. Fewer were also packing but starting toward the east with their master. She packed quickly, abandoned anything she wouldn't need, and hurried to mingle with Jesus' followers. Once she was among them, she found them walking in groups of two or three often talking together, so she kept pace, alone, many yards from Jesus, but not far from Simon. She eavesdropped as much as possible.

Jerusha would slowly blend into a group from behind, keeping her eyes in front or watching her step. She found most took no notice of her, or even knew each other very well, if at all. When their talk was not concerning the weather or other trivial subjects, it merely repeated or expanded on the subjects the rabbi had discussed the night before. Jerusha had found these topics boring enough then, and more so now. And even she could tell Jesus was often misunderstood or misquoted. Once in a while she overheard someone who was along only in the hope of witnessing one of the famous "miracles."

The word she heard most often, though, was "love." Jesus had used it repeatedly in his lecture on the hill. Not romantic love, but all-encompassing. Jerusha had often heard of God's love for Israel, but she had rarely heard the word applied to individual people. Prophets and other important people, yes. But for each person? Even a nonentity and sinner such as herself? Jerusha remembered one of the things that drove her from her faith was the wide gulf separating her, Jerusha, from God's supposed "Love." Her opinion had been proven by the horrors the Lord had done nothing to protect her from. But the people in this crowd had many and varied opinions.

Although these people were friendlier and politer to each other than any random gatherings Jerusha could remember, there were a few arguments she overheard, though none ever sank to the rude and personal level. One elderly man seemed anxious to profit from the Nazarene's cause.

"It stands to reason," he stated emphatically, banging his walking stick on the ground for emphasis, "if our master refused a rich follower and ordered him to sell all his goods and give the money to the poor, then we poor people have a lot coming to us as the master's movement grows!"

"You remember that the rich man declined, however sorrowfully," a younger man responded.

"Not *all* will. But maybe this should be made the Law."

"And if all the rich complied, the entire population would be passing the same goods around eternally, while accomplishing nothing but mass poverty," the younger speaker replied. "The Master's order that day was not for everyone." He was clearly more intelligent than the old man, but kept easy and sharp answers to a minimum.

"I won't 'pass it around'. I'll quit when I have enough."

"I know you heard Jesus' lectures on that one subject and memorized them. The Master has talked often about our duty to the poor. The Scriptures also make our duty clear. But can you find a quote in which the poor are told to *take* from the rich? Indeed, doesn't one of the Great Commandments specifically forbid this? And doesn't the last Commandment forbid even wishing for it? Lay up your riches in Heaven. Anything that competes with God for our love is dangerous, whether it's money, lust, or sloth.

"My name is Matthew," he continued. "I was a rich

tax-collector. I gave it up when I met our Master and became one of his earliest followers. Now I am richer, in his love."

"I'm talking about justice for the poor," whined the older man.

"Justice is between individuals, and we are all sinners. Jesus speaks more of mercy." The man Matthew moved away, with a parting shot. "Envy is a sin, old man. Perhaps the most dangerous sin if it were ever indulged by large numbers. But only God knows. God will provide."

The old man tried to hold on to his audience. "Were you there when our Master said it was easier for a camel to go through the eye of a needle than for a rich man to enter the Kingdom of Heaven?"

"I'm certain it is. The rich have so many temptations, distractions and so much business I wonder that any can keep their thoughts and hearts on God and eternal life. I know I could not have. It has been said the love of money is the root of all evil. Do you, my friend, harbor that love?"

When Jerusha looked back she saw the older of the conversationalists take a few more steps at random, then wander back toward Jerusalem, his head hanging.

Looks like the rabbi has lost a follower.

Jerusha had listened longer to these two than usual. Because she was rich? She wondered. She had no overpowering love of money. Wealth was useful for her purposes.

Before circulating further among the group of travelers, Jerusha felt again the need to know, for certain, the extreme ambition of this new rabbi because of whom her boys had died. She remembered Zachariah's conclusion was that an attractive personality—the ability to win the respect, admiration, and loyalty of large numbers of people—was the most important quality in a leader. Maybe this was the strange rabbi's plan; his path to kingship. Not an army; simply people. Perhaps the man Matthew, having dismissed material wealth just now, could give Jerusha an insight into his master's intentions. Unlike Simon, Matthew was unrelated to Jesus, and might provide an impartial view.

She would catch up with him and learn. Within a few strides she was walking beside Matthew. They walked alone.

Jerusha could see dark clouds and sheets of rain far to the north of their path, and had a fleeting thought that a storm would interrupt her investigation. But there was no wind from the north, and though she sensed the fresh smell of approaching rain, Jerusha concluded the storm would go no further south than central Jerusalem.

She addressed the man called Matthew.

"Sir, I couldn't help overhearing your talk with the man who just left us, about wealth and envy. Would you speak with a woman for a short while?"

"Certainly. Why not?"

"I would know more about your master, Jesus of Nazareth." She kept her eyes on the path ahead.

"So would I," said Matthew. "I have been taking notes for a long time, and intended to question others about his life before I joined them. Especially Simon called Peter, and the Master's mother, Mary. I wish to remember all I can."

"Yes, you said you had been a tax-collector before, and that would require much learning, as well as knowledge of the ruling classes."

Matthew shrugged. "Each of us is different, and has his own experiences and skills. Learning is only one of them, and not the highest. What would you like to know, that you couldn't learn by listening to him?"

Jerusha pretended to think for a while as if gathering her words.

"I have heard your master talk about the poor, and our duty toward them. Couldn't he help them more if he rose to prominent office? Become a magistrate, or even a minor ruler? I'm not talking about King, of course, for that is inherited. Or even a Temple priest, for the same reason. But there are other rulers. Someone who could help hundreds, or thousands, of the poor and unfortunate."

Matthew laughed, which altered his features enough to indicate he was not accustomed to mirth or outbursts of any kind. "Our Lord has no such high worldly aspirations. This I know. He has been offered many such opportunities. Yes, and even the highest, I'm told, by a being who had the power to grant such things. Don't you see that his acceptance would destroy his *real* mission?"

"I wasn't talking only of him, of course, but of *all* of us. Is that not what our duty to the poor is? Would Jesus not wish to enforce righteousness as a ruler?"

Matthew began to speak in a condescending tone, but quickly amended it. "What does the Master, or any of us, have to give, in material goods? Surely you aren't suggesting he should rise to earthly power to take money from the Nation or the Temple, all of which comes from the people, and give it to those he favors or pities? This would not be charity; it would be theft. It would be what a Herod or a Caesar might do. Our master speaks to each of us and asks us each to look into his or her own heart, and give of what we own. There can be no charity with the Nation's or other people's goods, or any funds taken by force. That was how I justified my previous life as a tax-collector. One shouldn't do evil that good will come."

Jerusha blurted, "But think of the general prosperity!"

"God's Will shall be done, in times of scarcity or plenty, so long as there are men of good will. And even if there be none. Nor would Jesus interfere with the free will his Father gave to mankind."

Jerusha realized she would get no more out of Matthew. He spoke sense. But she was in no way satisfied. Her plans were based on the cruel ambitions of the Nazarene's family, and she could not reconsider them now, and deny her life.

She sought to excuse herself from Matthew's presence by humbly saying, "I am only a poor woman, an empty vessel to receive what I am given by learned men." Jerusha demurely cast her eyes downward.

Matthew was clearly irritated by her last statement. "Sister, you do me and my Lord an injustice. You are a child of God just as we are."

"Then why are there so few women among those following Jesus?" Jerusha could not resist a last shot.

Matthew mastered his irritation. "Many are home with their children. Teaching them the Law of God. Teaching them what our master has taught us. Some cannot travel far as we can. Perhaps their work is more important than ours, or will be to future generations. Of course, Mother Mary was and is more important than anyone of our master's followers. I hope you will meet her, as she is often among us."

Jerusha took long strides to get away from Matthew. He was clearly biased, and his mind belonged to his master. There were still many others she could listen to. Or overhear.

One thing became clear from her eavesdropping: None of the people she had joined yet had any special interest in her, except for the very occasional potential customer. Assuming they were not all hypocrites and liars, Jerusha had to conclude none was assigned to watch or guard against her. Had Simon spoken to *no* one?

Jerusha began to hear about a funeral toward which they were heading. Some friend of Jesus'. Jerusha was becoming more bored than tired, and perhaps it was time to join Jesus' closest two or three people, and, try to complete her mission.

Meanwhile, Jerusha continued to mingle and talk with Jesus' other disciples. She questioned them, but heard nothing sinister. When she got too close to Jesus, she looked at him and changed direction. *Why did I turn away? What am I here for, anyway?* Each time Jerusha went through these curious steps, either Jesus didn't happen to be looking her way, or had exactly the same facial expression he displayed to everyone in the crowd.

There was...something...unique about Jesus. At first she dismissed it as his robes being extra clean and white, but certainly he did not have his own laundress? Besides, the vague glow seemed to be around him—though from him alone. Jerusha could think of no trick of sunlight which would account for this effect. His closest disciples did not seem to notice any difference in Jesus' appearance from other times they had seen him. Surely the strange lighting shouldn't make Jerusha afraid of him? Thirty years of hunting her prey only to turn coward? What could he do to her that she had not imagined a hundred times without the slightest nervousness?

Just as the sun began its descent, Jerusha, like the others, prepared her blankets and oilcloths for a tent. Maybe during the night she would take action if she could get her dagger.

Once again, there was no stream nearby where she could bathe, so she had nothing better to do than build a fire for her supper. She was staring at the dead grass and twigs in the center of the shallow hole she had scratched when she heard a slight *thud* beside her. She spun to see her dagger lying there.

Simon had approached again. "I decided to risk your violence rather than see you starve to death due to an inability to cut bread which must be like stone by now," he said. "Limestone, I think, or our pink or yellow sandstone. At your age, if you used your teeth, you'd probably lose them all. So there's your knife."

Jerusha invited Simon to sit and share her meal, "stones and all". He arranged his robes and made himself comfortable.

"Well now that you've met almost everyone in camp, did you recognize anyone?" Simon asked.

"No. Should I have?"

"I guess not, it was so long ago. One of the men was but a boy when you last saw him. He was an archer serving under you in the wilderness, when you killed Marcus and his Roman detachment."

Now Jerusha remembered, though not enough of his facial features to have recognized him after so many years, which must have changed him. She mostly remembered that the boy had seemed hopelessly attached to her and she would in no way encourage a mother-child relationship to grow in his mind, even when she had been bandaging his wound. "If he was a Zealot, what is he doing with your people now?"

"He changed, as I did."

"Or is this entire gang leading people into just another branch of the Zealots? You never have told me what your group has as its goal, or even its reason for existence."

"At our first meeting, I told you that I was searching for God. Finding him and learning from him and living with him and sharing him is our only reason for existence."

"Are you living with God now?"

"Yes. We are all within his love."

She changed the subject. "What of this funeral I hear about? Was the dead man beloved of God?"

"Lazarus was a dear friend of Jesus, and our Master has asked us to come to Bethany, where Lazarus lived and is buried."

"Though Jesus is your younger brother, you constantly call him 'Master'."

"He is our teacher. Also, as you should have known long before now, Jesus is of God, and merits the title. My friend also named Simon like me, but called 'Peter' among us, was the first to realize this about Jesus. I don't know why it has taken you so long to put all this together. That's why Jesus is neither my blood-brother nor my half-brother, but my foster-brother. Maybe you haven't understood because you never saw his miracles. That's the reason for miracles. Somehow I thought you were above such signs."

Jerusha could not speak for a moment through her rekindled fury, but her curiosity proved temporarily stronger. "Then he *does* claim—it's not just a rumor—to be the Messiah, the Son of God, the Son of the House of David? His ambition knows no bounds?"

"For the time being, this is confidential except among a few of us, and others Jesus may have told. I kept all of *your* confidences. Except from Jesus, but you have nothing to fear from him. He knows the course of his life. You saw no suspicious looks from anyone, did you? If most of the people had a hint of *your* goal, some hot-head among us would have assured your death before the sun had risen far today."

"So Jesus still claims the throne?"

"No. He has never claimed or wanted earthly royalty. What makes you think he ever did? I came to eat, but I suppose you have nothing but boulder-bread."

"You know I kept the best food for myself and now, I suppose, you."

Simon settled in more comfortably.

Jerusha said, "So we're back to this 'Son of God' cult, are we? I suppose the Romans follow their pagan cults; the Edomites have heroes and gods I can't even pronounce. Among ourselves we have Pharisees, Zealots, Essenes. Might as well have yours. What do you call yourselves?"

"We are often called 'Nazarenes', as that was Jesus' home."

Jerusha shrugged. "All the same to me. Fortune-tellers, reincarnations, whatever. We who are—or were—poor, cross paths with these more often than you richer sorts because they think we're stupid and easily won over."

"So if one cult is false, all are?"

"Why not?"

"Tell me," asked Simon, "if you found a false gem, would you throw all gems away? If you hired a dishonest factor, would you fire them all and go back to poverty because, being illiterate, you could make no contracts? If you tasted a sour fish..."

"Never mind; I get your point. But I might ask a magician who wanted my trust to do some trick for me. Finally, the only miracle I've seen so far, though done by others, was to kill all the male, and some female, children in Bethlehem."

"Finally it begins to come together for me, too," mused Simon aloud. "Tell me about it."

Jerusha sighed. "I told you some of it before. Herod the Great heard that a rival to his throne had been born in Bethlehem. So he ordered all male children in that town under the age of two years be...killed." Jerusha was unaware of the tears forming in her eyes and spilling down her dusty cheeks. She was more accustomed to feeling anger, often silent, when thinking of her story. She did not remember being demonstrative in public. She usually kept her sorrow in the locked box of her brain.

She continued, "I had three boys—one was over two years old, but Herod's men were not fussy. I saw them die; arms and legs hacked off. I seem to remember seeing one head fall off the loft, but the details get worse each time I think about them. One or two tried to scream, I think, but my own head was screaming by then, and I don't know."

"Yes," Simon said quietly, his eyes growing impossibly more soft and large, until they were all she could see of his face. "Herod was that cruel and jealous. But God's love is greater."

"One of the killers has died, rather fittingly, I think, at my hands. I only hope he was still young enough to know why he suffered. Herod is, of course, long dead. The only one left who must pay still lives."

"How is my brother mixed up in all this?"

Jerusha replied, "Jesus was the *cause* of all that happened. The child who created Herod's fear and jealousy."

Simon almost laughed, then choked on it, and said, "After all the horrors you have told me, I cannot but offer my deepest condolences. If I were not so certain of eternal life, this knowledge would be unbearable. Since you do not have that certainty, I can only grieve for you. If you only knew how much God loves you and your children."

"Do you mean *me*, personally? All of scripture that has been read or told to me talks of God's love for Israel. I don't remember hearing that He cares about any individual people. Gentiles and Heathens, for example. The Arab merchant I overheard when I was young was right: his race is without God's love. Then why should God get even more narrow and love *one* person, me?" *Especially after all I have done*, she thought.

"He created you for his love. Just as He created the Gentiles and Heathens. And everyone else, all of whom are sons of Adam. And you, and each other sinner, can experience God personally through Jesus, his Son. Repentance, and God's forgiveness. That's what He came on earth to tell us."

"I've experienced quite enough from his 'Father,' when he left me all alone. And Jesus hasn't ever spoken to me."

"He did in a crowd, on a hill. And if your heart were open, he would when you are alone. Jesus knows all about you, Jerusha. And loves you more than you can imagine. Do you, of all people, desire emotional demonstrations? But one day he will give his life for you."

That last he will, though he doesn't know it. Jerusha thought.

Simon's eyes remained large and damp; now unmistakable tears were just visible in his curly beard. "But I must know how your attitude against Jesus came about? How long ago was this atrocity perpetrated on your children?"

"About thirty years."

Under other circumstances Simon would have laughed. "Then this is all a mistake on your part, Jerusha! Can't you see that? Jesus was an infant himself. You can ask James, my other brother, who is with us at this moment. He will tell you Jesus' age. And we all lived in Nazareth and other areas near Gallilee, the farthest north you can live from Bethlehem. Are *you* now claiming miracles, and evil ones, for an infant away across the country?"

"And do you, Simon, forget the Roman census? Jesus' family had to come to Bethlehem, being of the House of David, as you claim. Now your thick-headedness has made me lose my appetite."

"And yours has mine. I now remember my father and step-mother, who was with child, set out for Bethlehem for the census. So Jesus was born in your town. But he and his family returned to Nazareth when He was still a small child. Could one of his young years have such ambition to become a king, and anger Herod?"

"...Perhaps not," Jerusha conceded. "I have thought of this question for many years. But his parents could have, especially now that I know he wasn't poor."

Simon confessed, "I was again, unforgivably, on the verge of laughter. If you only knew his mother, Mary. Or had known her husband Joseph—you slander my father. And me; would I not have known of my family's royal ambitions? Back at headquarters did I give you any hint of such?

"But appealing to common sense: Would this 'ambitious' family have returned to isolated Galilee? And later, let their own son and would-be king wander all over the country, with little money, not a hovel for a house, few rich or important friends and avoiding all centers of influence and power to the point that the crowds who listen to him aren't certain of even his name, but talk of his love and his miracles? Healing the lame and blind? Curing the ill? Creating food out of almost nothing to feed the hungry?"

Jerusha replied, "Zachariah and I talked about Jesus' wanderings when I last saw my brother, and even we could see

that it is the population of the countryside and towns which you
need to unite behind you if you wish to form an army to start an
insurrection."

Simon said, "You have now seen the disciples we have with
us, and talked with a number of them. You met the people on
the hill at Jesus' latest talk, and heard his words. That was one
of the largest crowds we have had. I saw you talking to many of
them while playing peddler. Did they strike you as the core of a
revolutionary army? The same scene has been repeated throughout
Galilee and Judea as long as I have been with my brother. What
does Herod Antipas, or anyone, have to fear from such a crowd
or Jesus' words when talking to them?"

Jerusha had no answer, but was certain there was one.

Simon continued, "I beg of you to give it some more thought
and remember Jesus' age when the horrors were visited upon you.
What a shame you can't read; it is through reading that we learn
the wisdom of the ages." Jerusha felt a speech coming on Simon
but was too mentally tired to stop him.

"What you lived through in Bethlehem was not the first
time innocents were slaughtered by an evil ruler. Our master
encourages us to read Scripture. Almost a thousand years ago,
Queen Athaliah, who had seized the throne, murdered all of
her own grandchildren and all others of David's seed, except one
who was hidden from her. Why did she do this? Because her late
husband, whom she hated, was of the House of David and such
slaughter would assure the end of that line. Despite all the blood,
Queen Athaliah failed because of the one remaining man of the
House of David."

Jerusha murmured, "Coincidence."

"Coincidence? Two events in the House of David which
we know occurred, the first of which, if successful, would have
assured that my Master had never been born, and the second of
which would have killed him as an infant, had something not

stepped in both times and saved two children of the same family from two evil rulers?"

Jerusha smirked, still too caught up in the argumentation to consider supper or anything else. "All you talk about are facts and logic, and now just told a story which is based on nothing, being a thousand years old, according to your own admission. I don't suppose you have an extremely old witness standing by?"

"Very strange," Simon looked up and over her head. He paused between thoughts. "I'll wager you who have never been ten miles away from where you were born; you cannot read or write; you have probably spent almost every waking moment of your life in your home or at Zealot headquarters; you have no friends, and have surely not met a hundred people in your life, few of them educated; you might believe me if I said the sky was made of blue linen. Yet you have the nerve to doubt when I tell you Queen Athaliah killed her family. Why? Only because it happened a very long time ago, and nothing that old could be true. After all, you weren't born at the time, so evidence and logic go out the window. This has been called 'Temporal bigotry': dismissal of anything in the distant past as 'impossible'. You yourself have witnessed equal acts of evil, but the ones in the past are 'impossible'. Your brain is as twisted as a snake.

"To get back on the subject, Jerusha, I am convinced you would not have devoted yourself to your cause so fanatically merely as a victim. You're stronger than that. Bethlehem was full of victims. I mentioned to you when you were with the Zealots that victimhood was not the greatest motivator of hatred. There is something else which happened that night. I know your brother Zachariah had children of the same age. They must have been killed at the same time, but you have not mentioned them. Why not? Nor have you mentioned his wife who was raising them. I do not judge people I know personally, and I believe God forgives all who ask Him for it. I pray and believe He will forgive me my sins."

The sun had gone down and not having lit their own cook fire, Jerusha blamed the darkness on what she was about to say.

"Perhaps you are right, Simon, though I cannot hope for forgiveness." Jerusha described how she had actively participated in the killing of Leah and her family.

"Leah's boys were a bribe! A sacrifice I knowingly arranged. I did not count on Leah's motherly violence which caused such a thorough search and slaughter of my own boys. But I did entice Leah. And nothing you say can change that. Only Leah can forgive me. She, may I be cursed forever, is dead. Only she, and God if he exists, could forgive my betrayal of my own kin. *And* what I did with the Zealots, later."

"You speak truly."

"I suppose your brother is now God?" Her disgust was palpable.

Simon replied, "You will understand someday. Meanwhile, know that your children are happy and love you, as do your nephews, as does, to an infinitely greater degree, Almighty God, the Father."

"The children are dead." Tears were now running freely down her face.

"My Master is sorrowing now, for you and for the other parents who were left bereft that night long ago."

"I know nothing of this, and it defies sense."

Jerusha then dismissed Simon with such strong words he had no choice but to leave, with the saddest face she had ever seen on a man. But she still had her dagger.

Jerusha wished she had bought a real tent before setting out on her journey. Instead, she had decided to maintain the image of a poor peddler with only a few blankets and an oilcloth out of which to make sleeping quarters. She had picked furze bushes and attached the center of the blankets to the highest and opposing branches, more like twigs, stuck the side edges of the cloths into the dirt with stronger twigs, and spread the oilcloth over the whole misshapen mess. Which left her, of course, no front or back opening, at least tonight. She crawled in the space left her on one of the wider sides.

She could have sworn that she had chosen the rockiest, shrubbiest area in the neighborhood, complete with slants in every direction she could imagine. If it rained, Jerusha was certain the deepest depression would be directly under her back. She had even forgotten to pick a broad, flat stone for a pillow, or smooth, soft dirt she could mold into one. With her luck, if she found soft earth it would have been an anthill.

The deepest reflections came to her after about an hour of trying to sleep. The thought crossed her mind that it was her brain keeping her so uncomfortably awake. Though usually introspective, she dismissed this consideration at once. *It is the fault of the ground I have chosen. What else could it be? Tomorrow I will complete my mission or use my dagger on myself—a coward has no right to live. Thinking is not hesitation. Prudence is necessary in any endeavor. I have killed a band of Romans, and a single Roman official. And one of Herod's men-at-arms. And even an apparently decent Jew against whom I had nothing. Perhaps the last was even devout, despite his dress—certainly more devout than I am. I was justified in everything I have ever done...In whose eyes? Oh, yes. In my eyes. Am I the only one that matters? I never even had a real friend to ask for advice. That God could ever be near enough to ask is ludicrous...much less some rabbi and former carpenter.* A rock worked its way into her side. *Simon is kind, but irritating. I am a victim, and more so, my children were victims, and Leah... and Leah's two children...what were their names? What right has Simon to doubt my actions? He was worse than I am...How many Romans did he kill as a Zealot? He said he would be forgiven. By whom—Ceasar? Simon hasn't shown any signs of guilt recently. Has he no conscience? Or are all of his speeches pure nonsense? But has*

it been he who has condemned my actions...or has it been I myself?
She was becoming confused.

My life is what it is; I have had no choices...or have I? I have always prided myself on my strength...my will. A thorn from one of the bushes to which she had attached her tent came loose and stuck her in the ribs. She tore it off, only to have two more jab her in her thighs. She broke them off more carefully. *No: I am no victim. Only cowards are victims; or remain so. Love...love is fine in a world in which everyone shares it. So some people live lucky lives and have no reason for hate...Hate and guilt. At least in this world. Is this the only world? Everyone seems to deny it, but most of them live as though it is. Simon claims a way to a better world. If there is one, why would so many try to improve their lot in this one? Even those who strive for improvement for everyone, talk about improvement only in this world... Why bother to improve this one, if the next world is better? This Jesus talks incessantly about his Father's Kingdom. Why would God—the Father?—put us in this living Hell, first? There is no God... only humanity. And myself. From what I have seen of humans,* they *cannot be the highest beings that exist and* I *certainly am not God.* That thought almost brought her to laughter. *Then who can judge right from wrong? I have heard of Satan...When will sleep sneak up on me? Wouldn't a just God kill Satan? Then we would all be good. We would have no choice. Do we need a choice? I have always prided myself on my choices—my free will. But haven't I doubted that earlier tonight? Then again, what choice did my children have? Can I keep my free will without Satan and evil in the world?* Confusion...

She must have dozed off for a moment for she jerked up and remembered she had forgotten to feed or water her donkey—for how long? She struggled out of her tent and took care of that chore, using up the last of the grain. She almost got lost on her way back, though the distance was only three or four yards. After fighting her way back into what was left of her "tent," her scattered thoughts began again as soon as she lay down.

Good...Evil. Simon seems good...and how many are bad? What good would paradise be for me? What good is this world to me? I have lived in it forever—and—do not remember joyfulness. Wealth certainly didn't bring it. Nor did power; or love, whatever that was. But at least I knew truth! How? Reason.—Facts, facts, facts. What facts have I seen indicating joy in this world, or in the next, or more importantly, in the existence of God? Or in His absence? What did it...

Jerusha did not know when, or if, she fell asleep, but sunrise was creeping in the many gaps that had appeared in her coverings during the night, which must have occurred due to her uncomfortable tossings. Surprisingly, the worst memories of this night had not involved the deaths of her children, but the future. *What possible future could I have?*

CHAPTER 14

Bethany

Jerusha worked her way out of her tent only to see Simon squatting again, almost where he sat last night.

"I've become too used to good food," said Simon, "or maybe I'm just lazy."

"You won't be used to this; I've run out of almost everything."

"You look terrible this morning," he commiserated. Then smiled, "Have you been given a mission requiring another disguise?"

"I didn't sleep well."

"I hope that doesn't affect your cooking skills." He actually looked hungry.

"My skills depend upon my ingredients." Jerusha tried to put together a meal out of whatever she had left. Hard, stale bread, crumbled in a large pot with all of her strength; lentils with more juice than bean, which improved the barley bread almost as much as it took the taste out of the beans; a few strips of dried, deboned, and slightly smelly fish, purslane which was more brown than green, a few spoons full of water in order to make the mess easier to stir, since she had no more sauces; a pinch of each spice she had left, including mustard, in order to disguise the flavor. There was no more olive oil or wine, which actually improved the mixture because almost all other foods Jerusha had previously prepared had one or the other, leaving this bowl slightly exotic by comparison. She ground the mortar and pestle together hard enough to make the concoction appear as much like a poultice as like food. She no longer cared what others thought of her cooking. She took it off the little fire she had built and handed her spoon to Simon without a word.

He swallowed his portion, and then said, "That is the worst thing you have ever prepared. Or anyone has, I honestly believe," he added with a smile. "Are you trying to poison me? Are you still that angry at me?"

Eating out of the same bowl, she said, "This answers your first question. What is in it is all that I had left. You could have watched me fix it."

"There are weeds that grow around here which would have improved it, but I don't know how to cook them, either. Anyway, we should be in Bethany by noon, and can eat there. Please give me another spoonful of that stuff so I can make it that far unstarved, if not satisfied. We had no supper last night, if you recall. Bethany will prove the old saying that funerals serve better feasts than the happiest celebrations." Simon and Jerusha said nothing for a while, looking into the bowl or at each other.

"I did get to speak with, or listen to, a few of those who have been with your master the longest, besides you. And later, I talked with the man you call Peter. He's a large, simple fisherman, but said he is now a 'fisher of men'. I don't understand this, but his devotion to your brother is undoubtable. You said that he was the first to understand Jesus' true nature. All I know is that Peter is a good man." *How could I know that?*

Simon thought aloud. "Perhaps you should have spent this entire trip with Peter. He knows how to address people in a straightforward manner. None of my involved explanations or lecturing."

"I met a couple of others, whose names I don't remember, but they were all different. Apparently, Jesus doesn't discriminate among those who sincerely choose to follow him. There was one, I think his name was Judas, who reminded me of one of my factors. Don't take that as a compliment. He seems weak, somehow. I was interested to learn that he is your treasurer. We talked finances for a while, and he wasn't very forthcoming. Of course, he had no reason to trust *me*.

"Oh, and the youngster, John. He reminded me of my young archer when I was with the Zealots. John thinks too much for someone of his tender years. I didn't recognize my archer himself, now that he's grown older. I met a few others.

"I must admit that I don't see your group as leaders of an insurrection against the king." *Am I disappointed?*

Simon smiled and asked, "What did you think of the small crowd that follows us now?"

"They're no better than most people. Perhaps a few are."

"Maybe you should have seen what they were like before they came to us. Only some have been with us for more than a short length of time. Did you think that giving our lives to Jesus would radically change our personalities?"

"No, and I hoped it wouldn't. Overly righteous and polite people are tedious."

Simon commented, on a slightly different matter, "A few days ago, before you came, when we were still southeast of Jerusalem we had one of our nastiest fights. That was when we heard that Jesus' friend Lazarus was dying in Bethany, and we knew that a word or a touch from the Master would keep him alive. Some of us loved Lazarus very much, especially Simon Peter. Jesus refused to risk our group by increasing the pace when there was a hostile group in front. This caused anger and hurt among us.

But we abided by his judgment. And Lazarus is now dead. But, as God wills."

"Or as your brother wills, as you would put it."

"Whatever else he is, Jesus is a man." Soon after this, Simon thanked Jerusha for the meal, such as it was, and prepared to leave.

"But, Simon, I have things I want to ask you. Things I thought about last night."

"Later," he said with a wave. But before Simon was a few paces away, he stopped, faced her, and made what he clearly meant as a final address. "I wouldn't have spent so much time with you if I had not heard one of Jesus' stories." He settled his stance more comfortably. "A certain shepherd had a hundred sheep, one of which had gone astray. The shepherd rejoiced when he found that lost sheep more than over the ninety and nine which had never strayed. But shepherds, sheep, and situations differ. Hope I will see you in Bethany."

"*More puzzles.*" Jerusha said to herself, "*Pompous.*"

Jerusha put the belongings she had left on the donkey to keep up with the remaining crowd.

Jerusha and her donkey wandered in and about the small groups of pilgrims, but she heard nothing else that interested her. She joined Simon again and complained, "Why have we had to come such a twisted way to Bethany?"

"So as not to provoke Jesus' enemies with a public procession along the roads. They cannot help it; their passions are being stirred by powerful personages who foolishly feel endangered by the Master's message. But, as Jesus has said, his time has not yet come. Though it approaches."

"And must he then die?" Jerusha asked ignoring the irony that she had spent three decades planning just that.

"He says so. And not too long from now; keep your voice down. Don't be concerned; you probably won't be the cause of his death."

How does Simon know my plans enough even to dismiss them?

Jerusha was puzzled more than ever before. "Then why must he die?"

Simon sighed. "We should have discussed this long ago. But you're not a good listener, and I am tired. I'll try once more, though you say I talk too much. The easy answer as to why the Messiah must die is because his death is prophesied in Scripture. Just as that night of blood in Bethlehem was inevitable. Your children did not die in vain. Jesus recently said 'the Son of Man came to give his life as ransom for many.' I have reason to hope he will rise again, and show us eternal life. But I'm wasting my time with you."

"No," said Jerusha. "I have been thinking about all you have said, and what your brother told the crowd. But this which Jesus offers, eternal life, is it that important? As for me, I have lived long enough and yearn for sleep."

Simon's large eyes expressed sadness, as they had so many times before. Jerusha was puzzled that his voice and eyes sometimes sent opposite signals. "Thirty years of hate and guilt is a long life on this earth. Too long. But did your children, also, live too long? They will live again, because of God's grace." Simon noticed that he and Jerusha were falling farther behind, were in danger of joining a trailing group, and he picked up his pace. "Just as your children will live, you could live forever, too...not bitter, not bent, white and old, but in a better world than this one. The choice to accept God's gift is yours. The opposite to such an eternity as Jesus offers is not just death. You will not like it. Compared to such an existence, you will consider your life here to have been paradise.

"See our Master up ahead? He carries your burdens. He

has taken your sins onto his own shoulders, as he has those of Herod's soldiers, cruel Romans, unfaithful spouses, ungrateful children, divorcers, thieves, the selfish, the prideful, the greedy, the slothful, the lustful—in fact, the sins of the world. With repentance on their part. But Jesus must die to atone for all these misuses of the free will which God has given mankind. Also, if you listened the other night, you noticed that almost every one of the Master's talks began with the word 'repent'. You and I must repent, accept him and try to follow his teachings."

Jerusha replied with one of her old sneers, "I would have been satisfied with justice, instead of paradise."

"Do you truly want justice, not just for Herod's men, but for yourself as well?"

An instance's retrospective of her victims from Leah to Habakkuk made her blurt, "I would also want mercy, I suppose. But I can't have that."

Simon sighed, a gesture of his Jerusha was as familiar with as her own sneers. "Jerusha, I don't know how to say this to you, but I'll try. Haven't you yet concluded from back at Zealot headquarters—though then it was for a different reason and by a different person—that I was personally assigned to you? I have failed."

"'Assigned to' me? By whom? Why?"

"You'll have to put up with another one of my little speeches. There are some people in the world who are very spiritual in their outlook on life. All they need is kindness, understanding and an equally spiritual nature to put their faith and trust in the Lord. In short, they need only to feel the love of God. Other people have no interest in the spirit as such—all they need is a miracle which they cannot explain away, and in the absence of any evidence or reasoning to the contrary, or motive for fraud, they will, rightly, believe what they see and hear. The love comes later, when they have meditated on it. There are probably hundreds of other types, many now the greatest among us—what my brother calls the 'salt of the earth.'"

Jerusha smiled, "I am none of these. You must have been surprised when you met me."

"Don't flatter yourself. Every infant is born a non-believer, and his lack is based on only one thing: abysmal ignorance. It takes years of teaching and study, sometimes without the learner's conscious effort, to achieve the knowledge. So I see unbelievers daily without much shock. The miracle of baptism has often been more direct, among us Nazarenes, at least. And God can approach infants or anyone He wishes, directly.

"Now I have discovered that there is another type of person: someone like you. From my experience, and apparently those of my brothers in the faith, this is the rarest type of person. Don't take that as a compliment. Freaks of nature are also rare, but not necessarily to be admired—get as angry as you wish. Observation, facts, and reason have absolutely no effect on this person. In your case, specifically, mixing bad and good characteristics together. You have shown yourself to be exceptionally cynical, and with a stubborn streak that nothing seems to penetrate. I think this comes from overwhelming pride stretching back as far as I can possibly imagine. You have an extremely intelligent mind, but without a hint of flexibility. You appear to have no interest in or liking for your fellow man, unless he or she strikes an irrational chord in you unrelated to the person's merit. You have spent your life apparently isolating yourself from mankind except when it serves your purposes. Yes, I know your tragedies, but you are not the only one to have lived through such horrors. And I'd wager the seed of your character was already there."

The two had by now set a pace to avoid those walking in front and behind them.

Simon continued, "In sum: I can think of no way to reach

you, though I have prayed about it continuously. I suppose you will have to be the one sheep that is abandoned for the other ninety and nine, at least by me. Someone else might have been better for the job. Like Peter. It's a shame; I really do like you more than almost anyone I ever met. My brother, doubtlessly, would be successful...Jesus can cast out devils, but I don't know if yours are self-made and, as I said before, I have not my brother's abilities...

"Feel free to follow us if you want, anyway."

"But I tried to call out to you after breakfast! I have some serious questions! My thoughts in the tent last night..."

"I'm afraid its too late for me,and our current mission. Maybe someone else will talk with you after Bethany."

"And I have fed and befriended you, all this way."

"All things come from God. Even that mustard plaster I had for breakfast. *Shalom.*" Simon walked ahead to catch up with the other leaders, glancing back only once to see that Jerusha kept her distance.

Gradually other people who had come directly from Jerusalem intermingled with Jerusha's group. They did not show any curiosity, as by that time people were coming from all directions. The number of mourners on the path to Lazarus' house was large by Jerusha's standards, but being unacquainted with rich men's funerals, she had no way to judge. She certainly now knew that Lazarus had been rich, for the walls around his house and outbuildings, which they were approaching, encircled a large area, containing as many flowerbeds as vegetable plots and vineyards, and several paths led to more out of view. Jerusha could even see a fountain in the distance, though she wondered how it could be fed without visible Roman aqueducts. The house was not only large but consisted of many wings with archways along them, giving every dweller or guest there cool verandas, windows, and privacy simultaneously. It was the first noticeable house in Bethany, surely built there because it stood on a hill, and looked down on somewhat smoother land.

With the crowd heading up the path from the gate to the front, Jerusha had no doubt who had owned the house. The path was lined with a banquet on both sides. Blinded by hunger, Jerusha grabbed handfuls of food at random and ate it while keeping up with the crowd. After receiving surprised looks she remembered that the banquet was for later. She could see several people rush to greet Jesus, though she was too far back to hear anything that was said. The greeters, as almost everyone in the crowd, were in mourning clothes and proper costumes, including torn clothing and ashes on their heads.

Jerusha approached Simon again by accident, and he told her, to fill in the time, that Lazarus had always been well-liked, and that he had been dead for four days, and his sister was distraught by grief. Then he assumed a puzzled look.

"This is the first time I have ever seen my Master—my brother—weep."

"Then why didn't he *save* the man if he can perform miracles?"

"That may be exactly the reason." Simon disappeared in the crowd.

At intervals Jerusha could see Jesus proceeding through the mourners. He walked toward some hillside caves not far either from the house or the village beyond it. The entire crowd followed or joined him. Not taking care, Jerusha found herself at the back of the crowd, where she could see nothing of interest until Jesus climbed a hill facing what was clearly a fresh grave, blocked, as were other graves, with a large stone. Jesus, still with the slight glow Jerusha had noticed earlier, was joined by two workmen. The men pushed the stone aside, struggling as though they were using all of their strength, which seemed strange since the stone had been smoothly carved into what must have been a perfect circle, lying on its edge. Jesus raised his arms upward to the sky, facing the grave.

Jesus then cried, loudly, "Lazarus, come forth!"

Even from the rear of the crowd Jerusha could hear him clearly. With the tomb fully exposed, but dark, the people saw nothing for a moment. But then a shock spread through the mass. Gradually they and Jerusha saw a man walking from the back of the tomb wearing only a winding sheet and headcloth.

The man took a few steps forward of the cave and stopped, amid universal gasps, moans, scattered screams, and shouts of "Lazarus! Lazarus! Let us see if it is Lazarus!" Jerusha couldn't have identified him if she had wanted to, but what just happened? She had found a small hillock to stand on and look over the heads of the crowd, several of whom were already moving toward the man, to unwind the cloths.

Just at that moment Jerusha herself saw not one person but four. Three were her own children—David, Jonathan, and Abraham—each with a look of rapture on his face, though Abraham, throughout his babyhood, almost always looked ecstatic. This was different, though. The three were as pale as Lazarus' cloths. They caught sight of Jerusha at the same time and began laughing and waving their arms, though the baby was waving all four limbs until he fell over backwards. David quickly reached aside and sat Abraham up again, causing him to laugh the harder. There was no sign of having been away from their mother for even a moment. *How can they recognize me, as old as I am? How can they accept me, after I failed them?*

Jerusha started pushing through the crowd. By then everyone was rushing toward the man Lazarus, a healthy-looking man in early middle age with the same expression of rapture that Jerusha had seen on her children. There were shouts of "He's alive", "He's come back from the dead", and "Jesus brought Lazarus back."

Just then Jerusha saw Leah's children brought out of the tomb by their mother. Again, the same look of paleness and ecstasy. To Jerusha's surprise and chagrin, Leah showed nothing but joy at seeing her sister-in-law; no hint of blame. *How can she forgive me?* Jerusha found herself now sharing in the joy, or rather release, as she felt that she had been redeemed from that Night of Horror. As if from slavery. This confused her.

Jerusha knew she could get no closer, and, with tears running down her face she shouted to a few people near her, "Do you see them? Are they still there? Aren't they beautiful?"

In return she received only puzzled looks and a few comments such as, "There's only Lazarus," and "She must be crazy." When she finally made it to the front she saw that neither her own children, nor Leah and hers, were there any more.

But they had been. Facts. Facts.

Jerusha changed direction and started a slow walk toward Jesus, who was now separated from Lazarus by the crowd. Jerusha looked into his face, where the tears—concerning Lazarus or her experience?—were still on his face. As she looked into Jesus' eyes, she was overwhelmed with awe. She felt that he knew her—and all her grief and guilt and anger—and that he loved and forgave her. Jerusha then went limp and fell to the ground at his feet. She had the sensation of Jesus reaching down to touch her head. If he spoke, it was more like a communication of infinite love, than of words.

When she regained full consciousness a moment later she was alone in the crowd. She quickly rose, and forced herself through the throng in the direction of Bethlehem. She neglected to search for her donkey or provisions, or to find the road, and headed across open countryside. Jerusha thought she heard Simon call after her, but was too far away to clearly recognize his voice. At intervals she thought she again heard someone who might have been Simon calling out to her, sometimes from near, sometimes from far, but she was too afraid of her feelings to respond. By nightfall she could no longer hear anything behind her. She slept in the open for awhile, and then continued on her journey, with, for the first time, an unerring sense of geographical direction.

Her *life's* path had radically changed.

CHAPTER 15

...Help Me In My Unbelief

At sunrise, several days after returning home, Jerusha was seated next to a young man with mounds of papyrus and parchment spread about him. Most of them were Aramaic translations of ancient Hebrew Scriptures. The hunger and thirst she had felt on her way back from Bethany had long been assuaged, and the scratches on her legs, arms, and face from the wild brush had healed almost entirely. Her feet were again fully usable. Her heart was still racing, much of the time.

The young man was a scholar and looked it, from his ascetic body and features to his weak, squinty eyes. He was trying to teach Jerusha how to read. Judging from his grimaces and mannerisms, she was a most difficult student. She learned quickly, but often interrupted. He exhibited not the slightest hint of a sense of humor. Or much patience.

Jerusha had hired him for only one reason, though she had sworn the man to secrecy. She wanted to read and understand something of Scripture: Those parts which concerned the prophecies of the Messiah. Jerusha was paying the man highly, not only to ensure his silence, and because the Passover was beginning, but because he, like most men, thought it was useless to give women an education, a point he had made clear. But her studies had progressed faster than she, or he, had thought possible, despite her interruptions.

Today, Jerusha was arguing with her tutor that passages in the Psalms of King David would, logically, not be talking about the Messiah, as King David never claimed to be he, and, speaking in the first person, must have been describing his own suffering, real or imagined. Her teacher tried to explain, at least to her satisfaction, that King David's use of the first person could refer to someone else in the distant future. Similarly, some Messianic passages from Isaiah and Daniel seemed muddled to Jerusha.

Nevertheless, her aging mind was still agile.

It all made sense to her if the Messiah came not just for the salvation of the Nation of Israel, but for individual people, including her children...and her. Then his "Father's Kingdom" was not of this fallen world.

"Who is the 'Son of Man'?" Jerusha asked the scholar.

"That is one of the titles of the Messiah, whom I've been talking about," he replied, tiredly.

"Oh. I heard it somewhere."

Jerusha feared what would happen to Jesus if any of the following were true:

> "He is despised and rejected of men; a man of sorrows, and acquainted with grief...Surely he has borne our griefs, and carried our sorrows...But he was wounded for our transgressions, he was bruised for our iniquities...with his stripes we are healed...

"They pierced my hands and my feet...they part
my garments among them and cast lots upon my
vesture."

Jerusha read enough to know that this torture would lead to
a humiliating death.

Some of the other passages of Scripture were becoming much
clearer to Jerusha. At times she felt that she was becoming closer
to God—"the Father"—and occasionally she was unsure whether
her seemingly random thoughts could actually be considered
prayers. Loud and showy prayers were a Pharisee habit, and these
people had not seemed to merit any special favor from her Master.

Jerusha still felt Jesus' love flowing over, and through her,
just as she had in Bethany. Also, she felt his offer of complete
forgiveness. But the latter left her with an obligation: Full
repentance, and sharing love and forgiveness with others. This
would be the hard part, given her nature and the habits of a
lifetime. But with God's help she could make some progress.

Jerusha kept very busy. She went to each of her factors whom
she suspected of cheating herself or others, or of any manner of
sharp dealings, and, while not forgetting that she had previously
encouraged many of them, now dismissed each one. She was
careful never to leave the impression that she was too righteous
for such things, or, contrary-wise, that the factors had not been
ruthless enough. She spaced out such actions so that those who
knew each other might not be tempted to meet and compare
notes.

Jerusha's reason told her that repentance must also include at
least an attempt at restitution for the victims of her sins. Although
this would be impossible in the most serious cases, she could at
least try to perform minor favors to substitutes. She spent all
one morning searching out the few beggars in Bethlehem and
dropping a handful of valuable coins into each bowl. How this

could balance out the tortures and killings she had committed, she had no idea. The concept was laughable; especially considering her previous thoughts on the uselessness of alleviating beggary. But it seemed like the right thing to do that day. Maybe she was remembering a gold coin dropped in her bowl many years ago.

She used her own imaginary, elderly illnesses as an excuse to close down entirely that part of the slave trade in which she had an ownership interest. She had observed and heard of the countless sins it occasioned among her employees and contractors. Jerusha liquidated every enterprise in which she was involved that appeared morally doubtful to her. During these transactions she remained curt, so that no one would see an immediate change in her personality.

This was not a difficult front for her to maintain, for she still had to work on her indifference toward most people, and contempt for some. She did make an effort to be courteous to all strangers, and to help those in need whom she recognized to be so, though she could not yet be attuned to them all. Throughout this work her fortune continued to grow, even though she took no special notice of results and after all these years a considerable amount of her investments were not only legitimate, but beneficial. On one occasion two of her paid "enforcers" came to her for work, and she dismissed them with loud oaths, not only from new found emotion but to maintain some confusion about her reputation as a hard business-woman.

Jerusha was unsure as yet whether these actions were what the Master would have wanted of her, but this was what she was trying to learn.

She tried to pray on a regular basis, though often felt self-conscious and unworthy. Attempting to make up her own prayers sometimes left her at a loss for words, while reciting half remembered children's prayers, by rote, allowed her to actually think about the old words simultaneously, but felt somehow artificial. She finally settled on simply talking conversationally to the Lord about whatever was on her mind. Jerusha gradually came to feel God could hear her, whichever manner she used, giving her comfort and encouragement.

Jerusha sought out a small group of Nazarenes who suggested baptism after repentance, as a man called John the Baptist had taught them, and explained the process. She grasped at the chance, believing she repented all of her sins, even those she had not yet atoned for. She was surprised to find that some of her dislike for others was slipping away with the waters of her baptism. The Nazarenes also taught her what they called "The Lord's Prayer." She need no longer feel self-conscious during prayer.

On this morning, the one that would become Jerusha's last with her tutor, they were interrupted by a knock on her door. Jerusha no longer cared what sort of omen that was, but shouted for the stranger to enter.

The teacher growled—whined?—giving in to all the indignation he could muster, "I am missing out on part of the Passover to be here, a serious omission, and this is what I get."

"I'm missing out, too," replied Jerusha, regretfully.

The knock had to be from a stranger, as far as she knew. Surely Zachariah would not come here again. The man who entered appeared middle aged, and he approached Jerusha as though he was going to throw his arms about her.

When Jerusha showed only puzzlement, he said, rapidly, "I'm sorry to interrupt you when you have company, but I ran here from Jerusalem, where I heard from a follower of...a friend of ours, and saw things going on, and wanted to tell you, first," he was breathing hard. "Don't you remember me? I knew you first in the wilderness when..."

Jerusha immediately understood and ordered her tutor from the house abruptly, with what she knew as an inadequate excuse, but it would have to do. She tossed him a small sack of coins, which was many times what she owed her teacher and might make some amends, as his now grateful expression indicated.

"...I had a bow and arrow and fought alongside you." The visitor finished his sentence after the door closed.

"You must not have learned much if you don't know to keep your mouth shut about your time with the Zealots."

"I'm sorry. I was overcome by seeing you."

"What could you possibly have to do with me now?" Jerusha asked, though with a gentler voice than she had used previously.

"I saw you at Bethany and before, among us followers of Jesus."

"So what if that's so?"

"I left the Zealots to follow the Lord, and I have important and terrible news. The Sanhedrin arrested Jesus, and the Romans have sentenced him to crucifixion." The man spat the words out. "If you are one of us, you would want to know, so I asked at our old headquarters where you live."

Emotionally crushed, Jerusha could only stammer, "Want to know? What can we *do* about this?"

"I have no idea. Jesus is to be tortured and then executed today." Tears were now streaming down his face.

Could she at last have a positive mission? From God? For His Son?

"We can't do anything here. We must get to Jerusalem this morning. Now. This minute."

Jerusha rushed to assemble a few provisions from her cupboard, not knowing how long they would be gone. Out of her peripheral vision she saw an old dusty box, smaller than her hand and made of acacia wood, in the back left corner of the lowest shelf. She was nonplussed for a moment, then remembered the old parchment writing—the phylactery—her husband Mordecai had so prized and left her. When she had replaced her little food box for the new cabinet she must have placed the acacia box in the corner, for no particular reason she could think of. It was a short note and now that she could read, though with difficulty, Jerusha would finally perform her husband's greatest wish.

She opened the box, dropping the top and a few other objects on the floor, and quickly ripped out the fragile parchment. Almost miraculously, it was not damaged further, beyond the cracks and stains the years had given it. Jerusha noted that it was in Aramaic rather than ancient Hebrew. Mordecai must have translated it for her ease, from what he had read or heard and memorized. All this, even the reading, took almost no time.

The Book of Proverbs, Chapter 1, verses 5 – 7. Jerusha guessed that a few less important words had been omitted:

> "A wise man will hear, and will increase learning; and a man of understanding, shall attain unto wise counsels...The fear of the Lord is the beginning of knowledge: But fools despise wisdom and instruction."

Jerusha thought, with her quick mind, that taking this writing to heart long ago, had her stubbornness permitted it, might have changed anything from her smallest errors to the course of her life. And the lives of others. She planned to think on this in quiet moments for however long she had left on this earth, and of the man who was better than she had thought him, Mordecai. And of other things, such as Simon's counsels. But, it was pitifully late, now.

The two set out at the same pace, the man's relative youth matched by her desperation and lifelong physical strength. Halfway to Jerusalem the sky turned as dark as night, yet both knew that it was about the middle of the day.

Jerusha was not shocked as much as angry. "We can't go fast, or even slowly, on this road without sunlight. We'd stumble and fall at every rock and pebble each step or two."

"God is mysterious. We need rest anyway. This might not last long," said the man whom she still thought of as her archer.

Jerusha settled on a rock by the road. "By the way," she said, "if something should happen to me and you survive, I have a fortune in gold coins under the ground next to the stove. I checked the surface and marking stone before I left. There's no lock on the lid. Dig it up and keep it or use it as you wish. The rest of my holdings are elsewhere, will be robbed by my factors, and you can't hope to get at them. I don't care about them."

"I will defend..."

"Oh, be quiet. I wasn't starting a conversation."

The archer expressed puzzlement about Jerusalem: "A short time ago it seemed as though the entire population turned out to greet Jesus as their savior, throwing palm leaves at the feet of his donkey. Now, a mob is demanding his crucifixion. What changed?"

"They were two different groups. No doubt the latter one you know of are the Sanhedrin and their followers who fear the diminishment of their power. You cannot blame the whole for the actions of a small but loud minority."

The sun came back out after awhile and the two broke into a run, praying all the while as they could. They headed toward Jerusalem and Golgotha, north of the city, the place of executions. They stopped for a moment's rest in the great city. They resumed running, though Jerusha was clearly showing her age by now.

The archer would have to run ahead, though not without a heartbroken glance behind him. Jerusha alternated running a few steps, then limping and hobbling in the direction he had taken. The city crowds became thick in going to or from Golgotha. She turned down a cluttered alley. Then she recognized one of the disciples who had spent most of his time close to Jesus, and had apparently been highly regarded by the Master. He was the large fisherman Simon Peter, who, despite his size and strength, was now stumbling along the cobblestones, in his obviously deep grief. This was confirmed when he looked up to the sky and called out:

"Master, I have denied You three times! Now that You, my Lord, are crucified, how can I live on?"

Jerusha wondered if Peter's loudness was to atone for the denial of his Lord. But she finally knew that it was too late to help Jesus. *Is there nothing I can do?* She paused and caught her breath, watching. Peter's words had been emotion-stricken but clear. By this time it was dark night except for the many torch lights.

A man armed and dressed as a Temple guard was not far behind Peter, walking in the same direction. He could not have missed Peter's noisy confession.

The guard stopped instantly and shouted at Peter's back, "You lied to me today, coward! You *are* a Nazarene Blasphemer!" Jerusha saw the guard draw back his arm to throw his spear at Peter.

Jerusha was next to the target, and intentionally threw herself to her left, knocking Peter, weak and unbalanced as he had become, to the street. Only the fisherman's bulk kept Jerusha upright for a short moment.

Jerusha was not surprised when the guard's spear plunged into her side. She fell, twisting to her right, and landing on the cobblestones on her side and face, at the foot of the wall. She used all her remaining strength to pull the spear, to press her hand against the wound, and to position her face mostly outward. The guard had disappeared in the crowd. Peter struggled to stand, and blindly stumbled out of her line of sight.

Since Jerusha was near some crates, she was not knocked about by the feet of the masses. The pain began. She breathed shallowly as the dew settled around her. For no particular reason it seemed important to keep torches in her sight, with their reflections on helmets, breast-plates, damp stones, and the sweating faces of the people. Everything glistened; the scene was almost beautiful. Jerusha felt she needed to watch the figures walking or pushing in all directions. People, good and bad, but, objectively, none worse than she. Why had she despised them most of her life?

She knew that her deep, bloody wound would shortly prove fatal. Having done similar things to others, but more efficiently, Jerusha considered it a not unwarranted form of justice. The pain had not yet arrived in earnest. Despite some growing confusion, Jerusha knew there was something else she was supposed to do, even, or especially, in her situation. She silently said what might be considered a confession, or a prayer, or something else useful.

Two more of Jesus' disciples—she recognized Simon the Zealot—passed near Jerusha, who was lying on the ground partly obscured by the crates.

"Who's that?" Simon stopped and asked of the bloody bundle, but Jerusha had no strength to move or answer.

"We should keep going. We're near where we are to meet, and Peter must be up ahead," his friend urged.

Something caught Simon's eye before he moved on, because he looked closer at the bundle, and said the last spoken words that she would ever hear on earth. "I knew her. Some would say that this killing is just. But I knew and loved her and I refuse to believe it. I saw something come over her at Bethany. And she tried to ask me something, that morning...I turned away, rather than get involved again. Later I tried to chase her down, calling out, but couldn't find her. Jesus is dead, but I know He will come back, as prophesied. He's gone to prepare a place for her." The other disciple tried to pull Simon on his way.

"*Leave me alone!*" Simon shouted. He started away at a slower and more thoughtful pace, and then looked back. "*Shalom,* Jerusha," he said. "You'll never leave my prayers."

Jerusha, having heard Simon's solemnity, laughed to herself, despite the pain. *He still talks too much, pompous ass, but he's kind... kinder than I deserve. I loved you, too, Simon, but I didn't know it. I love those fools who gathered around you and your brother. And the other true fools, as I was. Why didn't I understand them all as... children of God?* Jerusha's pain, much controlled by her considerable will, did not interfere with these thoughts.

Her silent laughter came back. *Tonight was going to be the first time I would have willingly observed the Sabbath meal in over thirty years.* Jerusha's smile, though it could not be seen, was pure and innocent, without irony.

It was You I was seeking, all along...my Lord and my God.

As she lay in the spreading pool of her own blood, gasping for each breath, she quivered while every fiber of her body struggled against the ebbing of life. Torch light lingered, setting the walls and buildings of Jerusalem aflame in hues of red and gold. Echoing out of the mists of her now agonizing pain, a strange yet vaguely familiar voice came to her mind.

He who believes in Me, though he may die, yet shall he live...

Jerusha's chest heaved for the last time.

Printed in the United States
By Bookmasters